New Directions in Irish-American History

HISTORY *of* IRELAND *and the* IRISH DIASPORA

James S. Donnelly, Jr.

Thomas Archdeacon

SERIES EDITORS

Sinn Féin: A Hundred Turbulent Years

BRIAN FEENEY

New Directions in Irish-American History

EDITED BY KEVIN KENNY

HISTORY *of* **IRELAND**
and the **IRISH DIASPORA**

New Directions in Irish-American History

EDITED BY

Kevin Kenny

The University of Wisconsin Press

The University of Wisconsin Press
1930 Monroe Street
Madison, Wisconsin 53711

www.wisc.edu/wisconsinpress/

3 Henrietta Street
London WC2E 8LU, England

1   3   5   4   2

Printed in the United States of America

Library of Congress Cataloging-in-Publication Data
New directions in Irish-American history / edited by Kevin Kenny.
p. cm. — (History of Ireland and the Irish diaspora)
ISBN 0-299-18710-1 (alk. paper)
ISBN 0-299-18714-4 (pbk. : alk. paper)
1. Irish Americans—Historiography. I. Kenny, Kevin, 1960– II. Series.
E184.I6 N475   2003
973'.049162—dc21   2003002454

Contents

General Introduction

New Directions in Irish-American History

KEVIN KENNY

OVER THE LAST GENERATION, from the late 1960s to the present, the writing of Irish-American history has been transformed in line with a wider transformation in American historical writing as a whole. While American historians have by no means abandoned the study of high politics, diplomacy, and business that once dominated the field, the emphasis in recent decades has been on history "from the bottom up" rather than "from the top down." American historiography since the 1960s has focused on the history of the oppressed, the downtrodden, and the marginal, without losing sight of the broader framework of power and politics in which history has unfolded. Of central importance has been the formation of identities along the lines of class, race, ethnicity, and gender.

Irish-American history has been no exception to this shift in emphasis. But, just as some American historians before the 1960s were always interested in questions of labor, class, and race, so too were some historians of Irish America. In examining historiographical shifts, one needs to be careful of sweeping generalizations: new sources, methodologies, and interpretations certainly emerge over time, but the "new" historiography rarely represents an absolute departure from the "old." Elements or precursors of the newer scholarship can always be found in the work of preceding generations. Each new generation of historians necessarily builds on the work of its predecessors. These considerations are certainly germane in the case of Irish-American history, which has always been in large part a story of an impoverished, disadvantaged people uprooted from one side of the Atlantic to the other. At the heart of their story lies the great catastrophe of the 1840s, when 1 million Irish people died of famine and 2 million more fled the coun-

1

try.[1] How could such a history ever ignore the plight of ordinary people struggling to survive?

The answer is that it never did. Historical writing on Irish America has always been concerned to some extent with the poor, with working people, and with popular culture. The spectacular history of the Kennedys has received plenty of attention since the 1960s, but the mundane and fundamental process of mass migration and settlement has long been a focus of historical inquiry, as for example in the classic works of William F. Adams (1932) and James G. Leyburn (1962). Robert Ernst (1949) pioneered the field of modern social history with his painstaking analysis of life and labor among the German and Irish immigrants of antebellum New York City. Carl Wittke (1956) and George W. Potter (1960) gave plenty of attention to migration and settlement, class and race, and the participation of Irish-American workers in the labor movement. William V. Shannon's classic work (1963) balanced interpretations of high politics and culture with equally gripping portraits of prizefighters like John Morrisey, John L. Sullivan, and James J. Corbett. Lawrence J. McCaffrey (1976) concentrated on Irish domination of urban politics and the Catholic Church, but not to the exclusion of popular culture and the evolution of ethnic identities. And, as far back as 1937, the heavily Irish underworld of nineteenth-century New York City—featuring such colorful Irish gangs as the Shirt Tails, Forty Thieves, Plug Uglies, and Dead Rabbits—had been brought vividly to life by Herbert Asbury. In the "old" Irish-American history, then, there was no shortage of working people and popular culture.[2]

So what is new about the "new" directions in Irish-American history as it is being written today? The essays presented here provide the answer. Study of Irish-American history, literature, and culture is flourishing as never before. To mark this new upsurge in scholarship, the interdisciplinary Irish studies journal *Éire-Ireland* recently published two special issues devoted exclusively to the American Irish and covering the full sweep of history from the late eighteenth through the late twentieth centuries.[3] Most of the essays are historical, though they were written not only by professional historians but also by historically minded practitioners of related disciplines like geography, sociology, literary criticism, and American studies. The best of these essays from *Éire-Ireland* are presented here, and together they constitute some of the most innovative recent scholarship in the field.

The essays have been arranged into four thematic sections, each accompanied by a substantial historiographical introduction written specially for this volume. The first section deals with the process of transatlantic migration, the second with politics and race, the third with labor and gender, and the fourth with twentieth-century issues of representation, historical memory, and return migration. While each section has its own thematic introduction, it will be useful here to offer some reflections of a more general nature.

The new scholarship can make three claims to originality, each of which represents a shift or intensification of emphasis rather than something entirely new. The new Irish-American history investigates Irish as well as American history; it seeks to incorporate the Protestant dimension of the story; and it deals with new themes of race and gender as well as class. First, the new history pays much closer attention to the social, economic, cultural, and political history of Ireland itself, in the conviction that American immigration history cannot make proper sense without a good knowledge of old-world antecedents. Historians of Irish America have always had an interest in the premigration society of Ireland, but the work of Kerby A. Miller (1985) raised this dimension of the field to a new level.[4] The essays in this collection are all in some way transnational in their approach, dealing with Irish culture on both sides of the Atlantic simultaneously, and thereby moving beyond the restrictions of self-contained national historiography. They deal with the process of transatlantic migration, patterns of immigrant settlement, the Irish origins of American racial and ethnic identities, representations of Ireland, American memories of Irish history, and the return to Ireland of Irish-American migrants. A second original characteristic of the new history is that it has begun, for the first time, to integrate the Protestant migration of the eighteenth and early nineteenth centuries into the same framework of Irish Atlantic history as the later, more substantial Catholic migration that came to define Irish America. Irish Protestant migration has been intensively studied on its own terms, but hitherto as a separate story from the larger migration of which it was one integral part.[5] Third, again in keeping with broader trends in American historiography, the new Irish-American history has pushed onto center stage the existing interest in the poor, the marginal, and the excluded. Migrants, women, and workers are among the central players in the new historiography, which features sophisticated analysis of class, ethnic, racial, and gender identities.

The first group of essays in this book deals with transatlantic migration. It might be thought that this topic has by now been exhaustively studied, but each of the essays breaks important new ground.[6] Maurice J. Bric examines Irish migration in the late eighteenth century in the broad context of Atlantic history, showing how it was part of an exten-

sive network of trade connecting Ireland and America. While most
accounts of the eighteenth-century migration stop in 1776 and give only
scant attention to the postrevolutionary period, Bric focuses on the last
two decades of the century. Kerby A. Miller's essay takes up where Bric's
leaves off, examining nineteenth-century Ulster Protestant migration to
America, one of the most neglected topics, not only in Irish-American
history, but also in American immigration and ethnic history generally.[7]
Taking as his subject the peregrinations of William Murphy, a Protestant
migrant from Ulster in the era of the Great Irish Famine, Miller presents
an example of the new Irish-American history at its most innovative.[8]
Timothy M. O'Neil's essay offers another fine example of transnational
history, examining in detail the complex trails of ongoing "chain" and
"step" migration that brought copper miners from rural Ireland to the
mines of Michigan and then out west to Butte, Montana.[9] Finally,
Matthew J. O'Brien's essay examines a phase of Irish transatlantic migration that, once again, has been almost entirely neglected, the era between the two world wars. Although Irish transatlantic migration
declined in the 1920s (due mainly to its diversion to Britain rather than
to American immigration restriction laws), it was not until the Great
Depression that it declined absolutely. Those migrants who continued
to come in the 1920s, O'Brien demonstrates, were part of a dense network of reciprocal economic, social, and cultural links between Ireland
and the United States.

If these studies of migration fill major gaps in a story that has always
formed the starting point of Irish-American history, the essays in the
second section present new perspectives on questions of politics and
race. Irish domination of American urban politics in the century after
the Civil War has been intensively studied. But what were the origins of
Irish-American political power?[10] To find out, Tyler Anbinder takes us
back to the rough-and-tumble world of New York City's Sixth Ward in
the 1840s and 1850s. He shows how the juxtaposition of mass Catholic
immigration with the abolition of property qualifications for voting
placed the Irish in the position of power brokers, an opportunity they
exploited through membership in volunteer fire departments and police
forces and ownership of taverns and liquor stores. A central issue in this
boisterous antebellum world was the relationship between Irish immigrants and African Americans. Historians' investigations of that topic
have given rise to an important debate in recent American historiography concerning "whiteness," the argument being that immigrant workers expedited their assimilation by adopting white racial (and racist)
identities.[11]

Catherine M. Eagan's essay examines this topic by using a source that social historians are inclined to overlook, Irish-American popular fiction.[12] Rather than searching for more examples of how their enemies described them in racially derogatory terms, Eagan concentrates on how Irish Americans saw themselves. She finds that they had a well developed sense of white identity, which they persistently strove to convey to others. But there is much more to the history of race in Irish America than "whiteness." Irish sentiment for and against abolitionism, for example, which was of considerable interest to historians of previous generations, now seems to have fallen out of favor, and renewed examination of this topic is surely overdue.[13] One possible direction is suggested in Fionnghuala Sweeney's essay, a fascinating account of how Frederick Douglass began to reinvent himself when he resided in Britain and Ireland in the 1840s. His time there, she concludes, can only be understood in terms of a broader Atlantic history of race embracing both Ireland and the United States.

The racial dimension of Irish-American history was interwoven with, and indeed dependent on, a larger question of labor. Recent investigations of whiteness by American scholars emerged from the study of workers in the mid–nineteenth century, at a time when the Irish-born accounted for about a quarter of the population in cities like New York and Philadelphia. Irish workers have therefore been a particular focus of inquiry. Section 3 offers some new interpretations of labor history.[14] William Jenkins offers a masterly account of the development of an Irish enclave in Buffalo, New York, during the famine era and its persistence well into the twentieth century. Analyzing patterns of settlement, residence, labor, and politics, he shows how the city's First Ward retained its distinctive Irish character across several generations. Drawing on some of the central concerns in recent American labor history, Patricia Kelleher's essay looks at how class and gender informed the identities of young Irish immigrants in Gilded Age Chicago.[15] Ruth-Ann M. Harris also explores the history of women's work, finding in the letters sent home to Ireland by young female immigrants a generally optimistic portrait of life and labor in America. Diane M. Hotten-Somers paints a somewhat darker picture, but she finds some empowerment for Irish-American women in the reciprocal nature of the mistress-servant relationship, with each side influenced by and helping to constitute the identity of the other.

Finally, while the classic period of Irish-American history has been the "long nineteenth century," from the American Revolution through the end of World War I, some of the most exciting work currently being done involves the relatively neglected twentieth century.[16] Characteristic of that work, as section 4 demonstrates, is a strong emphasis on the interconnections and interactions between the Irish at home and abroad, and between Ireland and the United States more generally.[17] Harvey O'Brien's essay examines the multiple representations of Ireland in American and Irish tourist films in the mid–twentieth century, contrasting the pastoral idylls portrayed by the films with the realities of Irish economic and political life. Mary E. Daly tracks the shifting and ambivalent attitudes of the Irish government toward the United States in the decades after World War II, examining such themes as emigration, tourism, and nationalism and detecting an uneasy dialectic between pan-Irish sensibility and economic self-interest. While these two essays offer some memorable examples of how the Irish on opposite sides of the Atlantic have seen each other in the twentieth century, Thomas J. Archdeacon's essay takes us onto the thorny ground of Irish-American (and American) historical memory, specifically the recent controversial measures mandating the inclusion of the Irish potato famine in American high school curricula.[18] These proposals unleashed a predictable storm of criticism, not least by the British government, especially concerning the question of genocide. Analyzing the fraught and complex politics involved, Archdeacon gets to the heart of history's relevance to the present.[19] In conclusion, quite fittingly, Mary P. Corcoran examines a remarkable new phenomenon in Irish migration history, the return to a newly prosperous Ireland of large numbers of people who had emigrated during the economically depressed 1980s. For only the second time since the Famine, the Irish population is growing rather than declining, and more people are entering the country than leaving it.

Today, the American Irish enjoy unprecedented economic and political power, a renewed sense of ethnic identity, the erosion of older forms of prejudice, and a remarkable cultural vibrancy. In some ways, connections between the Irish at home and abroad are closer than ever before. Ireland and the United States are linked by a complex web of economic, political, and cultural ties, and one can fly to Dublin from Boston or New York in little more than five hours. But the paths of Irish and Irish-American history have also diverged in several important respects. Even as Irish Americans continue to celebrate their ethnic heritage, their sense of "Irishness" is increasingly unrecognizable to many in Ireland itself. It is from the confluence of these two linked but divergent cultures, Irish and Irish-American, that the conception of history presented in this book has emerged. The scholars represented here constitute their own modest diaspora: six of them are based in Irish universities, three more (including the editor) were born and raised in Ireland, and all are equally at home in Irish and American scholarly traditions.

While the new Irish-American history has broken important new ground and is in several respects broader and more inclusive than before, it might be noted in closing that it also has some limitations. It has not yet expanded the field of study beyond the United States to encompass North America as a whole, a peculiar omission given its otherwise impressive transnational framework.[20] Business history, and especially the emergence of an Irish-American middle class, has also been neglected. And, simply by virtue of being new, much of the recent scholarship ignores some of the central concerns of the old history, most notably urban and national politics, nationalist movements, and the institutional history of Catholicism.[21] Given that the "old" history gave considerable attention to "history from below" as well as to high politics, institutional religion, and anti-Irish political nativism, the "new" history will remain incomplete until it too tackles history both "from the bottom up" and "from the top down." Without this dual perspective, immigrant and ethnic history becomes uncoupled from the realities of social and political power in the host society, unfolding in a self-contained narrative rather than intersecting with bigger questions of national development. The formation of ethnic identities was a reciprocal rather than an autonomous process; immigrants made their own lives, but in a context in large measure determined by others before their arrival. Most of the essays presented here do address questions of power, some explicitly and others implicitly, but these questions will require more attention from future historians. For the present, however, the new Irish-American history can be justifiably proud of its accomplishments.

NOTES

1. The figures refer to the "Famine decade" of 1845–55, when 1.8 million Irish came to North America (1.5 million of them to the United States) and 300,000 went to other foreign destinations. Many more went to England and Scotland.

2. Arthur Schlesinger Jr., *A Thousand Days: John F. Kennedy in the White House* (Boston: Houghton Mifflin, 1965); Theodore White, *The Making of the President, 1960* (New York: Atheneum Publishers, 1961); William V. Shannon, *The American Irish* (New York: Macmillan Co., 1963); William F. Adams, *Ireland and the Irish Emigration to the New World from 1815 to the Famine* (1932; repr., New York: Russell & Russell, 1967); James G. Leyburn, *The Scotch-Irish: A Social History* (Chapel Hill: University of North Carolina Press, 1962); Robert Ernst, *Immigrant Life in New York City, 1825–1863* (1949; repr., Syracuse, N.Y.: Syracuse University Press, 1994); Carl Wittke, *The Irish in America* (1956;. repr., New York: Russell and Russell, 1970); George W. Potter, *To the Golden*

Door: The Story of the Irish in Ireland and America (Boston: Little, Brown & Co., 1960); William V. Shannon, *The American Irish* (New York: Macmillan Co., 1963); Lawrence J. McCaffrey, *The Irish Diaspora in America* (Bloomington: University of Indiana Press, 1976); Herbert Asbury, *The Gangs of New York: An Informal History of the Underworld* (New York: Knopf, 1937).

3. *Éire-Ireland: An Interdisciplinary Journal of Irish Studies* 36 (spring/summer 2001) and 37 (spring/summer 2002).

4. Kerby A. Miller, *Emigrants and Exiles: Ireland and the Irish Exodus to North America* (Oxford: Oxford University Press, 1985). Recent similar efforts include Patrick Griffin, *The People with No Name: Ireland's Ulster Scots, America's Scots Irish, and the Creation of a British Atlantic World, 1689–1764* (Princeton, N.J.: Princeton University Press, 2001); Kevin Kenny, *The American Irish: A History* (London and New York: Longman, 2000) and *Making Sense of the Molly Maguires* (New York: Oxford University Press, 1998).

5. Leyburn's *Scotch-Irish* and R. J. Dickson's *Ulster Emigration to Colonial America, 1718–1775* (London: Routledge and Kegan Paul, 1966) offer excellent, but self-contained, accounts. Miller's *Emigrants and Exiles* integrated the Protestant component into his general history of Irish migration, as does Kenny, *The American Irish*. Donald Akenson, in various works, calls for the Protestant dimension to be included, e.g., *The Irish Diaspora: A Primer* (Belfast: The Institute of Irish Studies; Toronto: P. D. Meany Co., 1996).

6. For a discussion, see the introduction to section 1, below. Standard works include Miller, *Emigrants and Exiles* and the following by David Fitzpatrick: *Irish Emigration, 1801–1921. Studies in Irish Economic and Social History, No. 1* (Dundalk, Ireland: The Economic and Social History Society of Ireland, 1984); "Emigration, 1801–70," in W. E. Vaughan, ed., *A New History of Ireland*, Vol. 5, *Ireland Under the Union, 1, 1801–70* (Oxford: Clarendon Press, 1989); "Emigration, 1871–1921," in W. E. Vaughan, ed., *A New History of Ireland*, Vol. 6, *Ireland under the Union, 2, 1870–1921* (Oxford: Clarendon Press, 1996).

7. Earl F. Niehaus, *The Irish in New Orleans, 1800–1860* (Baton Rouge: Louisiana State University Press, 1965) and David Gleeson, *The Irish in the South, 1815–77* (Chapel Hill: University of North Carolina Press, 2001) both deal with southern Protestants of Irish extraction.

8. See also Kerby A. Miller, "'Scotch-Irish,' 'Black Irish,' and 'Real Irish': Emigrants and Identities in the Old South," in Andy Bielenberg, ed., *The Irish Diaspora* (London: Longman, 2000).

9. Chain migration involves joining friends or relatives (or potential employers) who have already moved abroad, while step migration involves moving to one's final destination by stages, often with periods of residence in one or more cities, regions, or countries along the way.

10. Edward M. Levine, *The Irish and Irish Politicians: A Study in Social and Cultural Alienation* (Notre Dame, Ind.: University of Notre Dame Press, 1966); Steven P. Erie, *Rainbow's End: Irish Americans and the Dilemmas of Urban Machine Politics, 1840–1985* (Berkeley: University of California Press, 1988).

11. For a full discussion, see the introduction to section 2, below. The two most influential books in the Irish case have been David Roediger, *The Wages of Whiteness: Race and the Making of the American Working Class* (New York: Verso, 1992) and Noel Ignatiev, *How the Irish Became White* (New York: Routledge, 1995).

12. On Irish-American literature see Charles Fanning, *The Irish Voice in America: Irish-American Fiction from the 1760s to the 1980s* (Lexington: University Press of Kentucky, 1990) and Charles Fanning, ed., *The Exiles of Erin: Nineteenth-Century Irish-American Fiction* (Notre Dame, Ind.: University of Notre Dame Press, 1987).

13. See, for example, Gilbert Osofsky, "Abolitionists, Irish Immigrants, and the Dilemmas of Romantic Nationalism," *American Historical Review* 80 (October 1975): 889–97 (quote, 892); Douglas Riach, "Daniel O'Connell and American Anti-Slavery," *Irish Historical Studies* 20 (March 1976): 3–25.

14. See the introduction to section 3, below. Important works on this aspect of Irish-American history include David Noel Doyle, "The Irish and American Labour, 1880–1920," *Saothar: Journal of the Irish Labour History Society* 1 (1975): 42–53; David M. Emmons, *The Butte Irish: Class and Ethnicity in an American Mining Town, 1875–1925* (Urbana: University of Illinois Press, 1989); Eric Foner, "Class, Ethnicity, and Radicalism in the Gilded Age: The Land League in Irish-America," in Eric Foner, *Politics and Ideology in the Age of the Civil War* (New York: Oxford University Press, 1980); David Montgomery, "The Shuttle and the Cross: Weavers and Artisans in the Kensington Riots of 1844," *Journal of Social History* 5 (1972): 411–46, and "The Irish and the American Labor Movement," in David Noel Doyle and Owen Dudley Edwards, eds., *Ireland and America, 1776–1976* (Westport, Conn.: Greenwood Press, 1980); David Gerber, *The Making of an American Pluralism: Buffalo, New York, 1825–1860* (Urbana: University of Illinois Press, 1989); Ernst, *Immigrant Life in New York City*; Kenny, *Making Sense of the Molly Maguires*.

15. Other studies include Carol Groneman Pernicone, "Working-Class Immigrant Women in Mid-Nineteenth-Century New York: The Irish Woman's Experience," *Journal of Urban History* 4 (1978): 255–73; Thomas Dublin, *Women at Work: The Transformation of Work and Community in Lowell Massachusetts, 1826–1860* (New York: Columbia University Press, 1979); Carole Turbin, *Working Women of Collar City: Gender, Class and Community in Troy, 1864–86* (Urbana: University of Illinois Press, 1992). On Irish-American women's history more generally, see Hasia Diner, *Erin's Daughters in America: Irish Immigrant Women in the Nineteenth Century* (Baltimore: Johns Hopkins University Press, 1983); Janet Nolan, *Ourselves Alone: Women's Emigration from Ireland, 1885–1920* (Lexington: The University Press of Kentucky, 1989); Pauline Jackson, "Women in Nineteenth-Century Irish Emigration," *International Migration Review* 18 (winter 1984): 1004–20; Patrick O'Sullivan, ed., *The Irish World Wide. History, Heritage, Identity. Vol. 4. Irish Women and Irish Migration* (Leicester, England: Leicester University Press, 1995).

16. McCaffrey's *The Irish Diaspora* gave extensive coverage to the twentieth century, and Kenny's *The American Irish* devotes two of its six chapters to this period. Other relevant works include Linda Dowling Almeida, *Irish Immigrants in New York City, 1945–1995* (Bloomington: University of Indiana Press, 2001) and Ronald H. Bayor and Timothy J. Meagher, eds., *The New York Irish* (Baltimore: Johns Hopkins University Press, 1996), parts 3, 4, and 5.

17. See the introduction to section 4, below.

18. See Maureen Murphy and Alan Singer, "New York State's Great Irish Famine Curriculum: A Report" and James Mullin, "The New Jersey Famine Curriculum: A Report," *Éire-Ireland: An Interdisciplinary Journal of Irish Studies* 37 (spring/summer 2002), 109–18 and 119–29.

19. Recent books on the Famine include Mary E. Daly, *The Famine in Ireland*

(Dublin: Dublin Historical Association, 1986); Peter Gray, *The Irish Famine* (London: Thames and Hudson, 1995) and *Famine, Land and Politics: British Government and Irish Society, 1843–1850* (Dublin: Irish Academic Press, 1999); James S. Donnelly, Jr., *The Great Irish Potato Famine* (New York: Sutton Publishing, 2001); Christine Kinealy, *This Great Calamity: The Irish Famine, 1845–1852* (Dublin: Gill and Macmillan, 1994) and *A Death-Dealing Famine: The Great Hunger in Ireland* (London: Pluto Press, 1997); Cormac O'Gráda, *Black '47 and Beyond. The Great Irish Famine: History, Economy, and Memory* (Princeton: Princeton University Press, 1999).

20. Donald Akenson has repeatedly emphasized the need to do so.

21. On politics see Erie, *Rainbow's End;* Edward M. Levine, *The Irish and Irish Politicians: A Study in Social and Cultural Alienation* (South Bend, Ind.: University of Notre Dame Press, 1966); Thomas H. O'Connor, *The Boston Irish: A Political History* (Boston: Northeastern University Press, 1995); George E. Reedy, *From the Ward to the White House: The Irish in American Politics* (New York: Charles Scribner's Sons, 1991). Standard works on nationalism include Thomas N. Brown, *Irish-American Nationalism, 1870–1890* (Philadelphia: Lippincott, 1966); Foner, "Class, Ethnicity, and Radicalism in the Gilded Age: The Land League in Irish-America"; David A. Wilson, *United Irishmen, United States: Immigrant Radicals in the Early Republic* (Ithaca, N.Y.: Cornell University Press, 1998); John Belchem, "Nationalism, Republicanism and Exile: Irish Emigrants and the Revolutions of 1848," *Past and Present* 146 (February 1995): 103–35; Victor A. Walsh, "'A Fanatic Heart': The Cause of Irish-American Nationalism in Pittsburgh During the Gilded Age," *Journal of Social History* 15 (1981): 187–204; Andrew J. Wilson, *Irish America and the Ulster Conflict, 1968–1995* (Belfast: Blackstaff Press, 1995). On Catholicism see, for example, John Cogley, *Catholic America* (New York: Dial Press, 1973); Robert D. Cross, *The Emergence of Liberal Catholicism in America* (Chicago: Quadrangle Books, 1967); Jay P. Dolan, *The American Catholic Experience: A History From Colonial Times to the Present* (Garden City, N.Y.: Doubleday, 1985) and *The Immigrant Church: New York's German and Irish Catholics, 1815 to 1865* (Baltimore: Johns Hopkins University Press, 1975); Andrew M. Greeley, *The Catholic Experience* (New York: Doubleday, 1967); Thomas T. McAvoy, *History of the Catholic Church in the United States* (South Bend, Ind.: University of Notre Dame Press, 1969); Charles R. Morris, *American Catholic: The Saints and Sinners Who Built America's Most Powerful Church* (New York: Times Books/Random House, 1997).

Part 1

Patterns of Migration

Editor's Introduction

NOTE: For greater ease of reading, these section introductions are presented without notes. The relevant literature is cited in the notes to the general introduction at the beginning of the book. For a full bibliography, see Kevin Kenny, *The American Irish: A History* (London: Longman, 2000).

THE HISTORY OF MASS MIGRATION is the starting point for any account of the American Irish. The sheer scale of migration from Ireland is staggering. Since 1700, more than 7 million Irish men, women, and children have left Ireland for North America, Australia, New Zealand, South Africa, and elsewhere (along with 3 million more to Britain). The total number of emigrants—about 10 million—exceeds the entire Irish population at its historical peak on the eve of the Great Famine of the 1840s and is almost double the current population of Ireland, north and south. The majority of Irish migrants settled in the United States, with almost 5 million coming in the century after 1820, along with perhaps 300,000 more arriving in the colonial era. Only Germany and Italy sent more emigrants to America, but their populations today are between twelve and sixteen times greater than Ireland's.

Mass migration was among the most critical developments in modern Irish history. No other European country lost so large a proportion of its people to migration in the eighteenth and nineteenth centuries. Without this massive social hemorrhage, the nature of modern Ireland would have been radically different. In the year 1890, to give just one revealing example, two out of every five Irish-born people were living abroad. Two-thirds of the overseas Irish, or one-quarter of all Irish-born people, lived in the United States at that time. With 275,000 Irish-born

13

residents, New York City and Brooklyn (which had not yet incorporated into a single city) had the largest Irish urban concentration anywhere in the world, exceeding the total populations of both Dublin and Belfast. If the 600,000 or so second-generation Irish New Yorkers and Brooklynites are added, these figures become all the more impressive.

The story of the American Irish makes little sense without a prior understanding of the origins, scale, and significance of the mass migration that brought them across the Atlantic. On this subject there is an exceptionally well developed literature, certainly one of the best in the historiography of American immigration and ethnicity. The bulk of the literature, understandably enough, covers the century after 1820, the classic period of Irish Catholic migration to North America. It offers a sophisticated analysis of the economic, demographic, social, political, and cultural history of Ireland, as well as a comprehensive account of transportation and conditions of passage. Historians have paid particular attention to regional origins, class background, religious affiliation, and gender and the impact of these patterns of Irish history on developments in North America. Some of the best recent work has traced the history of immigrant communities in America to specific localities and regions in Ireland.

A common perception of Irish-American history is that it began with the Great Famine of the 1840s, which sent more than 2 million people across the Atlantic to North America. Of these migrants, 1.8 million went to North America (of whom 1.5 million went direct to the United States and 300,000 to Canada, with many of the latter soon migrating southward). With another 1 million dying of starvation and disease, the Irish population was cut by one-third in a single decade. Although 2 million people left Ireland in the single traumatic decade of 1846–55, four times that number left the country during other periods and almost three times that number came to North America. Irish transatlantic migration to America began in the seventeenth century and assumed the character of a mass movement in the eighteenth century. A conservative estimate for Irish Protestant migration to America in the latter century is 250,000, with an undetermined number of Catholics coming as well. Between 800,000 and 1 million Irish crossed the Atlantic in the first four decades of the nineteenth century. By far the heaviest period of migration was the postfamine era, from 1855 through the 1920s, when more than 3.5 million Irish came to the United States and hundreds of thousands more went elsewhere. Significantly smaller numbers of Irish— fewer than 200,000 in all—came to America after 1930, most of them in the 1950s and 1980s.

As concerted study of the twentieth century gets underway, historians have also begun to integrate the migration of the eighteenth century into its broader Irish, American, and Atlantic contexts. The great majority of Irish migrants before the 1830s were Protestant, most of them Presbyterians from the northern province of Ulster. Although the volume of eighteenth-century migration was much lower in absolute numbers than the mass Catholic migration of the following century, it was just as high when measured as a proportion of both the Irish and the American populations. When the first federal census was taken in 1790, people of Irish origin accounted for an estimated 14 to 17 percent of the white population, the dominant presence being those of Ulster Presbyterian origin, who made up about 10 percent. Because this story has often been excluded from the larger history of Irish America, it is worth dwelling on here.

Migrants from Ulster came to colonial America in search of land and religious toleration. In furtherance of both causes, they moved away from the eastern seaboard onto the isolated and dangerous frontier, where many became Indian fighters. By the eve of the Revolution, the Ulster Irish had settled all the way along the southern backcountry, from Pennsylvania to Georgia. If one were to stop the clock in say, 1800, and look for Irish America, it would be found primarily in the state of Pennsylvania and in a long line of states heading southward from there down the Appalachian mountains. In America, Irish Presbyterians came to be called "Scotch Irish," though that term had apparently not been used in Ulster and is uncommon there today. The term "Scots Irish" is preferable, but better yet is "Ulster Scots," for most of the Irish Presbyterians who migrated to America were descended from Scottish settlers who had come to Ulster in the seventeenth century. Asked to identify themselves, the people in question might simply have said "Presbyterian" or, perhaps, "Dissenter."

Should they be included in the story of Irish America? If they are included, then the first Irish president of the United States was Andrew Jackson, who was born in the Carolinas only two years after his parents emigrated from County Antrim, rather than John F. Kennedy, the privileged great-grandson of a Famine immigrant. James Buchanan, another son of Irish immigrants, was the second Irish president, and depending on who is counting, there were another twelve, thirteen, or even sixteen Irish presidents after that. But filiopietism of this sort makes for poor history. Few if any of these Ulster-descended Protestant politicians regarded themselves as Irish in any meaningful way, and many ignored or suppressed their heritage altogether. Claiming to be Irish, regardless of religious affiliation, was not the best way to launch a political career in America in either the eighteenth or nineteenth centuries. Only after 1960 did an Irish (by then Catholic Irish) pedigree begin to carry a political dividend.

On the other hand, recent polls suggest that of the 45 million Americans who claimed "Irish" as their primary ethnicity in the 1990 census, slightly more than half were Protestant. Evidently they regard themselves as "Irish" now, even if their ancestors did not in the past, a development that is in keeping with the rediscovery (or perhaps invention) of "white ethnicity" in the United States since the 1960s. Given this disjunction between the present and the past, what is the historian to do? The typical grounds for excluding the "Scots Irish" from true Irishness have been religious, regional, or even racial. Clearly, none of these criteria stands up to scrutiny; an Ulster Protestant of Scottish descent can be "Irish" if he or she so chooses. Better grounds for exclusion are needed, and they are to be found in the complex history of the nineteenth-century Atlantic world. For, if Catholic Irish nationalists on both sides of the ocean excluded Protestants from Irishness, Ulster Scots in America were more than willing to follow suit. Irish-American Protestants excluded themselves, laying claim to the term "Scots Irish" as the basis of a new ethnic identity that would differentiate them from the incoming Catholic Irish masses. Ulster Americans fade from the historical record thereafter, and we lose sight of them as the nineteenth century develops. They occasionally remerge in political and nativist organizations, in religious disputations, and at times of crisis like World War I, World War II, or the outbreak of "The Troubles" in Northern Ireland in the late 1960s, indicating the survival of some sense of ethnic identity. But the most pressing question for future investigation is what happened to Ulster immigrants and their descendants in the nineteenth century, especially in the rural South.

Ultimately, the movement of Presbyterians from Ulster to America is best seen as one part of the larger Atlantic story of Irish migration. Though separated by region, time, religion, and patterns of settlement, the Presbyterian and Catholic migrations had very similar economic causes. Both groups left the same divided island of Ireland and embarked on a common Atlantic history. In America, their lives can be studied in much the same terms of social and geographical mobility, religious identity and discrimination, involvement in nationalism, and the evolution of ethnic identities. Whether Protestant or Catholic, they were, after all, American immigrants, part of the great movement of population from Europe that helped create the United States.

Patterns of Irish Emigration
to America, 1783–1800

MAURICE J. BRIC

THE GENERAL FEATURES of Irish emigration to colonial America
are clear and relatively undisputed: it was largely of Ulster origin; the majority sailed for the Hudson and Delaware valleys; and the
departures peaked at three points: 1717–20, 1725–29, and during the nine
years prior to the outbreak of the American Revolution. As such, when
the passenger trade resumed after the Treaty of Paris (1783), it did so
within structures that were well established and familiar as well as along
shipping lanes that were managed by commercial networks and families that often spanned the Atlantic. But the later emigrants also sailed
during a period of more coordinated passenger travel, while the agents
who managed the business preferred to engage paying passengers
rather than indentured servants. Thus American independence not only
redefined political relationships between the old and new worlds,[1] but
it also marked a reorganization of the passenger trade between Ireland
and America.

-1-

After 1783, most Irish emigrants saw the new republic, in the words of
one emigrant letter, as a "Plentifull Country" [sic], which "before a year
or two . . . will be extremely enviable."[2] Despite the impact of such letters, the presentation and understanding of the emigration process were
even more greatly influenced by the management and fortunes of Ireland's two major industries, linen and provisions. Also, the commercial
structures of these industries, more often than not, determined the
choice of one American destination over another and where the majority of Ireland's emigrants would actually land.

In the northern province of Ulster linen had long been central to the economy and, although Dublin remained its major port of export, most of the eighteenth-century product came from the northern part of the island. In the nature of things Ulster also emerged as a major market for American flaxseed, 96 percent of which originated in the two ports of New York and Philadelphia in 1766–67. Moreover, several Irish merchants, through either full or occasional partnerships with houses in America, owned much of the tonnage that sustained this flaxseed/linen roundabout and managed it through networks of personal, family, and church connections that were geographically split only by the Atlantic. For example, the Belfast firm of John & James Holmes sent its ship *Barclay* on at least one trip to the Delaware every year, principally because the Holmes's brother, Hugh, was a partner in the Philadelphia-based firms of Holmes & Ralston and Holmes & Rainey. In any event, both the Delaware and the Hudson were central to Ulster's external trade, and this was reflected in the region's shipping advertisements for America. Of the 442 sailings that were advertised in the provincial press between 1750 and 1775, 53.5 percent and 18.5 percent were for Philadelphia and New York, respectively.[3]

The corollary of these connections was that prior to the American Revolution the middle colonies became the major attraction for Ulster's emigrants, especially if they were servants. After all, the holds of the flaxseed vessels had to be filled for the return journey to America. John and Robert Ogle suggested to their Philadelphia correspondent in 1774 that servants and redemptioners "make an advantageous returning freight to vessels loaded from you to us, & is *all paid down at Shipping*."[4] Thus the management of servants was central to the cash flow of Ulster-American trade, and merchants and ship-captains as well as their agents traded in people as they would in any commodity. As a result, the networks that linked the weavers, brokers, and merchants of the linen industry were also used to promote emigration from Ulster, while on the other side of the Atlantic the central role of the middle colonies in both the importation and distribution of servants and other Irish immigrants was assured.

After 1783 Ireland's linen industry underwent a remarkable revival. Between 1783–84 and 1791–92, linen exports almost doubled, and they continued at unprecedented levels of growth until the end of the century. As during the colonial period, Philadelphia emerged as the industry's major American *entrepôt*. For all that, however, there was also a new awareness that the American market was more competitive and no longer cushioned for Irish merchants by common membership in the

British empire. Moreover, as one correspondent remarked in 1786, the considerable increase in transatlantic trade gave "singular satisfaction . . . [only] if due attention is paid to the *goods proper for the American market.*"[5] While some ports, such as Derry, responded by building on their pre-revolutionary strengths in the linen and flaxseed trades, others, such as Dublin, diversified their trade and widened the geographical range of their American connections. The year 1783 thus inaugurated a more calculated approach to the Atlantic trade, while the opportunities afforded by peace were taken up in different ways in the various ports of Ireland.

Ireland's other staple industry was provisions and, as with linen, most areas of the country derived some prosperity from it. In this case, however, the external trade was concentrated on the ports of southern Ireland.[6] Before the revolution the export to the mainland American colonies had surged during the 1760s and early 1770s, although even at this peak it was a poor second to the trade with the Caribbean. In any event, the internal structures of the industry were less integrated than those relating to linen. In part this can be explained by the dependence of the southern ports' extensive West Indian trade on the long-term credit of the London commission system, as a result of which substantial consignments of southern linen were diverted to America through English ports during the course of the eighteenth century. The Treasury records for the period December 1773 to March 1776 highlight the implications of these commercial arrangements for the region's emigrant trade: significant numbers of passengers (although not all) followed the triangular patterns of southern Irish shipping and sailed for American ports through Britain.[7] However, while they sometimes pursued routes that were less direct than those from Ulster, American clearances from southern ports had a more varied list of destinations than those that sailed from Ulster. Thus, whereas Ulster's major ports focused on the middle colonies, shipping patterns suggest that Dublin, Cork, and Waterford had a relatively broader range that also included an important traffic to Maryland, New England, Virginia, and the West Indies.[8]

Relative to Ulster, however, the southern merchants were not unduly interested in the passenger trade. Popular empathy with America was also not as strong as in the north, and the connections and structures of its commerce and trade did little to counter this. Moreover, there was a long-established culture of seasonal labor in southern Ireland, and the Newfoundland fisheries, which attracted between three thousand and five thousand men every year, were part of this world.[9] Given that the negative images of the seventeenth-century emigration also lingered for most of the eighteenth, it was difficult to promote emigration in southern Ireland as a more positive alternative to seasonal labor. From the 1760s, however, there was a noticeable shift in attitudes, and southern Ireland did begin to develop a new appreciation for America as a "land of liberty." Indeed, Audrey Lockhart records that of 439 ships that left southern Irish ports between 1681 and 1775, the majority did so after 1750.[10]

The American Revolution left an indelible mark on the nature, structures, and orientation of Ireland's export of provisions. Between two-thirds and three-quarters of Irish beef had been taken by the English and French colonies of the West Indies before 1776. Thereafter, however, most of these exports were directed toward the English and other European markets.[11] Irish merchants never recovered their domination of the Caribbean market, and many West Indies-based agents of Irish and English houses returned home during the 1770s and 1780s. As a result, those merchants who stayed in the provisions export trade after 1783 were encouraged to forego their traditional West Indian routes and triangular trade patterns in favor of *direct* contact with the United States. The implications of these changes for the flow of Ireland's emigrants to America would become more obvious as the century drew to a close.

The passenger trade had always had a closer relationship with linen exports, however. After 1783, not only was the urge to emigrate resumed from the linen centers of Ulster but, as Norman Gamble has shown, the emergence of more specialized emigration brokers in Belfast in particular can be related to the city's increased trade in the commodity. Indeed, the Belfast merchants who were confidently rebuilding their American interests after 1783, either as owners of, or as agents for, American-bound vessels, ultimately relaunched and supervised emigrant traffic as well. Of their Atlantic routes, those to the Delaware valley were the most popular, and between 1783 and 1798 forty sailings were advertised for there in the provincial press. These were managed as operations that were exclusive to that region, as were twenty-four others that were advertised for New York and twenty-six for Baltimore. A further thirteen vessels sailed to a combination of two of the three destinations. However, such shared ventures were far less common among Belfast merchants than those that were managed directly to only one American port. The route to Baltimore was the least constant, and after 1789 sailings to Baltimore began to decrease. As they did, however, those leaving for New England increased, and between 1789 and 1796 sixteen vessels were advertised between Belfast and the region, especially for Massachusetts.[12]

Although advertised sailings from Derry to America just exceeded those from Belfast between 1783 and 1798, they did not have Belfast's geographical variety. As they had done before the revolution, they focused on the Delaware, which attracted over three-quarters of the city's clearances, outstripping those between Belfast and the Delaware by 300 percent to 400 percent between 1784 and 1793. Ulster's other major port, Newry, also had strong links with the Delaware (thirty-two sailings). It also split a number of additional sailings between the Delaware and the Hudson (thirteen) and developed a significant and enduring direct link with New York between 1785 and 1789 (eight sailings), when this route was not as actively pursued from the other Ulster ports. As ever, these connections were associated with the promotion of linen. Indeed, on 26 August 1784, the *New York Packet* published an address, signed by no fewer than eighty merchants, publicizing Newry's newly opened linen hall and protesting that "all Merchants from thenceforth at all times may depend upon a regular and constant supply of linens, diapers, *&c. &c*" from the port.

Dublin took to "the happy effects" of peace with great enthusiasm and on 11 March 1786, *Saunder's [Dublin] Newsletter* announced that there were "more American ships now in the port of Dublin than have ever been known since the Revolution and the encouragement for the export of our manufactures wears a more favourable aspect than it has ever done." The American connections of these ships were as geographically varied as those of Belfast, although the volume from Dublin was higher. The Delaware (sixty-two sailings), the Hudson (sixty-seven), and—between 1783 and 1789—the Chesapeake (twenty-eight) were the strongest attractions for the city's advertised shipping, but after 1795 New York became Dublin's most popular destination. Also after 1795 the number of sailings to New England began to increase, and in 1799 it equaled those for New York. Few domestic letter-books of firms involved in Dublin's American trade have survived, and advertisements published in the capital city contain less detailed information than those of Belfast and Derry. However, some light was thrown on the trade when allegations of incompetence were made against the captain of the ship *Success* (Dublin to Philadelphia, 1783) and its owners, the Dublin firm of Galloway *&* Stillas. The charges were widely publicized at the time, but there were hints that some houses were "malicious[ly] reporting" the affair in order to get an edge on their rivals in the passenger trade.[13] As such, the affair highlighted the new energy with which Dublin's merchants were approaching the American routes after 1783 and, in particular, how they were competing for emigrants.

After 1783, Cork continued some of its pre-revolutionary associations with the West Indies, Nova Scotia, and Baltimore. Of the three destinations, however, it was only the last that developed a significant passenger traffic during the seventeen years to 1800. As with the other Irish ports, Cork's shipping connections with the Delaware (fifty-two sailings) and the Hudson (thirty-three) were also strong after the war and were almost always managed as separate enterprises. Regardless of their American destination, however, the vessels that sailed from Cork were particularly vulnerable to privateers and impressments, and during the 1790s this influenced the decision to redirect most of them to New York and New England.

-2-

On the American side of the Atlantic, Philadelphia's interest in the passenger trade was sustained by a number of commercial connections with the old country. Some merchants, such as John Barclay, Benjamin Fuller, and Blair McClenachan, had been born in Ireland. In 1784, Fuller introduced to his brother Abraham, of Cork, the distinguished Philadelphia merchants John Donnaldson and Francis West, who would be visiting "most of the principal places [in Ireland] . . . in order to form connections." With a similar intention McClenachan, one of Philadelphia's leading pre-revolutionary correspondents with Ulster, visited his native city of Derry in June 1784 and was reported to have made a conspicuous display of his "opulence." As if to confirm that his vessel, the 600-ton ship *Congress*, was indeed what its advertisements stated, "a remarkable fine ship," he entertained on board two hundred of the city fathers with "an elegant breakfast [and] a dance, enlivened by good humour and a joyous innocence." If Ireland made "proper use" of such American interest in Irish trade, the Dublin *Freeman's Journal* concluded that it "must unavoidably become, in less than half a century, great, rich, and flourishing."[14]

Other Philadelphia merchants were involved in the Irish trade through the ownership or joint ownership of, or the local agency for, vessels on the several routes from Ireland. For example, Haynes & Crawford co-owned the 400-ton ship *America* (Dublin to Philadelphia, 1784) and the 350-ton ship *Dublin Packet* (Dublin to Philadelphia, 1785–87 and 1789) and acted as agent for nine of the thirty-one Irish entries in 1787: five from Derry, one from Belfast, two from Dublin, and one from Cork. The Irish associations of Conyngham & Nesbitt were particularly strong, and as John Campbell has noted, "Quite a number of [the Philadelphia Irish Society of] the Friendly Sons of St. Patrick came to

America through connections of the firm, several of them with letters of recommendation from friends or relatives in Ireland."[15] As during the colonial period, most of these traveled from Ulster ports. During the late 1780s, however, Philadelphia's shipping entrances from Ulster and southern Irish ports drew closer, and between 1788 and 1790 they came to within 1, 4, and 4, respectively, of parity (13/12; 15/11; 16/12). After 1790 the predominance of the Ulster ports was more clearly re-established, as was the particularly strong connection with Derry.

Peace also enabled New York to develop its trade with Ireland, and during 1785–86 the British consul recorded twelve and fourteen entries from, and twenty and twenty-six clearances for, Ireland.[16] While the clearances reflected the relaunching of the flaxseed trade, they also chart an ongoing rivalry with Philadelphia. Accordingly, it was with no little pride that on 14 January 1792 the *New York Journal* reported that for the year ending 30 December 1791, the numbers of marine arrivals in New York and Philadelphia were 2,537 and 1,828, respectively, or a balance of 709 "in favour of New York." Although the corresponding figures from "foreign ports" were 718 and 567, it was not until 1793 that New York supplanted Philadelphia as the major focus of Ireland's American vessels (twenty-six/twenty-five sailings). This happened because of New York's developing connections with the ports of southern Ireland, which especially increased during the second half of the 1790s and included relatively regular traffic from ports such as Waterford and Limerick that had not figured very prominently in the port's biography up until then.

Baltimore's Irish entrances between 1783 and 1790 were from southern rather than northern Ireland (fifty-five/thirty). Nonetheless, the port was situated in a region of great promise, as suggested in the following advertisement for the ship *Cato* (Belfast to Alexandria, 1791): "It is within a few miles of the spot lately chosen and now building for the Federal Town and constant seat of Congress, and where labourers and tradesmen of all denominations will meet with higher wages than in most other parts of America." Among the merchants who were involved in the city's Irish trade were William Patterson, Oliver Simms, William and Joseph Wilson, and John Stevenson, who together sought to establish Baltimore as an alternative to the more established routes to the Delaware and Hudson. The lane was particularly associated with the 300-ton ship *Paca*, advertised in 1784 as a "new vessel" from Belfast and owned by a consortium of six Baltimore merchants, including the Limerick-born Wilson and the Ulster-born John Brown, the latter of whom traveled to Baltimore on the maiden voyage with another owner, Captain Thomas Kell.

By 1785, however, the vessel had abandoned its Ulster connections for the ports of southern Ireland, changing its advertisement of that year from Belfast to Cork and Limerick, whence it could make two trips every year and return flaxseed and staves for redemptioners and servants, who were then sold at "the average price of £14.2.5 each."[17]

The biographies of ships such as the *Paca* and the *America* underline the influence that American merchants and their Irish agents could have on an emigrant's choice of destination in America. In Ireland these agents usually worked within wider networks that linked the manager of a given sailing to a mosaic of subagents in outlying towns and villages. This was especially true in the northern province of Ulster, where personal and family ties were often reinforced by those nurtured by the linen industry. In the hinterlands of the southern ports of Cork and Dublin, the activities of the emigration manager were more casually organized and advertised. These were areas of high mobility and seasonal labor which, for the Cork region, David Dickson has related to the seasonality of the Newfoundland fisheries, hiring fairs for the potato and slaughtering seasons, the development of rural commissions in grain, and recruitment for the Irish brigades of Catholic Europe.[18] While these activities are difficult to define by virtue of their informality, they were as important in facilitating southern emigration after 1783 as was the extended organization of the linen industry to the passenger trade of Ulster.

The most public record of the promotion and management of late eighteenth-century Irish emigration is to be found in the shipping advertisements of contemporary Irish newspapers. From the themes of these notices one can get a sense of how the passenger trade responded to the demands and needs of the traveling public after 1783. Invariably, "plenty" and "good" provisions were promised. For example, the ship *Independence* (Belfast to Philadelphia, 1783) promised that "strict attention will be paid to the quality of the provisions, to have the Ship well stored with every thing [sic] proper and necessary for the voyage, so as to render the passage agreeable." To its assurance of the "very best Provisions," the ship *Paca* (Belfast to Baltimore, 1785) added that it would give a rebate for any "overplus" that would be left over after its presumed "swift" passage between Ireland and America. The age and build of the vessel were also usually mentioned. For example, the ship *Barclay* (Derry to Philadelphia, 1790) was "but 6 months off the docks," while the ship *Three Brothers* (Derry to Philadelphia, 1783) was "strong and well built of live Oak and Cedar." The ship *Hannibal* (Belfast to Philadelphia, 1789) was said to be especially sturdy and, "having been built for a Ship of War, she is superior in accommodation for passengers, to any other in the trade." In some cases passengers were also invited to assess for themselves the conditions on board before they made any commitments. For those who wanted to sail on the ship *Richard and Thomas* (Belfast to Philadelphia, 1784), boats would "take down any persons desirous of seeing her, every Friday during her stay here."[19]

The advantages of one vessel over another were also conveyed by suggestions that, as in the case of the ship *Three Brothers* (Derry to Philadelphia, 1783), it was "a remarkable fast Sailer." However, the length of the passage to America did not alter very much from the colonial period. On average the voyage from Ulster ports to Philadelphia took from sixty-four days in the early spring to forty-nine during the high season of July to September, with vessels from Dublin and Cork taking a little less time to make the crossing. For the port of New York the data are similar, but on the longer routes to Charleston the average duration of the voyage, usually initiated in the fall, was eight to nine weeks, while the span to Baltimore ran a week to ten days shorter.[20] In some cases purpose-built vessels led to improvements on these averages during the 1780s and 1790s, and these were duly incorporated into shipping advertisements. For example, the ship *Dublin Packet* (Dublin to Philadelphia) often boasted of its quick passages of 30 to 35 days to Philadelphia, while "more than once, it performed its voyage from Philadelphia to Dublin, in 21 days." The *Paca* (Cork to Baltimore, 1785) insinuated its speed by referring to its "twice yearly sailings" from Ireland, and its advertisement, as published in the *Belfast Newsletter* on 25 January 1785, noted that its

> last voyage . . . [had been] made in seven weeks and three days with 459 souls on board, who arrived at Baltimore all well, being the same number he [the captain] took in at Belfast; and a circumstance which scarce has not been equalled, the passengers not being able to use their full allowance of provisions during the voyage.[21]

For all that, dates of departure were often altered, and this could involve Irish travelers in additional expense. For the colonial period Dickson has suggested that on average there was a five-week delay between advertisement and departure, although during periods of heavy emigration delays were longer, given that it was often impossible to predict when a vessel would arrive in port. From the early 1770s, however, a better organized trade often saw Irish passengers provisioned from the day that they were issued with a "positively final" notice to depart, although this was far more usual after 1783. During the 1780s voyages were still deferred, as they had been prior to the revolution.

Such delays were usually presented as being "at the request of a number of passengers." However, they also highlighted the occasional problems of managing a trade that was drawing on increasingly wider catchment areas. Nonetheless, promoters had to address the problems that postponement caused. In 1792, for example, the managers of the brig *Rachel* (Newry to Philadelphia and New York) promised that "should the vessel be detained after the 14th of April, any passengers who have then engaged, will be maintained on board from that day." However, potential travelers were less interested in such schemes than in the assurance that the captain, as the managers of the *Philadelphia and Dublin Packet* (Dublin and Philadelphia, 1791) put it, was "well known for the Punctuality of sailing at all Times."[22]

From the early 1770s emigration brokers also began to respond to concerns about ventilation by including more and larger portholes in the designs of their newer vessels. The ship *Mary* (Derry to Philadelphia, 1783) was reported to be "very lofty" between decks, with six portholes on each side, while the ship *Betsey* (Derry to Philadelphia, 1790) was "6 Feet high between Decks, Cabin and Steerage, Ditto." There were also undertakings not to overcrowd vessels. Thus the owners of the ship *Alexander* (Derry to Philadelphia, 1788) warned that they would close their register at "a certain number of passengers," after which "none" would be taken.[23] Such promises were not always kept. However, the managers of Ireland's late eighteenth-century passenger trade were not insensitive to the comforts (and criticisms) of those to whom they promoted the Atlantic crossing and were less ready to dismiss potential Irish emigrants to the bit parts to which they had usually been assigned for much of the colonial period.

Advertisements also implied that the conduct of the ship captain was vital in determining whether conditions on board would be pleasant or pathetic. Some passengers were told of the "humanity" and "care and attention" of the captain, while others were reassured that captains were experienced and had been "long in the passenger trade." In 1786 it was reported that Captain William Cheevers of the ship *Anne and Susan* (Newry to Philadelphia and New York) had already made sixty-nine voyages "across the Western Ocean," while Captain William McDonnell of the ship *Richard and Thomas* (Belfast to Newcastle and Philadelphia, 1784) was not only "an experienced master but had latterly [been] an officer under captain McBride of the Artois frigate." Passengers could later comment on the accuracy of such descriptions and on occasion did so to considerable effect through testimonials and letters of thanks that were often published in the contemporary press. Although such memorials first appeared in the early 1770s, they became more common during the following decades. In 1783, for example, Captain James Gillis was thanked as follows:

> We, the under-named persons who sailed from Belfast to Philadelphia on board the Three Brothers, should think ourselves wanting both in gratitude to our worthy Captain (Mr. James Gillis) as well as in regard to such of our friends and countrymen who at any future period may choose to visit America, were we to omit declaring, in the most public manner, the humane and friendly treatment we met with from that Gentleman during the whole of our passage.
>
> PHILADELPHIA, NOV. 20TH, 1783.

In the following year Captain William Cheevers of the brig *Congress* (Newry to Philadelphia) received what was perhaps the ultimate accolade: his "good treatment" of his passengers was described as being too "well known" to bear detailed repetition.[24]

As might be expected, such citations were not always spontaneous productions. However, they did reflect the increasing importance of the passenger in the promotion and even in the vindication of a particular vessel. As the [*Philadelphia*] *American Daily Advertiser* remarked on 16 August 1791,

> the bare silence of the passengers would . . . be looked on as sufficient condemnation of both the Captain and vessel . . . and if once the Captain of one of these Ships, suffers the "*Mark of the Beast*" to be written on his forehead, or on the stern of the vessel, he will probably never again be able to procure a single passenger.

In any event, aggrieved passengers were not as intimidated about taking the captain or owners to court as they had been earlier in the century. In 1788, for example, a Philadelphia court found against an Irish captain "for brutality and ill-treatment of his passengers." Eighteen months later, the Hibernian Society for the Relief of Immigrants from Ireland was founded in the same city. This society lost no time in denouncing Captain Robert Cunningham of the brig *Cunningham* (Derry to Philadelphia, 1790) for his "flagrant violations of the precepts of humanity" and later sponsored his indictment on charges of overcrowding and scarcity of provisions, despite the vessel's advertisement to the contrary. As a result, Cunningham was fined £500 and spent several months in prison. He was eventually released in April 1791 after "friends of the master" had petitioned for "relief" and "clemency." However, the appeal was not effective until the Hibernian Society itself was seen to formally support such leniency.[25] This case showed that the complaints of newly arrived Irish immigrants, as coordinated by their immigrant-aid societies, could not be ignored. Moreover, shipowners were again reminded that their passengers were no longer mere ballast for their holds.

-3-

The number of those who sailed from Ireland after 1783 is difficult to calculate. For the 1780s and 1790s Maldwyn Jones has estimated that the annual average outflow was "about 5,000." Not surprisingly, what the British consul in Philadelphia, Phineas Bond, described as "the rage for emigration" was especially noticeable from Ulster, and newspaper reports of booked-out sailings from the province and the refusal of passengers "for want of room" were not uncommon. However, increased emigration from outside Ulster was also a feature of these years. From Dublin one newspaper reported that "not less than 1,000 persons" had embarked for America in February 1784, while the *Pennsylvania Packet* observed on 3 August 1784 that "it is imagined [that] ten more vessels could shortly be filled, were they to sail with emigrants to that part of the world [Philadelphia] from the city and county of Dublin only." The flow of people continued into the 1790s and established Dublin as a newly important exit-point for Irish emigration to America. For the other southern ports of Cork, Galway, Limerick, and Waterford, there were also several "alarming instances of emigration." From Limerick, for example, it was suggested in 1784 that "such is the rage of emigration, that above 1,000 persons offered, but were rejected for want of room" on the *Intrepid* (Limerick to Baltimore, 1784).[26]

Whatever their Irish origins, most late eighteenth-century emigrants headed for the Delaware Valley. This region had a long-established and central role in Ireland's passenger trade, which was well documented in the contemporary press as well as by official and semi-official observers. Among the former one account from mid-1784 reported that "5,000 natives [of Ireland] had arrived in Philadelphia alone," with "many more" expected. Even in the "five or six sail of Vessels" that had arrived in American ports from Ireland in the late-season month of October 1784, "at least" seven hundred to eight hundred passengers were reported to have landed at Philadelphia.[27] Of the official observers, Bond paid closest attention to the incoming Irish traffic. He had a peculiar access to information because of the requirement that on arrival British and Irish captains had to deposit their registers and Mediterranean Passes with his office.[28] Accordingly, his data for the 1780s are of particular interest and suggest that not only was the flow from Ireland higher than before the revolution, but that the "the migrations hither since the Peace, have been much greater from Ireland than from all the other Ports of Europe."[29]

For the 1780s Bond listed the figures as follows:

CONSULAR REPORTS ON IMMIGRATION
INTO THE DELAWARE VALLEY, 1783–89

Year	1783	1784	1785	1786	1787	1788	1789
Passengers	3508	9436	5866	2340	1220	1050	2296

Source: (London) Public Record Office, FO/4/7–8.

Of these 25,716 arrivals, the number of *Irish* passengers was 23,823. Although Bond suggested in 1790 that the number of these passengers, while still "important," had fallen "very short of the general expectation," he did not keep these reports in as much detail as he had kept those of the previous seven years. However, my own reconstruction from newspaper and other sources suggests that nearly 75,000 passengers entered the Delaware Valley from Ireland between 1783 and 1800, almost half of them between 1783 and 1789. During the first six years after independence the majority came from Ulster, and the difference between these (23,214) and those who had sailed from southern Irish ports (13,311) is striking. For the 1790s it is even more so, and, indeed, from an annual average of over 1,900 between 1783 and 1789, the identifiable immigration from southern Ireland fell sharply to an annual average of a mere 176 between 1793 and 1799. In the meantime emigration from Ulster ports continued throughout the 1790s, and, although it declined by nearly two-thirds after 1797, its combined total between 1790 and 1797 was, at nearly 32,000, even greater than that for the preceding seven years, 1783–90. By any standards, these figures represent a major flow and suggest that Ulster immigration into the Delaware valley continued at peak levels well into the 1790s.[30] They also imply that while the attraction of the Delaware was both definite and obvious from both parts of Ireland after 1783, war and the fear of impressment had a greater impact on the passenger trade from southern Ireland than it had on that from Ulster.[31]

For the port of Philadelphia per se, computing Irish immigration is complicated by the fact that passengers often disembarked at the Delaware ports of Newcastle and Wilmington. During the colonial period these ports had evolved as stopovers for ongoing traffic to Philadelphia, especially after Pennsylvania imposed duties on incoming servants and, later, when it adopted strict quarantine regulations for immigrants.[32] As a result, passengers often broke their journeys in Delaware and completed them either overland or by separate tender. The port of Newcastle remained intertwined with Philadelphia well into the early national period, and several Irish vessels continued to advertise for Philadelphia (and other destinations) "by way of" Delaware. For example, the ship *St. James* (Belfast to Newcastle and New York, 1789) announced that it would not travel up-river but that there were "frequent vessels" to take passengers onward to Philadelphia. With this in mind "most" of the four hundred passengers on its 1791 voyage expected to land at Newcastle, while of the three hundred fifty who sailed on the ship *Nancy* (Derry to Newcastle and Philadelphia, 1791), two hundred "came ashore in New-Castle [sic] [and] the remainder came up to this city [Philadelphia] in good health."[33] In addition to these kinds of notices, the special relationship between the two ports is also implied by the 40 percent difference between my estimated figure of 36,525 entrants for the first six years after independence and the 23,823 given by Bond. On one level this discrepancy is a matter of focus: mine on the Delaware valley as a whole, Bond's on Philadelphia. However, as during the colonial period, it again confirms that Newcastle was a port of dispersal through which passengers traveled both onward to Philadelphia and to other ports, including New York to the north and Baltimore and Charleston to the south.[34]

The Irish emigrants who entered the Hudson valley were also welcomed as "a most valuable acquisition." Data on this passenger flow are less detailed and more difficult to quantify in the way that I have been able to do for the Delaware valley. However, some general observations can be made. It is clear that, at least on purpose-built vessels, no fewer passengers were carried into New York than on trips to the Delaware. In 1791, for example, the *Anne and Susan* ferried four hundred fifty passengers from Derry to New York, while six years later, the *Elizabeth* landed "upwards of 300 passengers" from Waterford. There were also reports that a number of vessels from Ireland entered with unspecified numbers of "passengers" and that testimonials were published from satisfied travelers along with accounts of people entering New York *via* Newcastle, Delaware. Such notices suggest that Irish immigration into the Hudson valley was no less important than that into the Delaware, and this is confirmed in the official reports of Sir John Temple, the British consul-general, who was based in New York. In April 1789, Temple informed the Duke of Leeds that "considerable numbers" had landed at New York and Baltimore between 1783 and 1787, while two years later he wrote that immigration from Ireland had been "very great the year past." However,

Temple had less cause to worry than Bond. In general terms it can be stated that Irish immigration into the Hudson valley was only between a quarter and a third of that into the Delaware.[35]

For Baltimore, Bond recorded that during 1783 and 1784 the port attracted "from 6 to 800 Irish passengers." Contemporary newspapers confirm these figures and add that the southern Irish predominated. As noted above, the flagship of the port's Irish connections was the ship *Paca*, which sailed from both Belfast (1784–86) and the southern ports of Cork and Limerick (1784–88), sometimes making two trips per year. On 8 September 1785 the *Cork Hibernian Chronicle* noted that over the previous fifteen months, the ship had carried seven hundred fifty passengers to Baltimore on its first three sailings. However, the vessel's numbers did not continue at these levels, and on its last trip (1788) the *Paca* brought as few as sixty-nine servants from Limerick, after which it was directed to non-Irish routes. For these years of the late 1780s Bond noted a decline in Irish immigration and reported that "scarcely any" Irish emigrants arrived between 1785 and 1789.[36] In part this was due to the impact of negative reports about the treatment of servants in the area. Irish immigration into Maryland did not cease, but, unlike that into Philadelphia, it was drawn from the ports of southern rather than northern Ireland.

Charleston had strong connections with Ulster and in particular with the Larne merchant John Montgomery. Although Montgomery was involved in other vessels, his principal interest was in the three-hundred-ton ship, the *Irish Volunteer*, which he owned and which between 1788 and 1796 made an annual trip between Larne and Charleston. The ship had been purposely built as a passenger vessel and usually carried between two hundred and three hundred sixty passengers. With the help of the Rev. Douglas of Clough, Larne's Anthony Sinclair also sent his ship *Ann* to Charleston between 1788 and 1790. The involvement of clergymen in such ventures was neither new nor rare (at least on this route) and had emerged as a feature of the various schemes of assisted emigration that colonial Carolina had developed during the 1730s and 1760s. These projects had also encouraged better organized and prearranged *bloc* sailings, and this approach to emigration endured with respect to the Carolinas until the late 1790s.[37] Toward the end of the century the patrols of French and English privateers operating out of the West Indies all but stopped Charleston's direct Irish passenger trade until the following century. In terms of numbers the best snapshot was given in January 1790 by the British consul in Charleston, George Miller:

Within the last two years, there have arrived in South Carolina, 1017 Emi-grants, in three Vessels from Larne, and one from Belfast. These people paid for their passage generally. . . . Some also have arrived in North Car-olina, from the same place. . . . Formerly they used to suffer considerably on their arrival, on account of their not planning their departure so as to arrive always at a favourable season of the year. . . . Those who have late-ly emigrated have been more prudent, by arriving in the beginning of Winter, which afforded them an opportunity of travelling through the swampy and unhealthy part of the Country at the most proper time of the year.[38]

Every Irish immigrant was given "great" and "proper encouragement" to seize their opportunities in the newly proclaimed "land of liberty." After 1783 the choices on offer were wider and more thoughtfully pre-sented than they had been before the revolution. Thus, as Irish immi-grants arrived in Philadelphia, the official capital of the new republic after 1790, they were seen as more discriminating characters than their pre-revolutionary cousins. In Philadelphia, Irish immigrant-aid soci-eties, such as the Hibernian Society, also encouraged America's post-revolutionary Irish immigrants to develop a clearer sense of national identity than had been the case in the more undifferentiated culture of the colonial years. They also urged them to challenge America's estab-lished élites and their systems of social and political leadership. During the 1790s the changing nature of America's more substantial, self-assured, and politically experienced Irish communities would be reflected in the ways in which they became involved in the politics of the new republic, especially in Philadelphia and New York. Indeed, the growth of "ethnicity" and "party" are mirror images of each other, and while they interacted in different ways in the other cities of the union, in these two cities they not only contributed to the broadening of the early national polity but also were a testament to the arrival of a "new Irish" immigrant in the new American republic.

NOTES

1. R.J. Dickson, *Ulster Emigration to Colonial America, 1718–1785* (London, 1966); Audrey Lockhart, *Some Aspects of Emigration from Ireland to the North American Colonies between 1660 and 1775* (New York, 1976); Marianne S. Wokeck, *Trade in Strangers* (University Park, Penn., 1999). For the period 1700–1820 the estimates of the passenger flow vary between 250,000 and 450,000; see Henry A. Gemery, "European Emigration to North America, 1700–1820," *Perspectives in American History*, new series, I (1984), 286.

2. Belfast, Public Record Office of Northern Ireland (PRONI), D1752, Andrew Martin to his father, 5 July 1787.

3. Thomas M. Truxes, *Irish-American Trade, 1660–1783* (New York, 1983), 199, Chapter 9. For the ownership of the vessels cited in this article, see Maurice J. Bric, "Ireland, Irishmen, and the Broadening of the Late Eighteenth-Century Philadelphia Polity," 2 vols. (Ph.D. diss., Johns Hopkins University, 1990), I, Chapter 4. The data on the sailings have been derived from Dickson, *Ulster Emigration,* Appendix E.

4. Library of Congress, Blair McClenachan Papers, letter dated 15 August 1774.

5. Louis M. Cullen, *An Economic History of Ireland since 1660* (London, 1972), 62–63; *Saunder's [Dublin] Newsletter (SN),* 2 October 1783, 15 July 1786.

6. I am using the word "southern" to refer to the principal ports outside Ulster: Dublin, Cork, Waterford, and to a lesser extent, Limerick and Galway. The "northern" ports include Belfast, Derry, and Newry as well as the lesser ports of Larne and Portrush.

7. Truxes, *Irish-American Trade,* 147, 154, Chapters 3, 4, and 9. For Ireland's trade with the Caribbean, see R.C. Nash, "Irish Atlantic Trade in the Seventeenth and Eighteenth Century," *William and Mary Quarterly (WMQ)* 42 (1985), 329–56. The Treasury records are analyzed in Bernard Bailyn, *Voyagers to the West* (New York, 1986), 67–239. For more general comment, see Francis G. James, *Ireland in the Empire, 1688–1779* (Cambridge, Mass., 1973) and "Irish Colonial Trade in the Eighteenth Century," *WMQ* 20 (1963), 574–84.

8. In this article data on the patterns, extent, and ownership of shipping between Irish ports and America are drawn from an updated analysis of contemporary newspaper advertisements and marine notices published in my *Economy of Irish Emigration to America, 1760–1800* (forthcoming, 2001). For a preliminary survey of these references, see Bric, "Ireland, Irishmen, and the Broadening of the Late Eighteenth-Century Philadelphia Polity," II, Appendix IV.

9. The extent of the Newfoundland connection is conveyed by, among others, a report in *SN,* 20 April 1784, that during the previous week four vessels had sailed for the fisheries from Cork, sixteen from Waterford, three from Baltimore (in Cork), and two from Crookhaven.

10. Lockhart's figures are analyzed in David Noel Doyle, *Ireland, Irishmen, and Revolutionary America* (Cork and Dublin, 1981), 65.

11. Cullen, *Economic History,* 9; Nash, "Irish Atlantic Trade," 329–56; William O'Sullivan, *The Economic History of Cork City from the Earliest Times to the Act of Union* (Cork, 1937), 327, 335, 342.

12. Norman E. Gamble, "The Business Community and the Trade of Belfast, 1767–1800" (Ph.D. diss., Trinity College, Dublin, 1968), 93, 25–41, 45. For data on the routes, see n. 8 above.

13. The *Success* ran aground in the Delaware in November 1783, allegedly after the captain had "knowingly and willingly" mismanaged the vessel, and its "owners and merchants of Dublin . . . [were] totally ignorant of naval affairs." See (Philadelphia) *Independent Gazetteer (IG),* 3, 4 October 1783; *SN,* 23 October, 29 November 1783.

14. Historical Society of Pennsylvania (HSP), Benjamin Fuller Letterbook, 24 June 1784; *Belfast Newsletter (BN),* 15 June 1784; *Londonderry Journal (LJ),* 8 June 1784; *BN,* 16 July 1784; Dublin *Freeman's Journal (FJ),* 25 November 1788. For Philadelphia's Irish merchants, see Thomas M. Doerflinger, *A Vigorous Spirit of Enterprise: Merchants and Economic Development in Revolutionary Philadelphia* (Chapel Hill, N.C., 1986).

15. HSP, Port of Philadelphia, Port Entry Books (1784–87); John H. Campbell, *A History of the Society of the Friendly Sons of St. Patrick and of the Hibernian Society* (Philadelphia, 1892), 107; Doerflinger, *Vigorous Spirit of Enterprise*, 59, 236–38.

16. London, Public Record Office (PRO), Records of the Foreign Office (FO), FO/4/3, FO/4/4.

17. *BN*, 25 January 1791, 26 March 1784; Maryland Historical Society (MHS), MS. 1149, William Wilson Account Book.

18. Dickson, *Ulster Emigration*, Chapter 7; David Dickson, "An Economic History of the Cork Region in the Eighteenth Century" (Ph.D. diss., Trinity College, Dublin, 1977), 330n., 409–10, 435–36, 465–66, 487–91, 629.

19. *BN*, 11 July 1783, 25 January 1785; *LJ*, 10 August 1790, 22 July 1783; *BN*, 29 December 1789, 15 June 1784.

20. *LJ*, 22 July 1783. The data on the length of voyages have been taken from Bric, *Economy of Irish Emigration*, Chapter 4.

21. *BN*, 9 June 1789. For the *Paca*, see also the *Cork Hibernian Chronicle (CHC)*, 27 March 1786, 5 April 1787.

22. Dickson, *Ulster Emigration*, 122, 202–03; *BN*, 6 March 1792, 15 June 1784; Dublin *Hibernian Journal (HJ)*, 7 January 1791. In 1783 the departure of the brig *Rose and Betty* (Newry to Baltimore and Virginia), originally advertised for 20 April, was put off no fewer than three times before it finally sailed on 23 May; see *BN*, 7 March, 30 May 1783.

23. *BN*, 27 May 1783; *LJ*, 4 May 1790, 8 April 1788.

24. *BN*, 28 March 1786, 14, 11 May 1784, 1 April 1783. A similar testimonial to Captain Gillis was printed in *BN*, 25 March 1785.

25. *FJ*, 30 August 1788; Philadelphia *American Daily Advertiser (ADA)*, 4 March 1791. For the Cunningham case, see J. Franklin Jameson, ed., "Letters of Phineas Bond, British Consul at Philadelphia," *Annual Report of the American Historical Association for the year 1897* (Washington, 1898), hereafter cited as "Bond Letters," 472–73, 482 (Phineas Bond to the duke of Leeds, 3 January, 3 May 1791); *Journal of the First Session of the House of Representatives of the Commonwealth of Pennsylvania* (Philadelphia, 1790), 339; *Journal of the Senate of the Commonwealth of Pennsylvania* (Philadelphia, 1791), 253, 255, 257; and Erna Risch, "Immigrant Aid Societies before 1820," *Pennsylvania Magazine of History and Biography (PMHB)* 60 (1936), 31–32.

26. Maldwyn A. Jones, "Ulster Emigration, 1783–1815," in E.R.R. Green, ed., *Essays in Scotch-Irish History* (London, 1969), 50; PRO, FO/4/11, Bond to Grenville, 8 October 1791; *SN*, 27 February 1784; *Pennsylvania Packet (PP)*, 19 November 1784; *SN*, 20 March 1784; *PP*, 5 October 1784. See also a letter dated from Galway, 2 August 1784, in *SN*, 7 August 1784, where it was stated that only half of those who had sought passage on the ship *Anne and Francis* (Galway to Baltimore, 1784) could be received "for want of room."

27. *HJ*, 17 November 1784; *BN*, 9 November 1784; *HJ*, 7 January 1785.

28. By arrangement with the Barbary powers these passes were issued by the British government to protect British-registered vessels on the high seas from piracy and impressment.

29. PRO, FO/4/8, Bond to Leeds, 10 November 1789.

30. PRO, FO/4/7; "Bond Letters," 464, Bond to Leeds, 1 November 1790. My own figures are principally drawn from a trawl of the following sources: American and Irish newspapers, port entry books, and the archives of the Foreign Office, as held in the PRO. The detailed tables will be published in Bric, *Economy of Irish Emigration*, Appendix XI.

31. In February 1793, France declared war on Britain. Although the United States proclaimed its neutrality and thus that its "free ships [made] free goods," this was not accepted by either of the belligerents; see Alexander DeConde, *Entangling Alliance: Politics and Diplomacy during the Administration of George Washington* (Durham, N.C., 1958).

32. Richard J. Purcell, "Irish Settlers in Early Delaware," *Pennsylvania History (PH)* 13 (1947), 95; Dickson, *Ulster Emigration*, 32–34; John A. Monroe, *Colonial Delaware: A History* (Millwood, N.Y., 1978); Wokeck, *Trade in Strangers*, Chapter 5.

33. *BN*, 14 April 1789; [Philadelphia] *General Advertiser (GA)*, 19 August 1791; *New York Daily Gazette*, 27 July 1791.

34. My figure of 36,525 is the sum of the 23,214 and the 13,311 who entered from Ulster and southern Irish ports, respectively; see above. See also John A. Monroe, "The Philadelawarians: A Study in the Relations between Philadelphia and Delaware in the Late Eighteenth Century," *PMHB* 69 (1945), 62–80.

35. *New York Journal*, 10 August 1791; (New York) *Time-Piece*, 16 August 1797; *PP*, 11 February 1788; *New York Daily Advertiser*, 29 August 1791; PRO, FO/4/7, Temple to Leeds, 23 April 1789; FO/4/11, Temple to Grenville, 5 October 1791.

36. "Bond Letters," 455, Bond to Leeds, 3 January 1790; *PP*, 25 May 1784; Washington, D.C., National Archives, Port of Baltimore, Port Entry Books (1784–88); MHS, MS. 1149, William Wilson Account Book. The Limerick-born Wilson owned a quarter-share in the *Paca*.

37. *BN*, 7 April 1789. The colonial connection with South Carolina is discussed in Dickson, *Ulster Emigration*, 49–52, 56–57, 165–70, and *passim*, and Warren B. Smith, *White Servitude in Colonial South Carolina* (Columbia, S.C., 1961). For the role of clergymen in the post-1783 emigration, see the shipping advertisements for colonial Carolina in *BN*, 22 January, 22 July 1790, 23 July 1791.

38. PRO, FO/4/8, Miller to Leeds, 28 January 1790.

The Famine's Scars:
William Murphy's Ulster and American Odyssey

KERBY A. MILLER AND BRUCE D. BOLING
WITH LÍAM KENNEDY[1]

UNTIL VERY RECENTLY, scholars have neglected the Great Famine's impact on the northern Irish province of Ulster and especially its impact on Ulster's Protestant inhabitants. This neglect stemmed in part from historians' reading of published census and other data indicating that the North's *general* experience of excess mortality and emigration in 1845–52 was indeed less catastrophic than that of southern and western Ireland. Thus, whereas between 1841 and 1851 the populations of Munster and Connacht declined by 22.5 and 28.8 percent, respectively, that of Ulster fell "only" 19.8 percent.[2] To be sure, Joel Mokyr and other scholars have noted that several counties in south or "outer" Ulster—Monaghan, for example, and especially Cavan—witnessed high rates of famine mortality, but this is commonly understood by reference to the fact that their populations were composed predominantly of Catholic petty farmers and cottiers.[3] By contrast, conventional wisdom holds that Northeast Ulster or, even more broadly, the six counties that later became Northern Ireland—and particularly their Protestant inhabitants—escaped the famine with comparatively minimal damage, whether measured in excess mortality or in abnormally heavy out-migration. To explain this apparent phenomenon, historians often have cited socio-economic and cultural factors relatively unique to Northeast Ulster, such as industrialization and urbanization, the prevalence of tenant right and comparatively congenial landlord-tenant relations, and, among the rural populace, a greater variety of income sources and less dietary dependence on potatoes than prevailed in Munster and Connacht.[4]

However, some scholars may inadvertently have repeated contemporary claims by Irish unionists, who argued that "Ulster"—i.e., its Protestant inhabitants—eluded the famine because of the province's superior "character" for industry, virtue, and loyalty. But in reality, many Protestant as well as Catholic Ulstermen and -women suffered grievously. Between 1841 and 1851 Ulster's population fell by nearly one-fifth—significantly more than the 15.3 percent decline that occurred in heavily Catholic Leinster. During the same period the number of inhabitants of the future Northern Ireland fell 14.7 percent (or 13 percent if Belfast's burgeoning population is included), and in the four northeastern counties that in 1861 had Protestant majorities (Antrim, Armagh, Down, and Londonderry), the comparable decline was 12.1 percent (or, including Belfast, nearly 10 percent).[5] Of course, it is likely that northeastern Catholics suffered more severely than did Protestants, and it is probable that population losses in the region, particularly among Protestants, were primarily due to out-migration rather than to the effects of starvation and disease.[6] However, as David Miller has argued, in the prefamine decades the contraction of rural weaving and spinning had created in Ulster an impoverished Protestant underclass whose members' vulnerability to the crisis of 1845–52 can be compared with that of Catholic cottiers and laborers in the South and West. Furthermore, Miller points out, some poor Protestants in Northeast Ulster *did* perish of malnutrition or "famine fever," even in areas adjacent to thriving industrial centers. And Mokyr's estimated excess-mortality rates for heavily Protestant County Antrim, as well as for the roughly half-Protestant counties of Armagh, Fermanagh, and Tyrone (all four in the future Northern Ireland), exceed those in most parts of Leinster.[7]

Unfortunately, not until 1861 did the official Irish censuses record religious affiliations, and so it is impossible to gauge precisely or compare population losses among Ulster's Protestants and Catholics between 1841 and 1851. And although the Irish Commissioners of Public Instruction compiled parish-based religious censuses in 1831 and 1834, few scholars have tried to correlate these data with those of 1861.[8] Thus the authors of the most recent comprehensive study of the famine in Ulster made few attempts to distinguish between Protestant and Catholic experiences,[9] and the subject awaits detailed research in church, estate, and other records. Yet much evidence indicates that Protestants suffered heavy losses, primarily through emigration but also to a degree from disease and malnutrition,[10] in many areas of Northeast Ulster. For example, David Miller concludes that between 1845 and 1861 the Presbyterian population of Maghera, Co. Derry, fell by about 30 percent.[11] Likewise, between 1841 and 1851 the number of inhabitants in ten heavily Protestant, contiguous parishes in mid- and East Antrim declined overall by more than 14 percent,[12] and losses in some parishes were comparable to those in parts of Munster and Connacht. For example, in 1841–51 the population of Glenwhirry parish (92 percent Protestant in 1831) fell nearly 23 percent, that of Raloo (84 percent Protestant) by more than 24 percent, and that of Killyglen Grange (81 percent Protestant) by nearly 21 percent.[13]

Significantly, the Protestant inhabitants of these Antrim parishes were in 1831 overwhelmingly Presbyterians: for instance, nearly 100 percent in Glenwhirry; 92 percent in Raloo; and 97 percent in Killyglen Grange. Indeed, much evidence suggests that the famine's effects were *not* evenly distributed among Ulster's Protestants, and that Presbyterians experienced substantially greater attrition than did members of the legally established Church of Ireland. For example, during the period 1831–61, spanning the famine crisis, Ulster's Presbyterian population fell by nearly 18 per cent, compared with a less than 13 percent decline among Anglicans (and a 19 percent decrease among Catholics).[14] In 1831–61 proportional losses among Ulster's Presbyterians were greater than for Anglicans in eight of the province's nine counties; only in Fermanagh, with its minuscule Presbyterian population, did the percentage decline among communicants of the Church of Ireland exceed that experienced by Presbyterians (or by Catholics). Moreover, only in Antrim (excluding Belfast) and in Down were Presbyterian attrition rates slightly less than those of Catholics. In Antrim (excluding Belfast), for instance, between 1831 and 1861 the Presbyterian and the Catholic populations declined by 7 and 10 percent, respectively, but the number of Anglicans increased by more than 12 percent. Likewise, Armagh's Anglican population fell merely 8 percent, compared with a 31 percent decline among Presbyterians (and a 16 percent decrease among Catholics); and in County Londonderry the number of Anglicans rose by 1 percent, while that of Presbyterians fell 28.5 percent (and of Catholics, 13 percent). Even in the predominantly Catholic "outer" Ulster counties of Cavan, Donegal, and Monaghan, proportional losses among Presbyterians in 1831–61 exceeded those among Anglicans and Catholics alike.

To be sure, between 1831 and 1861 the Catholic proportion of Ulster's total inhabitants declined from 53 percent to 50.5 percent. However, whereas the famine and the emigrations immediately preceding and following that crisis made Ulster more heavily Protestant, they also made the North and its Protestant populace less Presbyterian and more Anglican. Thus, between 1831 and 1861 the Presbyterian proportions of

Ulster's overall and Protestant populations declined from 27 percent to 26 percent and from 57 percent to 53 percent, respectively. In northeast Ulster, the heartland of the future Northern Ireland, the changes in the balance between Presbyterians and Anglicans were more striking. For instance, in Antrim (excluding Belfast), the Presbyterian percentage of the Protestant population declined from 76 to 70.5, while the Anglican proportion rose from less than 22 percent to more than 24 percent; in Armagh the comparable Presbyterian decrease was from 40.5 percent to 32 percent, and the Anglican rise from 58 percent to 60 percent; in Down the Presbyterian decline was from 71 percent to 66 percent, and the Anglican increase from 27 percent to 30 percent; and in Londonderry the Presbyterian decrease was from 73 percent to 64 percent, while the Anglican share of the county's Protestants rose from 25 percent to 31 percent.[15] These trends would continue for at least the next half-century: between 1861 and 1926 the Protestant share of the population in the area that in 1920 became Northern Ireland rose from 57 percent to 66.5 percent, whereas the Presbyterian proportion of the statelet's Protestant inhabitants declined from 60 percent to 46 percent, while the percentage of Protestants who were members of the Church of Ireland rose from 38 to 40.[16]

Scholars have scarcely examined these demographic trends, although the shifting balance between Ulster's Presbyterians and Anglicans may have begun with the heavy "Scots-Irish" emigrations of the mid- and late eighteenth century. Nor have historians considered their possible political ramifications—e.g., for the consolidation of Ulster Protestant loyalism and conservatism, both traditionally Anglican projects—although the remarkable attrition of Presbyterians in many mid-Ulster parishes between 1766 and 1831, accompanied by equally startling proportional increases among the area's Anglicans, suggests that local Dissenters, no less than Catholics, may have suffered severely from the rise of Orangeism and the triumph of loyalism in the 1790s and early 1800s.[17] More pertinent to this study, however, is that quantitative as well as qualitative evidence indicates that many of Ulster's Protestants, especially its Presbyterians and even in its most economically "advanced" counties, did not escape the horrors of Black '47 and other famine years.

-1-

How did ordinary northern Protestants, particularly Presbyterians, respond to the travails they endured and witnessed between 1845 and 1852? In the famine's aftermath contemporaries observed, and historians subsequently have confirmed, the famine—and Irish and Irish-American nationalists' anglophobic interpretations of that crisis—engendered lasting bitterness among Irish Catholics both at home and in the US, fueling desires for vengeance against the British government and Ireland's Protestant landlords that found expression, from the 1860s through the early 1920s, in Catholic Irish and Irish-American support for the Fenian, Land League, Home Rule, and independence movements. In addition, some scholars have argued that such expressions also served hegemonic and psychological functions, enabling Catholics in Ireland and overseas to project onto alien "others" feelings of anger and shame: anger that might have been directed against wealthier co-religionists—shopkeepers and "land-grabbers"—who benefited from the plight of starving peasants and evicted neighbors; and shame—for their poverty, humiliation, and self-saving violations of communal ties and constraints—that, if not externalized, might have had destructive personal consequences.[18]

During the famine years a few Ulster Presbyterian emigrants wrote letters revealing anti-British and anti-landlord sentiments comparable to those expressed by Irish and Irish-American Catholics.[19] In general, however, Ulster Protestants' political culture, as it had developed on both sides of the Atlantic since the Act of Union, allowed for neither a nationalist nor a class-based interpretation of the famine experience. In Protestant Ulster itself, for example, although Anglican-Dissenter and landlord-tenant conflicts remained common, between the early 1800s and the 1840s a combination of socio-economic, religious, and political factors (not least of which was mass emigration by disaffected Presbyterians) had virtually eradicated among northern Protestants the ecumenical radicalism of the United Irishmen—creating instead a pervasive, hegemonic loyalism to the union with Britain and to its Irish upper- and middle-class Protestant champions, as well as a corresponding hostility to Irish nationalist movements that were now almost exclusively Catholic in composition and identity. Likewise, by the mid-nineteenth century Irish-American Protestant political culture was dominated by what later critics would call a "Scotch-Irish myth" that encompassed nearly all non-Catholic Irish immigrants and their descendants in a shared sense of social and cultural superiority.[20]

Indeed, it is arguable that the famine in Ulster played a crucial role in the consolidation of Unionist ideology (just as famine immigration, heavily Catholic and generally impoverished, undoubtedly spurred Irish-American Protestants' efforts to distinguish themselves as "Scotch-Irish").[21] This was because Ulster Protestant distress during the famine belied Unionists' most basic assumptions in at least three crucial respects. First, it contradicted their fundamental conviction that Protestantism and its associated social virtues would inevitably produce material rewards, win God's favor, and thus shield its adherents from poverty, famine, and eviction—that is, from the "natural" consequences of the social and moral degradation that Irish Protestants conventionally attributed to Catholic peasants, and from the divine punishment that the latter deserved for their wickedness and disloyalty to the crown. Second, Ulster Protestant suffering in 1845–52, and especially the deficiencies of official relief, had the potential to call into question the practical value of the union with Britain even among the queen's most proverbially dutiful subjects. For instance, in 1849 the Ulster Presbyterian MP, William Sharman Crawford, warned the British government that its rate-in-aid bill, which levied extra taxes on solvent poor-law unions in east Ulster for the relief of bankrupt unions in western Ireland, might dissolve the ties of loyalty that bound the North's Protestants to the "British connexion."[22] And third, famine conditions and the inadequacy of local relief exposed and exacerbated the overlapping class and denominational conflicts within Ulster Protestant society.

Thus ideological and political imperatives converged with economic and social concerns to ensure that Anglican landlords and other Ulster Protestant spokesmen would interpret or "explain" the famine by escalating Unionist and sectarian rhetoric so as to counteract the crisis' divisive and educational potential. For example, as rents fell and relief costs and poor-rates rose, Protestant proprietors and middle-class ratepayers became less likely to be charitable and more prone to contend that, thanks to "Ulster's" thrifty, Protestant character, there was no famine in their province at all. Moreover, loyalist pronouncements not only denied the famine's very existence in loyal, industrious, and Protestant "Ulster," but ascribed hunger and misery only to the "lazy, vicious and indolent" Catholics of southern and western Ireland, and attributed the latter's plight to "the almighty's wrath" against "idle," "feckless," and "sabbath-breaking repealers."[23]

Such arguments—repeated in Protestant newspapers, speeches, sermons, and public resolutions—helped to justify the exceptionally parsimonious relief measures implemented (or denied) by many northern poor-law boards, especially in eastern Ulster. Those measures won high praise for "efficiency" and "frugality" from Whig officials in London, but must have exacerbated distress among lower-class Protestants as well as Catholics. Hence, public works, soup kitchens, and outdoor famine relief, generally, were employed less often in Ulster (especially in its northeastern counties) than in any other province, while local landlords and poor-law guardians publicly rejected accusations of misery and starvation among their dependents as malicious slanders on "the peaceable and industrious inhabitants of the north of Ireland."[24]

This rhetoric of course obscured the harsh realities of contemporary experience for poor northern Protestants, but it also served to cloak the actions of many Anglican landlords—and of affluent Protestant head tenants and employers of rural laborers—who, in East Ulster as elsewhere, often evicted insolvent farmers and cottier-laborers or, at the least, viewed with equanimity the famine's "thinnings" of their properties.[25] Furthermore, as David Miller has argued, Unionist rhetoric during the famine also reflected Ulster Presbyterianism's contemporary transformation from "an inclusive communal faith" to a bourgeois, "class-based denomination"—and, in consequence, its clerical and lay leaders' increasing tendencies to ignore poor, un-churched Presbyterians and to interpret "class" problems, such as those posed by the crisis of 1845–52, in crudely sectarian terms.[26] Finally, therefore, it may be very significant that the greatest outpouring of Unionist and sectarian rhetoric occurred in the famine's latter years and coincided not only with the controversy over the rate-in-aid, which threatened upper- and middle-class Ulstermen with higher taxation, but also with the beginnings of Sharman Crawford's tenant-right movement, designed to mobilize ordinary Presbyterian farmers against the authority of landlords and their middle-class allies.

In short, Ulster Protestant victims of famine, evictions, and parsimonious relief measures could not express their pain, their grievances, and their resentments within the context of a hegemonic religious and political culture that denied their very existence. Consequently, whereas the letters of some famine immigrants suggest that the crisis of 1845–52 scarred them psychologically and adversely affected their adjustment to American life, this may have been particularly true of those who were poor Protestants. In contrast to Irish Catholic immigrants, Protestant migrants from Ulster generally lacked large, cohesive, and supportive working-class ethnic communities and subcultures in a mid- and late nineteenth-century America where the prevalent "Scotch-Irish myth" also denied that Irish Protestant immigrants might be permanently destitute. More crucially, as loyalists to both the British crown and the ideology of Protestant superiority, Ulster Protestant immigrants could only internalize feelings of anger and shame that Irish Catholics could project outward on their traditional oppressors.[27] Such may have been the situation of William Murphy, a skilled or semi-skilled Protestant laborer from County Antrim, who never settled physically or psychologically in the US. Often homesick, burdened by guilt, and a frequent sufferer from severe depression, Murphy was unable to form close attachments to persons or places to replace the relationships that had been tragically sundered in his formative years. Other famine emigrants no doubt shared similar problems, but Murphy was unusual in his ability to articulate a sense of anomie or spiritual exile that others felt but could not express so eloquently.[28]

-2-

William Murphy, the son of a shoe- and bootmaker, was born in 1841 and spent his childhood in the townland of Rory's Glen, in Kilwaughter parish, Co. Antrim, adjacent to the seaport and manufacturing town of Larne, just north of Belfast.[29] His parents, Alexander and Anne Murphy (born in 1806 and 1807, respectively), resided on the Agnew estate, a property of nearly ten thousand acres that included the entire parish. Married in 1832, Alexander and Anne Murphy had at least eight children by 1851, three older and four younger than William. The Murphys were Presbyterians, as in 1831 were nearly three-quarters of the parish's inhabitants (96 percent of them Protestants)—who were described in 1840 as "very bigoted in their religious opinions."[30]

Prior to the mid-1820s Kilwaughter parish, like nearby Larne, was a center of cotton manufacturing, but the industrial depression of that decade bankrupted the local mills, and by 1841 a majority of the local families were engaged exclusively in agriculture. Only one-third of the parish was arable, the rest "mountain and waste land," dominated by bogs and the imposing mass of Agnew's Hill, which loomed over the landscape. Consequently, the area was more suitable for large grazing farms than for tillage, but in 1841 over 87 percent of the holdings—the great majority of which were undoubtedly subtenancies—were still devoted to raising oats and potatoes and were too small to employ paid laborers. Before the famine the average size of a farm on the Agnew estate was merely twenty acres, and over 80 percent of the occupiers inhabited one- or two-roomed thatched cottages. Nevertheless, half the men and almost one-third of the women in the parish could read and write, and local literacy rates were significantly higher than in County Antrim, generally.

William Murphy's father and mother were both literate, and his father's skilled trade and his parents' obviously superior education not only maintained the Murphys above poverty but also ensured them a certain stature in the parish, no doubt enhanced by the ability of at least one family branch, which emigrated to Upper Canada (now Ontario), to prepare its sons for the ministry. Moreover, in 1840 an Alexander Murphy was recorded by the Ordnance Survey as butler at Kilwaughter Castle, the Agnew estate house, and as superintendent of a Presbyterian Sunday school which boasted a lending library of one hundred religious books. If this was William Murphy's father, then his family indeed enjoyed relatively high status during his formative years—which makes his parents' subsequent descent into poverty more traumatic, and his own sense of loss and maladjustment in America more comprehensible.

For the documentary evidence and hints in his own letters suggest that the security of William Murphy's childhood crumbled dramatically during and shortly after the Great Famine. In the late eighteenth and early nineteenth centuries Kilwaughter's landlord, Edward Jones Agnew, had granted his tenants leases of twenty-one years and two "lives," one of which was his own; thus his death in 1834 meant that the expiration of most leases would coincide with the onset of the potato blight. Margaret Jones, Agnew's successor as proprietor, enjoyed a benevolent reputation and apparently did not evict *head* tenants during the crisis. However, the prior collapse of cottage spinning, the introduction of power looms in Belfast factories at mid-century, and the overcrowded and impoverished conditions that characterized Kilwaughter's smallholdings made the parish highly susceptible to the same demographic processes which operated in the poor, mountainous districts of mid- and South Ulster during the Great Famine. Whether forced or "voluntary," wholesale clearances of subtenants, cottiers, and weavers *must* have occurred, for between 1841 and 1851 the populations of both Rory's Glen and Kilwaughter parish declined by a remarkable 36 percent (compared with merely a 15.5 percent decline in County Antrim, generally), and by the latter year a consolidation of holdings had radically altered the local landscape: in 1851 nearly half the farms were over thirty acres in size and over three-fourths of the parish's arable land had been converted to grazing. Perhaps few of the inhabitants actually perished from malnutrition or disease during the famine, but out-migration from the parish—hitherto rare—was extensive. If Alexander Murphy had indeed been butler at Kilwaughter Castle, one can only speculate how or why he lost or relinquished his position, but apparently he suffered the same fate as his poorer neighbors. Given the family's size, the Murphys could not afford to emigrate overseas, but with many others they moved to the growing industrial city of Belfast.

Between 1851 and 1854 the Irish census and the Belfast city directories list Alexander Murphy, "boot and shoemaker," his wife, and eight children as living in south Belfast alongside other petty craftsmen at 9 Bradbury Place, a terrace of houses and shops on the west side of the roadway, near the present Shaftesbury Square. In 1851 young William Murphy was attending a school taught by James McMullen at 24 Fifth Street, in the virtually all-Protestant Shankill neighborhood. Perhaps it was McMullen who taught William and his brothers the lines by Thomas Hood and other popular poets which the Murphys later would quote in their letters from America. However, in 1854 Alexander Murphy moved his family yet again: across the Lagan River to the industrial sub- urb of Ballymacarrett in East Belfast, where until 1862 he resided at Wheeler Place and was first listed as a "mechanic," later as a "mechanic and grocer," in city directories.[31] Thus, expelled from the relatively homogenous and even bucolic environs of Rory's Glen, William Mur- phy spent his late childhood and adolescent years in a city that was grossly overcrowded with poor migrants from the Ulster countryside, riven by violent sectarian conflict, and beset by severe problems of san- itation and disease.

Between 1841 and 1851 Belfast's population increased by almost one- fourth, to 87,000 inhabitants.[32] Many of the newcomers were famine refugees; in 1847 alone 14,000 persons were admitted to the city's work- house, and hundreds perished in the streets. By 1861 Belfast's inhabi- tants numbered 122,000, a rise of 39 percent in ten years, and in 1861–71 the population grew by another 43 percent, to 174,000. Many migrants found employment in the city's expanding linen factories and shipyards, and by Irish or even British standards mid-nineteenth-century Belfast was relatively prosperous. However, wages were low, and both Protes- tant and Catholic workers, not yet fully segregated into discrete neigh- borhoods, expressed their grievances in fierce competition and some- times violent conflict with each other, rather than in cooperation against their employers. In 1861 Presbyterians constituted 35 percent, members of the Church of Ireland 25 percent, Methodists and other Protestants 6 percent, and Catholics 34 percent of the city's inhabitants. Protestant street preachers such as the Presbyterian minister "Roaring" Hugh Hanna acted as catalysts of sectarian strife; the Murphys would have witnessed Rev. Hanna's anti-"papist" harangues and the conse- quent riots of 1857, when Catholic and Protestant workers—many of the latter members of the Loyal Orange Order—engaged in bloody street battles throughout the summer.

However, the aspect of life in working-class Belfast that apparently affected the Murphys most severely was the prevalence of disease. In 1833–40 the Ordnance Survey had described Kilwaughter parish and its inhabitants as remarkably healthy. By contrast, mid-nineteenth-century Belfast had the highest death rate in Ireland and probably in the entire UK: water and sewage systems were grossly inadequate; epidemics of cholera, typhus, and typhoid were frequent; tuberculosis and bronchial disorders were chronic; and infant mortality rates were so high that the average life expectancy at birth was merely nine years. Although the Murphys do not appear to have resided in neighborhoods that were unusually congested or squalid, all working-class areas suffered from impure water, filth (25,000 houses had no privies or sewer lines), and endemic disease. After 1862 Alexander Murphy's name disappears from the city directories, and his son's later letters (especially that of 1880) strongly suggest that in the late 1850s or early 1860s both of William Murphy's parents and four of his siblings died within a relatively short time, perhaps from the effects of their unhealthy environment. Meanwhile, another brother, James, contracted the tuberculosis that would shorten his life in America.

Murphy himself emigrated in about 1862–63, in his early twenties, apparently alone and perhaps in a manner that justified some of his American relations in accusing him of deserting his orphaned and only surviving sister—to whom he wrote his later letters, often in an exculpatory vein.[33] We do not know Murphy's motives for emigrating, but it may be credible to speculate that his traumatic early experiences, the losses of community (twice) and family, and perhaps a drinking problem (hinted at in his American letters) drove him to leave Ireland in search of a security and identity lost forever in Ireland. Sadly, however, his correspondence indicates that those same traumas made it impossible for him to form close or permanent associations in America—or even to identify with anyplace or anyone except the scenes and the few relatives he had left behind. Moreover, the fragmentation and fatalism of his personality, the latter perhaps conditioned by his church's predestinarian outlook,[34] may have been exacerbated by his participation in the carnage of the American Civil War, which he describes in his first surviving letter, written from one of Pittsburgh's industrial suburbs.

William Murphy, Lawrenceville, Pennsylvania, to his brother,
James Murphy, Belfast, 8 November 1865.

Lawerenceville [sic]
Nov 8th 1865
Dear Brother
　　I suppose youl think it strange that I didnt answer your letter sooner but I have tramped a good deal since I got your letter and I hope you will

pardon me not writeing sooner I couldnt go to work for a long time after I wrote to you last I doctered till my money was about all gone and I had given up all hope of ever being well when I met with an old Indian docter who gave me some herbs and two weeks affter I begun to take them I was abel to go to work and to day I beleve I am stouter and better than I ever was. I went to work in Erie [Pennsylvania] but I hadnt worked long before they took down our wages and there was a genreal[35] strike amongest the hands I might have stoped in Erie as long as I had a mind to for I have lots of friends there but I didnt want to stop when I couldnt get work so I started on tramp I tramped all over ohio and hauled up at last in the far famed Iiron City of Pittsburgh Pennsilvania the reason I have my letter headded Lawrencevill is becaus the part of city I work in goes by that name[36] however when you answer this drect to Erie Wm Murphy box 207 because I cant tell how long I may be in this place but I have friend in Erie who will send all letters to me no matter where I be his name is Alex maxwell him and I shiped in the Navy to gather and stuck by [each] other like brothers through it all   if ever you should come across him and let him know you were a brother of mine there would be nothing to good for you times are rather dull here but for all that dear James I wish that you and robert were here for if you were here and the three of us stick to gather we could make lots of money I dont know how it is but I cant get along myself at if have had[37] good chances many a time but some how luck always went againest no matter there is a good time comeing yet. I often in my black moods have wished that some Southern bullet had strecthed me along side my fallen Shipmates on the banks of the Cumberland Tennesee or Missisippy river but Im getting over all that I wish I had that letter of Elizas I will write to aunt Eliza as soon as I get settled down again tell W^m McCoulloh and Hugh Nelson that I will give theme a long decription of the war Millatary and political some day if I knew roberts adress I would write to him James when you write please let me know your plans give my best respects to hugh Nelson W^m McCoulaugh and all the rorysglen follk remember me to Charlie Jonson give my love to Grandmother Aunt Eliza and our own Eliza and robert God bless and keep you

YOUR AFFECTIONATE

BROTHER WILLIAM MURPHY

Murphy's subsequent "black moods," suggesting manic depression, may never have been as severe as in the war's immediate aftermath, but the preceding letter exposes several contradictions at the heart of this immigrant's career and personality. On the one hand, for example, Murphy craved comradeship and guidance, especially from his remaining kin and even from younger brother James (born ca. 1843–44). Indeed, in his next letter, written in early 1866 from Pittsburgh to his older sibling

Robert (born ca. 1837–38),[38] William expressed his own needs and inadequacies more explicitly and poignantly, practically begging his brothers to join and look after him in America:

> . . . I thought I would write you these few lines merely to let you know that I [am] well and expecting to see you both before long   there [is] some mistake about me   Id like to do well but I cant   the fact of the matter is this bob I want you here to lead me   I have no thought for the future and soon forget the past   I form good resolutions but soon forget them and if you and James dont come here and kick me along I'll[39] never be worth ten cents. . . .[40]

However, although his brothers *did* emigrate in 1866–67, William Murphy spent only relatively few months with them during all their years in America. During part of 1867–68 William and Robert apparently worked together in Pittsburgh and Chicago, and in 1869–70 he and James labored for a ship's captain in the Hudson River port of Poughkeepsie, but after that date he rarely saw them—although they wrote sporadically and affectionately to each other. In part, such separations reflected the exigencies of unmarried life for immigrant artisans and laborers, as all three brothers were involved in the carpentry and building trades, and as Robert admitted, "a wife is rather an expensive luxury in this country."[41] Nevertheless, after 1870 Robert and James were inseparable during their travels in the Far West, until the latter's death from consumption in San Francisco in 1879, and William's social and spiritual isolation seems more a function of personality than of occupation.

Likewise, despite his avowed affection for fellow ex-soldiers, and his subsequent career as a member of sizable, albeit transient, workgroups, close-knit by necessity, William remained remarkably disconnected from the overlapping ethnic and working-class associations, both formal and informal, that structured the lives of most Irish immigrants, Protestants as well as Catholics. For instance, during the 1870s, 1880s, and 1890s Murphy was either headquartered or permanently resident in or near Pittsburgh, over a tenth of whose inhabitants were Irish immigrants, over 20 percent of whom were skilled and semiskilled workers (plus over 50 percent unskilled), and about one-fourth of whom were Ulster Protestants.[42] However, judging from his letters, the tumultuous events that shook that city in those decades and which involved so many of its Irish workers (the temperance crusade of 1876, led by Francis Murphy, an Ulster Protestant immigrant; the great railroad strike and riots of 1877; the rise of the Knights of Labor, the Greenback-Labor Party, and the Irish American Land League in the late 1870s and 1880s; the struggles of the Amalgamated Iron and Steel Workers' Union, culminating in the Homestead strike of 1892) made no impression upon him, save perhaps to confirm his alienation from what he called "this Wicked World."[43] Moreover, Murphy never resided in any of Pittsburgh's Ulster Protestant enclaves (Lawrenceville's Irish were primarily Munster and Connacht Catholics), and in his letters he never remarked on the ethnic or religious affiliations of any nonrelatives he encountered in America. Indeed, in his later correspondence specific references to wartime comrades or fellow workers disappeared almost entirely, and he seemed to attain psychological equilibrium by an almost total emotional detachment from people and places in the US and by projecting his affections and hopes overseas to his younger and only surviving sister, Eliza[beth] (born ca. 1849–50), and her husband, David Gilmore.[44] "[D]ont think Eliza," Murphy wrote plaintively from Poughkeepsie in early 1869:

> that either him [brother Robert] or me have ever forgot our Sister for I tell you Eliza and I tell you truely in some of the hardest fought battles of the late war when men fell like grain before the sickel, above the roar and din of battle above the wild cheers of the combatants the heartrending shreicks of the wounded and dying something seemed to whisper in my ear never fear your little Sister prays for you and I sometimes think that although she has got to be a big married woman she sometimes prays for me yet, [even] if I shouldnt be quite as good as I ought to be.[45]

By 1870, after a short career aboard a coastal steamer, Murphy had settled into what would be his livelihood for at least the next decade, working for a Pittsburgh-based bridge-building firm, probably Andrew Carnegie's Keystone Bridge Manufacturing Company, traveling in crews throughout the country constructing iron bridges to accommodate the enormous contemporary expansion of the nation's railroad lines.[46] In the following letter Murphy describes his new trade and rationalizes his personal anomie, expiating his guilt and evading responsibility for leaving his orphaned sister in Belfast, by sentimentalizing his homesickness and, ironically, by conforming (albeit in nonpoliticized ways) to what were generally Irish *Catholic* conventions of involuntary "exile" from the "old country."

William Murphy, Pennsylvania, to David and Eliza Gilmore,
Belfast, 5 April 1870.

April 5th 1870.
Dear Brother & Sister
    after a long silence I sit down to write you a few lines   I hardly know how to excuse myself for not writeing to you sooner but the truth is I have contracted such a habit of moveing from place to place that I am

never in one place long enough to here from the old country   when I
wrote to you last I was sailing on an American coaster   in that trade I
have been all along the seaboard from Maine to Mexico I have seen the
ornge groves of Cuba yes Dave I have seen all the glourious beauties of
the Sunny South and a great many of her horrors to[o] but after all many
a time I have thought as I trod the deck in the lonely watchs of the night
or gaezed on the dark bleu waters of the Gulf how much better and hap-
pier I was when I took my first trip down the bay to bangor[47]   the people at home think that we exiles in a forigen land soon forget the home
and freinds of our youth but the[y] are greatly mistakeing   abesence
makes the heart grow fonder   I have seen many a sunbrowned wander-
er drop a tear as he told some little anicdote of his boyish days in his far
distant Island home   yes Dave I have made some good freinds and true
in this country yet I have never forgoten my old freinds at home and far
above them all my little sister   I know there is plenty around her to tell
her that I am not worthy to be her brother. now David I know I have done
wrong often   I have been acused of not helping Eliza when she was battling with the world alone but circumstances over which I had no control
prevented me for God knows I would give my hearts blood to aid Eliza if
it was required   the reason I have writen this is because I have seen a relative of mine[48] sometime ago who called me a scoundrel and a reprobate
and among other thing[s] cast up to my teeth that before Eliza was married I did'nt care wether she starved or not   alas for the raririty of chris-
tan charity under the sun. I felt for Eliza keenly the more so because I
could'nt help her.   but let us drop this and take up something else   well
I have given up Salt water and taken to bridge building   dont think that
I have turned stone mason   bridges here and the long bridge[49] diffrs
here the[y] are built of iron or wood as the case may be and it takes only
a few weeks to put one up so that I am travelling around from place to
place with a bridge company helping to put up New ones and pull down
old ones   I am at present in the State of Pennsylvania but I cant tell what
state I'll [be] in when you get this perhaps the State of matrimony   I
sometimes think it would be better for me if I was but however I'll think
it over and let you know some other time   I suppose you have a dozen
bouncing boys and girls by this time   I hope so at any rate   I would like
to be called uncle once to see what it was like   but I must stop this
nonsence   answer this as soon as you can and I wont be so long of writeing again   [no signature]

Despite his speculations, Murphy never married, and for the next
decade, at least, he roamed the country building bridges, primarily in
the South and West. Between construction jobs he boarded with various families in the Lawrenceville district of Pittsburgh, where his
neighbors were a mixture of Irish, German, and British iron workers,

artisans, and saloonkeepers congregated along Butler Avenue between 40th and 42nd Streets.[50] Interestingly, in 1880 Murphy boarded with the family of a German shoemaker: on the one hand, a reflection of his lack of close ties to his fellow bridge-builders or to other Ulster immigrants; on the other hand, perhaps an unconscious effort to replicate the vanished securities of his shoemaker father's Irish household. However, during the 1870s Murphy apparently became reconciled to having no fixed abode: "the wide world is my home now," he wrote to his sister and brother-in-law on New Year's Eve, 1871:

> if I had settled in one place at first it might have been different but I was bound to see the world   well i have seen it and I must confess I feel no happier for the sight   the bad far outweighs the good as far as my experience goes[51] and it is wide and varied. there is some times I think I will settle down then the old yearning to see more comes over and I drop the idea at once in fact Davy I have got a rovers commison and do my best I cant get rid of it.[52]

However, in 1880 news of his older brother's death in San Francisco, and the prospect that his sister's family might join him in America, forced Murphy to abandon, at least temporarily, the pretence that his transient, solitary life was either voluntary or more than tolerable.

William Murphy, Keokuk, Iowa, to David and Eliza Gilmore,
Belfast, 18 December 1880.

Keokuk Iowa
Dec 13th 1880
Dear Brother & Sister
    I hardly know how to commence a letter to you it is so long since I heard from you direct   I here from you right along thru Robert but that would scarcly excuse me from writeing to you   I wrote to you last winter from Indiana but Bob informed me you never got my letter   the fact is Dave & Eliza I have to knock around so much at the work I follow that I hardly know what to do very often. I am hardly ever more than a week or two in one place and I make up my mind to write every place I go but when I get there I think this way well I'm not going to be long here   perhaps the next place I go I can wait and get an answer and so it gos but I hope you will forgive me and I know you will for my neglect. I asure you I never for a moment forget you. no doubt you think why dont I settel down like other peopel   I have asked myself that question a thousand times, I have went further   I have tried to do so   I know that I can make as good a liveing perhaps better by staying in one place all the time but when I try it I soon get tired and the restless spirit gets the best of me all the time.   the fact is traveling is so natural to me that I might as well try

to live without eating as withou[t] wandering around   but what difference does it make[?]   life is but a dream and although I know that my last
days will be spent in all probability amongst strangers, I almost wish
sometimes the dream was over   Dear Brother & sister dont think for a
moment that I am despondent or downhearted for I am anything but that
but just think for a second of the past that has gone never to be recalled.
it seems but yesterday since we were a happy and United famly Mother
Father Brothers and Sisters   where are they now.   they grew togather side
by side   they filled one hall with glee   there graves are scaterd far and
wide by mountain stream and sea   six of that once happy family sleep
the last long sleep beneath the Green sod of their native land and James
the latest of our loved and lost laid him down to rest in the far away
Calaifornia   he like thousands more tried to find a fortune and instead
he found a grave but where could he find a more fitting resting place
than in lone Mountain   the last rays of the setting Sun kiss his grave as
it sinks behind the waters of the Great pacific, and his spirit has crossed
the great divide and joined the others in that better land beyond   there
are but three left now and thousands of miles of land and sea seperate
them three   robert is away up on top of the rocky mountains whilst I like
the wandering jew cannot call one spot of earth my home, and you dear
Sister (and I thank God from the very bottom of my heart for it) are a
happy wife and mother   although you may think me cold hearted
because I dont write oftner still I never forget my littel Sister and if you
only knew how my heart yearns to see you once again you would forgive
my aparient neglect but I will promise to do better in the future   I have
made arrangements with a freind so that letters will be forwarded to me
no matter where I am   I had a letter from Robert a day or two since   he
says you were wanting [to] know something about the Climate &c of Colrado   well Dave my boy Southren Colrada has a splended Climate dry
and warm not to[o] warm   the princple biusness in the state is mineing
although there is considreble farming done in some parts of the state but
as a genrel thing the Climate is to[o] dry for farming   Northren Colrado
is very montainous and the winters are very severe the thermomenter
going way down to 40 below zero   but Dave if you have any notion to
leave old played out Europe and come to this live and pogreseve land I
would advise you to go to some of the older states   California has the
finest Climate in the world   nither to[o] hot nor to[o] cold but nearly a
uniform temprature all the year round   in fact with a few exceptions in
some of the Southren and middel Westren States the Climate of this
country is healthy   but I must come to a close this time but next time I
write I will give you all the information I can   I hope you are both well
and happy   give my love to aunt Eliza and let me know [how] she gets
along   also to Lizzey Martin   I dont know her name now but that makes
no diffrenc   I suppose she is a sedate old married woman now but I think

of her only as the lively littel girl she used to be   and Dear Brother and
Sister may God bless and perserve you is the ernest Prayer of your affectionate Brother—

WILLIAM

IN CARE F SMITH NO 4018 BUTLER STREET

PITTSBURGH PENNSELVAINA

After the above there is a ten-year gap between William Murphy's
surviving letters. In March 1889 brother Robert reported from Montana
that William was still building bridges, then in North Carolina,[53] but on
17 August 1891 William wrote from Braddock, a grimy steel-town just
east of Pittsburgh, that he had been unemployed for an unspecified
length of time and forced to work at "common labor," probably at the
mammoth J. Edgar Thomson steelworks that dominated Braddock,
alongside "the very lowest scum of Europe Itilians & Hungarians as
filthy and ignorant a class of people as God ever put the breath of life
into."[54] Seven years later, according to his last surviving letters, also
from Braddock, Murphy was again working, probably for a steel mill or
a coal-gas company, but a coal miners' strike made his employment
"rather ticklish," and, buoyed up by remittances from the Gilmores, he
hoped to return at last to Ulster in the fall.[55] Whether Murphy indeed
returned is unknown, but he was still alive in 1910, when he sought confirmation of his birth-date from the Irish Public Record Office in order
to gain the Civil War pension, which hitherto had eluded him.

Recent studies of late nineteenth- and early twentieth-century Pittsburgh describe a city which, especially after 1890, was increasingly
dominated by economic and political forces beyond the individual or
collective control of the Irish and other old-stock workers who, in the
1870s and 1880s, had struggled with some success against corporate
power. The technological and managerial revolutions associated with
the displacement of iron by steel and of numerous competing firms by
industrial giants such as Carnegie Steel and its successor, U.S. Steel,
plus the huge influx of black migrants and new immigrants from eastern and southern Europe, proletarianized and fragmented the city's
workforce, weakening labor solidarity and often destroying union
power, as in the great Homestead strike of 1892. In Lawrenceville and
other districts the Irish were displaced from their old jobs and neighborhoods, and it seems likely that in 1889–90 William Murphy was one
of many victims of these developments. Ironically, for personal reasons
centered in Ulster, Murphy had already undergone the often severe
psychological consequences that the degradation of status and the

atomization of community wrought among many American workers. And for that reason perhaps he was better able to cope with what was, for him, only another round of potentially devastating change and loss—from which he could again escape by recrossing the Atlantic.

Thus, although Murphy's experience of the Great Famine—and his inability to externalize its psychological impact within the religio-political constraints of Ulster Protestant culture—may have inhibited his ability to adjust to American society, that same experience may have helped to cushion him emotionally from the "future shocks" that corporate capitalism dealt him in his adopted land. Unfortunately, if he did return to northern Ireland, we can only speculate how well Murphy (in Pittsburgh a self-described "rabid democrat,"[56] despite his ethnic prejudices) was able to re-adjust to an Ulster Protestant society that in the early 1900s was not only rigidly stratified but in which Unionist mythology was even more hegemonically powerful and pervasive than it had been in the late 1840s and 1850s—when its upper- and middle-class purveyors had effectively erased from public memory the famine's harrowing effects on the poor inhabitants of Rory's Glen and of similar northern Protestant communities.

NOTES

1. An earlier version of this article was written several years ago for a collection of essays on the American and Irish-American responses to the Great Irish Famine, to be edited by Professor Timothy Sarbaugh of Gonzaga University. Tragically, however, Tim suffered an untimely death, and his project was aborted. Hence, we are grateful to editor Kevin Kenny for including our greatly revised essay in this volume as well as for his helpful suggestions.

2. W. E. Vaughan and A. J. Fitzpatrick, eds., *Irish Historical Statistics: Population, 1821–1971* (Dublin: Royal Irish Academy, 1978), 15–16. See also Líam Kennedy, Paul S. Ell, E. M. Crawford, and L. A. Clarkson, *Mapping the Great Irish Famine: A Survey of the Famine Decades* (Dublin: Four Courts Press, 1999).

3. Joel Mokyr, *Why Ireland Starved: A Quantitative and Analytical History of the Irish Economy, 1800–1850* (London: George Allen & Unwin, 1985), 267. See also Cormac Ó Gráda, *Ireland before and after the Famine: Explorations in Economic History, 1800–1925* (Manchester: Manchester University Press, 1988), 87.

4. On the socio-economic developments in prefamine Ulster, especially in the northeastern counties, that generally stemmed the famine's effects in the region, see, for example, the relevant chapters of Jonathan Bardon, *A History of Ulster* (Belfast: Blackstaff Press, 1992); L. M. Cullen, *An Economic History of Ireland since 1660* (London: B.T. Batsford, 1972), and Cullen, ed., *The Formation of the Irish Economy* (Cork: Mercier Press, 1969); and Líam Kennedy and Philip Ollerenshaw, eds., *An Economic History of Ulster, 1820–1939* (Manchester: Manchester University Press, 1985).

5. Calculated from the data in Vaughan and Fitzpatrick, *Irish Historical Statistics*, 5–16.

6. Cormac Ó Gráda, *Black '47 and Beyond: The Great Irish Famine* (Princeton, N.J.: Princeton University Press, 1999), 110.

7. David W. Miller, "Irish Presbyterians and the Great Famine," in J. Hill and C. Lennon, eds., *Luxury and Austerity: Historical Studies* 21 (Dublin, 1999), 168; and Mokyr, *Why Ireland Starved,* 267. See also Christine Kinealy, *This Great Calamity: The Irish Famine, 1845–52* (Dublin: Gill and Macmillan, 1994), 233–34.

8. For the 1831 and 1834 religious censuses, see the *First Report of the Commissioners of Public Instruction, Ireland,* British Parliamentary Papers, H.C. 1835, xxxiii. Since 1985–86 Kerby Miller and Líam Kennedy of Queen's University, Belfast, have worked on a project to organize and compare the 1831–34 census figures with earlier and subsequent demographic data; for some preliminary results, see Kennedy and Miller, "The Long Retreat: Protestants, Economy, and Society, 1660–1926," in Raymond Gillespie and Gerard Moran, eds., *Longford: Essays in County History* (Dublin: Lilliput Press, 1991), 31–61; and Appendix 1 of Miller, Arnold Schrier, Bruce D. Boling, and David N. Doyle, *To Ye Land of Canaan: Letters, Memoirs, and Other Writings by Immigrants from Ireland to Colonial and Revolutionary America, 1675–1815* (New York: Oxford University Press, forthcoming). Because much of the demographic data presented below stems from Kennedy's and Miller's joint efforts, the former is included as an author of this essay; however, we gladly absolve him of any responsibility for the accuracy of our computations or for the interpretations contained herein.

9. Christine Kinealy and Trevor Parkhill, eds., *The Famine in Ulster: The Regional Impact* (Belfast: Ulster Historical Foundation, 1997).

10. Ó Gráda, *Black '47 and Beyond,* 89.

11. Miller, "Irish Presbyterians and the Great Famine," 168.

12. The parishes surveyed were Ballycor (including Doagh Grange and Rashee), Ballynure, Carncastle (including Solar), Glenwhirry, Glynn, Inver, Killyglen Grange, Kilwaughter (see below), Larne (not including its workhouse inhabitants in 1851), and Raloo; 1841–51 data in British Parliamentary Papers, H.C. 1843, xxiv, and H.C. 1852–53, xcii (Vol. 3, Ulster).

13. The Protestant proportions of the parishes' populations in 1831 were calculated from the 1831–34 religious censuses, in the *First Report of the Commissioners of Public Instruction, Ireland,* British Parliamentary Papers, H.C. 1835, xxxiii. Even higher losses occurred in Kilwaughter parish (see below).

14. These and the following percentages are based on analyses of data in the 1831 religious census (see n. 13) and in the official 1861 Irish census in the British Parliamentary Papers, H.C. 1863, liv (Vol. 3, Ulster).

15. It is noteworthy that the Presbyterian proportion of Belfast's Protestant population also declined between 1831 and 1861—from 57.5 percent to 53 percent—whereas the comparable Anglican percentage fell from 40 to 37.5, while "other Protestants" increased their share of Belfast's non-Catholic population from 3 percent to 9 percent. (In the same period the Catholic proportion of the city's total inhabitants rose slightly from 33 percent to 34 percent.) In nine-county Ulster as a whole between 1831 and 1861, the 252 percent increase in the number of members of "other Protestant" denominations—primarily of evangelical churches such as the Methodists and Baptists—is a complicating factor, but we see no reason to assume that Presbyterians were more susceptible to the lures of evangelicalism than were members of the Church of Ire-

land. However, in the eighteenth century it was common for ambitious or upwardly mobile Presbyterians to convert to the legally established church; if this trend continued during the nineteenth century, it would help to explain the shifting balance between the two denominations, although we suspect that differential emigration rates were most significant. Also, conversions to Anglicanism among ordinary Presbyterians may have increased during times of unusual political or economic stress, as during the loyalist repressions of suspected United Irishmen in the 1790s (see n. 17); perhaps the Great Famine had similar effects (were northern Presbyterians as well as western Catholics subject to the blandishments of "souperism"?), but local research is needed to investigate this possibility.

16. Calculated from the 1861 and 1926 data in Vaughan and Fitzpatrick, *Irish Historical Statistics,* 4, 10–13, and 69–73. Again, the increasing proportion of "other Protestants"—comprising 13.5 percent of Northern Ireland's non-Catholic inhabitants in 1926—is a complicating factor, as is the possibility of Presbyterian conversions to the Anglican faith (see n. 15). In Belfast, between 1861 and 1926 the Presbyterian proportion of the city's Protestant inhabitants declined from 53 percent to 43 percent, while the Anglican share rose from 37.5 percent to 42 percent, and that of "other Protestants" increased from 9 percent to 15 percent. (Between 1861 and 1926 the Catholic percentage of Belfast's total population fell from 34 to 23.)

17. See Miller, Schrier, Boling, and Doyle, *To Ye Land of Canaan.*

18. See, for example, Kerby A. Miller, *Emigrants and Exiles: Ireland and the Irish Exodus to North America* (New York: Oxford University Press, 1985), Chapter 7; Miller, "'Revenge for Skibbereen': Irish Emigration and the Meaning of the Great Famine," and Miller and Bruce D. Boling, "The Pauper and the Politician: A Tale of Two Immigrants and the Construction of Irish-American Society," both in Arthur Gribben, ed., *The Great Famine and the Irish Diaspora in America* (Amherst: University of Massachusetts Press, 1999), 180–218. Our argument here does *not* imply, however, that Catholic Irish and Irish-Americans were largely unjustified in attributing famine suffering to landlords and to inadequate or hardhearted government relief policies.

19. See, for example, the Kerr brothers' letters, 1843–53 (MIC 144/3–23, Public Record Office of Northern Ireland, henceforth PRONI).

20. See, for example, Miller, *Emigrants and Exiles,* 68–69, 84–88, 228–35; Kerby A. Miller, "'Scotch-Irish' Myths and 'Irish' Identities in Eighteenth- and Nineteenth-Century America," in Charles Fanning, ed., *New Perspectives on the Irish Diaspora* (Carbondale: Southern Illinois University Press, 2000), 75–92; and Miller, Schrier, Boling, and Doyle, *To Ye Land of Canaan.*

21. Although we argue elsewhere that in its modern, formal expression "Scotch-Irish" identity first emerged in late eighteenth-century America; see Kerby A. Miller, "'Scotch-Irish' Myths"; and Miller, Schrier, Boling, and Doyle, *To Ye Land of Canaan.*

22. James Grant, "The Great Famine and the Poor Law in Ulster: The Rate-in-Aid Issue of 1849," *Irish Historical Studies* 105 (May 1990), 35–36. Also on the rate-in-aid, see James S. Donnelly, Jr., "The Administration of Relief, 1847–51," in W. E. Vaughan, ed., *A New History of Ireland, V: Ireland under the Union, I, 1801–70* (Oxford: Clarendon Press, 1989), 328; Peter Gray, *Famine, Land, and Politics: British Government and Irish Society, 1843–50* (Dublin: Irish Academic Press, 1999), 317; and Kinealy, *Great Calamity,* 257–60.

23. See, for example, Bardon, *History of Ulster,* 299; Grant, "Great Famine and Poor

Law in Ulster," 36, 43; Kinealy, *Great Calamity,* 259; Kinealy and Parkhill, *Famine in Ulster,* 11–12; and David W. Miller, "Irish Presbyterians and the Great Famine," 174.

24. Grant, "Great Famine and Poor Law in Ulster," 31–33; Bardon, *History of Ulster,* 287; and Kinealy and Parkhill, *Famine in Ulster,* 11–12.

25. Kinealy, *Great Calamity,* 218; Cahal Dallat, "The Famine in County Antrim," in Kinealy and Parkhill, *Famine in Ulster,* 28.

26. Miller, "Irish Presbyterians and the Great Famine," 167–75.

27. Alternatively, they could follow the logic of Ulster Protestant mythology, rooted in communal "memories" of Catholic sieges and massacres, and blame their plight not on Protestant landlords and relief officials, but on fellow sufferers who were Irish "papists." To be sure, in parts of mid- and outer Ulster, where Protestant-Catholic competition for land was keen, such sentiments were often grounded in the realities of sectarian strife. Yet as noted above, in general it was not Catholics but members of the Church of Ireland who were likeliest to inherit Ulster from Presbyterians, who, in proportion to their numbers, were most commonly subject to economic displacement immediately before, during, and shortly after the famine. Nevertheless, it is possible that the Protestant interpretation of the famine, as described above, heightened anti-Catholic and loyalist sentiments among Irish Protestant emigrants to America (just as the nationalist interpretation intensified Irish Catholics' animosities to the British government and to Irish landlordism). The single reference to Irish Catholics made in his surviving letters by William Murphy, the Ulster Presbyterian immigrant whose career is described and analyzed below, might reflect such sentiments (William Murphy to Robert Murphy, 27 January 1866; see n. 28 for the general citation to the Murphy correspondence; see n. 43 for Murphy's remarks on the Fenians).

28. The remainder of this essay is based largely on the immigrants' letters of William, Robert, and James Murphy, catalogued as D.3558/1/21 in PRONI. The collection also contains a certified copy of the since-destroyed 1851 Irish census schedule for the Murphy household in Bradbury Place, Belfast. The authors wish to thank the Public Record Office of Northern Ireland and W. R. Thompson, Esq., for permission to publish the Murphy letters. We also wish to thank Jennifer Altenhofel, then a Ph.D. candidate at American University, Washington, D.C., for her assiduous, albeit unsuccessful, efforts to locate William Murphy's Civil War military and pension records in the US National Archives.

29. The information on Rory's Glen, Kilwaughter parish, the Agnew estate, and County Antrim contained in this and the following paragraphs was derived from the following sources: the 1831, 1841, and 1851 Irish censuses, the 1831–34 Irish religious census, the Irish poor-law reports of 1837–38, and the 1841 and 1851 Irish agricultural returns, all published in the British Parliamentary Papers; Samuel Lewis, *A Topographical Dictionary of Ireland,* Vol. 2 (1837; reprinted Baltimore: Genealogical Publishing Co., 1984); Angelique Day and Patrick McWilliams, eds., *Ordnance Survey Memoirs of Ireland, Vol. 10: Parishes of County Antrim III* (Belfast: Institute of Irish Studies, 1991); *Land Owners in Ireland . . . , 1876* (reprinted Baltimore: Genealogical Publishing Co., 1988); and Vaughan and Fitzpatrick, *Irish Historical Statistics.* Information as to the birth dates and literacy of William Murphy and his parents is included in the 1851 census schedule, located in D.3558/1/21, PRONI.

30. Day and McWilliams, *Ordnance Survey Memoirs,* 114. In 1831 the population of Kilwaughter parish included 1,476 Presbyterians, 484 Catholics, 25 members of the Church of Ireland, and 31 other Protestant Dissenters (Quakers, Methodists, etc.).

31. Information derived from *Henderson's Belfast Directory and Northern Depository* (Belfast, 1852); *Belfast and Province of Ulster Directory* (Belfast, 1852–62).

32. Information on Belfast in this and the following paragraph derived from J. C. Beckett and R. Glasscock, eds., *Belfast: Origin and Growth of an Industrial City* (London: British Broadcasting Corporation, 1967); and W. A. Maguire, *Belfast* (Keele: Keele University Press, 1993).

33. In 1867 one Ann Murphy died in the Belfast workhouse. Her age, sixty, listed on the death certificate corresponds to the 1807 birth-date of William Murphy's mother. However, it is very uncertain whether this woman was Murphy's mother, for his letters of 1865–69 do not refer to her, as they almost surely would if she were alive or had recently died. Nevertheless, if this *was* William's mother, her death in the workhouse, and his abandonment of her by emigrating, would provide additional causes for his own guilt and his relatives' aspersions. See Civil Registry of Deaths, 1867, v. 11, 182 (originals in the General Register Office, Belfast; on microfilm in the library of the Church of Jesus Christ of Latter Day Saints, Hollywood, Co. Down).

34. Apparently, the Murphys were orthodox Presbyterians, as Alexander Murphy's Sunday school in Kilwaughter parish originated when the local Calvinists seceded from another school dominated by Unitarians.

35. genreal: general. With few exceptions, as when Murphy's misspellings or omitted words and letters might produce confusion among readers, we present Murphy's correspondence with minimal editorial insertions and annotations and in strict accordance with the original manuscripts.

36. Lawrenceville (population 3,260 in 1860) was one of several industrial villages east of Pittsburgh that were annexed to the city in 1868. In the late nineteenth century the Lawrenceville district comprised wards 17 and 18; in 1870 about one-fourth of its population was Irish-born, increasing to over a third by 1880, when nearly 70 percent of its Irish inhabitants were unskilled laborers, primarily in the iron and steel mills. See Victor A. Walsh, "Across 'the Big Wather': Irish Community Life in Pittsburgh and Allegheny City, 1850–1885" (Ph.D. diss., University of Pittsburgh, 1983).

37. I cant get along myself at / if I have had . . . : i.e., I can't get along myself at it / I have had . . .

38. In 1868 the *Belfast and Province of Ulster Directory* listed Robert Murphy, of Wheeler's Place, Ballymacarrett, East Belfast, as a laborer, although by this time he had emigrated to America.

39. I;ll in MS. Murphy frequently employs semicolons instead of apostrophes in his correspondence; for readers' convenience, in such instances we have silently restored apostrophes.

40. William Murphy to Robert Murphy, 27 January 1866.

41. Robert Murphy to David and Eliza Gilmore, 29 November 1875. Between 1875 and 1889, Robert Murphy wrote ten surviving letters to the Gilmores, primarily from San Francisco and Butte, Montana, where he alternated between carpentry and vain attempts at gold mining. Although Robert was more sociable than his brother William, Robert's letters express much the same sense of fatalism, especially with regard to his occupational failures ("I am very unlucky," he wrote on 18 March 1889), which may reflect the brothers' religious heritage as well as their common childhood experiences of famine, privation, and loss.

42. The information on Pittsburgh and the Irish in that city, contained in this and subsequent paragraphs, is derived from Walsh, "Across 'the Big Wather'"; Francis G.

Couvares, *The Remaking of Pittsburgh: Class and Culture in an Industrializing City* (Albany: State University of New York Press, 1984); Leland D. Baldwin, *Pittsburgh: The Story of a City* (Pittsburgh: University of Pittsburgh Press, 1937); Stefan Lorant, ed., *Pittsburgh: The Story of an American City* (Garden City, N.Y.: Doubleday, 1964); Erasmus Wilson, *Standard History of the City of Pittsburgh* (Chicago, 1888); and G. M. Hopkins, *Atlas of the County of Allegheny, Pennsylvania* (Philadelphia, 1876).

43. William Murphy to David and Eliza Gilmore, 31 December 1871. The sole exceptions to Murphy's apparent lack of interest in Irish-American political activities were his sardonic remarks on the Fenian movement, written from Pittsburgh in 1866: "The fenians are fighting amongst themselves here the[y] have got two Presedents for the Irish republic at a late Government sale of condemed Muskets warented to kill at every shot (if they dont kill the man the[y] shoot at theyl kill the man that shoots them off) one party of the finnegans bought 80,000 of these Muskets but whether they are going [to] use them against the English or themselves it dont state"; William Murphy, 27 January 1866 (parentheses added). Although Murphy's strictures are more facetious than harsh, certainly they suggest his inability to identity with the Fenians or, by extension, with their nationalist interpretation of the famine.

44. Elizabeth Murphy married David Gilmore, "grocer," in St. Matthew's Church (Church of Ireland), in the Shankill district on 24 October 1868. See Civil Register of Marriages, 1868, v. 16, 397 (General Register Office, Belfast; on microfilm in the library of the Church of Jesus Christ of Latter Day Saints, Hollywood, Co. Down). Elizabeth Murphy's husband may have been the son of the David Gilmore listed in the Belfast city directory as a baker, living in 1865–68 at 27 Welwynne Street, in the area between the Crumlin and Shankill roads. From 1868 to 1870 the Welwynne Street address was occupied by a Mrs. John Gilmore, listed in 1870 as a millworker. Between 1870 and 1899, David Gilmore, Elizabeth's husband, was listed as a grocer or as a provision dealer at various Belfast addresses: 101 Old Lodge Road, West Belfast (1870–76); M'Millen's Buildings, 81 Albert Bridge Road, East Belfast (1877–84 and again in 1894); and 203 Grosvenor Street, West Belfast (1894–99). See *Belfast and Province of Ulster Directory* (1865–84); *Slater's Ulster Directory* (Belfast, 1870–94); and *Slater's Belfast Directory* (Belfast, 1894).

45. William Murphy to Eliza and David Gilmore, 22 March 1869.

46. Between 1860 and 1890 the nation's railroad track expanded from less than 31,000 to nearly 160,000 miles, which generated an enormous demand for railroad bridges—as well as for timber, iron, and steel generally—which specialized bridge-manufacturing companies formed to supply. In 1865 Andrew Carnegie organized the Keystone Bridge Company of Pittsburgh, which built the superstructure of the famous Eads Bridge at St. Louis (1868–74), among many others. In 1888 Keystone employed about six hundred workers and was one of the nation's major bridge-building firms. However, in the late 1880s and 1890s American bridge-building, hitherto highly competitive among numerous companies (which often led to cheap, shoddy construction with unreliable wooden and iron trusses), shifted to steel and became consolidated under control of the railroad companies. The consequent transitions, both technological and organizational, may have cost Murphy his job ca. 1890 (see below). See George Rogers Taylor and Irene Neu, *The American Railroad Network, 1861–1890* (Cambridge, Mass.: Harvard University Press, 1956); J. A. L. Waddell, *Bridge Engineering* (New York: John Wiley and Sons, 1941); and Llewellyn N. Edwards, *History and Evolution of Early American Bridges* (Orono: University of Maine Press, 1959).

47. bangor: Bangor, a minor seaport on Belfast Lough, about ten miles from the city, in County Down.

48. Murphy's reference was to his Uncle Robert or Aunt Martha of Newburgh, N.Y., whom he visited unsuccessfully sometime in the late 1860s.

49. the long bridge: Murphy was probably referring to the Queen's Bridge over the Lagan River in Belfast, which replaced the old Long Bridge in 1842.

50. Data on William Murphy's household were found in the microfilmed schedules of the 1880 U.S. census for Pittsburgh. Unfortunately, his transience, plus the commonness of his name, made it impossible to locate Murphy himself in any US censuses or in Pittsburgh city directories.

51. "gois" in MS.

52. William Murphy, 31 December 1871.

53. Robert Murphy to David and Eliza Gilmore, 18 March 1889.

54. William Murphy to David and Eliza Gilmore, 17 August 1891. On Braddock, see George H. Lamb, ed., *The Unwritten History of Braddock's Field* (Braddock, Penn.: Braddock History Committee, 1917).

55. William Murphy to Elizabeth Gilmore, 23 August 1897; this letter is accompanied by another, of the same date, to Elizabeth's daughter Ann Gilmore. By this time Elizabeth's husband David may have died, for Murphy's 1897 letters do not mention him.

56. William Murphy, 17 August 1891.

Miners in Migration:
The Case of Nineteenth-Century Irish and Irish-American Copper Miners*

TIMOTHY M. O'NEIL

WHAT FORCES COMPELLED SO many in postfamine Ireland to resettle in North America? With an emigration rate more than double that of any other European country, Ireland in this period has received considerable scholarly attention.[1] Yet most studies focus on larger structural forces—chiefly the capitalist transformation of agriculture from tillage to pasture—to the neglect of local conditions and the role of specific migration links between Ireland and America. Allied to this, Irish-American community studies seldom determine where precisely in Ireland their subjects originated or what, beyond the larger structural forces, compelled them to emigrate.

While not centered on the study of Irish migration, David Emmons' award-winning *Butte Irish: Class and Ethnicity in an American Mining Town, 1875–1925* asked the important question: Where specifically in Ireland were the Irish in his story from? Emmons concluded that "the Irish-born among Butte's thousands of Irishmen were principally drawn from the idle copper mines of West Cork and from landless farm laborers and small farmers of the West of Ireland."[2] He based his conclusion on place-name association, noting that the six most common Irish surnames in Butte "are closely associated with Co. Cork."[3] To support his place-name

*The comments and suggestions of John J. Bukowczyk and Charles K. Hyde of Wayne State University and William Mulligan, Jr., of Murray State University are gratefully acknowledged.

association evidence, he also cited Riobard O'Dwyer's genealogical studies of the Beara Peninsula, a copper-mining district in West Cork, which confirmed considerable migration to Butte.[4] In a more recent work Emmons returned to the West Cork–Butte nexus and again concluded that the concentration of West Corkonians in Butte was "no historical accident," citing as further evidence that "West Cork had had the only copper mines in Ireland, at Hungry Hill, near Allihies."[5] What Emmons did not realize is that nineteenth-century Ireland contained several copper-mining districts, two of which (Knockmahon in County Waterford and Avoca in County Wicklow) equaled or exceeded Allihies in both production and number of workers engaged.[6]

While Emmons and O'Dwyer demonstrated a strong migration link between the Beara Peninsula and Butte, the existence of additional Irish copper districts raises important questions. Did the other mining districts send such numbers to Butte? If not, why? Moreover, while Emmons asserted that "County Cork in southwestern Ireland supplied a hugely disproportionate share of Butte's population,"[7] it must be remembered that Cork was Ireland's largest county and produced by far the greatest number of emigrants in this era.[8] It is therefore reasonable to assume that County Cork surnames predominated in many other Irish-American communities. This essay will also explore that supposition.

Emmons' scholarship has made an indispensable contribution to our understanding of the Irish in America. His discovery of chain migration between copper districts in West Cork and Butte invites further investigation into the migration patterns of nineteenth-century Irish copper miners. This essay endeavors to offer such an investigation. Its objectives are fourfold: first, to present a brief narrative on Irish copper mining and the role of Irish copper miners in the development of the two primary nineteenth-century American copper ranges, Michigan's Keweenaw Peninsula and Butte, Montana; second, to offer a more precise method of determining surname frequency in Ireland; third, to apply this refined method to the Beara Peninsula and the two other major Irish copper-mining districts, Knockmahon and Avoca; and, finally, to correlate the surname frequency of the three primary Irish copper-mining districts to the surname frequency of both Butte and the Keweenaw Peninsula. To determine surname frequency in Ireland, this study will utilize the indexes to *Griffith's Valuation,*[9] which, owing to the shortage of other complete Irish records, often serves as a substitute census.[10] Taken between 1848 and 1864, the survey lists all householders and lessees by parish, no matter how small, and the occupant and value of each separate piece of property. To ascertain

Irish surname frequency in the US, the study will use US census manuscripts and indexes.

-1-

Des Cowman, the leading authority on Irish copper mining, has noted that, despite the physical evidence of abandoned mine shafts, "[s]chool geography text books of a generation ago assured us that there had been no mining in Ireland."[11] While nineteenth-century Ireland did indeed yield coal, iron, zinc, manganese, sulfur, and even gold, its most productive mines, in both tonnage mined and workers engaged, were in the three large copper-mining districts at Avoca, Knockmahon, and the Beara Peninsula. Avoca and Knockmahon began mining during the eighteenth century and by the mid-nineteenth century directly employed 2,000 and 1,200 persons respectively. Mining operations on the Beara Peninsula started in 1812, and at their peak the mines employed about 1,200 workers.[12]

Mining on the Beara Peninsula brought employment to a region where tillable land was rare and work was scarce.[13] In the parish of Kilcaskan, for instance, less than one-sixth of the soil was suitable for agriculture.[14] Visitors to the County Cork mines often wrote of the pathetic conditions that the inhabitants endured.[15] In a letter to the *Cork Examiner* a Protestant minister at the mines, the Rev. G. T. Stoney, wrote: "I have frequently visited the log shanty of the slave on the cotton plantations in South Carolina, and chatted with the inmates. I have knelt on the mud cabins on the mountains of Connemara and the bogs of Roscommon, but never 'till I came to the Berehaven mines did I witness such wretchedness of eye-revolting poverty. . . ."[16] In that no ancillary industries developed to support the mines, mining did not produce an economic boom for the peninsula. As was the case with all Irish copper-mining districts, the Berehaven mines conformed to the colonial model of exporting raw materials and importing manufactured goods. The Irish mines shipped their raw copper to Swansea for smelting and imported their supplies (coal, timber, machinery, etc.) from England. Therefore, except for trade in British manufactured goods to miners, the copper industry produced little additional economic activity on the peninsula.[17]

The Beara Peninsula held no monopoly on "eye-revolting poverty." In one Knockmahon mine location, seven hundred people lived in ninety *bóthans* (mud huts).[18] Yet the community surrounding the Knockmahon mines was economically better off than the Beara Peninsula, reminding us that poverty in nineteenth-century Ireland was a matter of degrees. Although the land that directly encompassed the Waterford mines was "generally naked and uncultivated," within a few miles lay productive soil, and thus the region enjoyed a more diverse economy.[19] Much of the mines' labor force consisted of seasonal or part-time workers who remained primarily agricultural laborers.[20] During the harvest, when agricultural wages were at their highest, the mines of Knockmahon forfeited much of their work force.[21] Here geography was an important factor. Not only did the locality around the Knockmahon mines have productive soil, but the terrain also permitted agricultural laborers to walk daily to the mines. By comparison, the mountainous terrain of the Beara Peninsula would have made a daily commute difficult at best.

The Avoca miners experienced a higher standard of living than that of their Knockmahon counterparts and were certainly better off than the Beara miners.[22] Again, poverty in nineteenth-century Ireland was relative, as the comments of a French visitor illustrate: "Along the Avoca valley I saw cottages so miserable they are impossible to describe. Most of them have neither the size nor the type of organisation that one would find in a shed to house animals . . . ; the traveler could never suppose that these were human habitations."[23] Like Knockmahon, the area around Avoca had a comparatively diverse economic base.[24] Reflecting this economic diversity, both the Knockmahon and Avoca mines experienced periodic labor shortages. There appears to be no evidence that the Beara mines experienced any difficulty in attracting sufficient labor, probably owing to the lack of sustainable agriculture on the Beara Peninsula.

All three mining districts drew their capital, management, and captains from England, Wales, and Cornwall, while their labor was Irish—men, women, boys, and girls.[25] Cornish miners provided the technical experience for the Irish copper districts, but their influence varied in each district. At the County Cork mines Cornish miners and their influence seemed the greatest, while by 1849 the Cornish appeared all but absent from Knockmahon.[26] The importation of a Cornish mining élite (more precisely, the privileges in housing, food, and wages accorded to this élite) caused animosity among the native-born work force. At Allihies, for instance, Irish miners received £2 9s. per month while Cornish miners received up to £9 for the same work.[27] This animosity and labor-market competition, as this essay will suggest, also migrated to the mining districts of the US.

The "Cornish contract system" accompanied the Cornish miners to Ireland. Under this system Irish miners did not work for set wages, but rather teams of miners, usually based on kinship, bid against each other for a contract to remove a certain portion of rock or ore. At the end of the contract period the mining captain would measure their progress, and after deducting for the use of tools, candles, blasting powder, and services, would pay the miners. The mining companies also paid the surface workers by task. While working underground was a male preserve, women and girls worked on the surface. Girls "dressed" the ore by picking out rocks that contained no copper, and women hammered the rocks to separate the ore. Miners, mine laborers, and surface workers all protested that their employers manipulated the wage system to withhold a greater part of their wages.[28]

Irish copper miners withstood their all-too-often deadly work, withstood the Great Famine, and withstood the "eye-revolting poverty"; they could not, however, withstand the parallel forces of British imperialism and global capitalism. As early as the 1820s, the Swansea smelting interests endeavored to replace Russia as the principal supplier of copper to Europe, yet their suppliers, the mines of Cornwall and Ireland, could not meet even the British domestic demand.[29] In 1842 the British government attempted to alleviate the supply problem by halving the tariff on foreign copper. British capital responded by investing heavily in the development of copper mines in the Americas, particularly Chilean copper mining. Thus a combination of state action and the subsequent capital flight resulted in the decline of Cornish and Irish copper mines and the rise of copper mining in the New World.[30] During the 1850s and 1860s Irish mines became redundant, as did their miners, many of whom now needed to migrate in search of work.

Where did they go? Except for O'Dwyer's work on the Beara Peninsula, there are no statistical data on their destinations. For Avoca the *Select Committee on Industries (Ireland)* of 1888 simply reported that some went to England and some went to America.[31] From Knockmahon, to take one example, Ed Fitzgerald first mined in Australia, then in Butte.[32] Jer Cooney and Bill Roberts also left Knockmahon for "Bute City."[33] Oral traditions in County Waterford tell of miners who left for Montana.[34] The oral traditions of the Beara Peninsula also speak of miners emigrating to Michigan and Montana.[35] Clearly, then, miners left Ireland for American mining districts, but what remains unclear is how many Ed Fitzgeralds and Jer Cooneys there were. Was the fate of these two men typical of Irish copper miners in general? Or was their fate recalled only *because* they emigrated?

America experienced its first significant mining boom during the mid-1840s when copper mining began on Michigan's Keweenaw Penin-

sula. By the end of the American Civil War the Keweenaw Range produced three-quarters of all the nation's copper. In 1870 Michigan
accounted for 87 percent of American copper production, and the state
would account for at least half of the nation's production until 1886,
when western mines, particularly the mines of Butte, surpassed it.[36] The
Keweenaw Range drew its capital from the East, chiefly from Boston,
and its labor from Western Europe and Canada, then, after 1880, from
eastern and southern Europe. With 56.6 percent of its population foreign-born in 1870, the Keweenaw's Houghton County had the third
largest foreign-born population in America.[37] While in that year 71 percent of Americans had native-born parents, fewer than 5 percent of
Houghton County residents could make such a claim.[38] According to
one Irish American, the claim of native-born parentage held a negative
connotation for the resident of the Keweenaw:

> There ain't no natives on the range. We're all foreigners up here. Sure, I
> was born here; but my folks came from Ireland and they stayed Irish until
> the day we buried the two of them. Them Swedes, them Austrians and Pol-
> ish, they're all the same way. . . . What I mean, we're different from those
> people downstate [Lower Peninsula]. Hell's fire, half them fellows in Lans-
> ing are ashamed their folks come from Europe. Look at the way they
> changed their names. You don't see that stuff on the range. . . . We ain't the
> same as those stuck-ups downstate. That's why I say we're foreigners.[39]

During this period only Zapata County, Texas, on the Mexican border
(99.4 percent) exceeded Houghton County (95.8 percent) in percentage
of population that had at least one parent of foreign birth.[40]

The Irish were present in the Lake Superior copper district from its
inception, and by 1870 they were the largest single foreign-born group
(Table 1), accounting for nearly one-third (31.4 percent) of the total foreign-born population, followed by natives of England and Wales (22.2
percent), Canada (18.8 percent), and Germany (17.5 percent).[41] Not only
did the Irish dominate the range numerically during its early years, but
they also produced its greatest number of miners,[42] which on the
Keweenaw Peninsula was not a generic title to describe those who
worked underground, but rather the preserve of the skilled men who
"read the rock," drilled holes, set a charge, and then ignited it.[43]

After the blast laborers or "trammers" gathered the rock and brought
it to the surface. Although Irish miners outnumbered Cornish miners
in 1870, Larry Lankton's *Cradle to Grave: Life, Work, and Death at the
Lake Superior Copper Mines*, the definitive study on the range, spent several pages on the migration of Cornish miners to the range, but seems

TABLE 1

HOUGHTON COUNTY, 1870: RATIO OF LABORERS TO MINERS

Place of birth	Laborers	Miners	Ratio
England	40	433	1:10.82
Ireland	398	456	1:01.11
Germany	260	115	1:00.44
United States	147	19	1:00.12
Canada	422	9	1:00.02

Source: Ninth Census of the United States, 1870, Manuscript, Houghton County, Michigan.

not to have entertained the idea that the Irish miners might have mined previously in Ireland.

Does the large number of Irish miners on the Keweenaw Range in 1870 simply reflect the gradual advance to skilled positions of a significant number of laborers? If this were the case, we should find that other ethnic groups underwent a similar advancement. Table 1 suggests otherwise. Germans, the native-born, and Canadians over the same period of time, 1850–70, did not become miners in such numbers, even though the number of German-born exceeded the Irish-born. Canadians accounted for 10.6 percent of the Houghton County work force but produced less than 1 percent of its miners. More striking was that 43.3 percent of the population was born in the US, yet the native-born accounted for only 1.6 percent of the miners. Clearly, then, the number of miners in a given group did not simply correspond to that group's proportion of the population as a whole. Table 1 demonstrates that only the Irish and the Cornish produced more miners than laborers, strongly suggesting mining experience prior to their arrival. It should be remembered that place of birth is not the same as ethnicity. The US census manuscripts for Houghton County revealed several persons with Cornish and English surnames who stated their place of birth as "Ireland," and many with Irish surnames who stated their place of birth as "England." There was, of course, tremendous Irish migration to England, and English surnames in Ireland are common. Those enumerated with Cornish surnames who stated their place of birth as "Ireland," however, raise the possibility that they had also mined in Ireland.

The hostile relationship between Irish and Cornish miners in Ireland evidently crossed the Atlantic. Indeed, most histories of hard-rock mining refer to Irish miners only within the context of their antagonistic relationship with Cornish miners. Willis Dunbar's *Michigan: A History of the Wolverine State*, the standard text of a generation ago, mentions Irish copper miners only twice. In the first instance Dunbar noted that "antagonism between the Cornishmen, or 'Cousin Jacks,' and the Irish in mining towns became traditional."[44] In the second, Dunbar quipped that "the Irish, nicknamed 'Micks,' were about as numerous in the Copper Country as the Cousin Jacks. And there was a traditional rivalry between the two."[45] Most historical works explain this "traditional rivalry" in terms of religious/ethnic bigotry. Arthur Todd, in his study of Cornish miners in America, while not discounting religious bigotry, advances a "skill envy" theory to explain the rivalry: "The hatred of the Irish for the Cornish is understandable though it cannot be explained entirely in terms of Roman Catholic and Methodist bigotry. Celtic temperaments clashed when the exhausted Irish laborer found himself face to face with the acquired skills of centuries."[46] Todd, like many scholars of American mining, erroneously constructed a rivalry between skilled Cornish *miners* and unskilled Irish *laborers*, while statistically it is clear that the rivalry was between two ethnic groups competing for the skilled position of miner or mining captain. A more historically accurate explanation of this rivalry is an ethnicized labor-market competition having its origins in the copper districts of Ireland.

During the early period on the Keweenaw Range mining companies operated under the previously described Cornish contract system.[47] The system gave an obvious benefit to miners who previously had bid on mining contracts. These miners understood what to bid on and, just as important, what not to bid on as well as, of course, how much to bid on a given contact. This system would clearly have been advantageous to both Irish and Cornish miners, while it would have disadvantaged experienced miners from Germany and Scandinavia, who were not accustomed to it. While Irish miners might have found the familiar contract system on the Keweenaw Range, however, the copper industry there did not directly employ women and girls.

Although the Irish-born provided the largest number of miners on the Keweenaw Peninsula in 1870 and later dominated the copper mines of Butte, their numerical domination in these districts was exceptional. Nationally, Irish miners ranked third behind native-born and English-born miners.[48] With the large number of Cornish miners on the nearby Marquette iron range, Irish miners ranked second in the state of Michigan.[49] Does migration from idle Irish copper mines explain the unusually large, atypical, presence of Irish miners on the Keweenaw copper range during its formative years? And did many of the Keweenaw's Irish copper miners previously mine copper in Ireland? Perhaps surname-frequency analysis can add further evidence to support this proposition.

-2-

Because many Irish surnames derived from clans and thus from discrete geographical areas, surname-frequency analysis operates on the assumption that many Irish names can be associated with a given geographical area. Ireland's relatively low levels of urbanization, industrialization, and, consequently, permanent internal migration heighten the association between names and places. Of course, nearly every Irish surname exists in every Irish county, rendering surname-frequency analysis far from exact. Nonetheless, the difference in the frequency of surnames from one parish to a neighboring parish is quite remarkable, as is the concentration of surnames in a parish itself. For example, an examination of the thirty surnames representing the ten most common in each of the three major Irish mining districts (Table 2) reveals that only one, Murphy, appears twice. Murphy and Kelly, the two most common surnames in Ireland, are well distributed throughout the island.

TABLE 2

SURNAME FREQUENCY OF IRISH MINING DISTRICTS,
RANKED IN ASCENDING ORDER

Rank	Beara Peninsula[50]	Knockmahon[51]	Avoca[52]
1	Sullivan	Powers	Byrne
2	Harrington	Walsh	Doyle
3	Shea	Morrissey	Kavanagh
4	Murphy	Fitzgerald	Cullen
5	Leary	Whelan	Keernan
6	McCarthy	Foley	Brien
7	Lynch	Flynn	Murphy
8	Kelly	McGrath	Murry
9	Dwyer	Kiely	Neill
10	Crowley	McNamara	Tracy

Source: *An Index of Surnames of Households in Griffith's Primary Valuation and Tithe Applotment Book*, National Library of Ireland, Dublin.

TABLE 3

FREQUENCY OF IRISH SURNAMES IN HOUGHTON COUNTY,
BUTTE (DEER LODGE COUNTY), AND
PHILADELPHIA, RANKED IN ASCENDING ORDER

Rank	Houghton Co.	Deer Lodge Co.	Philadelphia
1	Sullivan	Sullivan	Kelly
2	Harrington	Harrington	Dougherty
3	Shea	Murphy	Murphy
4	Murphy	Kelly	Gallagher
5	McCarthy	Lynch	Collins
6	Kelly	Collins	O'Brien
7	Ryan	O'Brien	Quinn
8	Lynch	Powers	O'Neill
9	O'Brien	Flynn	Kennedy
10	Hanly	Dunn	Duffy

Source: Indices to the *U.S. Federal Census Manuscript,* Houghton Co., Michigan (1870), Deer Lodge Co., Territory of Montana (1880), and Philadelphia, Pennsylvania (1860).

According to Emmons, from 1886 to 1914 the six most common Irish surnames in Butte were Sullivan, Harrington, Murphy, Kelly, Shea, and O'Neill.[53] Employing *Griffith's Valuation* to narrow the County Cork surnames to the parishes that surrounded the mines of the Beara Peninsula (Table 2), we discover that five of the six Butte surnames appear among the ten most common surnames of the Beara Peninsula. Except for the ubiquitous Murphy, Emmons' list of Butte surnames does not match with any of the ten most frequent surnames from Avoca or Knockmahon (Table 2). Table 3 reveals that the first four most frequent surnames (Sullivan, Harrington, Shea, and Murphy) are, in order, identical for the Beara Peninsula and Houghton County. This matching of surname frequency surely transcends mere coincidence. In addition, the lists match McCarthy and Lynch. By expanding the Houghton County list (Table 3) to the fifteen most frequent surnames, we find Dwyer (11) and Crowley (13). Though not identical, these names are very similar to those of Butte. As with Emmons' list, again except for the ever-present surname of Murphy, none of the most common surnames from Avoca or Knockmahon are among the ten most common in Houghton County. Table 3 reveals Sullivan and Harrington in the first and second positions in Butte, which is identical for the Beara Peninsula and Houghton County. The names Powers and Flynn from Knockmahon also appear in Butte, suggesting perhaps an earlier migration to Mon-

FIGURE 1

HOUGHTON COUNTY, MICHIGAN: FOREIGN-BORN BY COUNTRY

AS PERCENT OF TOTAL FOREIGN-BORN POPULATION

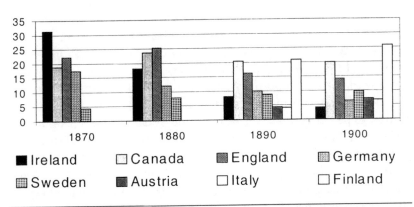

Source: *Ninth Census of the United States*, Vol. I: *The Statistics of the United States, Population*, Table VII—State of Michigan—"Selected Nativities By Counties," 359; *Tenth Census of the United States*, Vol. I: *The Statistics of the United States, Population*, Table VIX—State of Michigan—"Native and Foreign Born Populations by Counties," 514; *Eleventh Census of the United States*, Vol. I: *The Statistics of the United States, Population*, Table 33—State of Michigan—"Foreign Born Population Distributed According to Country of Birth by County," 633; *Twelfth Census of the United States*, Vol. I. *The Statistics of the United States, Population*, Table 93—State of Michigan—"Per 10,000 Distributed of Population of Each State and County, by Country of Birth," 1095.

tana—or, more likely, a continual migration on a significantly lower scale than that from the Beara Peninsula, driving their surnames further down the list. As with both the Butte and Houghton County lists, the most common surnames from Avoca are absent. The similarities between the surnames of Butte and the Keweenaw Peninsula not only suggest that both drew upon the miners of the Beara Peninsula and, to a much lesser extent, County Waterford, but that there was a migration link between the Michigan mines and the Montana mines.

In 1870 the Irish accounted for 17.8 percent of Houghton County's total population, placing it sixth nationally in percent of population born in Ireland.[54] After 1870 the number of Irish in Houghton County continued to decline in both actual numbers and in their percentage of the total foreign-born (Figure 1). By 1880 the number of native Cornish and Canadians had surpassed the number of native Irish. During the 1880s the number of native Finns, Germans, Norwegians, and Swedes also exceeded the Irish. By the close of the century, among the foreign-born of Houghton County, the Irish ranked only seventh. While the number of native Irish dropped dramatically from 1870 to 1900, as did their percentage of the foreign-born population, many second-generation Irish Americans presumably stayed on the Keweenaw Range.

Many Irish Americans, however, did not remain on the Keweenaw Range. According to the US census, Michigan was the most frequent state of birth among Butte's second-generation Irish.[55] Most likely, the majority of these Michigan-born second-generation Irish migrated to Butte with their Irish-born parents. From the 20 percent drop in the number of Irish in Houghton County from 1870 to 1880, and from the further 30 percent drop in the next decade, and discounting population losses owing to natural decrease, we might estimate the Irish out-migration from the Keweenaw Range, but this simple formula would not account for continuing Irish migration to Houghton County. It is reasonable to suspect that Irish emigrants continued to make their way to the Keweenaw Range, some of whom mined and remained, while others mined and then continued on to Montana.

The drop in the number and percent of the Irish foreign-born population in Houghton County corresponded with the rise of the Irish in Butte (Figure 2). In 1870 the Butte Irish ranked second behind the Chinese. With the prohibition on Chinese immigration in 1882 (owing to the success of a campaign often led by Irish miners), the main rival of the Butte Irish once again became the Cornish. At the turn of the century the Irish, with 25.9 percent of the foreign-born population, ranked first in Butte (Figure 2). The corresponding rise of the Butte Irish and the decline of the Keweenaw Irish do not, of course, necessarily denote migration from Michigan to Montana. Yet they add further evidence to the suggestion that there existed a migration link from the Beara Peninsula to the Keweenaw Peninsula and then on to Butte.

At the outset of this essay it was suggested that, given County Cork's predominance in Irish emigration to America, it is reasonable to suspect that Cork surnames (Sullivans, Harringtons, Sheas, etc.) would be the most frequent in many Irish-American communities, not just those engaged primarily in mining. Applying surname-frequency to random communities, this appears not to have been the case.[56] For instance, quite different Irish surnames seem to have dominated Philadelphia (Table 2). Again, except for the omnipresent Murphy and Kelly, these names have a decidedly Donegal/Ulster origin.[57] This, of course, is not to say that no Harringtons, Sheas, McCarthys, or Dwyers lived in Philadelphia, but rather that, although the city had *ten and a half times* as many Irish as Houghton County, it had fewer Harringtons, Sheas,

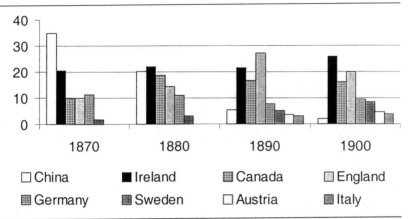

FIGURE 2

DEER LODGE/SILVER BOW COUNTIES, MONTANA: FOREIGN-BORN
BY COUNTRY AS PERCENT OF TOTAL FOREIGN-BORN POPULATION

Source: Ninth Census of the United States, Vol. I: *The Statistics of the United States, Population,* Table VII–Territory of Montana–"Selected Nativities by Counties," 363; *Tenth Census of the United States,* Vol. I: *The Statistics of the United States, Population,* Table VIX–Territory of Montana–"Native and Foreign Born Populations by Counties," 519; *Eleventh Census of the United States,* Vol. I: *The Statistics of the United States, Population,* Table 33–State of Montana–"Foreign Born Population Distributed According to Country of Birth by County," 640; *Twelfth Census of the United States,* Vol. I: *The Statistics of the United States, Population,* Table 93–State of Montana–"Per 10,000 Distributed of Population of Each State and County, by Country of Birth," 1105.

McCarthys, and Dwyers. Similarly, the surname Sullivan, the most common name in West Cork, appeared in large numbers in other communities, ranking fifth in frequency in Chicago, but nowhere near as common as in Michigan.[58] For instance, the ratio of Sullivans to Irish-born in Chicago was 1:115, while for Houghton County it was 1:12. The name Harrington is more telling; the ratio in Chicago was a mere 1:1085 while for Houghton County it was 1:30.

While the evidence has suggested that a well-defined migration network existed between the Beara Peninsula, the Keweenaw Peninsula, and Butte, Montana, and to a lesser extent from Knockmahon, the miners from Avoca seem to have been all but absent from the American copper-mining districts. What explains the disparities in emigration from three Irish mining districts that were similar in both the numbers of workers they employed and in mine closures? When Irish copper mining began to decline and then ended during the 1870s, each district afforded varying opportunities for miners to find other means of support in Ireland. The terrain of the Beara Peninsula made sustainable employment in agriculture exceedingly difficult. West Cork, one of the most economically distressed and congested districts in Ireland, produced tremendous emigration to the US. That generations of Beara Irish, who never could have seen the inside of a copper mine, continued to migrate to the Keweenaw and to Butte in the period from 1870 to 1920 points to an extensive migration network but also to the limited employment prospects on the Beara Peninsula.

The areas encompassing the Avoca and Knockmahon districts enjoyed a much more diverse economy than did the Beara Peninsula. In addition, the Avoca district was situated in County Wicklow, which experienced the lowest per capita emigration of any Irish county between 1851 and 1871 and again from 1871 to 1891. By comparison, County Waterford's per capita emigration rate was twice that of County Wicklow, whereas the County Cork rate was nearly two-and-a-half times greater than Wicklow's.[59] While emigration rates do not account for an individual's decision to emigrate, they do reflect economic opportunities and supplies of surplus labor and other structural influences. Moreover, Leinster's geographical proximity and economic ties to England extended to migration patterns. Thus those who emigrated from County Wicklow were likelier to migrate to England and, to a lesser extent, Australia. This perhaps serves as an explanation for the apparent absence of significant numbers of Avoca miners in Michigan and Montana. Those who emigrated from County Cork and County Waterford, as with the entire province of Munster, were likelier to select the US.[60]

This essay has suggested that a migration network existed between the Beara Peninsula (and to lesser extent Knockmahon), Michigan's Keweenaw Peninsula, and Butte, Montana. David Emmons demonstrated that many Butte miners had previously mined in Ireland. The same was clearly true for the Irish miners of the Keweenaw Range, something that has escaped previous students of this prominent mining region. The case of Irish copper miners offers an example of Irish immigrants who possessed industrial skills, and it raises the question of how many other Irish emigrants to America possessed industrial or proto-industrial skills. While the landless agricultural laborer remains the archetypal Irish immigrant, how common were the exceptions?

NOTES

1. Timothy J. Hatton and Jeffrey G. Williamson, "After the Famine: Emigration from Ireland, 1850–1913," *The Journal of Economic History* 53 (1993), 575.

2. David Emmons, *The Butte Irish: Class and Ethnicity in an American Mining Town, 1875–1925* (Urbana: University of Illinois Press, 1989), 18. Kevin Kenny, *Making Sense of the Molly Maguires* (New York: Oxford University Press, 1998) also uses surname frequency, among other sources, in tracing the Donegal origins of many of his subjects.

3. Ibid., 15.

4. O'Dwyer traced the histories of over 14,000 people on the Beara Peninsula. See Riobard O'Dwyer, *Who Were My Ancestors*, in four different volumes representing the parishes of Eyeries (1976), Allihies (1988), Castletownbere (1989), and Bere Island (1989), all published by Stevens, Astoria, Illinois.

5. David Emmons, "Faction Fights: The Irish Worlds of Butte, Montana, 1875–1917," in Patrick Sullivan, ed., *The Irish World Wide: History, Heritage and Identity*, Vol. 2: *The Irish in Their New Communities* (New York: St. Martin's Press, 1992), 82–98 (quote, 83).

6. Des Cowman, "Life and Labour in Three Irish Mining Communities, Circa 1840," in *Saothar: Journal of Irish Labour History* 9 (1983), 11.

7. Emmons, *Butte Irish*, 15.

8. The number of Irish emigrants from 1851 to 1911 is estimated at 4,080,753. Of this number, County Cork contributed 545,085, or roughly 13.5 percent. W.E. Vaughan and A.J. Fitzpatrick, *Irish Historical Statistics, 1821–1971* (Dublin: Royal Irish Academy, 1978).

9. *Griffith's Valuation* is indexed by county and is shelved in the main reading room of the National Library of Ireland, Dublin.

10. James G. Ryan, ed., *Irish Records: Sources for Family and Local History* (Salt Lake City, Utah: Ancestry Publishing, 1988), xviii.

11. Cowman, "Life and Labour," 10.

12. Ibid., 11.

13. Samuel Lewis, *A Topographical Dictionary of Ireland*, 2 vols. (London, 1837; reprinted Baltimore: Genealogical Publishing, 1984), Vol. I, 302.

14. Ibid., Vol. II, 59.

15. For a contemporary account, see Lady Chatterton, *Rambles in the South of Ireland during the Year 1838* (London: Saunder and Otley, 1839).

16. *Cork Examiner*, 3 March 1868, as quoted in Colman Mahony, "Copper-Mining at Allihies, Co. Cork," *Journal of the Cork Historical and Archaeological Society* 92 (January 1987), 79.

17. Lewis, *Topographical Dictionary*, Vol. I, 307.

18. Cowman, "Life and Labour," 14.

19. Ibid.

20. "Dicie" [Des Cowman], "Life and Work in an Irish Mining Camp, c. 1840: Knockmahon Copper Mines, Co. Waterford," in *Dicies* 14 (May 1980), 30.

21. British Parliamentary Papers, *Children's Employment Commission; Appendix to 1st Report of Commissioners of Mines*, H.C. 1842, Vol. 16, 865.

22. Des Cowman, "The Mining Community at Avoca, 1780–1880," in Ken Hannington and William Nolan, eds., *Wicklow History and Society: Interdisciplinary Essays of an Irish County* (Dublin: Geography Publications, 1994), 775.

23. *Excursions pittoresque et artistique en Irlande pendant les années 1836–7*, trans. Professor Garrick (Paris, 1839), 99, quoted in Cowman, "Mining Community at Avoca," 775.

24. Lewis, *Topographical Dictionary*, Vol. II, 511.

25. Cowman, "Life and Labour," 10; British Parliamentary Papers, *Children's Employment Commission; Appendix to 1st Report of Commissioners of Mines*, H.C. 1842, Vol. 16, 865–67.

26. "Dicies," "Life and Work," 36.

27. O'Mahony, "Copper-Mining at Allihies, Co. Cork," 75.

28. Emmet O'Connor, *A Labour History of Waterford* (Naas, Co. Kildare: Leinster Leader, 1989), 76.

29. William Culver and Cornel J. Reinhart, "The Decline of a Mining Region and Mining Policy: Chilean Copper in the Nineteenth Century," in Thomas Greaves and William Culver, eds., *Miners and Mining in the Americas* (Manchester: Manchester University Press, 1985), 70.

30. Ibid., 71.

31. British Parliamentary Papers, *Report from the Select Committee on Industries (Ireland)*, H.C. 1884–85 (288), Vol. 9, 746.

32. Joseph J. Walsh, *Waterford's Yesterday and To-Morrows and an Outline of Waterford's History* (Waterford: Munster Express, 1958), 22.

33. Ibid., 17.

34. Cowman, "Life and Labour."

35. The author visited the region in the spring of 1995 and was told this in numerous conversations.

36. Larry Lankton, *Cradle to Grave: Life, Work, and Death at the Lake Superior Copper Mines* (New York: Oxford University Press, 1991), 20.

37. *The Ninth Census of the United States*, Vol. I, *Population, General Nativity, and Foreign Population* (Washington: Government Printing Office, 1872), 299–325. Figure refers to counties with populations exceeding 10,000, of which in 1870 there were only five with a majority foreign-born population: Cameron County, Texas, 63.3 percent; Marquette County, Michigan, 61.4 percent; Houghton County, Michigan, 56.6 percent; Sanilac County, Michigan, 52.9 percent; Carver County, Minnesota, 51.1 percent. (Source: *Ninth Census of the United States*, Vol. I.)

38. *Ninth Census of the United States*, Vol. I, 313.

39. Angus Murdoch, *Boom Copper: The Story of the First U.S. Mining Boom* (1943; reprinted Hancock: Book Concern, 1964), 201.

40. *Ninth Census of the United States*, Vol. I, 299–325.

41. *U.S. Federal Census*, 1850, Manuscript, Houghton County, Michigan.

42. Ibid.

43. Lankton, *Cradle to Grave*, 30.

44. Willis F. Dunbar, *Michigan: A History of the Wolverine State* (Grand Rapids, Mich.: William B. Eerdmans Publishing Co., 1965), 358.

45. Ibid., 501.

46. Arthur Cecil Todd, *The Cornish Miner in America* (Glendale, Cal.: Arthur H. Clark Co., 1967), 242.

47. Lankton, *Cradle to Grave*, 65.

48. *Ninth Census of the United States*, Vol. I, 704.

49. Ibid.

50. The surname frequency for the Beara Peninsula was compiled from the following parishes: Kilcaskan, Kilcatherine, Killaconenagh, and Kilnamanagh, all in the Barony of Beara, Co. Cork, and the parish of Tuosist, Barony of Glanarought, Co. Kerry.

51. The surname frequency for the area around Knockmahon, a five-mile radius comprising a portion of County Waterford was compiled from the following parishes: Kilberrymeadan, Ballylaneen, Monksland, Stradbally, Fews, Rossmire, and Kilrossanty, all in the Barony of Dices without Drum; and Dunhill and Newcastle, both in the Barony of Middlethird.

52. The surname frequency for the area around the Avoca district, a five-mile radius comprising a portion of County Wicklow was compiled from the following parishes: Castlemacadam, Redcross, Ennereilly, Ballintemple, Kilbride, Killahurler, and Arklow, all in the Barony of Arklow; Ballykine, Barony of North Ballinacor; and Kilcommon, Barony of Newcastle.

53. Emmons, *Butte Irish*, 15.

54. *Ninth Census of the United States*, Vol. I, 359. The top ten counties with the highest percent of those of Irish birth were Suffolk, Mass. (21.8), New York, N.Y. (21.4), Hudson, N.J. (19.4), Stoory, Nevada (18.9), King's, N.Y. (18.6), Houghton, Mich. (17.8), San Francisco, Cal. (17.3), Providence, R.I. (17.3), Middlesex, Mass. (16.8), and New Haven, Conn. (16.1). (Source: *Ninth Census of the United States*, Vol. I, 345–76).

55. Emmons, *Butte Irish*, 17.

56. The communities examined were Brooklyn, New York; Buffalo, New York; Chicago, Illinois; Detroit, Michigan; Philadelphia, Pennsylvania; and San Francisco, California.

57. Ryan, *Irish Records*, passim.

58. *Index to the U.S. Federal Census*, 1870, City of Chicago, Illinois.

59. Emigrants from County Wicklow in the period 1851–71 accounted for 17 percent of the county's population in 1851. For the period 1871–91 they accounted for 13 percent of the 1871 population. For Waterford the corresponding figures for 1851–71 was 36 percent, and for 1871–91 it was 26 percent. The figures for County Cork were 41 percent in 1851–71 and 30 percent in 1871–91. (Source: T.W. Moody, F.X. Martin, and F.J. Byrne, eds., *A New History of Ireland*, Vol. IX: *Maps, Genealogies, Lists: A Companion to Irish History* (New York: Oxford University Press, 1976).

60. R.F. Foster, *Modern Ireland, 1600–1972* (New York: Penguin, 1988), 354.

Transatlantic Connections and the Sharp Edge of the Great Depression

MATTHEW J. O'BRIEN

IRISH TRANSATLANTIC MIGRATION has inspired a number of impressive works in a variety of fields, from the humanities to the social sciences. Yet the vast majority of these accounts end early in the twentieth century, often immediately after World War I. Although some works mention the sharp drop in traffic in the late 1920s and early 1930s, most simply attribute this trend to changes in American immigration policy. According to Kerby Miller, one of the foremost scholars of Irish transatlantic migration, "The Easter rising and the Anglo-Irish war occurred just before the well of Irish-American memories, duty, and guilt ran dry," as if seventy-year-old transatlantic diasporic links abruptly unraveled in the years immediately following World War I.[1] Patrick J. Blessing, another major contributor to the field, also sees 1920 as the point at which "the story of the Irish in America had become the story of Americans of Irish descent."[2]

The reliance on immigration restriction legislation as a monocausal explanation of the drop in Irish migration to the United States stems from an underestimation of the multifaceted and persistent nature of this transatlantic connection. Rooted in decades of postfamine movement, the transatlantic migration network continued to involve not only those Irish-born crossing the Atlantic themselves but also the Irish at home and Americans of Irish descent in the United States. The wide array of transatlantic links built up in the late-nineteenth and early-twentieth centuries functioned as far more than mere conduits of immigration. The network served as a two-way connection, with Irish-born labor moving predominantly westward while information and remittance money flowed in the opposite direction. These connections

78

remained central to the lives of Irish men and women both at home and abroad and continued to function after the Immigration Restriction Acts of the 1920s. Even after the stock market crash of 1929, thousands of Irish men and women continued to arrive in the United States.

Nonetheless, the interwar period brought a momentous change in Irish migration history. The various and diverse bonds between Ireland and the United States emerged relatively unscathed from the restrictionist legislation of the 1920s, only to unravel from the ensuing social tensions of assimilation and the economic strains of the Great Depression. In sharp contrast to the temporary ebbs and flows of the late-nineteenth century, the depression permanently disrupted the westward flow of postfamine migrants. By the time the American economy began to recover, the outflow from Ireland had been diverted eastward, setting the pattern for almost a half-century.

Transatlantic Networks and Immigration Restriction

Postfamine transatlantic migration was dominated by one-way westward movement in the seventy years after the mid-nineteenth-century famine, with the departure of an estimated 3.7 million Irish-born men and women to the United States between 1851 and 1921.[3] Despite improvements in Irish conditions in the seventy years after the famine, the return rate for Irish transatlantic migrants was the second lowest for all immigrant groups in the United States between 1908 and 1923.[4]

The westward flow of Irish men and women across the Atlantic created a reciprocal eastward traffic in correspondence and remittances. Letters from the Irish in America carried usually reliable information about current economic conditions back to Ireland, providing potential migrants with the latest news and advice about employment prospects in the United States. This responsiveness of transatlantic links became especially important during times of economic distress in the United States, reacting with "stop-and-go" fluctuations in volume and even in direction during the instabilities in the early 1860s, the middle 1870s, and the late 1890s.[5]

The counterflow of remittances and information from the United States to Ireland played a vital role in the lives of the Irish at home and abroad. Contemporary observers in the United States noted with amazement the large share of American earnings sent home, while accounts of rural life in Ireland described the vital role remittances from America played in the maintenance of the family farm.[6] In addition, the "American letter" linked expatriates with their families at home, providing the main connection to home in a system in which there were often severe societal strictures against permanent return to Ireland.[7]

Contrary to conventional understanding, the restrictions imposed on European immigration into the United States during the 1920s did not directly affect most Irish immigration. The National Origins System, established and modified by the Immigration Restriction Acts of 1921, 1924, and 1929, imposed numerical limits on each sending country. These caps adversely affected the "new immigration" from eastern and southern Europe, however, rather than those western and northern European countries of "old immigration."[8] Irish-American leaders exerted their influence successfully to secure a relatively generous allotment of visas to the Irish Free State. With an initial allotment of 28,567 slots annually through the Johnson-Reed Act of 1924 reduced to 17,583 in 1929, the Irish demand for visas never exceeded the supply during the forty-year existence of the system.[9] Although the effect of the Immigration Restriction Acts has often been exaggerated to provide a monocausal explanation of the decline in transatlantic migration between Ireland and the United States, the new criteria for admission would eventually be overshadowed by long-term assimilative pressures and the calamitous event of the Great Depression.[10]

Changes in American immigration policy contributed to the sharp reductions in Irish inflow in the late 1920s and early 1930s, but these restrictions were of an administrative, not a political, character and stemmed from earlier laws. The two main operative clauses pertained to the issuance of American visas by consular officials. First, an immigration restriction bill passed by Congress in 1917 allowed for the assignment of American medical staff to overseas consulates in order to regularize the medical exams administered to visa applicants. Second, during the late 1920s the consular staff was instructed to apply a "Likely to Become a Public Charge" (LPC) test to reduce the number of indigent arrivals. Both clauses allowed for a considerable range of administrative discretion in their application, unlike the clear (albeit politically determined) caps established in the National Origins System.

According to the Dublin consular staff, the effect of the latter change in screening, the LPC clause, could be "neither so clearly expressed nor so easily measured" as the appointment of American medical examiners. The initial criterion used for this requirement in 1917 merely denied visas to Irish men and women who were not able to demonstrate that they had enough money to cover the cost of the transatlantic voyage. The Immigration Bureau workers classified almost three-fourths of all

Irish visa holders as unskilled laborers or domestic servants, but less than one-half of one percent of them were turned back on account of the LPC clause.[11]

Economic instability in early 1929 brought further steps to increase the stringency of the LPC test, and officials now required migrants to show proof of material support or the necessary skills to guarantee self-sufficiency in the United States. Cornelius Ferris, the U.S. Consul General in the Irish Free State, admitted increasing reliance on the LPC clause for screening potential migrants during a June 1929 interview before the stock market crash.[12] A State Department circular explicitly spelled out the new, higher standard one year later.[13]

This reliance on administrative consular judgment rather than on congressional legislation set a precedent for American policy as the economic situation deteriorated in 1930. Unprecedented levels of joblessness forced even the most liberal opponents of restriction to yield, and the political debate shifted to the means of reducing inflow. Hard-line restrictionists pressed for reducing national quotas by 60 to 90 percent, and a proposal for a five-year moratorium on all non-relative immigration lost in a surprisingly close U.S. Senate vote, 37 to 29. Meanwhile, the erstwhile opponents of restriction contented themselves with an ad hoc approach through the tighter administrative enforcement of preexisting screening clauses, relying mainly on the LPC qualification. In the end this latter argument carried the day, as the first Democratic-majority Congress in fourteen years became preoccupied with matters of immediate and direct relief.[14]

Furthermore, the proponents of this ad hoc policy took steps to ensure that these new conditions remained temporary. The higher standard for the LPC qualification was explicitly tied to the high unemployment of "abnormal times, such as the present, where there is not any reasonable prospect of prompt employment for an alien laborer or artisan who comes hoping to get a job and live by it."[15] Instructions from Washington established a "waiting list" for prospective migrants who been denied visas because of the higher LPC standards, arranged by occupation in order to facilitate the process.[16]

Irish-American Acculturation in the 1920s and the Resurgence of Nativism

The sharp drop in Irish inflow during the early years of the Great Depression followed a decade of challenges and changes for previous Irish migrants and their American-born offspring. Despite the resurgence of nativism during World War I and the early 1920s, the Irish-American middle-class continued to grow during the 1920s, building on the socioeconomic advance toward "respectability" during the late-nineteenth and early-twentieth centuries. By the end of the decade the popular press recognized the pervasive effect of Irish-American influence in wider American culture—an achievement proudly celebrated by the Irish ethnic press. In part driven by xenophobic resistance to non-Anglocentric patriotism, as well as by expatriate disillusionment with the cause of Irish nationalism, their rise to prominence through the assertion of ethnic pluralism effected a change in outlook for many Irish Americans. Old World tenets gave way to New World motivations, and by the time the depression ended American experiences had taken a formative role in redefining Irish-American identity.

At the same time, American nativists targeted Irish Americans on a national basis in the years immediately after World War I. In the early 1920s anti-Irish Catholic sentiment expanded beyond its earlier provincial basis, as shown in the geographical incursions of the Ku Klux Klan.[17] Responding to these attacks, Irish Americans challenged the Anglocentric conception of American patriotism by emphasizing the immigrant experience as crucial in appreciating the land of opportunity. The Irish-American response redefined American patriotism with the assimilationist image of the "melting pot," although barriers to Irish-American assimilation or even acceptance remained strong among the upper classes throughout the decade. The incomplete nature of acceptance had long-term repercussions for Irish-Americans, fostering a sense of insecurity and often defensiveness among later generations.[18]

Soon after the end of World War I the leaders of the Ku Klux Klan strategically expanded their rhetoric of intolerance to include American Catholics in an attempt to attract members outside the Old South. As new chapters started up in northern and western states outside the old Confederacy, Klan leaders shifted their bigotry from racism to anti-Catholicism and xenophobia. The organization often garnered recruits in the major cities like Chicago (50,000 members at its peak), Detroit (35,000) and even seemingly Irish-dominated cities such as Philadelphia (35,000) and Boston (3,500). Over half of those enrolled in the postwar incarnation of the Klan came from metropolitan areas with more than fifty thousand residents, and about 32 percent lived in cities of over one hundred thousand people. In 1928 Hiram Evans, the imperial wizard of the Klan, boasted, "There is not a single eastern state where we do not have a strong and effective membership."[19] In contrast to the provincial night-riders of the Reconstruction era, Evans's Klan operated on a national scale, with the forty thousand marchers gathered in Washington, D.C., outnumbering any World War I parade.

Anti-Catholic prejudices also came in the form of several state attempts to close Catholic schools. Oregon passed the only compulsory public-school education measure in American history in 1922, with the Rev. James R. Johnson issuing sectarian threats: "I warn the Catholic church now, keep your dirty hands off the public schools."[20] Even for those Americans uninvolved in the parochial school debate, the backlash against Europe often included insinuations against, or open condemnations of, Catholicism. With the retrospective collapse of the American rationale for involvement in the war, disillusioned Americans condemned any "foreign entanglements" with Europe. Nativist attacks on Catholicism stressed the foreign nature of this religion, characterizing the Catholic church as "the Church of Rome" and characterizing American Catholics as subjects of a foreign head of state.

Irish Americans, particularly those striving to enter middle-class occupations, responded to such attacks on their loyalty with defensive public declarations of American patriotism, shying away from controversial organizations like the Clan na Gael and the Friends of Irish Freedom and instead emphasizing their ethnic identity through nonpolitical means.[21] Irish-American social and cultural groups consciously placed their members' Irish ethnicity in an explicitly American perspective. Assimilationist institutions such as the Friendly Sons of Saint Patrick in Philadelphia and the American Irish Historical Society placed their nonideological emphasis on "affirming Irishness [in] a particular way, with [their] emphasis on charitable activities, inter-religious fraternity, and concern for Ireland's well-being."[22]

The Ancient Order of Hibernians (AOH) was among the most prominent of these Irish-American associations. The AOH took an active role in the broad consensus for Irish independence during the second and third Irish Race Conventions. After a split between Eamon de Valera and the editors of the *Gaelic-American,* however, the Hibernians tried to distance their organization from the increasingly fractious state of Irish republicanism, "lest the harsh discord be transmitted to our side of the ocean."[23] Instead the AOH redoubled its efforts to foster immigrant assimilation. The revised Hibernian constitution in 1923 pledged members "to uphold and sustain the loyalty to the government of the United States of America" before mentioning the general cause of Irish independence. It also restricted membership to American citizens and those involved in the naturalization process.[24] In his sermon at the opening mass of the 55th National AOH Convention in 1927, the Archbishop John J. Glennon of St. Louis, the national chaplain of the AOH, reasserted the Hibernian commitment to the United States:

> Here I am in an American city speaking to Americans whose memories, sometimes attenuated, may be of the Ireland of your forefathers, but today who claim, and justly so, their first love and their service to the land in which they live, and the nation of which they are honored citizens. Be it so! . . . The struggle of the one nation parallels the struggle of the other, and . . . the ideals of both are identical.[25]

As part of this attempt to redefine Irish-American identity within the context of the American ethnic melting pot, the celebration of Saint Patrick's Day gained new prominence, especially within the Irish-American ethnic press. In 1929 the *Gaelic-American* proclaimed the following in its coverage of festivities:

> Saint Patrick's Day, observed as the great racial holiday of the Irish race in America, has been practically taken over and adopted by the entire American people of all races, classes, and creeds. . . . The observance of Saint Patrick's Day is more general and widespread than that of some of our legal holidays . . . [in contrast to] the numerous attempts to popularize Magna Carta Day in this country.[26]

J.W. Mason, a special correspondent to the *Irish Advocate*, went further in an open letter to the English press magnate Lord Beaverbrook, responding to allegations of sectarianism among Irish Americans. Mason proclaimed that "the hard political strife which formerly allowed itself in Ireland has not been carried into the Irish male of New York. Toleration has been the foremost principle for New York's Irish."[27] The *New York Daily News* took note of the new multi-ethnic character of the holiday with a description of the parade's audience: "Between lines of applauding citizens of English, Irish, Polish, Jewish, Swedish, Italian, and Russian extraction, the sturdy Sons of Saint Patrick swept up 5th Ave." The same article described the parade as uniquely American: "something that cannot be, nor has ever been duplicated in any other place in the world."[28]

Throughout all of these accounts Irish Americans tempered their ethnic pride in Ireland with American patriotism, as they defended themselves against xenophobia with an aggressively confident loyalty to the United States. This meant the aggrandizement of their adopted country in comparison to old Ireland, a stance that even influenced early academic works. In his 1932 book, *Ireland and the Irish Emigration to the New World from 1815 to the Famine,* William Adams imbued the story of Irish migration to the United States with a tone of Darwinian self-congratulation. Adams attributed Irish-American success in the face of Old World misfortune to the qualitative self-screening aspect of the migration process: "The superior development of the Irish in America suggests either that opportunity brought out the latent qualities of the race, or that America was getting the best Irish."[29]

Yet Irish expatriates also struggled with the special sacrifices required of Irish expatriates in the realization of American aspirations. In contrast to his satirical treatment of the professional Irish, Frank O'Malley's description of the ethnic cost of upward social mobility was poignant, verging on pathetic. Even if O'Malley challenged the veracity and sincerity of an Irish-American nationalist identity in the late 1920s, his account of the sacrifice of Irish Catholic ethnicity on the part of socially ambitious Irish Americans was far from liberating:

> These grueling, intense, quick climbs to the social register pages at which we Irish Americans are so adept call too for a unique and heroic trait of character that is unknown and necessary among American climbers of other blue bloods. In our struggle up the ladder we must leave behind us, even trampled savagely under foot, our earlier and most cherished prides. This sacrifice of ours is heartrending at times and always embarrassing.[30]

This sacrifice was made even worse, according to O'Malley, by the re-identification of the Irish Catholic climbers as they emulated their sectarian critics:

> So many of us financially—and therefore socially—successful in America go Scotch overnight because, I suppose, the Scotch route is an easy way out. . . . The Irish Catholics are so pitifully few on the top rungs of the ladder. The 'pervert' McCartney, a Protestant, shins up the ladder much more quickly than his cousins, the McCarthys, of Saint Rose of Lima's parish.[31]

The Great Depression

During the early 1930s, however, the Great Depression compounded the changes taking place within the transatlantic relationship between Ireland and the United States. Just as the assimilative forces in American society reached their peak, massive layoffs and bank closings severed the transatlantic migration and financial network in a catastrophic blow. The depression was particularly damaging in manufacturing and factory employment, on which many of the disproportionately urban Irish had come to rely. For the first time in the seventy years of postfamine migration, a steady flow of thousands of migrants recrossed the Atlantic as "Returned Yanks." The inflow of male and female workers from Ireland to the erstwhile "land of opportunity" almost completely disappeared, halting the resurgence of Irish immigration to the United States that had taken place after World War I.

The disruption caused by the depression also went far beyond the dramatic drop in net migration figures in the early 1930s. The loss of faith in American opportunity had traumatic sentimental effects for the Irish at home and abroad as well as economic repercussions. The prospect of a permanent return to Ireland was a dismal last resort for most Irish expatriates—an admission of failure that would marginalize them in their native society for decades. Those Irish migrants who did return usually carried the derogatory label of "Returned Yank" in their native country. This opprobrious identification often remained decades after their return to Ireland, as insinuations of failure in America often combined with the begrudgery of the initially spurned native society to deny full reacceptance into Irish society. The stigma of failure in America could not be hidden easily, as it was betrayed by Americanized accents, clothes, or phrases.

The return of thousands of economic refugees from the American Depression discouraged many prospective emigrants, embodying the human cost of failure in the United States. Contemporary commentators described worn-out returnees as "old people before their time," and many of the failed expatriates could not conceal their bitterness and dismay at the misleading image of the United States as a "land of opportunity." In November 1931, the *Donegal Democrat* mourned the arrival of failed Returned Yanks:

> Patriots foretold that a time would come when the exiles would come back to the motherland; they were only waiting for the dawn of freedom; then they would return. That day has arrived, but how very different from the one the prophets foretold. The wild geese are returning, but their footsteps are slow and their faces are haggard. They are here because they can no longer get bread or work in the land of their adoption.[32]

One returnee recounted having to walk the seventy miles from Dublin to his place of birth in Kilkenny after having arrived penniless back in Ireland. Another migrant who had lost his savings in an American bank collapse could not contain his bitterness: "He hates to talk about it, and he even hates the Yanks that come home. He said America ruined his life." The influx of return migrants, broken by their misfortunes in the United States, spread warnings of desperation and disillusionment, warning would-be transatlantic emigrants that the depression had killed American opportunity.[33]

The mounting economic hardships effectively cut Irish Americans off from friends and family in Ireland, including those people formerly dependent on remittances from the United States. Those failed migrants who remained too ashamed to return often cut off contact with family members back in Ireland because they were too embarrassed or guilty about their inability to meet their familial responsibilities. Even the Irish-American ethnic press vented exasperation at perceived recriminations from domestic Irish newspapers in its coverage of the disappearance of American opportunity.

By the early 1930s the depression had leveled the hopes of even the most responsible, prudent members of the Irish-American working and middle classes. Not only did cities cull their job rolls and industries close factories, but many of the families who had seemingly reached respectability over the previous twenty years lost their life savings with the widespread bank collapses. Labor unions, traditionally an important institution of upward mobility for many Irish-American workers, were quickly humbled and forced to accept wage cuts. Generations of hard work and saving came undone within a few years in a calamity from which many formerly ambitious migrants never fully recovered.[34]

Although the depression struck all American ethnic groups in the early 1930s, Irish Americans were among the hardest hit. Because of their overwhelming tendency to settle in American cities and rely on Irish-American support, Americans of Irish descent were particularly vulnerable. The traditional dispenser of public welfare, the urban political machine, proved inadequate in the face of declining revenues and widespread joblessness. Throughout the late-nineteenth and early-twentieth centuries the vast majority of Irish migrants settled in the large cities in the northern and midwestern United States. Census figures from 1920 and 1930 show that 87 percent and 90 percent of all Irish-born men and women lived in urban environments, with 39 percent of all the Irish-born living in Boston, New York, Chicago, Philadelphia, or San Francisco in 1920.[35] These migrants, most of who came from rural areas of Ireland, responded especially quickly to the calls to political participation issued by urban machines.

Irish immigrants who settled in large cities during this period were even likelier to become American citizens than earlier Irish arrivals, who traditionally had very high naturalization rates compared to other immigrant groups. According to the 1940 census, Irish-born men and women (from the twenty-six counties) were the likeliest to initiate naturalization proceedings of any foreign-born population in New York City. They were second only to those born in Northern Ireland in Boston and Chicago that same year. The Irish constituted the second smallest share of alien residents in Cleveland, the third smallest in Detroit, and the fourth in Philadelphia (where Northern Irish migrants had the smallest share of aliens).[36]

As urban budgets resumed their expansion after World War I, the machines had retained an indelible Irish-American character. The Tammany Hall-controlled leadership of New York City expanded the municipal budget by 125 percent between 1918 and 1932, and "sachems" (leaders of the Tammany organization, which had styled itself after Native American tribes when founded in 1789) channeled much of the money ($631 million in 1932) to Irish-American employees. The "American dream" for the Irish in the United States was a vision provided by public-sector employment, with over one-third of all Irish-American residents in the nation's fourteen largest cities making their living through patronage jobs.[37]

As the economic stagnation of the depression worsened in the early 1930s, however, the ensuing financial pressures forced urban decision-makers to cut municipal budgets radically. Urban real-estate values dropped by one-quarter through the early 1930s, and tax-delinquency rates more than tripled between 1929 and 1933. At the same time welfare costs mounted, consuming 25 percent of New York City's municipal outlays in 1933, up from a share of only 3 percent five years before. Caught between dropping revenues and rising welfare expenditure, politicians reluctantly turned to banking creditors who demanded retrenchment, most notably through deep cuts in municipal employment. In Chicago, Mayor Anton Cermak cut the number of city jobs by 10 percent over eighteen months and slashed salaries by one-fifth. The older political machines in cities like New York, Boston, and Worcester, Massachusetts, which had been the most Irish-friendly, were hurt the worst. Federal relief offered little respite to the old-time machine bosses. In President Hoover's Emergency Relief and Construction Act of 1932, only $3.5 million of the $300 million in federal loans trickled down to the municipal level.[38]

Even after Franklin D. Roosevelt started his New Deal spending, local and regional power-brokers like James Michael Curley in Boston found themselves ungratefully bypassed by their fellow Democrats. Instead, the president turned to his fellow Ivy Leaguers such as Harry Hopkins, a classmate of the president from Harvard.[39] To make matters worse, Curley's intransigence in resisting compromise with other Massachusetts elected officials, both as mayor and later as governor, meant that millions of dollars in federal relief went unclaimed.[40] Administrators drew Works Progress Administration districts purposefully to override congressional, county, urban, and ward district divisions. By the late 1930s it was apparent that urban politicians would have to abandon old-time ethnic loyalties in order to qualify for federal funds. According to the 1946 census, only 1 percent of all foreign-born workers was involved in public-relief projects, compared to 5 percent of native-born Americans.[41]

In contrast to the short-term panics of the late-nineteenth century, the depression maintained its hold on the American economy throughout the decade. American industries were still trying to recover as late as 1939, with lower levels of earned wages (22 percent), value of products (19 percent), and number of manual workers (11 percent) compared to the predepression levels of ten years before.[42] Mayor Maurice Tobin described the lasting effects to the Boston City Council in that same year in a succinct metaphor: "It's a quick ride down the toboggan chute, but it's a long way back."[43]

The survival of political machines usually rested on the amenability of federal supervisors. Chicago, for instance, where the Democratic machines evolved into a multi-ethnic organization, was rewarded with considerable patronage authority. There was a clear increase in the popular understanding of the responsibilities of the government, which could increasingly be met only by federal measures.[44] Edwin O'Connor focused on the correspondingly diminished stature of local-level power brokers, as illustrated in his thinly veiled account of James Michael Curley's career (with the main character, Skeffington, clearly modeled on Curley). O'Connor has a wizened politico explain this transition to Skeffington's nephew:

> The old boss was strong simply because he held all the cards. If anybody wanted anything—jobs, favors, cash—he could only go to the boss, the local leader. What Roosevelt did was to take the handouts out of local hands. A few little things like Social Security, Unemployment Insurance, and the like—that's what shifted gears, sport. No need now to depend on the boss for everything; the federal government was getting into the act. Otherwise known as a social revolution.[45]

The long-term effects of the depression struck with more poignancy on a personal level. Even when compared to the panics of the late-nineteenth century, the Great Depression of the 1930s was unparalleled in duration and scale, robbing a generation of working-class Americans of their ambition and confidence as workers and providers. An Irish immigrant who left Ireland for the United States in 1935 explained the permanence of the experience in an interview forty years after his arrival:

> One reason why I never got married, going through the horrible Depression and almost drowning to death myself, I couldn't see the responsibility of someone else. . . . I think the reason why I feel as I do is my upbringing, my childhood, what I went through when I came into this country—they left a scar.[46]

This dramatic fall in Irish-American fortunes had an immediate and lasting impact on the transatlantic relationship between Irish Americans and their ancestral homeland. Potential Irish immigrants could no longer rely on a large number of Irish-American sponsors to cover transportation costs and satisfy I.N.S. officials, as erstwhile sponsors tramped out of cities looking for work and could scarcely afford to set aside any money for remittances. In the mid-1920s such contributions had become a lifeline for most Irish migrants, accounting for approximately 95 percent of emigrants' fares in 1925.[47] Irish-American social and cultural organizations also succumbed to the economic desperation of the depression in the early 1930s. The gradual decline in AOH membership during the 1920s accelerated precipitously, and entire chapters folded all around the country.

The Effect of the Depression on Emigrant Connections with Ireland

The transatlantic lines of communication, which once related tales of unprecedented prosperity and the opportunity for economic and social advancement, now carried accounts of broken dreams and desperation. Irish-American newspapers made concerted efforts to dissuade would-be migrants. The *Irish Advocate*, 1 February 1930, warned prospective migrants to reconsider their decision to come to the United States:

> The United States has millions of unemployed, and if the Irish who go there are able to find work quickly and to get continual employment, they consider themselves very fortunate. . . . This is the great tragedy of Irish emigration; these young people learn in the hard school of experience that they have taken the wrong road [i.e., by migrating to the U.S.].[48]

The *Gaelic-American* concurred, painting a desperate picture of the American situation:

> If such skeptics [in Ireland] would only visit New York or any other city or town in the United States, and see the long breadlines of hungry men and women seeking a meal, and the thousands of poorly clad people

awaiting their turn to get into one of the free employment offices looking for people to work, they would have the ocular demonstration of the widespread misery and want now prevalent in America. They would then know that Ireland is not the worst place in the world to live in.[49]

Irish opinion soon caught on, agreeing with American commentators that transatlantic migration was "at best jumping from the frying pan into the fire."[50]

The number and size of remittances from the United States dropped rapidly in response to the depression. The postwar rise in Irish-American affluence helped to explain the steadily increasing remittances going to Ireland from 1925 to 1929. Nevertheless, the stock-market crash and the ensuing fallout brought about substantial reductions in the money sent back during the early 1930s. This amount continued to decline throughout the rest of the decade, until it fell to less than one-third of its peak predepression levels in 1939–40.[51]

The fallout was not just financial; there were serious breaches in the sentimental network between the Irish at home and Irish expatriates in the United States resulting from the inability of the latter to uphold their end of the unspoken bargain. Some of the early Irish accounts of decreasing remittances were mournful. As the *Irish Independent* predicted, "There will be a serious loss in the west, where the American letter is awaited with expectancy and hope on the eve of the Christmas season."[52] But the tone soon turned defensive, as Irish-American newspapers answered critical comments from Ireland, like those of the Dublin *Leader*, which wrote: "Our exports to the U.S.A.—the rhetorical 'greater Ireland beyond the seas'—shrunk from, in round numbers, £85,000 in May 1930 to £15,000 in May 1931. Is it not 20 million of the Irish race that we are supposed to have, when oratory flows, in the U.S.A.?"[53] The *Irish Advocate* fired back at charges in the *Leader* that "the Irish in America are lost to us":

> We can say without fear of contradiction that the Irish in America are more loyal to their native land than any other nationality who come here in large numbers. . . . Their people at home expect too much from their exiled children, and so also do business, political, and religious organizations. To the many demands made, the bulk of the Irish are more generous and kindly disposed than any other people coming here.[54]

The interruption of the return flow of remittances and the news of vanishing opportunities completed the phasing out of a transatlantic strategy for Irish men and women at home wishing to depart for the United States. Irish net immigration to the United States remained almost negligible even after 1937, when American policy-makers discarded the more stringent standards put in place during the depression.[55] The image of *Tír na nÓg* described by several generations of migrants was now relegated to the past by the Returned Yanks, sad tales of desperation and failed expectations.

Meanwhile, cross-channel migratory links between Ireland and Great Britain adapted to the interwar depression with geographic expansion and occupational diversification. The interwar economic malaise took a more gradual and regional form in Britain, with the decline of the so-called "sunset industries" of coal, iron and steel, shipbuilding, and cotton in western Scotland, Wales, and northern England. Yet this stagnation was matched by remarkable growth in the "sunrise industries" such as plastics, electronics, and automobiles, most of which were located in the midlands or the south of England. Free from familial and regional constraints on their mobility, Irish migrants developed auxiliary migration routes within Britain, moving south shortly after disembarking in erstwhile port destinations like Liverpool and Glasgow. This adaptation also involved a shift in migrant occupation away from customary jobs in the declining sunset industries. This entire process, often obscured by the anachronistic charges of nativists on the Clydeside and Merseyside, appeared in the more systematic reporting of several British parliamentary investigations. By the late 1930s, when American immigration restrictions were relaxed, the momentum had shifted within the Irish diaspora with the establishment of Irish-British networks that were to dominate the outflow of the late 1940s and 1950s.[56]

Conclusion

Over the last several decades the study of Irish migration has moved away from a split perspective on push and pull factors. This new emphasis on migration networks has carried great conceptual promise, allowing for a more comprehensive approach that preserves the unitary nature of the migration experience. Kevin Kenny's account of the transatlantic roots of the Molly Maguires has joined other master works such as Kerby Miller's *Emigrants and Exiles*, illuminating the way in which expatriate networks sought to integrate the experiences of the New World with their Irish backgrounds.[57]

Yet, little work has been done on the role of such networks after the very early-twentieth century, as if these once-taut connections merely slackened in the decades after World War I. The sharp edge of economic desperation struck hard at these diasporic cords, sending thousands of Irish-born men and women reeling into the desperate circumstances of the Great Depression. When they emerged in the late 1930s, their national identities had been primarily fastened to a new mooring—an indigenous American identity that offered the security of the New Deal. This process did not permanently sever the connections between Ireland and Irish America in the twentieth century; affinities between Irish Americans and their ancestral homeland continue to this day. Nonetheless, the Great Depression cut deeply into the postfamine transatlantic network between Ireland and the United States. When expatriates renewed connections between the United States and Ireland later in the century, the continuing lapse in migration and reduced remittances attested to the slackness of these postdepression ties. Irish-American identity had changed from an immigrant nationality to an ethnic identification.

NOTES

1. Kerby A. Miller, *Emigrants and Exiles: Ireland and the Irish Exodus to North America* (New York: Oxford University Press, 1985), 555. In a departure from the norm, Kevin Kenny's *The American Irish: A History* (New York and London: Longman, 2000) devotes two chapters to the twentieth century.

2. Patrick J. Blessing, "Irish Emigration to the United States, 1800–1920: An Overview," in P.J. Drudy, ed., *The Irish in America: Emigration, Assimilation and Impact. Irish Studies, no. 4* (Cambridge: Cambridge University Press, 1985), 31; Stephan Thernstrom, ed., *Harvard Encyclopedia of American Ethnic Groups* (Cambridge, Mass.: Belknap Press, 1980), s.v., "The Irish," by Patrick J. Blessing.

3. Ministry of Social Welfare, Report of the Commission on Emigration and Other Population Problems (Dublin: Stationery Office, 1954), 309–11.

4. Mark Wyman, *Round-Trip to America: The Immigrants Return to Europe, 1880–1930* (Ithaca, N.Y.: Cornell University Press, 1993), 11.

5. David Fitzpatrick, *Irish Emigration, 1801–1921* (Dublin: Dundalgan Press, 1984), 26.

6. "There is hardly a family in the West of Ireland that does not receive regular remittances from America." Louis F.A. Paul-Dubois, *Contemporary Ireland* (Dublin: Maunsel and Co., 1911), 305.

7. Conrad M. Arensberg and Solon T. Kimball, *Family and Community in Ireland*, 2nd ed. (Cambridge, Mass.: Harvard University Press, 1968).

8. Henry Gemery, "Immigrants and Emigrants: International Migration and the United States Labor Market in the Great Depression," in Timothy J. Hatton and Jeffrey G. Williamson, eds., *Migration and the International Labor Market: 1850–1939* (New York: Routledge, 1994).

9. Robert Divine, *American Immigration Policy, 1924–1952* (New Haven, Conn.: Yale University Press, 1957), 30–32.

10. Congress passed several other restrictions during the depression, such as the Jenkins Act, which temporarily cut national origins quotas to 10 percent of their previous size. "New Bill Will Serve as a Check on Immigrants," *Irish World and American Industrial Liberator*, 28 February 1931.

11. U.S. Department of Labor, Bureau of Immigration, "Aliens Debarred from Entering the United States, by Race or People, Causes and Sex" (Table 53 in 1925, 45 in 1926, 47 in 1927, 48 in 1932), *U.S. Bureau of Immigration, Annual Reports of the Commissioner General of Immigration*, 1925, 1927, and 1932 (Washington, D.C.: Government Printing Office, 1926, 1928, and 1933); U.S. Department of State, John Corrigan, Jr., American Consul, 1 December 1926 (approved by Charles M. Hathaway, Jr., American Consul General, Dublin), "Subject Correspondence, 1906–1932," R.G. 84, National Archives and Record Administration (hereafter NARA).

12. "Low Emigration from Ireland; Last Year It Fell Below the Quota," New York *Gaelic-American*, 29 June 1929, 7; Gemery, "Immigrants and Emigrants," 179.

13. U.S. Department of State, 15 September 1930, Diplomatic Serial No. 992, *Records of Foreign Service Posts, Diplomatic Posts, Éire (Ireland)*, Vol. 9, American Legation, 1929, R.G. 84, NARA.

14. U.S. Department of State, Letter, 8 September 1930. Diplomatic Serial No. 992, *Records of Foreign Service Posts, Diplomatic Posts, Éire (Ireland)*, Vol. 9, American Legation, 1929, R.G. 84, NARA.

15. U.S. Department of State letter, 15 September 1930, NARA.

16. Ibid.

17. The Klan's antipathy toward Irish Catholics was predominantly sectarian in nature. A large share of Klan membership was made up of Irish-American Protestants (or self-described "Scots-Irish"). In fact, the Ku Klux Klan attempted to enroll foreign-born Protestants from northern Europe in an associated organization known as the "Royal Riders of the Red Robe." Wyman, *Round-Trip to America*, 121.

18. For a self-critical view of Irish America in the early twentieth century, see Frank Ward O'Malley, "American Sons of th'Ould Sod," *American Mercury* 18 (1929), 25–32. See also Stephan Birmingham, *Real Lace: America's Irish Rich* (New York: Harper and Row, 1973); Andrew Greeley, *That Most Distressful Nation* (Chicago: Quadrangle Books, 1972); Marjorie Fallows, *Irish Americans: Identity and Assimilation* (Englewood Cliffs, N.J.: Prentice-Hall, 1979).

19. Kenneth T. Jackson, *The Ku Klux Klan in the City: 1915–1930* (New York: Oxford University Press, 1967), 184, 236.

20. Ibid., 200.

21. The growth of an Irish-American middle-class in the late-nineteenth and early-twentieth centuries was particularly important for Irish-America apologists. See J.W. Mason, "English Newspaper on New York Irish," *Brooklyn Irish Advocate*, 14 June 1930, 4.

22. Dennis Clark, *Erin's Heirs: Irish Bonds of Community* (Lexington, Ky.: University of Kentucky, 1991), 35; "What the Irish Have Done in the Building of the United States," *Irish World and American Industrial Liberator*, 14 February 1931, 3, 5.

23. "Hibernians Neutral in Fight on Ireland," *New York Times*, 7 August 1922, 3. For more information on the schism between de Valera and Cohalan and Devoy, see the hagiographic David Hogan (pseud.), *The Four Glorious Years* (Dublin: Irish Press, 1953); Patrick McCartan, *With De Valera in America* (New York: Brentano, 1932); Marie Veronica Tarpey, *The Role of Joseph McGarrity in the Struggle for Irish Independence* (New York: Arno Books, 1976).

24. *Constitution of the Ancient Order of Hibernians in America (Revised and Adopted at the National Convention held in Montreal, Canada, 17 to 21 July 1923)* (Chicago: J.S. Hyland and Co., 1923).

25. *Proceedings of the Ancient Order of Hibernians 55th National Convention, 1927 (Buffalo, New York, 19 to 20 July 1927)* (Chicago: J.S. Hyland and Co., 1927), 10.

26. "Saint Patrick's Day Has Become Largely American Holiday," *Gaelic-American*, 16 March 1929, 1.

27. "English Newspaper on New York Irish," J.W. Mason, *Irish Advocate*, 14 June 1930.

28. "Saint Patrick's Day is Observed as an American Holiday," *Gaelic-American*, 8 February 1930, 2.

29. William Adams, *Ireland and the Irish Emigration to the New World from 1815 to the Famine* (New Haven, Conn.: Yale University Press, 1932), 95.

30 O'Malley, "American Sons of th'Ould Sod," 30.

31. Ibid., 32.

32. *Donegal Democrat*, 7 November 1931, qtd. in "Notes of the Week: Conditions in Ireland Now and in the Past," *Irish Advocate*, 14 November 1931, 4.

33. Wyman, *Round-Trip to America*, 84.

34. Stephan Thernstrom, *The Other Bostonians: Poverty and Progress in the American Metropolis, 1880–1970* (Cambridge, Mass.: Harvard University Press, 1973), 70; Fallows, *The Irish Americans*, 86, 116; Charles Trout, *Boston, the Great Depression and the New Deal* (New York: Oxford University Press, 1977).

35. U.S. Department of Commerce, Bureau of the Census, *Sixteenth Census of the United States: 1940, Nativity and Parentage of the White Population: Country of Origin of the Foreign Stock, by Nativity, Citizenship, Age, and Value or Rent of Home, for States and Large Cities* (Washington, D.C.: Government Publications Office, 1943), Table 3: "Nativity and Parentage of the Foreign-Born White Stock, by Country of Origin and Sex, for the United States, Urban and Rural: 1940 and 1930," 12–18; U.S. Department of Commerce, Bureau of the Census, *Fourteenth Census of the United States, Taken in the Year 1920, Volume II: Population, General Report and Analytical Tables* (Washington, D.C.: Government Publications Office, 1922), Table 12: "Country of Birth of the Foreign-Born Population for Cities Having 100,000 Inhabitants or Over: 1920," 729–31.

36. U.S. Census, 1940, Table 11: "Nativity and Parentage of the Foreign-Born White Stock, by Country of Origin, for Cities with 50,000 or more Foreign-Born White, 1940," 76–80.

37. Stephen J. Erie, *Rainbow's End: Irish Americans and the Dilemmas of Urban Machine Politics, 1840–1985* (Berkeley, Calif.: University of California Press, 1988), 5, 111.

38. Ibid., 113.

39. Trout, *Boston, the Great Depression and the New Deal*, 134–43.

40 Ibid., 143–71.

41. D.S. Howard, *The Works Progress Administration and Federal Relief Policy* (New York: Russell Sage Foundation, 1943), cited in Gemery, "Immigrants and Emigrants," 187.

42. Trout, *Boston, the Great Depression and the New Deal*, 252.

43. Ibid., 252.

44. The effect of Roosevelt's New Deal on urban political machines remains at the center of a long-running historiographical debate. For several decades the standard

explanation of the New Deal and the demise of urban machines came from Edwin
O'Connor's thinly veiled biography of James Michael Curley, *The Last Hurrah* (Boston:
Little, Brown, and Co., 1956). Erie's *Rainbow's End* revised this monocausal explanation, pointing out the anomalous nature of Curley's organization in Boston and concentrating on the long-term problems for machines that predated the depression, as
well as their survival after the depression. For a more developed case-by-case analy-
sis of the New Deal administration and six different urban machines, see Lyle Dorsett,
Franklin Roosevelt and the Urban Bosses (Port Washington, N.Y.: Kennikat Press, 1977).
David M. Kennedy also marshaled an effective, if necessarily brief, array of evidence
to contradict Edwin O'Connor's "Last Hurrah" thesis in his recent treatment of the
American Depression, *Freedom from Fear: The American People in Depression and
War, 1929–1945* (New York: Oxford University Press, 1999), Vol. IX of C. Vann Wood-
ward, ed., *The Oxford History of the United States*, 253. See also Trout, *Boston, the Great
Depression and the New Deal*, 279, 315; Joseph O'Grady, *How the Irish Became Ameri-
can* (New York: Twayne Publishers, 1973), 149–50; George Reidy, *From the Ward to the
White House: The Irish in American Politics* (New York: Scribner's, 1991), 157–60;
Ronald H. Bayor, *Neighbors in Conflict: The Irish, Germans, Jews, and Italians of New
York City, 1929–1941*, 2nd ed. (Chicago: University of Illinois Press, 1988), 30–46; Fred-
erick M. Binder and David M. Reimers, *All the Nations Under Heaven: An Ethnic and
Racial History of New York City* (New York: Columbia University Press, 1995), 182–84;
Melvin G. Holli and Peter d'A Jones, eds., *Ethnic Chicago: Revised and Expanded*
(Grand Rapids, Mich.: William B. Eerdmans, 1984), 435–44, 454–55.

45. O'Connor, *The Last Hurrah*, 374.

46. Fallows, *Irish Americans: Identity and Assimilation*, 86.

47. R.C. Geary, "The Future Population of the Saorstát Éireann," *Journal of the Statistical and Social Inquiry Society of Ireland (J.S.S.I.S.I.)* 15 (1935–36), 24.

48. "The Drain of Irish Emigration," *Irish Advocate*, 1 February 1930, 4.

49. "Glenbeigh and Glencar Not Forgotten by the Irish Exiles," *Gaelic-American*,
24 January 1931.

50. "What the *Dublin Leader* Says," *Irish Advocate*, 28 February 1931, 4.

51. Department of Industry and Commerce, Irish Free State, Table 177. "Number
and Value of Money Orders issued in certain countries for payment in Eire, in each
year ended 31st March, 1932–33 to 1939–40," *Irish Free State Statistical Abstract, 1941*
(Dublin: The Stationery Office, 1941), 146.

52. "Slump in Christmas Gifts from America Foreseen," *Irish Advocate*, 13 December 1930, 1.

53. "What the *Dublin Leader* Says," *Irish Advocate*, 8 August 1931, 4.

54. *Irish Advocate*, 14 March 1929, 4.

55. U.S. Department of State, "Visa Instruction—Repatriated Aliens," to Foreign Service Posts of the Department of State, Ireland, Cork Consulate-General Records,
1936–46: 1938, *Correspondence, American Consulate Cork, 1938*, Diplomatic Serial No.
2917, 16 March 1938, R.G. 84, NARA.

56. For more information on interwar cross-channel migration, see *Report of the
Interdepartmental Committee on Migration to Great Britain from the Irish Free State*
(London: United Kingdom Stationery Office, 1939); Stephen J. Fielding, *Class and Eth-
nicity: Irish Catholics in England, 1880–1939* (Philadelphia: Open University Press,
1993); Viscount Astor, A.M. Carr-Saunders, G.D.H. Cole, L.F. Ellis, and Christopher
Turner, Economic Advisory Council, *Committee on Empire Migration Report* (London:

HMSO, 1932); R.S. Walshaw, *Migration to and from Merseyside: Home, Irish, Overseas,* New Merseyside Series #7 (University of Liverpool, Social Science Department: Statistics Division, 1938); Bronwen Walter, "Time-Space Patterns of Second-Wave Irish Immigration into British Towns," *Transactions of the Institute of British Geographers,* New Series (1980), 5; P.J. Waller, *Democracy and Sectarianism: A Political and Social History of Liverpool 1868–1939* (Liverpool: Liverpool University Press, 1981).

57. Kevin Kenny, *Making Sense of the Molly Maguires* (New York: Oxford University Press, 1998); Miller, *Emigrants and Exiles.*

Part 2

Politics and Race

Editor's Introduction

IN THE 1820S AND 1830S, most American states abolished property qualifications for voting, opening up the suffrage to white men and inaugurating an era of popular democracy. At the same time, they placed new restrictions on voting and civil rights for African Americans. Into this newly expanded but racially restricted democracy arrived the Catholic Irish, whose mass migration commenced in this period. From the confluence of popular democracy, racial subordination, and shifting patterns of immigration emerged the main contours of Irish-American history in the antebellum era.

Among the more colorful stories in the history of the American Irish is their conquest of Tammany Hall and subsequent domination of urban politics across the United States. That story is well known and does not need to be retold here. Less familiar is how the foundations for later successes were established in the antebellum years. With the expansion of suffrage, Tammany Hall, the Democratic political organization in New York City that had been founded in 1789, cast off its earlier anti-immigrant sentiment and courted the Irish vote. The Democratic Party, indeed, was one of only two major American institutions that welcomed the Irish unequivocally, the other being the Catholic Church. By contrast, the Irish associated the Whigs, and later the Republicans, with nativism and Protestant evangelicalism.

The basis of the Irish-Democratic alliance was laid down before the Civil War in an arrangement that seemed tailor-made for both sides. The Democrats gave the Irish access to political power, something they had always been denied in Ireland. The Irish were also attracted by the party's opposition to social reform movements, especially abolitionism. The Democrats could therefore rely on the increasingly critical Irish vote. Along with southern slaveholders, indeed, the Irish became a mainstay of the principal political proponent of proslavery sentiment and racially restrictive democracy. At the local level, the Irish-Democratic alliance was cemented in a series of deals and interactions featuring machine politicos, grocers, firefighters, policemen, and saloonkeepers. Saloonkeepers especially became important cogs in the Tammany machine, controlling the venues where favors were dispensed, advice was given, jobs were allotted, and neighborhood gangs were based. From this grassroots base, the Irish built a movement that culminated in the 1870s in their control of Tammany Hall. They dominated American urban politics for long stretches of the century that followed, voted solidly Democratic in national elections until 1968, and retain a strong affiliation with the party today.

Among the most salient features of nineteenth-century urban politics was race, especially the evolution of "white" racial identities among immigrants and workers. For the first time, historians have widely recognized that the category of "race" applies not only to so-called "minorities" but also to the dominant group in American society, those of Caucasian origin. The Irish, as is well known, were stereotyped in racially negative terms in nineteenth-century America, where they occupied the lowest rungs of the social ladder and worked largely in menial, unskilled occupations. African Americans, even those who were free and lived in the North, were even more disadvantaged. But while black people retained a subordinate place in the United States throughout the nineteenth century and for much of the twentieth, the Irish advanced quite rapidly in social, economic, and political terms, matching and then exceeding national levels by the era of World War I. How did this remarkable transformation come about? Through hard work and enterprise, certainly; but what was it that allowed hard work and enterprise to be translated into social success? The answer, according to several recent historians, lies in the story of "how the Irish became white." By embracing a white racial identity, it is argued, the Irish ensured their own assimilation and success, but only by driving an ever-deeper wedge between themselves and African Americans, with serious consequences for American labor history and the wider history of racial formation in the United States.

This line of argument has considerable merit but also some flaws. It tends to exaggerate the degree of racism the Irish faced, especially compared to that endured by African Americans or Chinese Americans, who faced systematic violence and could not vote, serve on juries, hold political office, or enter certain states in the Union. Racial prejudice, in other words, should not be confused with racial subordination. If, as some historians argue, the Irish were not seen as "white," this does not mean they were treated as "black" or "yellow." A second problem is that the existing work on "whiteness" tells us a great deal more about how the Irish were seen by their detractors than about Irish self-perception. This is to be expected, given that so many of the immigrants were poor and illiterate at this time. In claiming that the Irish were not "white," however, historians need to explain that this is how their enemies saw them, not how they saw themselves. If an Irish immigrant had been asked to state a racial identity, he or she would surely have answered "white," realizing that this was the appropriate response in the peculiar new racial hierarchy of America. This raises a third, related problem: In order to understand the racial behavior of Irish Americans in America, historians need to investigate the racial perceptions and identities of the Irish before their arrival. In many respects, Ireland and the United States shared a common Atlantic history, but the existence of chattel slavery on one side of the Atlantic generated a racial hierarchy quite distinct from that found on the other side.

The racial dimension of nineteenth-century Irish-American history also needs to be extended beyond the current confines of the "whiteness" debate. While that debate concentrates almost entirely on Irish racism, the time has surely come to revisit Irish anti-racism. Racism was clearly a central component of the emerging Irish-American ethnic identity, but the Irish were not racist by definition. Indeed, if the historians of "whiteness" are correct, they learned most of their racism in America. Were there no alternatives, no dissenting voices? Daniel O'Connell's is perhaps the best known. The foremost Irish nationalist of his age, O'Connell was also an active member of the British and Foreign Anti-Slavery Society, which helped abolish slavery in the British Caribbean. Hoping to unite his nationalist movement for repeal of the Act of Union with the international abolitionist movement, he reached out to the American Irish for support, arguing that the colonial oppression of the Irish and the racial oppression of the slaves were part of a single history. O'Connell's dream of a racially egalitarian transatlantic Irish alliance soon foundered, as the American Irish rejected his call to come out in favor of abolition. Nonetheless, O'Connell's powerful voice, and the support it received on both sides of the Atlantic, cries out for renewed historical inquiry. Like most white Americans in the nineteenth century, the Irish adopted racist views and practices. But given that they came from a country where race had a different history and significance, it is worth investigating this dimension of Irish history as a precondition to studying what happened in America.

THE VOTING-PLACE, NO. 489 PEARL STREET, IN THE SIXTH WARD, NEW YORK CITY.

The scene in a Five Points saloon/polling place on election day, 1858. Note the large posters advertising the candidacies of John Clancy and John Kelly. Few of the bar's patrons would have agreed with those who complained that the ticket was "entirely too Irish."

Source: Harper's Weekly, 13 November 1858, 724. Author's collection.

"We Will Dirk Every Mother's Son of You": Five Points and the Irish Conquest of New York Politics*

TYLER ANBINDER

NEW YORK'S FIVE POINTS neighborhood was the most infamous slum in nineteenth-century America. Located just north of City Hall in what is now Chinatown, the district was laid out in the first years of the nineteenth century when city officials decided to cover over a freshwater pond to create new space for the city's ever-increasing population. When the city added new streets to the irregular ones that had once skirted the lake, it created some unusual intersections, including a five-cornered one where Orange, Cross, and Anthony Streets converged. As a result, the neighborhood soon became known as "Five Points."[1]

Because the ground over the old lake was damp and unstable, the buildings in Five Points quickly began to sag and buckle, and as a result only the poorest New Yorkers and the least respectable businesses chose to locate there. By 1840 the district's concentration of seedy saloons, bawdy dancehalls, filthy tenements, and brazen prostitutes was notorious throughout the US—and much of Europe as well. Writers of every background visited Five Points to witness the depravity for themselves. Journalist and reformer Lydia Maria Child reported that "there you will see nearly every form of human misery, every sign of human degradation." Frontiersman Davy Crockett said of the Five

*I would like to thank Kevin Kenny, Kerby Miller, Richard Stott, and Tony Kaye for their comments on earlier drafts of this paper, which was originally presented at the 2000 meeting of the American Historical Association in Chicago. Those seeking a more detailed account of Five Points politics should consult my book *Five Points* (New York, 2001).

Points inhabitants: "I would rather risque myself in an Indian fight than venture among these creatures after night." Scandinavian author Fredrika Bremer asserted that "lower than to the Five Points it is not possible for human nature to sink."[2]

It is significant, I believe, that Crockett's account of Five Points—the earliest of the three—also speaks disparagingly of Five Pointers' political proclivities. The frontiersman (or his ghostwriter) noted that Five Points "is part of what is called by the Regency the 'glorious sixth ward'—the regular Van Buren ground-floor," a reference to the neighborhood's propensity to vote overwhelmingly for the Democratic party. Soon the Five Points political district would become known citywide as the "Bloody Sixth" Ward because violence and intimidation were more prevalent at its primaries and general elections than in any other portion of the metropolis. Five Points Irish-Americans helped to revolutionize urban American political culture with this rough-and-tumble style of politics. Their use of these tactics helped Irish-Americans to gain their first real positions of power in New York City politics.

Like all New Yorkers, Five Pointers in the early nineteenth century deferred to their neighborhood's élite citizens in political matters. Prominent merchants and manufacturers occupied most elective offices of importance. This deference began to wane, however, in the early 1830s. A terrible election riot in 1834 announced the sea change in Five Points, with the violence reflecting non-élite voters' determination to take political power into their own hands. The modern historian of antebellum New York rioting has accurately portrayed this riot as a watershed in New York City social and political history. "Never before had an election pushed the city so near the brink," he writes. "Never before had there been such anarchy." Because the well-to-do in these years were already rapidly leaving the Sixth Ward—the political district in which Five Points sat—for more prestigious neighborhoods, few of the old élite bothered to contest this transfer of power to the brawling multitude. The 1834 riot was in some senses a last-ditch attempt by the old guard to "keep those damned Irishmen in order." Five Pointers were among the first New Yorkers of modest means to take control of their political destiny, and as a result they were the first to experience the new riotous style of mass politics.[3]

In the new political environment, manufacturers and wealthy merchants were replaced by saloonkeepers, grocers, policemen, and fire-company foremen in the district's positions of political leadership. The political power of these four groups resulted from their particular ability to influence voters. As many writers have previously noted, the saloonkeeper's prominence in the immigrant community, relative wealth, ability to find his customers jobs, and status as creditor, bail bondsman, and all-around neighborhood sage made him the ideal candidate in the new political order. Because many Five Points groceries sold little more than alcohol, grocers were as well positioned as saloonkeepers for political advancement.[4]

An alternative route to political prominence in antebellum Five Points ran through the volunteer fire department. Fire companies wielded political clout because these well-drilled units were just as likely to turn out to support a particular electoral slate as to extinguish a fire. Intimidation was an important weapon in the world of Five Points politics, and the renowned fighters of the Sixth Ward fire companies often determined the outcome of a primary meeting or general election. Most companies—whether dominated by native-born Americans or Irish immigrants—admitted at least a few members to their exclusive ranks specifically for their fighting skills.

The popularity and respect that carried a Five Pointer to a leadership position within a fire unit were the same qualities that political kingmakers sought in their candidates. Future Five Points political leaders such as Matthew T. Brennan, his brother Owen, alderman Thomas Walsh, assemblyman Michael Fitzgerald, and police justice Joseph Dowling all began their political careers in the ward's Engine Company No. 21. Because of its role as a means of political advancement, competition for places in No. 21 was fierce. As a result, some of its members created an auxiliary unit, the Matthew T. Brennan Hose Company No. 60, named in honor of No. 21's most prominent and politically powerful alumnus and dominated by his political allies. Its first foreman, John Clancy, became president of the board of aldermen and city register. Other early members included future alderman Morgan Jones, future county supervisor Walter Roche, and future city councilman Michael Brophy.[5]

Another path to political power wound its way through the police department. "There is no patronage . . . that a district leader desires so much and seeks so eagerly as places on the police force," noted postbellum attorney and reformer William Ivins. Politicos usually reserved positions in the police department for young men who had demonstrated party loyalty through previous campaign efforts. In return for such a high-paying and secure job (about $12 per week in the mid-1850s), the officer was expected not only to continue laboring for the party at election time, but to contribute a portion of his salary to party coffers and to use his influence to assist party members who might run afoul of the law. In this "unobtrusive and quiet way," Ivins recognized, a

policeman could render "valuable service" to both the political bene-
factor who secured him his job and the party as a whole. Such "service"
enabled many a Five Points policeman to rise out of the ranks to both
party leadership and elective office.[6]

The liquor dealers, firemen, and police officers battling for Five
Points political supremacy were all Democrats. In the twenty years before the Civil War, Whigs and their Republican successors won only a
single Sixth Ward political contest, and then only because the Democrats divided their votes among four different candidates that year. By the
late 1850s Republican candidates had trouble garnering even 15 percent
of the district's vote. But it is important to note that substantive discussions of issues rarely entered into Five Points political contests. Plat-
forms and policy statements are conspicuously absent from neighborhood political campaigns, even the few covered thoroughly in the press.
Instead, Five Points political struggles were usually decided by three factors: the personal popularity of the individual factional leaders; their
ability to deliver patronage to their followers; and their skill at wielding
violence and intimidation at primary meetings and on election day to
secure power and maintain it thereafter.

The career of Constantine J. Donoho, the first Five Points political
leader to emerge in the tumultuous new world of mass politics, exemplifies many of these rules of political life. What little we know about
Donoho's career comes from the memoirs of Frank "Florry" Kernan, a
self-described "sporting fireman" whose colorful reminiscences provide
some of the most vivid depictions of political and cultural life in Five
Points. Kernan remembered Donoho as "a zealous, firm, hard-fisted Democrat of the old school" who emerged as "king of the politicians of the
sixth ward" during "the reign of Felix O'Niel." O'Niel served as Sixth
Ward alderman from 1841 to 1842, which made him the titular leader of
the district's Democrats, but Donoho's role as king-maker gave him
every bit as much, and perhaps more, influence and power.[7]

Donoho's political support rested on the twin foundations of liquor
sales and patronage. "Con" (as he was universally known) operated a
grocery at 17 Orange Street, a half-block south of the Five Points inter-
section. "The steps that led to the barroom from the street, although
wide," recalled Kernan, "afforded only room for one customer at a time,
as upon each step a barrel stood containing two or three brooms, another with charcoal, another with herrings nearly full to the top, while
upon its half-open head lay piled up a dozen or two of the biggest, to denote what fine fish were within." Inside was "a bar quite ornamental,"
well stocked with liquor, pipes, and tobacco.

Seats there were none, as Con kept no accommodations for sitters, unless they found it on a half-pipe of gin, 'Swan brand,' that lay on its side near the counter, or a row of Binghamton whisky-barrels, interspersed here and there with barrels of pure spirits, much above proof, that told the fact that Con Donoho was a manufacturer of ardent spirits as well as ardent voters.[8]

The bulk of Donoho's power derived not from his status as saloon-keeper but from his position as Sixth Ward "street inspector," a post he had held since at least 1839. In this capacity Donoho hired men to clean, pave, and repair the ward's streets, giving him more patronage power than any other man in the ward. Con filled these dozens of positions not merely with loyal Democrats but with "all the roaring, fighting, brawling heroes of his locality" who could be trusted to battle for whichever party faction he chose to support. Donoho also rewarded men who could deliver the votes of a particular tenement or of an ethnic or regional constituency within the neighborhood. Con would be sure to stretch his hiring budget to the limit in the month or so before an election in order to ensure that influential Democrats and their friends and families had received a share of the proverbial "loaves and fishes." Donoho's status as street inspector benefited his grocery business as well. Those hoping for a job were sure to visit Con's establishment to remind him of their willingness to labor (both physically and politically) upon his behalf. Five Pointers whom he had favored with the coveted patronage posts would likewise show their gratitude by patronizing his bar. Rainy days in particular were "Con's harvest-time, for then the streets could not be swept, and knights of the broom, hoe, and shovel kept holiday at their chieftain's rendezvous."[9]

Securing the support of Con Donoho and other local men of influence was the most important asset that an aspiring politician could acquire to position himself for a nomination at the ward's annual Democratic primary meeting. As a prerequisite to running for alderman, a Five Points liquor dealer had not only to establish himself as one of the most powerful Democrats in his own election district, but to earn endorsements from party leaders in others as well. This would take years of service on behalf of the party, along with building popularity in the neighborhood and doling out patronage to influential neighborhood residents. In advance of the primary the would-be alderman would treat potential voters in the ward's saloons and make deals with other party leaders to obtain their support. Endorsements might be offered in return for a promise of patronage, the pledge of a reciprocal endorsement in the future, or an up-front cash payment. Sixth Ward Democrats were generally divided into two factions, so in most cases the aldermanic hopeful would canvass support from just one and then hope to rally that faction to victory at the primary.

The leaders of each Democratic faction drew up slates of candidates in advance of the annual (or in some cases semi-annual) primary meetings and hoped to get that ticket selected by a majority of those in attendance. Ivins explained in the 1880s that "a point of utmost consequence is the determination of the place at which the primary is to be held," and that "the voting is usually done at that liquor store, cigar store, livery-stable, or other place where the contestant favored by the [ward] leader can best control the house, its exits and entrances, and can most easily and speedily gather his voters together." The situation in the Sixth Ward was somewhat different prior to about 1858. Until that date all Democratic factions agreed that the ward primary meeting should be held in the neutral territory of "Dooley's Long-Room," the large barroom in the Sixth Ward Hotel. Kernan wrote in 1885 that in Dooley's Long-Room "there has come off more Irish jollifications, benefit balls, raffles for stoves, primary meetings, and political rows than in any other public place in the city." In the antebellum years, he noted, "Dooley's Long-Room was as famed in politics as was ever Tammany Hall. To hold a meeting there made it orthodox and regular." All factions consequently "struggled hard, even to bloody rows, to obtain an indorsement" at the annual primary meeting held there.[10]

In a city that became renowned for its rough and bloody primary meetings, those in the Sixth Ward were the most violent of all. Kernan recalled that "regularity in the old Sixth was ofttimes only won by black eyes, torn coats, and dilapidated hats. The knowing politicians of the ward never went well dressed to a caucus meeting at Dooley's Long-Room." The very first vote at the meeting was the most crucial, because whichever faction managed to elect the convention chairman controlled the proceedings and could, with official sanction, use its fighters to "maintain order," the excuse given for expelling the weaker faction's supporters from the building. If one faction's strongmen failed to appear promptly, disaster loomed for even the most popular and seemingly invincible clique. Kernan remembered,

> once, when John Emmons was the candidate [for alderman], nothing gave him the victory but the fact that Bill Scally [a noted pugilist], with Con Donoho and his men, arrived just in the nick of time to save the chairman from going out of the window, and the secretary following him; but their timely arrival changed the complexion of things, and sent the opposition chairman and officers out through the same window.

Candidates for even the most prestigious Sixth Ward offices could not sit idly by while hired bullies did the rough work for them. Kernan noted that those nominees who did not "take a hand with their friends in battling for their cause" at the Sixth Ward primary meeting would be derided as cowards and "would lack votes on election days."[11]

Often, the ticket that was defeated at the primary meeting decided to stay in the race anyway as an alternative Democratic slate, a practice known as running on the "split." One of Con Donoho's most important jobs was to use his influence to ensure that the "regular" nominees outpolled these renegades. To this end he employed every means at his disposal. Kernan observed:

> When Con was away on business, his good woman, Mrs. Donoho, stood behind the counter to attend to all customers; and an able helpmate was she to just such a rising man and politician as Con gave promise to be. Should Mrs. Conlan, or Mrs. Mulrooney, or the wife of any other good voter of the old Sixth, come for her groceries, or with a milk pitcher for a drop of good gin, or a herring to broil for the good man's twelve o'clock dinner, she would avail herself of the opportunity to have a bit of a talk with her concerning how her James, Patrick, or Peter would vote on the approaching aldermanic election . . . , and heaven help the customer if she talked up in favor of John Foote [or Bill Nealus] on the split. . . . If she did, the smallest herring or potatoes to be found in the barrel would be dealt out with a jerk, and a wink with it, that said when she had sense, and wanted to see her old man with a broom in his hand and ten shillings a day, work or no work, and pay from Con's own hand on Saturday nights, she had only to make her husband send the Nealuses to the devil, and hurrah for Felix O'Niel! In this way, Mrs. Con Donoho made many a convert to the banner of her liege lord, the bold Con Donoho.[12]

Even if defections to candidates running on the split had been kept to a minimum, party leaders such as Donoho had plenty of work to do on election day. If the renegade Democratic candidates managed to use their fighters to gain control of the polling places, they might discourage many voters from casting ballots and carry the election by intimidation. One such struggle for the polls occurred in 1848, when Democrat Frederick Kohler challenged incumbent Thomas Gilmartin in the race for Sixth Ward alderman. Although it is not evident which candidate was the party's "regular" nominee, Gilmartin clearly held the upper hand at one polling place. According to the *New York Tribune*, "Gilmartonians . . . occupied the [polling place's] staircase for the purpose of exercising a wholesome supervision over the ballots of democratic voters. As soon

as a man came up to vote they demanded to see his tickets, and if he refused snatched them out of his hand for examination. If a Whig, he was
suffered to go up and vote; but if a Kohlerite," he was thrown down the
stairs. Around 4:30 in the afternoon a large contingent of Kohlerites arrived to remove the obstacle to their voting, "when all of a sudden the
Gilmartonians brought forth a store of stout and heavy bludgeons, all
ready for fight." The similarly armed Kohlerites initially routed their opponents, but the Gilmartonians soon returned with bricks. "The struggle now became really fearful; hard blows were given, heads broken and
blood flowed freely. Several men were cut severely." Such gory struggles
made the Sixth Ward "notorious for the free indulgence of election privileges." Such violent battles for control of Five Points polling places were
especially common in the two decades from 1835 to 1855.[13]

By the end of the 1840s, as Donoho aged and his influence waned,
his place at the head of the district's Democrats was taken by Matthew
T. Brennan, who unlike Donoho eventually established himself as the
undisputed leader of the Sixth Ward Democratic party. Brennan was
born in New York in 1822. After attending primary school, he helped his
widowed mother at her vegetable stand and was briefly apprenticed as
a molder. When his older brother Owen, eight years Matthew's senior
and an active Whig, opened a Five Points saloon in the mid-1830s, the
teenaged Matthew became a bartender there. Although a childhood accident had left Matthew with "a perceptible limp," he "was fleet of foot,
and . . . possessed of extraordinary strength," precisely the traits of the
ideal fireman. Emulating Owen, Brennan entered the fire department
and eventually gained a place in the Sixth Ward's politically active Engine Company No. 21. In the meantime, as Owen ascended in Whig circles, he turned over control of the saloon to "Matt," as he was by now
universally known.[14]

Brennan exuded an air of confidence, strength, and congeniality that
made him a natural leader and helped him to achieve his prestigious
position as company foreman. In a neighborhood in which fighting and
toughness were prerequisites to political power, Brennan's imposing
physical presence also helped him. A friend and newspaper editor described Brennan at age forty as

> a large and robust man, with spreading shoulders, large and arching
> chest; throat muscular and massive; face singularly open, strong and
> honest; black hair curling closely round his forehead; a dark brown im-
> perial dropping down from his lower lip, and merging into a small black
> growth of throat-beard; hazel gray eyes, full of kindly humor and pene-
> tration, set under eyebrows rather slight and short; immensely broad

round the base of the forehead; and with a nose, not long, but prominent and indicative of energy and courage.[15]

Brennan possessed both the physical and personal traits necessary to ascend through the rough world of Irish-American ward politics.

As fire-company foreman, Brennan commanded a gang of forty or so tough young men who could be counted on to fight at primary meetings and on election day. Such influence had its rewards. In January 1848 he received his first patronage plum—appointment as one of the two ward residents to whom chimney fires were to be reported. But it was Brennan's election at about the same time as foreman of Engine Company No. 21, noted the *Times* years later, that served as his "stepping-stone to political preferment."[16]

Despite Brennan's rapid advancement, his political career seemed in jeopardy at mid-century due to the ambitions of Isaiah Rynders—a political fighter feared even more than Brennan or Donoho. Rynders' life, his *Times* obituary noted without exaggeration in 1885, "forms one of the most romantic of histories." Born near Albany in 1804 to a German-American father and a Protestant Irish-American mother, Rynders moved to the South in 1830, acquiring some notoriety as a riverboat gambler and horse trainer. He returned to New York in the mid-1830s and became a prominent "sporting man," that colorful "combination of gambler, horseman and politician." One admiring journalist described Rynders as "a lithe, dark, handsome man of medium size and sinewy form, with a prominent nose, and piercing black eyes." Unlike others in the "sporting fraternity," Rynders was not an especially skillful pugilist. But as a *leader* of fighters, Rynders was unsurpassed.[17]

Rynders rocketed to Democratic prominence in 1844. Realizing that Democrats needed to form an organization with which to rally the faithful for the tight presidential contest between Polk and Clay, Rynders established the Empire Club, which rallied New York Democrats and intimidated their Whig opponents. Whigs and Democrats alike gave Rynders a significant share of the credit for Polk's razor-thin margin of victory in New York, and the grateful new president rewarded Rynders with a lucrative no-show job in the New York customhouse.[18]

After 1844, Rynders and the Empire Club became real powers in New York politics, practicing on a citywide level what Donoho and Brennan had perfected at Five Points. Rynders and his comrades dominated primaries, disrupted the meetings of those they opposed, and caused havoc on election day. In a typical scene, recalled one eyewitness, Rynders mounted a box and shouted, "*I am Isaiah Rynders!* My club is here, scattered among you! We know you! Five hundred of you are from

Philadelphia—brought here to vote the Whig ticket! Damn you! If you don't leave these polls in five minutes, *we will dirk every mother's son of you!*" Within five minutes "five hundred men left the polls . . . and went home without voting, for fear of assassination." Rynders treated his Democratic opponents no better than Whigs. The *Evening Post* complained in 1845 that no man before Rynders had ever so boldly and impudently dominated the public meetings at Tammany Hall.[19]

By mid-century Rynders had reached the peak of his influence— helping to foment the bloody Astor Place riot of 1849 and receiving national attention for completely disrupting an abolitionist convention organized by William Lloyd Garrison and Frederick Douglass. Yet because the most powerful positions within Tammany were chosen by ward-based delegates, Rynders needed to establish a base of power in a single ward in order to progress further within Tammany's ranks. Given the important role that violence and intimidation already played in Sixth Ward politics, it should come as little surprise that Rynders resolved to concentrate his political operations in the "bloody Sixth." Rynders consequently bought a Sixth Ward saloon in the late 1840s, "hired a residence [there], located his family, and quietly awaited an opening."[20]

Rynders made his move in the autumn of 1850. Yet when he announced his intention to become active in Sixth Ward politics and to take the nomination for state assembly as well, remembered Kernan, it "did not suit the bone and sinew of the ward," who saw Rynders and his Empire Club thugs as "squatters." Not easily deterred, Rynders arrived at Dooley's Long Room for the primary meeting accompanied by noted sporting men Bill Ford, Tom Maguire, "Country McCleester," and "Hen" Chanfrau—"men who seldom met defeat"—as well as "hundreds of . . . the captain's friends." But Brennan, Donoho, and the other Five Points Irish-American leaders were not about to concede control of the ward without a fight. Kernan recalled that

> when the hour came to name the chairman, the fierce onset of Rynders's friends to defeat it was met with a bold response. The ball opened and the strife commenced, and ere ten minutes passed away, the hall was cleared of all who stood in opposition to the regular voters of the ward. Rynders and his men met defeat, and his ambition to get a foothold in the glorious old Sixth was quieted ever after.[21]

Rynders' come-uppance was engineered in large measure by the efforts of the increasingly influential Irish-American Democrats of the Sixth Ward. Although Sixth Ward Democrats opposed Rynders' assembly bid, the captain won the endorsement of Democrats in the Third Ward, which along with the Sixth composed the second assembly district. When city Democrats met at Tammany Hall to choose their legislative candidates, Rynders captured the nomination. On election day, however, the captain's Whig opponent defeated Rynders by 200 votes. Disgruntled Five Points Democrats had cast far fewer ballots for Rynders than for the other Democratic candidates (967 for Rynders versus 1328 for the Democratic candidate for assistant alderman, for example), and this had cost him the election. Realizing that he did not have the support in the Sixth Ward necessary to make it his political base, Rynders soon moved across the Bowery to the Seventh Ward. Stung by his electoral embarrassment, he never again ran for elective office. He remained a power in Democratic circles throughout the 1850s, and for his continuing loyalty to the party President James Buchanan made Rynders New York's United States marshal in 1857. But Rynders never again dominated New York politics with the swagger and impudence that had marked his conduct up to his showdown with the Irish-American Democrats of Five Points.[22]

With Rynders no longer a threat to dominate Five Points politics, Brennan could concentrate on his own advancement. In November 1851 he was appointed Sixth Ward police captain. Brennan used his new post to increase his already strong position in Sixth Ward political affairs. "A sergeant or captain is a real power if he takes any interest in politics," noted Ivins, and Brennan certainly proved this to be the case. He used his authority as captain to appoint a number of his most trusted allies to places on the force. At the end of 1854 these supporters established the M. T. Brennan Hose Company No. 60, both to demonstrate their gratitude to their patron and to rally support for his candidates at primaries and on election days. To ensure control of the polling places (and to discourage the turnout of his adversaries), Brennan moved some of the voting stations from neutral sites to locations associated with his supporters. By 1856, Five Pointers in the ward's second electoral district had to cast their ballots inside the Brennan Hose Company's club room at 123 Leonard Street (Brennan lived next door at 121 Leonard). Voters in the fifth district were required to venture inside the "low rum-shop" of Brennan loyalist Walter Roche at 19 Mulberry. Another polling site was located in a "hair-dresser's saloon" at 6 Franklin Street, across the street from the ward's police station at 9 Franklin, enabling Brennan's allies on the force to maintain control. Brennan was also probably behind the transfer of the ward's primary contest from Dooley's Long Room in the Sixth Ward Hotel, where it had been held for decades, to the friendlier confines of Elm Street's Ivy Green saloon, another haunt controlled by his allies.[23]

In 1854, after nearly three years as police captain, Brennan made his first run for elective office, seeking the influential post of police justice. Although police justices were the first judicial authorities before whom all those accused of misdemeanors and minor felonies were brought, legal training was not considered a prerequisite for the post. The judicial district in question covered not only the Sixth Ward, but also the Fourth and Fourteenth, each heavily Irish-American. While these demographics might appear to have favored Brennan, Democrats in the other wards nominated their own candidates for the highly prized office. On the eve of the vote these opponents attempted to blame Brennan for the police department's role in the arrest of an Irish patriot wanted by the British. Nonetheless, Brennan carried the election by a comfortable margin.[24]

Brennan had built up an effective electoral machine, but he was also a likeable man who made few personal enemies. He was "looked up to by all the poor of his ward and district as a protector and friend," reported his allies at the *Leader*. The *Herald* agreed that "he took a special and personal interest in the poor of his district, and always lent a willing ear to their grievances." Brennan was also a hard worker and devoted to "his fireside and family"—he married Margaret Molony in about 1850 and by 1860 they had five children. Unlike some of his fellow politicians, Brennan "lived a temperate life in all things. . . . His habits of living were of the old fashioned type, early to bed and early to rise, up at five o'clock in the morning, winter and summer, and in his office . . . hours before any of his subordinates thought of stirring." Though a native New Yorker, Brennan and his entire family "spoke Irish and took a pride in it," a devotion to Gaelic culture that undoubtedly impressed the many recent Irish immigrants among his constituents. Brennan's popularity was such that state Democrats nominated him for the post of state prison inspector in 1856. Although Brennan and his Democratic running mates were defeated in the November election, the nomination of a Five Points Irish Catholic for statewide office was unprecedented.[25]

One of the keys to Brennan's success was his young ally John Clancy, a Five Points native. Whereas the biography of virtually every Sixth Ward politician emphasizes his fighting prowess, Clancy's stressed that he had a "slender figure" and "blue eyes, soft as a woman's in their affectionate expression." Other Five Points politicos were known for their street smarts, but Clancy was bookish, erudite, and "a graceful and polished writer." Clancy's advancement in Sixth Ward politics was unprecedented. Without holding any of the usual minor patronage posts, or having served in the ward's police or fire departments, the twenty-four-year-old Clancy was elected in 1853 to one of the ward's seats in the city's new board of councilmen. In 1855 he was elected ward alderman. After his re-election in November 1856, Clancy's colleagues made him president of the board of aldermen, a great honor for a twenty-seven-year-old who four years earlier had been unknown in city political circles.

Clancy's remarkable rise to prominence was facilitated by several factors. One was his involvement with the *New York Leader*, a weekly newspaper that became the Tammany organ in 1855. Clancy began con-tributing to the *Leader* as soon as it became affiliated with Tammany, and his association with the journal made him familiar to all the city's Democratic strongmen. In February 1857, weeks after the aldermen chose Clancy as their president, the rising Sixth Warder became one of the paper's editors. Even more important to Clancy's success than his association with the *Leader* was his alliance with Brennan. Clancy prob-ably played a leading role in the founding of the Brennan Hose Com-pany, as the new company's members elected Clancy to be their first foreman. By early 1857 Brennan and Clancy had climbed further in Tam-many's ranks than had any previous Sixth Ward Irish Catholics.[26]

At the end of 1857, Clancy bought a controlling interest in the *Leader* and became its editor-in-chief as well. Now in complete command of the influential weekly, the ambitious and talented Clancy utilized the in-fluence and prestige that accompanied his new status to seek *citywide* office. No Irish Catholic Sixth Warder had ever held such a post. But Clancy was determined to be the first.

Clancy set his sights on the November 1858 contest for county clerk. Surveying the field and discovering that his main competition came from another rising Democratic star, Seventh Ward Supervisor William M. Tweed, the twenty-nine-year-old Clancy unabashedly utilized the pages of the *Leader* to explain why *he* was most deserving of the nomi-nation. An editorial noted sarcastically that the "small sprinkling of De-mocratic voters" in the Sixth Ward "have never, within the memory of any man connected with Tammany Hall, . . . received an acknowledge-ment of their existence." One non-Irish Sixth Warder had once been appointed receiver of taxes, but served for only a short period until he resigned

for a *Seventh* ward man, and in the distribution of patronage, both federal and municipal, the Sixth Ward seems to have had a back seat. There is an end to all things, and the idea of working every election to elevate other people and then get no thanks for it, is pretty well played out in the 6th Ward. For the past twenty years the democracy of that district have never

been recognized as they should be, except on election day, when they
are of some importance to county candidates; and during the several
democratic administrations at the Custom House and in this city, up to
the present time not one important place has ever been tendered to the
6th Ward.[27]

As all New Yorkers knew, the Sixth Ward was the most Irish and most
Catholic district in the city. Tweed, despite modern misconceptions, was
neither Irish nor Catholic. Clancy's plea was thus not merely one for his
ward, but implicitly one for the recognition of the debt that Tammany
owed to Irish Catholics as well.

The year 1858 was actually a watershed for Irish-Catholic politicians,
both in the Sixth Ward and all over New York, as they began an unprecedented push for a fair share of the nominations. The *New York Dispatch* had noted that summer that "there is beginning to be a good deal
of grumbling among the American and German Democrats, in consequence of these demands of the Irish." Such discontent became evident
at the Tammany nominating convention. Clancy's opponents argued
that because Irish-American John Kelly was the consensus choice to
head the ticket as the candidate for sheriff, Clancy's nomination for
clerk would mean that "the ticket would be entirely 'too Irish'." The convention nevertheless nominated him on the first ballot. "Mr. Clancy's
nomination," explained the *Irish-American* afterward, "was generally
conceded to the claims of the Sixth Ward" and implicitly to the Irish
Catholics who had dominated its politics for a generation but never
been granted the opportunity to run for citywide office.[28]

Clancy's triumph in the general election marked the climax of a remarkable quarter-century in Five Points politics. The election riots of
1834 had dramatically signaled the end of deference as the hallmark of
the neighborhood's politics, as Five Points' Irish-American residents
demonstrated their determination to take their political destiny into
their own hands. In the alternative political system that developed, violence, patronage, and party loyalty were the keys to advancement, as
was the ability to command the support of fire companies, police officers, and liquor dealers. Con Donoho was the prototypical Five Points
political leader of the 1840s. Using his patronage power and saloon connections to play king-maker in ward political battles, he nonetheless recognized that his rough tactics and Irish Catholic background made advancement to positions of influence beyond the ward impossible. As the
city became increasingly Irish with the flood of famine immigrants after
1845, and as the violent tactics of Five Points politicians became standard practice throughout the city, Sixth Ward Irish Catholics for the first

time discovered opportunities to advance their political careers beyond the ward's boundaries. Brennan was the first Five Points Catholic to become an important player in the Tammany hierarchy, and his influence was quickly matched by his protégé Clancy as well. Clancy's victory in the 1858 race for county clerk ensured that Tammany leaders would no longer be able to take Five Points Democrats for granted. Brennan's election in 1862 to the post of city comptroller confirmed that Five Pointers had once and for all shattered the glass ceiling that had kept them and Irish Catholics in general out of the highest Tammany ranks. By the time that the "Tweed Ring" had gained control of city politics at the end of the Civil War, Five Pointers would have the dubious distinction of being counted among the most influential of Tammany leaders. Nonetheless, Five Pointers could take some pride both in having helped to redefine the rules of ward electoral warfare and having paved the way for the eventual Irish conquest of New York politics.[29]

NOTES

1. Charles H. Haswell, *Reminiscences of an Octogenarian, 1816–1860* (New York, 1897), 84.

2. Lydia Maria Child, *Letters from New York*, 2nd ed. (New York, 1844), 26; [William Clark], *An Account of Col. Crockett's Tour to the North and Down East* (Philadelphia, 1835), 48–49; Fredrika Bremer, *The Homes of the New World*, 3 vols., trans. Mary Howitt (London, 1853), Vol. III, 409. See also Charles Dickens, *American Notes* (London, 1985), 80–82.

3. Paul A. Gilje, *The Road to Mobocracy: Popular Disorder in New York City, 1763–1834* (Chapel Hill, N.C., 1988), 140–41.

4. *The Nation* (4 November 1875), 288; Richard Stott, *Workers in the Metropolis: Class, Ethnicity, and Youth in Antebellum New York City* (Ithaca, N.Y., 1990), 239; Matthew P. Breen, *Thirty Years of New York Politics Up-To-Date* (New York, 1899), 233.

5. New York Board of Aldermen, *Documents* 25 (1858), doc. 6, 53–54, 161, 171; J. Frank Kernan, *Reminiscences of the Old Fire Laddies* (New York, 1885), 23–24 (Matthew Brennan), 501 (Fitzgerald); *Times*, 30 October 1884, 5 (Owen Brennan); *Manual of the Corporation of the City of New York for 1855* (New York, 1855), 168.

6. William M. Ivins, *Machine Politics and Money in Elections in New York City* (1887; reprint, New York, 1970), 13–14, 25; *Manual of the Corporation of the City of New York for 1856* (New York, 1856), 225; "A Policeman" in *Tribune*, 20 October 1856.

7. Kernan, *Reminiscences*, 47.

8. Ibid., 47–48; John Doggett, Jr., ed., *The New York City Directory for 1842* (New York, 1842), 100.

9. Kernan, *Reminiscences*, 50; *Proceedings of the Board of Aldermen*, 18 (1839–40), 324, 410; 21 (1841), 269. For extra hiring at election time, see *New York Tribune*, 13 March 1846.

10. Ivins, *Machine Politics*, 20; Kernan, *Reminiscences*, 49. The Sixth Ward Hotel

was also known in the early 1840s as "Dunn's Sixth Ward Hotel," by 1849 as "Pat Garrick's Sixth Ward Hotel," and later on as "Warren's Sixth Ward Hotel."

11. Kernan, *Reminiscences*, 49–50. On the influence of money and fighters in the securing of nominations citywide, see *New York Herald*, 29, 30 October 1850, 10 March 1855; Breen, *Thirty Years*, 40–43.

12. Kernan, *Reminiscences*, 48–50.

13. *New York Tribune*, 12 April 1848; *Manual of the Corporation of the City of New York for 1849*, 319; *New York Herald*, 6 November 1850 ("free indulgence"); *Harper's Weekly* (13 November 1858): 724; [George G. Foster], *New York in Slices: By an Experienced Carver* (New York, 1849), 49. Whig fighters sometimes instigated election brawls as well, though such cases were rare after 1845. See Tom Quick, "Old Sports of New York," *New York Leader*, 16 June 1860.

14. *New York Times*, 20 January 1879; *New York Tribune*, 21 January 1879 ("fleet of foot").

15. *New York Leader*, 22 November 1862.

16. *Manual of the Corporation of the City of New York for 1848* (New York, 1848), 100; *New York Times*, 20 January 1879.

17. *New York Times*, 14 January 1885; Thomas L. Nichols, *Forty Years of American Life* (London, 1864), Vol. II, 159.

18. *New York Times*, 14 January 1885; *New York Clipper*, 24 January 1885; Nichols, *Forty Years of American Life*, Vol. II, 159–61, 66–67; Breen, *Thirty Years*, 307–08.

19. Breen, *Thirty Years*, 303; Rev. Sherlock Bristol, *The Pioneer Preacher: Incidents of Interest, and Experiences in the Author's Life* (1887; reprinted Urbana, Ill., 1989), 66–67; *New York Evening Post*, 25, 27 January 1845. Rynders was not an ignorant thug, however. His election-night speeches at Tammany Hall, which became something of an institution, were "a mixture of terrible profanity with liberal quotations from the Scriptures and Shakespeare." He "could recite entire scenes from memory." *New York Times*, 14 January 1885.

20. *New York Herald*, 20 January 1850; *New York Tribune*, 9 May 1850; [Wendell P. Garrison], *William Lloyd Garrison* (1885–1889), Vol. III, 285–300; Kernan, *Reminiscences*, 53–54.

21. Kernan, *Reminiscences*, 53–54; *Manual of the Corporation of the City of New York for 1851* (New York, 1851), 345–46; *New York Herald*, 8 November 1850 (election results by ward).

22. One cannot be sure that the events described by Kernan took place in 1850, though given Rynders' eventual appearance in that year's race for the assembly, my inference that the primary Kernan describes took place in that year is probably accurate. Newspapers reported Rynders' nomination at Tammany Hall without comment (see *New York Herald*, 10 October 1850), so my assessment of how the captain captured the nomination despite the opposition of Sixth Ward voters cannot be confirmed, though it is hard to imagine an alternative scenario (except outright bribery or intimidation at the convention). Evidence of growing Irish-American resentment toward Rynders' attempts to influence Sixth Ward politics before the fall of 1850 can be found in the *New York Irish-American*, 24 February 1850. Following the lead of Breen, who said that Rynders "had long ruled the Sixth Ward with a rod of iron," a number of historians have erroneously stated that Rynders did for a time control Sixth Ward politics. But Kernan's account is the only one not contradicted by contemporary evidence (Breen would have been a young child in 1850). Breen, *Thirty Years*, 518–19; Herbert As-

bury, *The Gangs of New York: An Informal History of the Underworld* (New York, 1928), 43.

23. Ivins, *Machine Politics*, 13–14; *Manual of the Corporation of the City of New York for 1855*, 168; *New York Tribune*, 1 November 1856; *New York Leader*, 9 October 1858.

24. *New York Herald*, 3, 5, 6, 8 November 1854 (all advertisements except election result on the eighth). Brennan captured 2,823 votes to 1,854 for "Captain Kissner" of the Fourteenth Ward police; 1,145 for John McGrath; and 353 for Whig David W. Clark. *Manual of the Corporation of the City of New York for 1855*, 368–69, 379.

25. *New York Leader*, 22 November 1862; *New York Herald*, 20 January 1879; John Ridge, "The Hidden Gaeltacht in Old New York," *New York Irish History* 6 (1991–92), 17. Brennan can be found in the 1860 federal census in the Sixth Ward, fourth district, dwelling 265, where he is listed as a thirty-nine-year-old police justice with $14,000 in real property and $1,000 in personal property, along with his thirty-three year-old wife Margaret (also a New York native, who owned $2,000 in real estate), five children aged nine, seven, five, three, and one, and two servants. State Democrats realized that victory in 1856 was virtually impossible, and it is likely that Brennan would not have received the nomination for prison inspector had the party had a realistic chance to carry the contest.

26. *New York Times*, 2 July 1864 ("graceful and polished writer"); *New York Leader*, 2 July 1864 (all other quotations); *Doggett's New York City Directory for 1850–51* (New York, 1850), 101. Because Clancy edited the *Leader* at the time of his death, I have relied on its biographical details when they conflict with those of the obituaries in the other major dailies.

27. *New York Leader*, 2 October 1858.

28. *New York Leader*, 23 October, 6 November 1858, 2 July 1864; *New York Irish-American*, 14 August (quoting *New York Dispatch* of 31 July 1858), 23 October 1858. Clancy captured 38,077 votes, while his Republican opponent received 30,092. *Manual of the Corporation of the City of New York for 1859*, 413.

29. For the later careers of Brennan, Clancy, and the other Five Points politicians mentioned above, see Anbinder, *Five Points*.

Frontispiece portrait of Frederick Douglass from the variant first Irish edition of the *Narrative* (Dublin: Webb and Chapman, 1845). Although this edition bears the date 1845, it did not actually appear until 1846.

Source: Goldsmith's Special Collection of Economic Literature, Senate House, University of London.

"The Republic of Letters":
Frederick Douglass, Ireland,
and the Irish Narratives

FIONNGHUALA SWEENEY

ONE OF THE MOST NOTABLE VISITORS to Irish shores during the nineteenth century was Frederick Douglass, author, abolitionist, and fugitive slave.[1] Douglass had left the United States following the publication in 1845 of his autobiography, *Narrative of the Life of Frederick Douglass, an American Slave, Written by Himself,* in order to avoid recapture and re-enslavement, and to generate support for the anti-slavery cause in Europe. His travels throughout the then United Kingdom in the two years from 1845 to 1847 had profound effects on Douglass' social and intellectual status. Alan Rice describes him as arriving in "Britain [and Ireland] as raw material of a great black figure; [and leaving] . . . in April 1847 the finished independent man, cut from a whole cloth and able to make his own decisions about the strategies and ideologies of the abolitionist movement."[2]

Douglass' personal and political transformation is evident in the shifting form of his literary work, itself enmeshed in those same strategies and ideologies. In Ireland his autobiography was republished by the Dublin Quaker printer Richard Webb shortly after Douglass' arrival in September 1845, and it went into variant and second Irish editions in 1846.[3] Just as Douglass' personal and professional standing were deeply affected by the experience of being outside the US, the reprinting of the *Narrative* in Ireland marks the beginning of a stage in Douglass' literary career that has profound implications for contemporary readings of his life and work. Taken in conjunction with his other literary output at this time—the letters to Garrison from Britain and Ireland that were subsequently published in the abolitionist newspaper, the *Liberator*—the Irish

123

Narratives mark a transitional phase in Douglass' emergence as a modern subject and in his negotiation of nineteenth-century models of socio-cultural identity.

For with the republication of the *Narrative* in Dublin came several and various changes in the form of the work, with often contradictory implications. These changes included the incorporation of a resolution of the Hibernian Anti-Slavery Society on the flyleaf; varying portraits of Douglass on the title spread; a verse from John Greenleaf Whittier on the title page; and a "preface" written by Douglass and inserted before the preface to the US edition. New appendices included the "Address to the Friends of the Slave"; a reproduction and contestation of A.C.C. Thompson's refutation of Douglass' *Narrative* in the *Delaware Republican*; a selection of favorable critical notices from US and British newspapers; and two testimonies from Protestant clergymen in Belfast. All of these changes, most notably the new preface written by Douglass himself, illustrate the strategies he used in negotiating the social, economic, and ideological landscape of the Atlantic world.[4]

The new "preface" first appears in the variant first Irish edition published in March 1846 and, in an extended version, in the second Irish edition of May of the same year. Both editions were produced after Douglass had left Ireland for Britain and was lecturing on his famous "Send Back the Money" campaign against the Free Church of Scotland.[5] The first introduction, therefore, was written in Ireland in 1845 and extended while Douglass was in Glasgow in 1846. As such, the appearance and meaning of the "preface" can be seen as bearing directly on Douglass' Irish experience—an experience marked by economic success, social mobility, and increasing ideological independence.

The preface is important both as autobiographical and ideological commentary on Douglass' changing status within abolitionism and his increasing awareness of the risks and opportunities of engagement with the society and politics of the Atlantic world. While the American edition confined itself to the exposure and abolition of slavery as part of an ongoing domestic campaign against that institution in the US, the Irish editions reconfigure—through the addition of the preface—the anti-slavery debate and the slave-subject in the international discourse of Western modernity. The confessed purpose of the preface is to clarify what Douglass calls the "threefold object" of his visit to Britain and Ireland. "I wished," Douglass explains,

> to be out of the way during the excitement consequent on the publication of my book; lest the information I had there given as to my identity

and place of abode, should induce my *owner* to make measures for my restoration to his "patriarchal care!"

My next inducement was a desire to increase my stock of information, and my opportunities for self-improvement, by a visit to the land of my *paternal* ancestors.

My third and chief object was, by the public exposition of the contaminating and degrading influences of Slavery upon the slaveholders and his abettors, as well as the slave . . . as may tend to shame (her) [the United States] out of her adhesion so abhorrent to Christianity and to her republican institutions.[6]

It is clear from Douglass' remarks that he attached significant personal as well as political meaning to the visit. In an ironic rereading of his fugitive status he even went so far as to interpret his British/Irish visit as an opportunity for "self-improvement" and the demonstration and furtherance of his intellectual liberty. But the preface also provides an explanatory note to Douglass' deterritorialized presence in the then United Kingdom, acting as an autobiographical extension of the core narrative. Written from Ireland, a site on the margins of western modernity and politicized in American and British terms by immigration and anticolonial struggle, respectively, the preface upsets any easy correlation of the slave-subject with American territory.

More remarkably, particularly given the audience at which the Irish editions were directed, the preface undermines the morally prestigious position held by Britain, in US abolitionist circles at least, after the abolition of slavery in the West Indies in 1833. Rather than a paradigm of enlightened reason and a place of safety from persecution, Britain is ironically recast by Douglass as "the land of my *paternal* ancestors." This echoes Douglass' contention in the body of the narrative that, though he is himself a slave, born of a slave mother, his father "was a white man."[7] Ironically restating his paternity in the preface to the Irish editions had repercussions exceeding the immediate abuses of power implied in the narrative proper. Foregrounded was Douglass' feminized and disinherited position within the patriarchal matrix of modernity,[8] thus implicating not only the individual concerned—Douglass' father, who was also, we are led to believe, his master—or, indeed, the institutional structures of the US, but the colonial process through which the US, as an independent nation, eventually emerged. Britain, the initiator of that colonial process and indeed of slavery in North America, is repositioned in the personal, and by extension transatlantic, history in which slave-subject and slave text were created. By tracing and stating his British paternity, Douglass invented himself as consequence, and representative figure, of that early transatlantic (colonial) alliance.⁹

As such, the preface has transhistorical as well as transatlantic effect, as past and present fuse in the physical and textual presence of the slave-subject. The later Irish editions therefore point to an inherent instability in the identity of the emerging modern subjectivity represented by and in the text of the slave narrative. The Irish "preface" resists any absolute interpretation of the narrative's central fiction—the author—within paradigmatic structures of American national-historical or geographic circumstances. Thematically, the preface assaults polarized Enlightenment models of subjective or political understanding; Douglass produces himself as cultural hybrid of a historical union between master and slave, as emblem of an erased colonial past and enslaved republican present.

But, although the preface can be seen as moving toward more integrated, transnational forms of historical understanding, a reading of it as an unqualified expression of empowered black subjectivity is impossible. Any such reading is complicated by the linguistic play between the need to escape the "patriarchal" institution of slavery and subsequent intellectual affiliation to a long unacknowledged "paternity." Indeed, the content of the preface, which remains couched in Garrisonian terms, provides ironic confirmation of that addition's concurrent contribution to the work's formal fragmentation, providing yet another narrative frame to the central account of Douglass' life in slavery.

Rather than the conventional effect of such narrative framing devices, however, which uphold the truth-claim of the work while maintaining the distance between audience and speaker, the preface—written in Ireland and addressed to a British audience—underlines the physical and subjective proximity of slave narrator and implied reader. And the placement of the preface has further significance for any reading of the *Narrative* within the newly defined, transatlantic context of its production. For, as was standard practice in such publications, Douglass' *Narrative* carries framing testimonies from respected members of the Anti-Slavery Society as to his personal integrity and the veracity of the narrative of his life in slavery. The existence and placement of the preface therefore renegotiate the metadiscourse of power relations exemplified in the intermediary frames of the slave narrative that typically define the relationship between the black narrator and the white reader. Nevertheless, Garrison's testimony had its virtues. In an ironic twist to this tussle for representative authority embedded in the Irish narratives, Garrison stated in his American preface: "I am confident that

[Douglass' account] is essentially true in all its statements; that nothing has been set down in malice, nothing exaggerated, nothing drawn from the imagination."[10] The letter from Wendell Philips that follows confirms this, assuring readers that "we have known [Douglass] long, and can put the most entire confidence in [his] truth, candor and sincerity."[11] In the American and first Irish editions of Douglass' *Narrative,* therefore, the text and the man are to be understood within the subjective and political framework of Garrisonian abolitionism. It is Garrison and Phillips, rather than Douglass, who act as mediators of the American narrative; the black text comes enclosed in the proverbial "white envelope" of abolitionist control.

Given Douglass' increasing acceptance and influence in upper-class and abolitionist circles in Ireland, it might be expected that those testimonies would disappear in the Irish editions. Certainly, the need to establish credibility and moral rectitude diminished as Douglass' range of consequential friends and acquaintances in Britain and Ireland increased.[12] Indeed, the very existence of the preface points to Douglass' increasing self-confidence, a confidence that reduced the need for third-party interpretation of the text. Nonetheless, the Irish narratives retain the testimonials of individuals accredited by the value systems of "enlightened" modernity. It is the placement of the preface to the Irish editions, however, where it precedes that of the American production, which provides the best indicator of Douglass' increasing authority over the text and its interpretation. Now framing Garrison's testimony, Douglass' preface usurps the textual and ideological authority previously held by American abolitionism. Douglass, in the light of his Irish experience, presumably decided that he rather than Garrison was the most appropriate mediator of the narrative of his life in slavery. Nevertheless, Garrison's testimony had its virtues: in an ironic twist to this tussle for representative authority, the retention of the American preface in the Irish editions suggests that, although Douglass no longer felt the need for the abolitionist crutch, he was willing to capitalize on the Garrisonian name and reap its social and economic rewards.

The preface to the Irish editions therefore has formal and thematic impact on any interpretation of the *Narrative,* particularly in the light of its transatlantic and transhistorical effect. Douglass the slave-narrator, bound by the ideological framework of abolitionism, is mirrored in and unfettered by the empowered persona of the Irish "preface," who both mediates the meaning of the central narrative and establishes a new hierarchy of interpretation in which the modernized slave-subject finally acquires textual authority. The inclusion of the preface therefore requires the recategorization of the *Narrative* as a whole, which, in its Irish editions, takes one step further toward the *bildungsroman* form it will assume in his later autobiographies, with concomitant implications for Douglass' subjective status and shifting relationship to modernity.

Against this, the retention of the American preface indicates the ongoing importance, if declining authority, of the abolitionist movement as an international ideological and economic context for the work. The introductory frames of the Irish *Narratives* illustrate the tension between Douglass—the emerging black subject—and American abolitionism, shifting the meaning and interpretation of the text in the new transatlantic context of slavery and abolition in which it is inscribed. However, even as the preface points to Douglass' increasing ideological and literary independence, suggesting a decreasing need for narrative framing devices, the number of testimonials progressively increases in the Irish *Narratives*. All of the Irish editions (first, variant first, and second) include an additional frame to that provided by the testimonies of Garrison and Phillips in the original publication, *viz.* the Hibernian Anti-Slavery Society's acknowledgment of Douglass' arrival in Ireland and its recommendation of him to fellow Irish abolitionists.[13] Arguably, this tendril of antislavery extends the geographical reach of the American movement to Ireland. And, as with the framing testimonies provided by Garrison and Phillips, the frame appears to be an attempt to mediate between the slave narrator and his (new) reading public, while simultaneously limiting that narrator's representative authority. Ireland rather than the US is now the arena of that mediation.

Economically, the Irish resolution, like the Garrisonian preface, had undoubted merit in the marketing of the work—an important consideration given Douglass' reliance on sales of the *Narrative* for an independent income. This aside, the frame has other, less material effects. Most obviously, it appears to wrap the text more tightly in the Garrisonians' embrace by rendering official Douglass' status as a noteworthy abolitionist "just arrived from the United States on an Anti-slavery mission to Great Britain and Ireland."[14] Somewhat ironically, Douglass' status within the abolitionist movement in Ireland is achieved by confirmation of the worth of his American sponsors—"some of the most distinguished and faithful friends of anti-slavery in the United States"—rather than of Douglass himself. More remarkably, and like the preface to the variant and second Irish editions, the resolution acts as a biographical extension of the core narrative. The new, opening frame of the Irish editions bears further textual witness to Douglass' deterritorialization in Ireland, recasting the narrative as a work of transatlantic scope and impact. Rooted in the discursive framework of American slavery, the text, in its Irish editions, begins to trace a formal "route" through peripheral sites of modern subjective emergence.

This voyage, reflected in Douglass' "preface" to the Irish editions and the introduction from Webb, reappears in the second Irish edition in the intertextuality established by the "critical notices" at the end of the work. Taken from a variety of US and British newspapers, the reviews register the ever-increasing circle of influence in which the narrative is active, and include articles from Philadelphia, New York, London, and Edinburgh. Much the same could be said of the personal notices by Protestant clergymen in Belfast, which provide the closing frame of the Irish editions. The Rev. Thomas Drew, D.D., describes Douglass' writing as "a metaphysical illustration of a mind bursting all bonds, and winning light and liberty for his own good and the good of millions," while the Rev. Isaac Nelson claims that Douglass "is indeed an extraordinary man—the type of a class—such an intellectual phenomenon as only appears at times in the republic of letters. . . . His name may yet be quoted both as an abolitionist and a literary man by those very States of America who now deny him a home."[15] The perspicacity, not to say prophetic insight, of these remarks with regard to Douglass' subsequent canonization notwithstanding, the notices provide an indication of the kind of politico-literary mask constructed by Douglass during his Irish tour.

In literary terms this involved the re-creation of Ireland as a space of social mobility that allowed the crystallization of the modern subjectivity that Douglass was so painstakingly constructing. Ireland, a liminal and empowering space—like Douglass himself, on the margin of modernity—provided the context of his political and literary evolution.[16] Comparisons between Douglass' experiences in the US and his reception in Ireland were consistently and publicly made, with many of his early speeches and letters dealing with the absence of color prejudice in Ireland and the warm welcome afforded him there, and otherwise creating a supporting myth of social and literary success. Writing to Garrison from Cork, for example, Douglass remarked of a soirée given in his honor: "[i]t was decidedly the brightest and happiest company, I think, I ever saw, anywhere. . . . Among them all, I saw no one that seemed to be shocked or disturbed by my dark presence. No one seemed to feel himself contaminated by contact with me." "I think," he continues, "it would be difficult to get the same number of persons together in any of our New England cities, without some democratic nose growing deformed at my approach. *But then you know the white people in America are whiter, purer, and better than the people here. This accounts for it!*"[17] Just two months later, Douglass was to write: "I have spent some of the happiest moments of my life since landing in this country. I seem to have undergone a transformation. I live a new life."[18]

These remarks were contained in one of a series of open letters to Garrison written while Douglass was in Ireland and later published in the *Liberator*. In these letters Ireland—represented by the upper and middle classes—provides a foil to the racialized, discriminatory, and enslaving environment of the US. "Instead of a democratic government," wrote Douglass from Belfast, "I am under a monarchical [sic] government. Instead of the bright blue sky of America, I am covered with the soft grey fog of the Emerald Isle. I breathe, and lo! The chattel becomes a man."[19] These letters meant that Douglass was in effect witness and spokesman for Irish society and its attitudes toward the slave; their publication provided official recognition of Irish enlightenment *and* of Douglass' liberated Irish persona.

This laudatory picture certainly had some basis in truth. Typically, black abolitionist speakers were wholeheartedly embraced by the upper echelons of British and Irish society, often becoming an emblem of the enlightened principles of the visitors' surrogate country—a monarchy— in opposition to the oppressive reality of the American republic they represented. Audrey Fisch contends that the success of black speakers in nineteenth-century Britain was in part due to that country's need to discredit US democracy and political institutions.[20] In Britain blackness, Fisch argues, was lionized, as the "spectacle" of the abolitionist movement (i.e., the black abolitionist) fused with a rising British nationalism aimed primarily at allaying the country's growing class conflict. Certain class-related as well as moral benefits therefore accrued to British, and by extension Irish, upper-class espousal of the antislavery cause, serving to displace arguments concerning human, civil, and labor rights to a safe distance in the Americas.

In Britain Douglass exploited that need for moral displacement by appealing to British nationalist sentiment. A speech given in Ayr, Scotland, provides just one illustration of the deliberate conflation of national and moral territory in his antislavery rhetoric. Predictably, the conceit involves the persecuted slave fleeing the spreading shadow of the republic in search of safety and succor in the bosom of the British nation. Speaking of the US he claims: "'There is no spot on the vast domains over which waves the star-spangled banner where the slave is secure;—go east, go west, go north, go south, he is still exposed to the bloodhounds that may be let loose against him; there is no mountain so high—no valley so deep—no spot so sacred, but that the man-stealer may enter and tear his victim from his retreat.' (Cheers.)" "[H]e rejoiced," the report continues, "that he now found in the paw of the British Lion the safety which had been denied him under the wide-spread wings of the American Eagle."[21]

Similar rhetoric was used in Ireland, though the tone was less that of popular (British) nationalism than that of the civilizing mission of empire.[22] In addition to emphasis on the differences between British and US socio-racial stratification and *domestic* policy so evident in Douglass' British speeches, his rhetoric in Ireland shows a more general interest in the power of British *foreign* policy, notably that relating to US expansion and of course slavery. A speech in Cork on 3 November 1845 on the annexation of Texas finds Douglass declaring that "Americans should be considered a band of plunderers for the worst purposes. . . . The conduct of America in this particular has not been sufficiently dwelt upon by the British Press. England should not have stood by and seen a feeble people robbed without raising a note of remonstrance."[23] That Britain was extending its own empire into Asia and Africa with equally regrettable consequences, and engaged in a long-running struggle to suppress Irish anticolonial resistance, is conveniently overlooked. Indeed, Douglass' rhetoric in Ireland actively encouraged the propagation of the ideology of progress that provided the ethical backbone of British colonial practice, displacing moral and political authority to Britain and reconstructing the United States as an unenlightened, amoral, and nonmodern space ripe for Christian conquest.

Douglass' use of the analogy between moral suasion and colonial evangelization is progressive. In his first speech in Cork on 14 October 1845 he asks only that moral pressure be exerted on American slave-holders in order to force an end to slavery:

> We would not ask you to interfere with the politics of America, or invoke your military aid to put down American slavery. No, we only demand your moral and religious influence on the slave[holder] in question, and believe me the effects of that influence will be overwhelming. (Cheers.) . . . We want to encircle America with a girdle of anti-slavery fire.[24]

Three days later, the object and objective of British influence had changed considerably. At a meeting held at Cork's Wesleyan Chapel, Douglass announced to an assembled company of "highly intelligent and influential people," including numerous church leaders of various denominations, that:

> Three millions of these poor people [are] deprived of the light of the Gospel, and the common rights of human nature; [are] subjected to the

grossest outrages— . . . the poor bondsman rattle[s] his chain, and
clank[s] his fetters calling upon the Christianity of the world to relieve
him. There [is] a wide field in America for missionary operations. (Hear.)[25]

The link between the liberation of the slave and British moral expansion was restated in Douglass' farewell speech in Cork at the Independent Chapel, George's Street, when he pushed the analogy between missionary zeal, Christian "enlightenment," and freedom to include the
acquisition of literacy, and, by inference, the concomitant absorption
into Western subjectivity:

> To you who have a missionary spirit I say there is no better field than
> America—the slave is on his knees asking for light; slaves who not only
> want the bible but some one to teach them to read its contents (hear,
> hear). Their cries come across the Atlantic this evening appealing to
> you![26]

Clearly, Douglass was keen to harness the interest of Irish élites in
overseas reform and did so by representing the slave population of the
US as a worthy and eager recipient of the benign attentions of evangelical zeal and the civilizing mission. This marks a stark contrast with the
tone of the *Narrative,* in the body of which religion and ministers of
religion are vilified, and the first American and Irish editions of which
contain an appendix explaining the negative light in which US religion
is portrayed, as well as detailing Douglass' personal religious stance. "I
love," he claims, "the pure, peaceable, and impartial Christianity of
Christ: I therefore hate the corrupt, slaveholding, women-whipping,
cradle-plundering, partial and hypocritical Christianity of this land.
Indeed I can see no reason, but the most deceitful one, for calling the
religion of this land Christianity." The appendix ends with the poem "A
Parody": "a portrait," Douglass claimed, "of the religion of the south . . .
which I soberly affirm is 'true to life', and without caricature or the
slightest exaggeration."[27] This "parody" provides the closing frame of
the American edition, which ends with Douglass "subscribing myself
anew to the sacred cause."[28] Robert Stepto describes the American *Narrative* as fusing, "in one brilliant stroke, the quest for freedom and
literacy," and ending, according to its own logic, with Douglass step-
ping heroically forward to his public duties as abolitionist and public
speaker.[29] Those public duties, Douglass' Irish rhetoric seems to suggest, involved securing not just the emancipation of the slave but his or
her salvation.

The tone of Douglass' rhetoric during his Irish visit therefore illustrates the complexity of his relationship with his Irish supporters and

the public he addressed. Stressing for his Irish audience the enthusiasm of a nonmodern, (allegedly) non-Christian, population for enlightenment, distracted from, and perhaps compensated for, a more intransigent population somewhat closer to home. Meanwhile, emphasis in his letters to Garrison on the allegedly unqualified support he received and absence of racial discrimination buoyed Irish abolitionist spirits and provided an unflattering comparison with the situation in the US. But the letters to Garrison were, like the rhetoric, above all an exercise in transatlantic self-fashioning. For while Douglass was widely fêted in abolitionist circles in Ireland, the response to his stance on the abolition of slavery, the role of religion, and even the consensus on the virtues of the *Narrative* was far from unanimously approving.

Considerable chagrin, for example, was expressed by some Irish abolitionists at the emphasis placed in Douglass' speeches on the links between churches in Ireland and those in the US. In Cork, at a speech given in the city courthouse, Douglass had caused a stir by, it was alleged, unfairly singling out Methodists for attack in his denunciations of the American churches.[30] At his next speech in Cork, Douglass was taken to task for his remarks by the Methodist clergymen Rev. William Reily, who remarked that "he could not but observe that an animus was evident in the language of Mr Douglas[s] not at all favorable to Methodists. Now it was well known that the Methodists did everything in their power, and never ceased until they banished slavery from the British Colonies (hear, hear)."[31] Douglass subsequently qualified his remarks, even going so far as to state (falsely) that he was himself a Methodist.[32] Writing to Webb from Belfast, Douglass claimed that

> the enemies of anti-slavery have been busy in creating prejudice against me, on the ground of my heterodoxy. From what I can learn, the Methodist minister in Cork as well as Dublin, have [sic] written here against me. So you see mine will be no bed of roses. These Revd Gentlemen are determined to identify themselves with their slaveholding brethren in America. They must take the consequences.[33]

These "consequences" were also to be felt by Douglass, who carried his own preconceptions concerning various religious denominations. Next day, he wrote to Webb informing him of his "success in getting the Methodist meeting house, in the face of letters prejudicial to me both from Cork and Dublin," an indication that he had survived the unfavorable reaction of southern Methodists. The same letter describes Belfast as "a field ripe for the harvest; . . . the very hotbed of presbyterianism and free churchism," concluding that "a blow can be struck here

more effectively than in any other part of Ireland." Free Church Presbyterians were certainly high on Douglass' list of desirable converts to the
antislavery cause. The "Send Back the Money" campaign, which formed
the basis of Douglass' Scottish tour, targeted the Free Church of Scotland, which was in receipt of monies from slaveholding co-religionists
in the American South.[34] The campaign against the executive of the Free
Church actually began in Belfast, though the results, despite Douglass'
declarations that he was everywhere met with approbation, were not
always happy. On one occasion on which the "Send Back the Money"
jingle backfired, Belfast was during the night placarded with the anti-
Douglass slogan: "Send Back the Nigger."[35]

The incident was blamed on the presence in the city of an American
Methodist clergyman, Rev. Smith, although, presumably, he was not acting alone. No mention is made of the incident in the famous "We don't
allow niggers here" letter written to Garrison from Belfast on 1 January
1846 and later published in the *Liberator*, in which Douglass once again
draws comparisons unfavorable to the US between his treatment there
and in Ireland.[36] "The people here know nothing of the republican
negro hate prevalent in our glorious land," wrote Douglass; "[t]hey
measure and esteem men according to their moral and intellectual
worth, and not according to the color of their skin."[37] Ireland was presented to US abolitionists as a place of uniform and unqualified support
for Douglass; no crack was to be allowed to be seen to have appeared in
the myth of a stalwart antislavery wall in Ireland.[38]

The second Irish edition of the *Narrative* reflects the complex sectarian negotiations in which Douglass engaged, as well as marking the
qualitative shift that occurred in his attitudes to religion during his Irish
tour. Gone is the stinging "parody" of Southern slaveholding Christianity, and, as noted, its place is taken by the "personal notices" of two Irish
Protestant clergymen. These were included in defiance of Webb, Douglass' staunchly anticlerical publisher.[39] Despite the objections of the
man who was undoubtedly one of Ireland's leading abolitionists, Douglass insisted on the inclusion of the notices in the second Irish edition,
informing Webb that he "ought to have thought of [his] prejudice
against priests sooner. If clergymen read my narrative and approve of it,
prejudice against their office would be but a poor reason for rejecting
benefit of such approval. The enclosed is from Mr Jackson, the Presbyterian Minister. I wish both it, and that of Dr Drew, to be inserted in the
second edition." "To leave them out because they are ministers," he
somewhat disingenuously continues, "would be to show oneself as
much and more sectarian than themselves."[40]

In the event, the notices were included, underlining once again the extent to which Douglass had evolved as a political and literary agent during his time in Ireland. The notices also give some inkling of his class affiliations in Britain and Ireland, where, according to his biographer William McFeely, Douglass' social leanings evolved "upward rather than outward."[41] These tendencies can be detected in Ireland in the religious composition of his audiences, which were predominantly upper-class and Protestant. The inclusion of the notices from members of that audience therefore recalibrates the socio-political stance of the text, whose new alignment reflects Douglass' rising status in the moral politics of the Atlantic world by underscoring his power to reward enlightened attitudes with textual recognition. Free Presbyterianism and Anglicanism, through their acknowledgment of Douglass' moral and literary status, and their support of the abolitionist cause, are welcomed into the prestigious antislavery fold now represented in and by the *Narrative*—an inclusion that has the added advantage of leaving the myth of unfaltering support for Douglass in Ireland unscathed.

Thus Douglass' representation of the success of his Irish visit in his open letters to Garrison show him availing of the personal and literary opportunities provided in Ireland by a reforming upper class eager to establish its enlightened credentials, which were finally established by the incorporation of letters from Irish clergymen as closing frames to the *Narrative*. In common with the "preface" to the variant and second Irish editions, these notices are testimony to Douglass' increasing literary and ideological independence. Ireland was central to the realization of that independence: not just as a refuge from re-enslavement and a safe platform from which to attack the US's "peculiar institution," but as an imaginary space which marked an important step in the development of his writing *and* of a distinctive narrative persona which escaped the racial confines of the US and the ideological control of the transatlantic abolitionist movement. Douglass' sojourn in Ireland made possible his emergence as a major cultural and intellectual force, an emergence that occurred in parallel with, and was bound to his self-representation as arbiter of his own text. The *Narrative*, in its Irish editions, traces the complicated path of that subjective and literary emergence, formally marking Douglass' accession to the coveted "republic of letters."

NOTES

1. Biographical accounts of Douglass include William S. McFeely, *Frederick Douglass* (New York and London: Norton, 1991), and Benjamin Quarles, *Frederick Douglass* (1948; New York: n.p., 1964).

2. Alan J. Rice, "Triumphant Exile: Frederick Douglass in Britain, 1845–47," in Alan J. Rice and Martin Crawford, eds., *Liberating Sojourn: Frederick Douglass and Transatlantic Reform* (London and Athens: University of Georgia Press, 1999), 3.

3. Both the first Irish edition and the variant carry the date 1845, though the latter was not in fact published until 1846.

4. Paul Gilroy has proposed the triangular relationship between Africa, Europe, and the Americas stemming from the African slave trade as a formative influence on Western cultural identity and a cornerstone of Western modernity. This triangular space permits a more nuanced evaluation of the complex trade in people, cultures, and ideas in the transatlantic context. However, Gilroy's framework does not acknowledge the complications presented by colonization, either in the Americas (beyond the figure of the post-emancipation Afro-American colonial subject) or worldwide, as similarly influential. In the Irish case the colonial relationship with Britain during the nineteenth century significantly complicates the status, influence, and effect of African-American visitors traveling to Ireland on an abolitionist ticket. See Paul Gilroy, *The Black Atlantic: Modernity and Double Consciousness* (Oxford: Blackwell, 1993).

5. The Free Church was established in 1843 and immediately embarked on a fundraising drive in Britain, Ireland, and the US. By 1844 it was estimated that £9,000 had been donated by Presbyterians in the American South. Douglass' campaign urged churches to have "no union with slaveholders" and specifically targeted the Free Church with the "Send Back the Money" slogan. See Alaisdair Pettinger, "'Send Back the Money': Douglass and the Free Church of Scotland," in Rice and Crawford, eds., *Liberating Sojourn*, 31–47.

6. Frederick Douglass, "Preface," *Narrative of the Life of Frederick Douglass, an American Slave, Written by Himself*, variant first Irish edition and second Irish edition (Dublin: Webb and Chapman, 1845, 1846), 3.

7. "He was admitted to be such," Douglass continues, "by all I ever heard talk of my parentage. The opinion was also whispered that my master was my father; but of the correctness of this opinion, I know nothing." Frederick Douglass, *Autobiographies*, ed. Henry Louis Gates, Jr. (New York: Library of America, 1994), 15.

8. The gendering of the black male subject derived from the "chattel" status that the institution of slavery imposed on the African-American subject in slavery and the related discrimination against free black persons who were denied many of the civil and political liberties enjoyed by "white" males, including the right to vote and stand for public office. The discourse of slavery and of abolitionism was itself overdetermined by a gendered discourse involving the abolitionist movement as a political vehicle for élite women and the re-creation of male slave subjectivity through the objectification of slave women.

9. The "preface" echoes the theme of a speech given by Douglass in Limerick on 10 November 1845, when Douglass informed his audience that "the Americans, as a nation, were guilty of the foul crime of slavery, whatever might be their hypocritical vaunts of freedom. It was . . . not a true democracy, but a bastard republicanism that

enslaved one-sixth of the population." John Blassingame, ed., *Frederick Douglass Papers,* Series One: *Speeches, Debates, and Interviews,* 1 (New Haven: Yale University Press, 1979), 76–86. Hereafter referred to as *FDP.*

10. Douglass, *Autobiographies,* 7.

11. Ibid., 12.

12. See Lee Jenkins, "Beyond the Pale: Frederick Douglass in Cork," *Irish Review* 24 (1999): 80–95, especially 89.

13. The text, inserted on the flyleaf, reads as follows:

> "At a meeting of the Committee of the Hibernian Anti Slavery Society, held in Dublin, the 20th of September, 1845 it was
>
> RESOLVED—That as FREDERICK DOUGLASS (who is now present) has just arrived from the United States on an Anti-Slavery mission to Great Britain and Ireland, we take the opportunity of recommending him to the good offices of all abolitionists with whom he may meet. He has long been known to us by reputation, and is now introduced to us by letters from some of the most distinguished and faithful friends of the Anti Slavery cause in the United States.
>
> JAMES HAUGHTON, *Chairman*
> RICHARD D WEBB, *Secretary.*"

14. *Narrative of the Life of Frederick Douglass,* first, variant, and second Irish editions (Dublin: Webb and Chapman, 1845, 1846), flyleaf.

15. Ibid., cxxxii.

16. For discussions of Irish marginality and the ongoing ambivalence of the relationship to Western modernity, see Seamus Deane, *Strange Country: Modernity and Nationhood in Irish Writing since 1790* (Oxford: Oxford University Press, 1997); Raymond Crotty, *Ireland in Crisis: A Study in Capitalist Colonial Underdevelopment* (Dingle: Brandon Books, 1986); David Lloyd, *Anomalous States: Irish Writing and the Post-Colonial Moment* (Dublin: Lilliput Press, 1993) and *Ireland after History* (Cork: Cork University Press, 1999).

17. Douglass to William Lloyd Garrison, 28 October 1845, in *Liberator,* 28 November 1845.

18. His letter goes on to contrast his treatment in the US with "the warm and generous co-operation extended to me by the friends of my despised race—the prompt and liberal manner with which the press have flocked to hear the cruel wrongs, has rendered me its aid—the glorious enthusiasm with which thousands of my downtrodden and long-enslaved countrymen portrayed—the deep sympathy for the slave, and the strong abhorrence for the slaveholder, everywhere evinced—the cordiality with which ministers of various religious bodies, and varying shades of religious opinion have embraced me, the kind respects constantly proffered to me by persons of the highest rank in society." Douglass to Garrison, in *Liberator,* 30 January 1846.

19. Douglass to Garrison, ibid.

20. "'Negrophilism' and British Nationalism: The Spectacle of the Black Abolitionist," *Victorian Review* 19 (Summer 1993), 2047, especially 2537.

21. *FDP,* 1: 1, 2001.

22. An exception to this occurred at a speech in Limerick on 10 November 1845, when, describing the *Cambria* incident, Douglass identifies Gough, the Irish captain of the ship, as one of the heroes of the piece. In the middle of recounting the story Douglass called for "three cheers for old Ireland." *FDP* 1: 1, 84. Other flirtations with

Irish nationalist sentiment can be seen in Douglass' frequent references to Daniel O'Connell, the mention of whose name was practically guaranteed to raise a cheer. Though Douglass referred to O'Connell as the "Liberator," he confined the application of that title to O'Connell's stance on American slavery, thereby emphasizing the enlightened credentials of the Irish upper classes while avoiding any possible conflict with his hosts over the issue of popular nationalism or repeal. Later, Douglass was to recall that at the 1845 repeal rally where O'Connell and Douglass met (the only occasion on which they did so, despite Douglass' ongoing self-identification with the repeal advocate), O'Connell had "called me 'the Black O'Connell of the United States.'" Douglass, *Autobiographies*, 682. See also Lee Jenkins, "'The Black O Connell': Frederick Douglass and Ireland," *Nineteenth-Century Studies* 13 (1999): 22–46, especially 28.

23. *FDP*, 1: 1, 74.

24. Cork, 14 October 1845. *FDP*, 1: 1, 42.

25. Cork, 17 October 1845. *FDP*, 1: 1, 52.

26. Cork, 3 November 1845. *FDP*, 1: 1, 75.

27. Douglass, *Autobiographies,* 97–102.

28. Ibid., 102.

29. Robert B. Stepto, *From Behind the Veil: A Study of Afro-American Narrative* (Urbana: University of Illinois Press, 1979), 26.

30. The remarks that appear to have given offense were the following: "It must also be stated that the American pulpit is on the side of slavery, and the Bible is blasphemously quoted in support of it. The Ministers of religion actually quoted scripture in support of the most cruel and bloody outrages against slaves. My own master was a Methodist class leader. (Laughter, and 'Oh'), and he bared the neck of a young woman, in my presence, and he cut her with a cow skin. He then went away, and when he returned to complete the castigation, he quoted the passage, 'He that knoweth his master's will and doeth not, shall be beaten with many stripes.'" (*FDP*, 1: 1, 43). This speech was one of the very few given in Ireland directed at a populist audience, and its tone differs significantly from much of Douglass' other rhetoric at this period, relying more on vernacular forms and appealing to popular nationalist sentiment.

31. William Martin defended Douglass from an attack by the Rev. Joseph Mackey, who said that "he felt offended at the language used by Mr Douglas[s], at the meeting in the Court-House, as it was calculated to cast opprobrium on Methodists in particular, whilst the Roman Catholic and other sects were passed by; and he need scarcely remark that the majority of the audience at that meeting was composed of persons who required but little incentive to induce them to cast opprobrium on their sect." Douglass, somewhat disingenuously, in reply said that "he was a fallible man; and it would be requiring too much that he should know men's religion by their faces." *FDP* 1: 1, 53–54.

32. The newspaper report reads: "He was a Methodist himself; but he cautioned his fellow religionists how they defended their brethren in America, for in doing so they would be defending the men . . . who scourged his . . . female cousin until she was crimsoned with her own blood [from] her head to the floor (hear, and oh, oh)." *FDP* 1: 1, 54. The admission is interesting, as Douglass habitually denied any sectarian affiliation, declaring on more than one occasion that "as to religion, I belong to none." A letter to Webb from Belfast, detailing his experiences on a brief visit to Birm-

ingham made in December of 1845, confirms this: "I called on the Rev. John Angel James DD to whom I had a letter of introduction. . . . He wished to know if I came recommended and if I . . . was a member of any Church—and if any to what Church. I told him I was not a member of any Church." Douglass to Webb, 20 December 1845: Boston Public Library (hereafter BPL), Boston Anti-Slavery Collection, MS. A.1.2, v.15, 89. Although the events went unrecorded in Blassingame's "Partial Speaking Itinerary," Douglass arrived in Liverpool on 14 December, spoke in Birmingham's Town Hall on the 16th for "25 minutes amid cheers," and arrived back in Belfast on 19 December 1845. A letter from Webb to Mary Weston Chapman indicates that Douglass briefly revisited Dublin in October 1846 in the company of Garrison: "I forgot among the droppers in last night to mention Frederick Douglass who looked stately and majestic—with an air that makes Garrison a mere baby beside him": BPL, Weston Papers, Dublin, 31 October 1846, MS. A.9, 2, v.22, 1846, no. 109.

33. Douglass to Webb, Belfast, 5 December 1845: BPL, Boston Anti-Slavery Collection, MS. A.1.2, v.15, 85.

34. The campaign provides the only example of Douglass mobilizing popular support while in Britain and Ireland.

35. According to Webb, "In Belfast a Carolinian Rev. Smith, a Methodist, endeavoured to injure Douglass by calumnious reports against his morality & by imputing infidelity to him. One night the town was placarded with large bills SEND BACK THE NIGGER." Webb to Maria Weston Chapman, 16 July 1846: BPL, Weston Papers, MS. A.9.2, v.22, 1846, no. 75.

36. The manuscript text, throughout which the phrase "We don't allow niggers in here" appears nine times, details Douglass' experience in the US where he alleged that he was repeatedly met with this remark and refused entry to churches, public buildings, and eating houses. In contrast, Douglass claimed that in Ireland "I find no difficulty . . . in gaining admission into any place of worship, instruction or amusement on equal terms with people as white as any I saw in the United States. I meet nothing to remind me of my complexion. I find myself regarded and treated at every turn with the kindness and deference paid to white people. When I go to church, I am met by no upturned nose and scornful lip to tell me 'We don't allow niggers in here'! etc." Douglass to Garrison, 1 January 1846: BPL, Anti-Slavery Collection, MS. A.1.2, v.16, 1.

37. Ibid.

38. See Richard Blackett, "Cracks in the Anti-Slavery Wall: Frederick Douglass's Second Visit to England (1859–1860) and the Coming of the Civil War," in Rice and Crawford, eds., *Liberating Sojourn*, 187–206.

39. In a letter to Maria Weston Chapman, Webb, himself a member of the Society of Friends, went so far as to state that "the people here in Dublin are stagnant—weighed down by Popery and Episcopalianism which would smother the life out of any people. They are the curse of Ireland." R.D. Webb to Maria Weston Chapman, 16 July 1846: BPL, Weston Papers, MS. A.9.2., vol. 22, 1846, no. 75.

40. Douglass to Webb, 16 April 1846: BPL, Anti-Slavery Collection.

41. McFeely, *Frederick Douglass*, 141.

"White," If "Not Quite":
Irish Whiteness in the Nineteenth-Century Irish-American Novel[1]

CATHERINE M. EAGAN

OVER THE PAST TEN YEARS, an increasing number of American-ist historians have suggested that Irish and other European immigrants, in an attempt to secure the prosperity and social position that their white skin had not guaranteed them in Europe, lobbied for white racial status in America. The success of this effort was by no means assured. While American laws concerning who could immigrate, be naturalized, and be enslaved accepted Irish people's pale skin color and European roots as evidence of their white racial pedigree, the dis-crimination that Irish immigrants experienced on the job, and the simi-an caricatures they saw of themselves in the newspapers, suggested that they were "racially" inferior to white Anglo-Americans and thus some-how nonwhite, perhaps even "black."[2] Many historians, focusing their attention on the Irish-American working class, have argued that Irish immigrants worked to counter suggestions of their racial affinity with African Americans and thus ensure the recognition of their whiteness through their participation in labor agitation and in popular cultural forms like blackface minstrelsy.[3] Some historians of Irish America, by contrast, have questioned whether Irish Americans actively pursued white racial status, citing desperation for jobs as the chief source of con-flict with African Americans and pointing to examples of Irish opposi-tion to antiblack racism.[4]

Be that as it may, the Irish-American novel, particularly as written by the embattled famine generation of immigrants, makes it clear that "whiteness" was an identity to which Irish Americans not only felt enti-tled but actively pursued. Although these novels should not be taken as

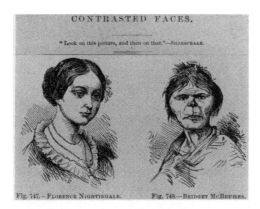

"Contrasted Faces." The juxtaposition of these two images starkly illustrates how the Irish were racialized in the mid-nineteenth century.

Source: Samuel R. Wells, *New Physiognomy: Or Signs of Character, as Manifested Through Temperament and External Forms and Especially in "The Human Face Devine"* (New York: Fowler & Wells, 1866). Widener Library, Harvard University.

exact reflections of Irish-American realities or sensibilities, they do reveal some of the modes through which Irish people argued for a white racial identity that they regarded as their entitlement, while also revealing the conflicting agendas that informed their articulations of this white racial belonging. This article will use the rarely studied Irish-American novel to offer a more complex understanding of how Irish Americans lived and lobbied for their whiteness. In doing so, I hope to bridge the gaps between Americanist and Irish-Americanist historians and between labor and cultural historians of Irish America.

Irish-American novelists, who were most often immigrant priests, journalists, and publishers, only occasionally asserted their white racial credentials by denigrating African Americans. A much stronger challenge to Irish whiteness than any ostensible link of Irish people to Africans was the Anglo-American concern that Irish Catholicism and nationalism made the Irish unfit for assimilation into the white American mainstream. For by the mid-nineteenth century many native-born Americans had come to believe that their cultural, national, and even religious and political differences with Irish and other European immigrant groups meant that the immigrants were racially inferior, despite their white skin color and European origins, and that such racial inferiority was biological and permanent. According to this logic, immigrants' undesirable characteristics would not disappear once they became accustomed to American society, but would persist and prevent assimilation into "white America" as Anglo-Americans defined it.[5] Irish-American novelists' attempts to allay concerns over Irish racial incompatibility with whiteness were usually indirect; they elaborated Irish whiteness through narrative reminders of the European, Christian, civilized, and free history of the Irish in Ireland and America. Sometimes, these reminders were articulated in the dialogues between characters or in the voice of the narrator in the form of long discourses on the sophistication of the Irish religion and culture.[6] Most often, the novelists simply assumed the whiteness of the Irish; the most positive characters speak proper English and are able to pass for Protestant, and the sentimental conventions of the novel invite Anglo readers to identify with Irish characters as equals.[7]

Irish-American novelists' pursuit of whiteness was not unqualified, however. For example, even as their novels praise the illustrious European heritage of the "Celt," they attempt to distance the Irish from whiteness as identified with "Anglo-Saxon" culture in America, for it threatens their religious and national particularity.[8] But the novels show how difficult it was to argue for white racial membership held in common with Anglo-Americans if one scorned any connection with the Saxon "race." If the literary theorist Frederic Jameson were to read these novels, he might say that one can see the novelists attempting to sustain the "political fantasy" of racial harmony between Irish-American and Anglo-American culture by engaging in complicated maneuvers to repress that fantasy's instability.[9] Though the Irish identified with whiteness and clung to the political and economic security that white racial status could bring, the sense of racial difference from the Saxon that they brought from Ireland, in combination with their antagonistic relationship with the Anglo-Saxon Protestant power structure in America, meant that their articulation of their whiteness would at times be convoluted. But the argument for Irish whiteness was nevertheless made; the specific form of that argument in literature is the subject of what follows.

Catholic, Civilized, Celtic, and White?

One of the primary goals of the famine-generation Irish-American novel, whether set in Ireland or America, was to refute the myths about Catholicism spread by everyone from sensationalist writers to elected officials. Authors were careful to arrange dialogues and plot situations so that the novels' heroes got plenty of opportunities to enlighten English and American Protestant characters as to Catholicism's respectability and sophistication.[10] Characters insist time and again that they are not pagans who pray to graven images. Rather, they explain that Catholics only pray to the Virgin Mary and the saints as intercessors, not as separate deities.[11] They also insist that the rite of confession does not give Catholics license to commit crimes without fear of punishment—as the heroine of John McElgun's *Annie Reilly* (1873) puts it, there are "'conditions necessary for a good confession.'"[12] Contrary to the Protestant assumption that priests and nuns forbid their parishioners to read the bible, Catholic characters make it clear that they are carefully instructed as to the teachings of their religion, and that they are not merely vessels for information but active thinkers.[13] Sensationalist rumors about the Catholic hierarchy are also strenuously rejected—readers are told that convents are not havens for prostitutes and baby killers, that the pope is not a despot, and that priests do not kidnap Protestants to convert them.[14]

This fiction also takes time to praise Irish priests for their discernment and intelligence, in an effort to counter Protestant stereotypes of them as corrupt or uneducated primitives. In Mary Meany's *The Confessors of Connaught* (1865), for example, an English visitor to Ireland praises one Father Dillon's sermon as "'the most thrilling sermon I ever heard, abounding in poetic passages and beautiful imagery,'" and as "'an intellectual treat.'"[15] Even the more humble priests, like Philippus O'Sullivan of Mary Anne Sadlier's *Confessions of an Apostate* (1864), are no less intelligent, if their manner is one of peasant simplicity and provincial scholasticism. These priests possess a "world of truthfulness and genuine kindness" in their hearts.[16] The nuns featured in these novels are no less distinguished. Peter McCorry, in his *Mount Benedict; or, The Violated Tomb* (1871), highlights the intelligence and grace of Sister Mary Bernard, an Irish scholar of modern languages, by juxtaposing her with the woefully ignorant Protestant firebrands who burn her convent in Charlestown, Massachusetts. No reader can possibly believe that she harbors prostituted nuns and infant skulls within her convent's walls, as the arsonists' handbills claim.[17]

As suggested by the examples above, defenses of Catholicism flowed easily into suggestions of its claims to cultural and civilizational distinction. These fictional characters frequently remind readers that Ireland was the "school of the civilized world" for centuries, and a few characters and narrators compare Ireland to ancient Greece and Rome.[18] Paeans to the religious and civilizational superiority of the Irish in turn supported assertions of the strength of Irish "racial" stock. In Father John Boyce's *Shandy M'Guire* (1848), his description of Ellen O'Donnell demonstrates the inextricable connection between Irish religious and racial strength. Boyce describes Ellen thus:

[A]s a Catholic, she was gay, cheerful and happy; as an Irishwoman,
impulsive and enthusiastic; as both together, inheriting as she did the
oldest faith in Christendom, and the oldest royal blood in the universe,
she was what you see her—a proud worshipper at a humble altar.[19]

But as Boyce's depiction of Ellen reveals, Irish-American novelists'
praise of Irish blood tended to assert not merely its equality to the blood
of the Anglo-Saxon but its superiority. Even as they assumed that the
European consanguinity of Celt and Saxon would entitle them to the
status of whiteness, they touted the superiority of the Celtic "race" to the
Saxon. In Father Hugh Quigley's *Profit and Loss* (1873), for example, Mul-
roony is proud that he has no Saxon blood in his veins, just "old stock."[20]
Similarly, in Boyce's *Mary Lee* (1860), Mr. Lee denies his daughter's hand
in marriage to the visiting Yankee suitor Mr. Weeks by declaring that
while Ireland is a noble country, Weeks's "'godless liberalism'" and
"'national vanity'" indicate that Americans "'must have sadly degenerat-
ed since the revolution.'"[21] Much of the praise of Irish religion and civilization cited above has the same chauvinistic flavor. As a friendly
Catholic woman reminds the orphaned Burke children in Sadlier's *Willy
Burke* (1850), "'you, as Catholics, stand on a high vantage-ground over
all other religious persuasions, and, as you love your own souls, see that
you never forget this fact.'"[22] Another definitive sign of Catholic superiority is the fact that many of the good-hearted Protestant characters in
the novels convert to Catholicism.[23] As a merchant who converts on his
deathbed in Quigley's *Profit and Loss* explains to his wife, it is hardly a
"'disgrace'" to convert to the "'oldest Church in the world.'"[24] Irish-American efforts to prove their whiteness were made additionally conflicted
by their insistence on retaining some portion of what they believed to be
their "Celtic" distinctiveness. In her *Con O'Regan* (1864), Sadlier claims
that American depravity, not Irish inferiority, is the cause of Irish immigrants' criminal, disobedient, drunken, and disrespectful behavior in
America, and her characters dream of emigrating west, where they can
live as they did in Ireland.[25] Sadlier's and Quigley's novels repeatedly
warn against abandoning the Irish culture and religion and describe the
hardship that comes to those who do so.[26] Irish Americans may have
begun to claim the benefits of white-skin privilege and leave their connections with African Americans behind, but they were uncomfortable
with the alliance with former "Saxon" enemies that claiming those benefits required, and with the loss of Irish Catholic particularity that an
alliance threatened.

These assertions of Celtic religious, civilizational, and sanguinary superiority had the potential to scuttle the "white racial project"[27] of the Irish, as they risked undermining the authors' talk of the racial strength that Irish and Anglo-Americans shared, and alienating the very Saxons who held the keys to Irish acceptance as whites in America. As early as 1849, Orestes Brownson brought this danger to the attention of his readers in *Brownson's Quarterly Review*. In a review of Boyce's *Shandy M'Guire*, Brownson warned that Irish-American authors' insistence on making "the tyrant . . . a Saxon and the victim a Celt" provoked readers' "wrath or contempt" and transformed "what should be a war against oppression for common justice into a war of races."[28] Though Irish-American authors did not abandon their Irish emphasis, they appear to have developed a series of strategies to compensate for these challenges to white racial sameness. Taken together, these strategies effectively argue for a kind of homogenized whiteness, a whiteness that may be threatening in part, but also has room for Celtic particularity within it. While somewhat undercut by the novelists' claims to Celtic superiority, these gestures toward brotherhood may have mitigated the Irish racial chauvinism in the novels and in American society generally.

Reassurances of White Racial Brotherhood

A key strategy for highlighting the whiteness of the Irish was to ensure that their physical descriptions impressed readers. Novelists resisted the assumption that the typical Irishman possessed a "simous nose, long upper lip, huge, projecting mouth [and] jutting lower jaw [and] sloping forehead," as L. P. Curtis has described it, by presenting characters with white skin, Roman noses, and high foreheads.[29] The rural Ireland in Patrick Cassidy's *Glenveigh* (1870), for example, is populated by lovers with "delicately-shaped" heads and "broad, square shoulder[s]."[30] Dillon O'Brien's *The Dalys of Dalystown* (1866) describes Henry Daly, the oldest son of the Norman Catholic landowning family, as blessed with "delicately chiseled nostrils," "a proud, disdainful smile," and a "tall, graceful figure."[31] O'Brien's peasants also display strong racial stock, and do not resemble the Celtic stereotype in the slightest, with their "erect and flexible carriage," "regular oval features," and "teeth of pearly whiteness."[32]

The exemplary physiognomy of the Irish is noted in the novels set in America as well, which bodes well for Irish acceptance as whites. Quigley emphasizes the physical perfection of the O'Clery children in *The Cross and the Shamrock* (1853). Parson Burly and his wife, who encounter the children in the poor house that they run, are astounded at Paul O'Clery's "'roman nose, raven hair, delightfully-carved mouth,

and lips, and eyes, and eyelashes quite indescribable, so beautiful are
they,'" find his sister "'a perfect Venus,'" and declare that the two younger
children, Patrick and Eugene, appear as if carved by "'some renowned
artist of antiquity.'" The parson's wife is so confused by their beautiful
appearance that she concludes they "'must belong to some race different from the Celtic half savages which we have read inhabit Ireland.'"[33]
Similarly, in *Mary Lee*, Boyce reminds his readers that there is no meaningful physical difference between the Irish and the English:

> [T]he Irish wear no horns of any description whatever, either behind or
> before—are endowed with the ordinary feelings and sense peculiar to the
> human family—and exhibit arms and legs, hands and hair, precisely like
> their Norman and Anglo-Saxon neighbors.[34]

The authors also assured their readers that the Irish were not only
physically similar to the Anglo-Saxon but possessed strength of character worthy of their society as well. The strength of Celtic racial stock was
used as a reassurance that the Irish would be good citizens, not as a
challenge to Saxon racial strength. One of the most beautiful Irish
women in these novels is Rose O'Donnell, the love interest of Henry
Daly in O'Brien's *The Dalys of Dalystown* and the daughter of the elder
Mr. Daly's former steward. Her physical beauty and "whiteness" is often
referred to, as well as her strength of character.[35] Raised by the Daly family after the death of her father, Rose serves as evidence that the Irish
can mix with those of the upper classes if given guidance, which bodes
well for Irish social mobility in America. Similarly, McCorry suggests in
Mount Benedict that regardless of the environment, the personal integrity and ambition of the Irish will assure their exemplary conduct.
McCorry writes of the Catholic Kate Crolly:

> [Her character] was not born with her; rather was it the result of severe
> training, and a devotion to virtue for virtue's sake. . . . That young lady's
> character was the result of constant prayer and vigilance. . . . Katie Crol-
> ly had to rise *above* nature before she became all that she was—not what
> she desired to be—for she aspired after divine perfection.[36]

If the physical and cultural similarities of Celts and Saxons were to
allow the Irish to excel in America, their ability to assimilate represents
both the promise of equality and the pitfall of complete assimilation, as
suggested earlier. Certain Irish-American authors endeavored to avoid
this pitfall by allowing some characters to "pass" even as they remain
recognizably Irish.[37] In Quigley's *Profit and Loss*, Father John, an Irish-
born priest who completed his seminary studies in Maryland, has "all
the vigor of a robust Irish frame, overlaid, as it were, by the studied and

assumed delicacy of a native American gentleman."[38] In Sadlier's *Confessions of an Apostate*, Simon Kerrigan moves to the country, changes his name to Kerr, and is accepted as a Protestant by his employer and the town in general, yet perceptive new acquaintances recognize his Irishness, and his cover is nearly blown; Sadlier implies that though Kerrigan has successfully assimilated, there is something Irish about him that will always be present and eventually reassert itself.[39]

All the novels, even as they emphasize Irish particularity and superiority on the one hand, contain scenes designed to assert the brotherhood of good-willed Protestants and Catholics. Though Mrs. VonWiegel, the Irish widow of a German Catholic in Sadlier's *Old and New* (1862), passes for white and is descended from an Anglo-Irish family, Sadlier hails her as a true Irish woman. No mention is made of her "racial" difference to the "Old Irish" Fogartys or Gallaghers, which implies that any lingering racial or religious prejudice against Catholics by American Protestants is a foolish denial of their common brotherhood. In Boyce's *Mary Lee* an Irish priest describes the Irish Protestant Kate as "'a genuine, true-blooded Irish girl, inheriting the enthusiasm and impulsiveness of her race. . . .'" Though Kate's ancestry is English, Irish "blood" can apparently be claimed by long-term residence and an affection for the Irish people.[40] In McCorry's *Mount Benedict*, this implication of brotherhood between the Saxon and Celt is solidified by marriage; Cecilia and Patrick are united once Cecilia converts.

The novelists' comparison of the Irish to white European and Christian populations also allowed them to emphasize the whiteness of the Irish by inappropriately referring to their oppression as "white slavery."[41] As Samuel Otter has pointed out in his examination of sailors' use of the white-slavery analogy in the nineteenth century, the "spectacle of white flesh being whipped" by cruel ship captains gained its power from the assumption that scarring "an unscathed body," in other words a white body unmarked by the difference of skin color, was a greater offense than scarring one already marked as inferior by its dark color.[42] White entitlement is assumed when characters or narrators make impassioned objections to the "enslavement" of the Irish or to Americans' failure to notice that "enslavement" because of the greater attention given to African Americans. In *Shandy M'Guire*, for example, Boyce tries to shock his readers by showing how Colonel Templeton regards his tenants as his property.[43] Later, a priest drives home the point that white slavery is a heinous evil by lamenting that slavery is especially hard to bear for the Irishman, who possesses blood "'transmitted him through the veins of a hundred kings.'"[44] Another example of frustration over Irish enslavement comes from D. P. Conyngham's *The O'Donnells of Glen Cottage* (1874). The narrator laments, "Oh, the famine years and a grasping landocracy have crushed and broken all the finer feeling of their nature; have made them what they wished them to be—helpless slaves in their own green land."[45]

Irish immigrant characters are even more offended than the Irish at being treated like slaves, and their shock at their treatment in the "land of the free" is dramatized. In Boyce's *Mary Lee* an Irish peasant named Mrs. Motherly responds to the abolitionist statements of Mr. Weeks by reading from a niece's letter, which charges that the Irish are treated worse by the Yankees than they were by the English. Mrs. Motherly then comments, "'It's a wonder they're not ashamed to purfess so much tinderness for the slaves, and trate the poor Irish so manely as that.'"[46] In Quigley's *The Cross and the Shamrock*, Van Stingey's cruelty to his Irish-American railroad workers, whom he calls "'darned paddies,'" makes an Irish priest wonder if America really is a free country if laborers receive store pay in lieu of wages, have to begin and end their days in the dark, and take orders from low sorts of men. "'I ask any man,'" the priest exclaims with anguish, "'Is this not slavery'?"[47] In Sadlier's *Con O'Regan*, Paul Bergen's long lost brother Felix pleads with him to come farm with him in Iowa, "'where a man can be his own master, and not be driven about like black niggers from post to pillar. . . .'"[48]

Often, the common racial heritage of the Irish and Anglo-Americans was emphasized using sentimental tactics. Sentimentalism encouraged potential Anglo-American readers to identify with Irish characters and sympathize with their struggles. Though Charles Fanning laments the didacticism and sentimentalism of Irish-American novels in this period, the use of sentimental convention had the most potential to convince native-born American readers of Irish racial sameness.[49] Nancy Armstrong, for example, has suggested that the sentimental novel's tendency to organize novel plots around the matching of characters with their appropriate marriage partners served to preserve racial purity.[50] As these novels manipulate their readers into caring about the births and deaths, romances and marriages, and hardships and triumphs of the Irish on both sides of the Atlantic, they indirectly assert the illogic and cruelty of English and American persecution of their fellow white, civilized Christians.

These novels generate sympathy for their Irish characters in the most basic ways. Aware of the American public's enjoyment of Irish quaintness, the novels feature many "local color" stories, fairy myths, and anecdotes of "the gay, light hearted Irish peasantry."[51] Appropriately, stories are often set in pastoral areas, and the characters demonstrate qualities supposedly endemic to Irish country life, like generosity and hospitality.[52] Like many American sentimental novels, these Irish-American novels often feature a child as the hero.[53] This child is usually faithful to his or her religion and refuses to convert or go to a mixed school. In *The Cross and the Shamrock* the O'Clery children steadfastly adhere to their religion even though they have been kidnapped by Protestants. Paul, the oldest child and the caretaker of the other children, ends up becoming a priest. In Sadlier's *Willy Burke*, Willy's behavior is exemplary—his brother, who falls into the clutches of a woman who promises him riches and education if he converts, reminds the reader of Willy's goodness.

Readers are also encouraged to identify with Irish Catholic characters in matters of love. The lovers, distinguished by the flawless physical traits of their race as outlined above, engage the reader's sympathy as they surmount various obstacles to their union. James and Annie are joined after a long separation in *Annie Reilly*; Frank crosses the class divide to marry Alice in *The O'Donnells of Glen Cottage*; Emily and Edward and Henry and Rose manage to preserve their relationships in the face of emigration in *The Dalys of Dalystown*, and Patrick and Cecilia marry despite their previous religious differences in *Mount Benedict*. The love relationships in all of these novels encourage readers to admit that Irish Catholics can enjoy a love as respectable as theirs.

Finally, another significant way in which famine-generation Irish-American authors attempt to evoke sympathy for their characters is by alluding to the horror of the dispossession and starvation of Catholics in Ireland. In Sadlier's novel *New Lights*, which ominously foreshadows the destruction of the 1847 famine year, one character cannot bear to revisit the horror of past starvation, saying:

> Oh pardon me, my country,—pardon me, my own, beautiful, sorrowing land,—if I shrink frow [sic] dwelling on your record. I have glanced at it, and it is so blistered with tears, so darkened with sorrow, that I may not now scan it too closely; for mine eyes are filled with tears, and my brain reels with indignant shame![54]

Because Sadlier has portrayed the Catholic Irish as fellow civilized whites concerned with religious faith and education, the starvation, property confiscation, and demoralization that they face would have been all the more horrifying to Anglo-American readers. When Meany's Mrs. Gillman finds out that her lighthearted, honest, hardworking, and charitable washerwoman lost four children in the famine, she marvels at the strength of a supposedly "simple creature."[55] The sentimental effect of these stories relies on the assumption that the outside reader should feel empathy, not just sympathy, for the tragedy experienced by their Irish brothers and sisters.[56]

The Irish use of cultural production to claim their whiteness has usually been discussed in terms of the blackface minstrel show. But it is no less important to examine this phenomenon in the Irish-American novel. In fact, it may be more important—for it is in this genre that the articulation of the Irish-American character as white was the most insistent and conflicted. Certainly, the stresses of such a perplexed approach to consolidating Irish whiteness may have compromised that message, despite novelists' efforts. Orestes Brownson's worries about the alienating tone of Irish-American fiction would have been magnified for nativists and Protestants who may not have read the novels, but were exposed to similar Irish-American arguments for whiteness in public discourse. Regardless of whether these famine-generation novels were able to further Irish Americans' "white racial project" in the nineteenth century, reading them provides important insight into the complexity of Irish-American racial identity in this period. Still shaped by and heavily invested in their politics and identity in colonial Ireland, the famine Irish struggled to benefit from their white skin color while retaining the religious and cultural distinctiveness of their Irishness. Historians have focused on the confused racial status of European immigrants mainly in terms of the establishment's unwillingness to grant them white racial status. What these novels reveal is that Irish immigrants were even more ambivalent about accepting it.

NOTES

1. My article title is an adaptation of Homi Bhabha's well-known description of the "*ironic* compromise" of the mimicry that happens under colonial systems. Bhabha defines "colonial mimicry" as the "desire for a reformed, recognizable Other, *as a subject of a difference that is almost the same, but not quite*" (emphasis in original). Homi Bhabha, "Of Mimicry and Man: The Ambivalence of Colonial Discourse," *The Location of Culture* (London: Routledge, 1994), 86.

2. For examples of English and Anglo-American comparisons of Irish and African racial inferiority, see Dale Knobel, *Paddy and the Republic: Ethnicity and Nationality in Antebellum America* (Middletown: Wesleyan University Press, 1986). Whatever the rhetorical strength of Americans' assertions of Irish and African racial similarities, it should be emphasized that the Irish retained their hold on white entitlement so as not to equate the oppression that they and African Americans experienced.

3. See Noel Ignatiev, *How the Irish Became White* (New York: Oxford University Press, 1971); David Roediger, *The Wages of Whiteness: Race and the Making of the Amer-*

ican Working Class (London: Verso, 1991) and *Towards the Abolition of Whiteness: Essays on Race, Politics, and Working-Class History* (London: Verso, 1994).

4. See, for example, David Brundage, "'Green Over Black' Revisited: Ireland and Irish-Americans in the New Histories of American Working-Class 'Whiteness,'" a paper delivered at the conference on "Racializing Class, Classifying Race: Labour and Difference in Africa, the USA, and Britain," St. Antony's College, University of Oxford, 11–13 July 1997; Graham Hodges, "'Desirable Companions and Lovers': Irish and African Americans in the Sixth Ward, 1830–1870," in Ronald H. Bayor and Timothy J. Meagher, eds., *The New York Irish* (Baltimore: Johns Hopkins University Press, 1996). Lauren Onkey provides a nice summary of Irish Studies scholars' reception of Noel Ignatiev's ideas in particular in her "'A Melee and a Curtain': Black-Irish Relations in Ned Harrigan's *The Mulligan Guard Ball*," *Jouvert* 4 (1999), 31 March 2000, <http://social.chass.ncsu.edu/jouvert/v4il/onkey/htm>.

5. For helpful analyses of the changing meaning of race in nineteenth-century Europe and America, see Knobel; Robert J. C. Young, *Colonial Desire: Hybridity in Theory, Culture, and Race* (London: Routledge, 1995); and Alexander Saxton, *The Rise and Fall of the White Republic: Class Politics and Mass Culture in Nineteenth-Century America* (London: Verso, 1990).

6. As Father Hugh Quigley, a former Young Irelander who had become an American missionary, described his mission in the preface to his novel *The Cross and the Shamrock* (1853), it was the "duty" of Irish-American writers to supply their community with literature that had "for its end the exaltation and defence of his glorious old faith." [Hugh Quigley], *The Cross and the Shamrock, or, How to Defend the Faith: An Irish-American Catholic Tale of Real Life, Descriptive of the Temptations, Sufferings, Trials, and Triumphs of the Children of St. Patrick in the Great Republic of Washington. A Book for the Entertainment and Special Instruction of the Catholic Male and Female Servants of the United States*, reprinted in *Wright American Fiction*, microfilm, Vol. 2, 1851–75 (Woodbridge: Research Publications, 1970–78), 7. Quigley's biographical information comes from Charles Fanning, *The Irish Voice in America: 250 Years of Irish-American Fiction*, 2nd ed. (Lexington: University Press of Kentucky, 2000), 141.

7. If these novels invited Anglo readers to hear their argument for white racial privilege, one must ask whether that argument was heard. Quigley's preface, cited in note 6, seems to indicate that Irish-American novels were primarily geared toward the Irish Catholic immigrant and the Irish and/or Catholic American. There is some evidence that the novels were intended for outside audiences as well. Though Fanning claims that famine-generation authors "wrote only for their own kind," extended discourses on Catholicism and Irish culture, and open-minded Protestant characters, may have been inserted in these novels to persuade Protestant American readers of the Irish people's white racial credentials. Certainly, these novels got some exposure before the general reading public through Orestes Brownson's periodical *Brownson's Quarterly Review*. Brownson, a former Protestant who had converted to Catholicism, addressed his journal to both Catholics and Protestants; if he was right that Catholics mainly bought "Bibles, Prayer-Books, and school-books, but scarcely a book of any other description," his review and the sales of Catholic-written literature thus relied in part on Protestant consumers. He also assumed a potential Anglo-American audience for the Irish-American novels that he reviewed when he criticized them for being overly nationalistic, or when he recommended them to "those who are pretending that Ireland is about to apostasize from the faith." See Brownson, review of *Rosemary,*

by J.V. Huntington, *Brownson's Quarterly Review*, 3rd New York series, Vol. 1, no. 4 (1860), 527; and Brownson, review of *New Lights: or Life in Galway. A Tale*, by Mrs. J. [Mary Anne] Sadlier, *Brownson's Quarterly Review*, 3rd series, Vol. 1, no. 3 (1853), 407.

8. The word "Celt" had a pejorative sense when used by Anglo-Americans perplexed by alleged Irish savagery, and was infused with a certain racial pride when used by Irish Americans seeking to differentiate themselves from "Saxons." For both groups the word suggested more than a national identity (it was typically identified with the Irish, though the word technically encompasses the Welsh, Bretons, and others), but an identity defined by race and by blood. The use of the words *Celt* and *Saxon* to suggest racial difference indicates that the newer notion of racial difference as permanent and biological was beginning to intersect with the older notion of race as a term used to designate national or cultural differences between peoples. Needless to say, this did not agree with definitions of race that counted both Irish and English as whites. Commenting on this type of inconsistency, Matthew Jacobson has called the "contest over whiteness" in nineteenth-century America "untidy." He writes: "Conflicting or overlapping racial designations such as white, Caucasian, and Celt may operate in popular perception and discussion simultaneously—despite their contradictions; the Irish simians of the Thomas Nast cartoon, for example, were 'white' according to naturalization law; they proclaimed themselves 'Caucasians' in various political organizations using that term; and they were degraded 'Celts' in the patrician lexicon of proud Anglo-Saxons." I would add, of course, that the Irish used the word Celt in a positive sense. Matthew Jacobson, *Whiteness of a Different Color: European Immigrants and the Alchemy of Race* (Cambridge: Harvard University Press, 1998), 5.

9. Frederic Jameson, *The Political Unconscious: Narrative as a Socially Symbolic Act* (Ithaca: Cornell University Press, 1981), 47–48.

10. If Protestant readers were not numerous, the novelists at least hoped to give Irish-American Catholic readers plenty of ammunition with which to defend their faith. The novelists feared that their fellow immigrants would convert to Protestantism in order to increase their potential for employment, and cast aside their love for their country in order to assimilate.

11. See, for example, Sadlier, *New Lights* 224; John Boyce, *Mary Lee; Or, The Yankee in Ireland*, reprinted in *Wright American Fiction*, microfilm, Vol. 2, 352 ff. Sadlier was the wife of James Sadlier, who with his brother Denis owned the largest Catholic publishing house in America: Fanning, *Irish Voice*, 114–15.

12. John McElgun, *Annie Reilly; or, The Fortunes of an Irish Girl in New York*, reprinted in *Wright American Fiction*, microfilm, Vol. 2, 170. See also Dillon O'Brien, *The Dalys of Dalystown* (Saint Paul: Pioneer Printing Company, 1866), 90–91.

13. The intelligence and devotion of the Catholic faithful, despite their lesser emphasis on scripture, was a favorite theme of many authors. See McElgun, *Annie Reilly*, 170; Boyce, *Shandy M'Guire; or, Tricks upon Travellers: Being a Story of the North of Ireland*, reprinted in *Wright American Fiction*, microfilm, Vol. 2, 32; Hugh Quigley, *Profit and Loss: A Story of the Life of the Genteel Irish-American, Illustrative of Godless Education*, reprinted in *Wright American Fiction*, microfilm, Vol. 2, 320; and Sadlier, *New Lights*, 224, *Con O'Regan; or, Emigrant Life in the New World* (New York: D. and J. Sadlier and Company, 1864), 308, and *Willy Burke; or, The Irish Orphan in America* (Boston: Thomas B. Noonan and Company, 1850), 158.

14. See especially Peter McCorry's *Mount Benedict; or, The Violated Tomb, a Tale of*

the Charlestown Convent, reprinted in *Wright American Fiction*, microfilm, Vol. 2. His novel is a fictionalization of the burning of the Ursuline convent in Charlestown, Massachusetts, in 1834. According to Fanning, McCorry was an "Ulster Catholic immigrant journalist and ardent Irish nationalist," who lived and wrote in Boston and New York. Fanning, *Irish Voice*, 79. For more on the riots and the exaggerated "captivity narratives" of convent life written by Protestants, see Jenny Franchot, *Roads to Rome: The Antebellum Protestant Encounter with Catholicism* (Berkeley: University of California Press, 1994).

15. Mary Meany, *The Confessors of Connaught; or, The Tenants of a Lord Bishop* (Philadelphia: Peter F. Cunningham, 1865), 58. For more learned priests, see Boyce's *Shandy M'Guire* and *Mary Lee*; Quigley's *The Cross and the Shamrock*; Alice Nolan's *The Byrnes of Glengoulah: A True Tale* (1869), reprinted in *Wright American Fiction*, microfilm, Vol. 2, 42–43; Sadlier's *Confessions of an Apostate* (1903; New York: Arno Press, 1978), 67; and D. P. Conyngham's *The O'Donnells of Glen Cottage: A Tale of the Famine* (1874; P. J. Kenedy, 1895), 64.

16. Sadlier, *Confessions of an Apostate*, 54–55.

17. McCorry, *Mount Benedict*, 113.

18. For comparisons of ancient Ireland to Greece and Rome, and reminders of its illustrious past as a center of civilization and religion, see Conyngham, *The O'Donnell's of Glen Cottage*, 83; Boyce, *Mary Lee*, 45; Quigley, *Profit and Loss*, 201; and *The Cross and the Shamrock*, 46.

19. Boyce, *Shandy M'Guire*, 254. Boyce, who wrote under the pseudonym Paul Peppergrass, was ordained at Maynooth and supported Young Ireland before emigrating to America, where he became an influential missionary priest in Massachusetts. See Fanning, *Irish Voice*, 97. For another instance of Irish religious and civilizational integrity being connected to racial strength, see Meany's *Confessors of Connaught* (55), in which the English missionaries and teachers in Ireland realize that the Irish race is just as strong as the Saxon race, which they had always assumed to be superior.

20. Quigley, *Profit and Loss*, 7–8. Ordained in Rome because he had refused to take Maynooth's required oath of allegiance to the British government, Quigley went on to incite his starving parishioners to theft during the famine and to involve himself with the Young Ireland movement before emigrating to America, where he was a missionary priest in New York, the Midwest, and California. Fanning, *Irish Voice*, 141.

21. Boyce, *Mary Lee*, 279. Cruel Anglo characters often had ugly physiognomies. See, for example, O'Brien, *The Dalys of Dalytown*, 63, 87; McCorry, *Mount Benedict*, 136, 157; Sadlier, *Confessions of an Apostate*, 61.

22. Sadlier, *Willy Burke*, 126.

23. See, for example, Meany, *Confessors of Connaught*, 315; Nolan, *The Byrnes of Glengoulah*, 336; Sadlier, *Confessions of an Apostate*, 66–67; Quigley, *Profit and Loss*, 20, and *The Cross and the Shamrock*, 19, 85; Sadlier, *Confessions of an Apostate*, 241, *New Lights*, 158, 330, and *Willy Burke*, 255.

24. Quigley, *Profit and Loss*, 207.

25. Sadlier, *Con O'Regan*, 16–28.

26. See, for example, Quigley, *Profit and Loss*; Sadlier, *Confessions of an Apostate* and *Old and New; or, Taste Versus Fashion* (New York: D. and J. Sadlier and Company, 1868).

27. This term comes from Howard Winant. See his "White Racial Projects: A Com-

parative Perspective," paper presented at a conference, "The Making and Unmaking of Whiteness," University of California at Berkeley, 12 April 1997.

28. Brownson, review of *Shandy M'Guire*, by Paul Peppergrass [John Boyce], *Brownson's Quarterly Review*, new series, Vol. 3, no. 1 (1849), 62. Brownson probably used the word "race" in terms of national or cultural difference; after all, he tirelessly argued that Irish Catholics were capable of assimilating. Nevertheless, he undoubtedly recognized that an insistence on racial difference, whether conceived of as cultural or biological difference, endangered the potential for white American unity.

29. L. Perry Curtis, Jr., *Apes and Angels: The Irishman in Victorian Caricature*, rev. ed. (Washington, D.C.: Smithsonian Institution Press, 1997), 29.

30. Patrick Cassidy, *Glenveigh; or, The Victims of Vengeance: A Tale of Irish Peasant Life in the Present* (Boston: Patrick Donahoe, 1870), 14. Cassidy became a journalist in America. Fanning, *Irish Voice*, 397, n. 12.

31. O'Brien, *The Dalys of Dalytown*, 92. O'Brien and his family emigrated to the American Midwest after the famine, where O'Brien taught in a mission school for the Chippewa Indians in Wisconsin and later edited the *Northwestern Chronicle*, a Catholic weekly published in St. Paul, Minnesota. Thomas O'Brien, "Dillon O'Brien," *Acta et dicta*, 6.1 (1933), 35–53.

32. O'Brien, *The Dalys of Dalytown*, 61.

33. Quigley, *The Cross and the Shamrock*, 63.

34. Boyce, *Mary Lee*, 18–19.

35. O'Brien, *The Dalys of Dalytown*, 33, 130 ff.

36. McCorry, *Mount Benedict*, 101–02 (emphasis in original).

37. While literary critics have assumed that racial passing is unique to novels written by people of color, the sacrifices demanded by "passing" for white are depicted quite similarly in these Irish-American novels, even though the characters in question have white skin. It must be remembered that the white racial credentials of Irish Americans were in question in this era; when these characters are revealed to be Irish, the jobs, marriages, and status that they have enjoyed while masquerading as white Anglo-Americans are often threatened. At the same time, the necessity, experiences, and consequences of passing are not as dire for Irish-American characters. The novels are organized to prove that passing for a white Anglo-Saxon Protestant is not necessary; those Irish characters who remain true to their Irish Catholic roots eventually have their white racial deservedness recognized, without having to masquerade. Needless to say, this recognition does not come to African Americans and other people of color who decide not to pass.

38. Quigley, *Profit and Loss*, 201.

39. See, for example, Sadlier, *Confessions of an Apostate*, 117–18.

40. Boyce, *Mary Lee*, 324.

41. For explicit reminders of Europeans' common Christian heritage, see Boyce, *Shandy M'Guire*, 24; Quigley, *The Cross and the Shamrock*, 5.

42. Samuel Otter, *Melville's Anatomies* (Berkeley: University of California Press, 1999), 68–69.

43. Boyce, *Shandy M'Guire*, 215. Colonel Templeton hopes that his tenants will not find out about American and French republicanism, or that their condition is the same as that of American slaves. Fanning, *Irish Voice*, 100.

44. Boyce, *Shandy M'Guire*, 265.

45. Conyngham, *The O'Donnells of Glen Cottage*, 89.

46. Boyce, *Mary Lee*, 234.

47. Quigley, *The Cross and the Shamrock*, 114.

48. Sadlier, *Con O'Regan*, 209.

49. See, for example, Fanning, *Irish Voice*, 144.

50. Nancy Armstrong, "Why Daughters Die: The Racial Logic of American Sentimentalism," *Yale Journal of Criticism* 7.2 (1994), 2.

51. Conyngham, *The O'Donnells of Glen Cottage*, 109. The popularity of Moore's *Irish Melodies* and of the plays of Tyrone Power attests to Americans' fondness for this image of the Irish.

52. See, for example, Meany, *Confessions of Connaught*, 17.

53. Armstrong ("Why Daughters Die," 4) says that Leslie Fiedler categorizes *Uncle Tom's Cabin* as an American novel in part because it is a little girl that triumphs, not a woman overcoming her seducer.

54. Sadlier, *New Lights*, 488.

55. Meany, *Confessions of Connaught*, 79.

56. For more allusions to the famine, see also O'Brien, *The Dalys of Dalytown*; Conyngham, *The O'Donnells of Glen Cottage*.

Part 3

The World of Work

Editor's Introduction

RECENT INVESTIGATIONS OF RACE in Irish-American history depend ultimately on the larger question of labor, which is fundamental to all immigration history and, indeed, to history as a whole. What did people do for a living? How did the immigrants survive and sustain themselves and their families? What measures did they take to ameliorate their lot? These questions are especially germane when considering a mass migration of impoverished and uprooted people, and rarely more so than in the case of the Irish in the nineteenth century. Until the last quarter of that century, the great majority of Irish-American workers were unskilled; most of the men were employed as laborers, and most of the women worked as domestic servants or factory hands. They were generally driven from Ireland by economic necessity and were attracted to America by the massive demand there for the work they could do. They helped build America's infrastructure—its roads, canals, railways, and buildings—and they freed middle-class women from the demands of daily labor, allowing them to engage in other pursuits, not least (and somewhat ironically) social and political reform. Unskilled workers have received little attention in American historiography, but the Irish are something of an exception to this rule; given that so few of them had marketable skills to begin with, studying the immigrant generation means studying menial workers.

If the history of domestic servants often remains concealed in the private realm, those workers who were more publicly visible responded to their conditions of life and labor in two ways: men engaged in faction fights and formed secret societies on the Irish model, and both men and women joined the more formal trade union movements typical of industrial capitalism. As a predominantly rural country, Ireland did not have a significant trade union movement in the nineteenth century. It did, however, have a strong tradition of faction fighting and secret-society violence, many signs of which emerged on the canals and railroads and in the mines of North America. In both Canada and the United States, there were Irish faction fighters with names like Corkonians, Fardowners, and Connaughtmen and secret societies like the Ribbonmen, the Whiteboys, and, most infamously, the Molly Maguires of Pennsylvania. These forms of protest gradually gave way to trade unionism, a more peaceful and generally more effective mode of labor organizing. Excluded at first from the unions organized by American-born skilled workers, the unskilled Irish formed their own organizations. Anti-Irish labor nativism soon dissipated, however, and by 1900 the American Irish dominated the trade union movement in the United States. Between 1900 and 1910, fully 50 of the 110 affiliate unions of the American Federation of Labor had Irish-American presidents. The Irish went on to play a central role in the labor movement during the century that followed.

The general poverty of Irish migrants in the United States meant that women, as well as men, typically had to work for a living. At any given moment in the nineteenth century, perhaps half of them worked as domestic servants, and the other half worked mainly in factories and sweatshops or in their homes, where they took in piecework, laundry, and boarders. The demography of Irish migration is especially important here. Men and women migrated from post-Famine Ireland to the United States in roughly equal numbers, and nearly all of them were unmarried. Only the Swedes had a similar profile. In other cases where sex ratios were equivalent, among Jewish migrants for example, most of the women were already married. Many other migrations, like those of Italians and Slavs, were overwhelmingly male. Unlike most young female immigrants in America, Irish migrants not only needed to work for a living outside their own homes but faced no obstacles in doing so. Free to work in the homes of others, they accounted for a large majority of domestic servants in the cities of the Northeast and other regions in the late nineteenth and early twentieth centuries.

Irish women so dominated domestic service in the United States that the prevailing term for a female servant was "Bridget." By contrast, many native-born and immigrant women avoided service altogether, whether because they saw it as beneath their dignity, because they were married, or because their culture would not allow single girls in public without a chaperone. Given the severely restricted opportunities at home in Ireland, in terms of both work and marriage, many young Irish women must have viewed coming to America as a form of escape rather than banishment. There they could rejoin siblings and renew old friendships. American cities were dynamic, exciting places to live. Factory wages were low but better than anything available in Ireland. Domestic service provided shelter and food and carried few expenses. Servants could send some of their earnings back to Ireland, spend some on their days off, and save the rest for the future.

This, at least, is the standard picture provided by historians who have written about the subject. But there is a danger of romanticism here. That Irish servants were better off in America than if they had they stayed in Ireland does not entail a simple progression from oppression to liberation. Servants were servants, after all. They made money but worked extremely long hours, typically rising an hour before the family and retiring an hour after it and sometimes serving through the night where there were young children. As impoverished Irish Catholics, they must have encountered considerable condescension in the genteel homes where they worked. And as young females living in the households of strangers, they doubtless encountered unwanted sexual pressures as well. Despite these obstacles, they generally prospered in the United States, carving out new lives for themselves, financing the passage of siblings to America, and supporting their families back in Ireland.

"In the Shadow of a Grain Elevator": A Portrait of an Irish Neighborhood in Buffalo, New York, in the Nineteenth and Twentieth Centuries

WILLIAM JENKINS

THE CREATION OF THE IMMIGRANT neighborhood is one of the central features of American urbanization since the nineteenth century. Irish settlements in North America since the early 1800s have been analyzed with depictions of various "Irishtowns" and "Cork-towns."[1] While images of ethnic homogeneity in urban neighborhoods in the period 1850–1930 have been dispelled by detailed research, the endurance of ethnically defined populations and identities has received scant attention.[2] Indeed, it has been assumed that the durability of such populations and identities in a given neighborhood seldom lasted beyond the immigrant generation, but rather represented a temporary or transitional arrangement in a city's social geography.[3] The urban ecologists of the University of Chicago in the 1920s and 1930s, with their "spatial assimilation" models, did not expect working-class immigrant neighborhoods to last for more than a generation. The descendants of the inhabitants of such places, they believed, suburbanized relatively quickly, paving the way for newer immigrant groups to occupy cheap housing close to downtown. The residential dispersal of the Chicago Irish from the notorious Stockyards district in the early twentieth century, for example, moved Paul Cressey to write that they had undergone "a more complete disintegration . . . and a greater degree of cultural assimilation" than the city's Germans.[4]

Though the exodus of the "lace-curtain" or "steam-heat" Irish from early shantytowns forms a key element in the story of Irish America at the turn of the century, little has been said of the primary settlement areas they left behind, or about how long such areas remained "Irish."

This paper explores, firstly, the socioeconomic milieu of the First Ward, the principal "Irish" district of Buffalo, New York, in the late-nineteenth century; and, secondly, it explores the conditions that contributed to the ward's durability as an Irish neighborhood into the twentieth century. In contrast to many other pioneer Irish neighborhoods in urban America, the identity of the First Ward as an Irish working-class neighborhood has endured far beyond the first generation of immigrants who settled there in the 1840s and 1850s.[5] And though the neighborhood has been hit hard by de-industrialization, with part of the housing stock now put to other uses, the neighborhood is still viewed by Buffalonians as the "Irish" part of Buffalo. Rather than being seen as a bounded "Irish world," neighborhood is conceptualized in this paper as a fluid entity. I argue that a variety of social territories co-existed alongside, and overlapped with, one another and were inextricably linked in a web of ethnic-based social relations. The First Ward, in other words, was not a world unto itself.

Profiling the economic and social structure of this Irish neighborhood and mapping its various social landscapes is possible through the analysis of census manuscripts, municipal records, personal memoirs, and a contemporary novel, Roger Dooley's *Days Beyond Recall*, set in the First Ward circa 1900.[6] The book chronicles the family and social relationships of Rose Shanahan, born in the ward to Limerick-born parents. Although Dooley, born in 1920, was writing about the previous generation who lived in the district, I argue that his status as a First Ward native of Irish background and his use of real place-names in the book offer a more nuanced picture of neighborhood life than can be gleaned purely through reliance on non-literary sources. As Mallory and Simpson-Housley argue, such novelistic descriptions of places "enable the essences of sense of place to be felt strongly by the reader."[7] In discussing the First Ward's Irishness, I explore not only the district's residential geography, but also its labor market and various social and political institutions, all of which functioned to produce an Irish-American neighborhood of long standing.

Initial Settlement

The completion of the Erie Canal in the 1820s transformed the young city of Buffalo into a grain port of world renown by mid-century. Grain arriving from the Middle West was stored in the city's waterfront elevators and later transferred onto Erie Canal barges for dispatch to markets on the Eastern Seaboard. In addition, the city's profile as a center of heavy industry rose through the second half of the nineteenth century, with the growth of the iron and steel and automobile sectors. By the 1890s, the socioeconomic pyramid of a small, wealthy élite and a large industrial proletariat had been firmly established. As Powell has noted, this period represented "the high noon of Buffalo capitalism. The city boasted 60 millionaires, twice the number in all the United States in 1850."[8]

The Irish, being among Buffalo's earliest settlers, had long been an integral part of the city's labor force. Upon the Erie Canal's completion, the various towns and villages in New York state along its length became heirs to "little colonies of Irish families. . . . In Buffalo, they were especially numerous simply because that was where the canal terminated."[9] "Numerous" did not necessarily imply a large community of settlers; John Timon, the first Catholic Bishop of the Diocese of Buffalo, estimated only four hundred Irish people to be present in Buffalo by the early 1830s.[10]

The nineteenth-century Buffalo Irish had much in common with Irish urban communities elsewhere in the northern United States. It appears that most of them were Catholic. In contrast to towns and cities in nearby Canada, Buffalo had too few Irish Protestants for them to develop a distinctive group life or presence.[11] Due to the efforts of the French, German, and Irish settlers, Catholicism in Buffalo was cast in stone with the building of St. Louis church in 1829, the parish and church of St. Patrick's being established in 1841.[12]

The famine-related immigration of the late 1840s had a significant impact on Buffalo and its Irish population. Over ten thousand individuals of Irish birth resided there in the early 1850s, overwhelming the pre-famine Irish settlers.[13] Most of Buffalo's Irish originated in Munster and Connacht, rather than Ulster or Leinster.[14] Like so many Irish in other American cities prior to the 1880s and 1890s, those in Buffalo occupied the lowest socioeconomic position among the city's two other main ethnic groups, the Protestant Yankees and German-speaking peoples from Central Europe. Buffalo's Protestant founders, mainly Episcopalians and Presbyterians, originated in New England and eastern New York. Germans, of a mostly artisanal background, both Protestant and Catholic, were also present in the city from the early nineteenth century.[15]

Although Irish households were present in all areas of Buffalo by 1880, the Irish remained closer to the waterfront and central business district than the Americans (who inhabited mainly the north and west sides) and Germans (on the east side). The First Ward accounted for 36 percent of all Buffalo Irish households of both the first and second generation in 1880.[16] In that year also, the "rambler," reporting for Toronto's

Irish Canadian, commented that "a large section of Buffalo—that towards the South—is largely inhabited by Irishmen and their immediate descendants."[17] This southern waterfront district, which consolidated itself as a blue-collar Irish-American district for more than a century, is the focus of the remainder of this essay.

The First Ward:
Location, Topography, and Territorial Evolution

Industry, residence, and ethnicity were interlinked in the shaping of the First Ward as one of urban America's most enduring Irish-American neighborhoods. Nineteenth-century Irish settlement in Buffalo did not extend very far from the city's waterfront, where the Erie Canal, Buffalo River, and City Ship Canal were lined by grain elevators, mills, warehouses, and other structures devoted to manufacturing and transportation. Irish settlers in the First Ward, located south of the city's central business district and covering an area of 634 acres, built wooden shanties along these waterways from the late 1840s. The various waterways through which Great Lakes tugboats, freighters, and canal barges alike traveled cut into the district's geography. Not surprisingly, rowing became a popular sport in the First Ward, particularly among grain elevator workers, and three clubs were established.[18] The ward was situated in one of the lowest-lying parts of Buffalo, whose swampy terrain made it undesirable for housing, prone to periodic flooding and, in the summer of 1849, the area of the city hardest hit by a cholera epidemic[19] (Figure 1).

Thirty years after the Great Famine brought thousands of Irish to the city, they remained the principal ethnic group of the First Ward but did not completely dominate. A 10 percent federal census manuscript sample of the ward's household heads in 1880 demonstrates that the Irish of at least two generations made up over 70 percent of the ward's population (Table 1). Of the 202 Irish households, a second-generation Irish male or female headed only 37, or 18.3 percent. The remaining nationalities were a mix of Americans of long generation, as well as immigrants from Germany, Britain, and other parts of northwestern Europe. The First Ward's residential geography reflected both its Irish flavor and its minorities. The latter were spread throughout the district; thus, while some streets, such as Kentucky, Tennessee, and Vandalia were heavily Irish, few were exclusively so. Single-family houses were strung along prominent east-west streets such as Perry, Elk, and Fulton, populated mostly by Irish laborers and their skilled or semi-skilled countrymen. Houses containing the families of Dutch, Danish, English, Scottish, and

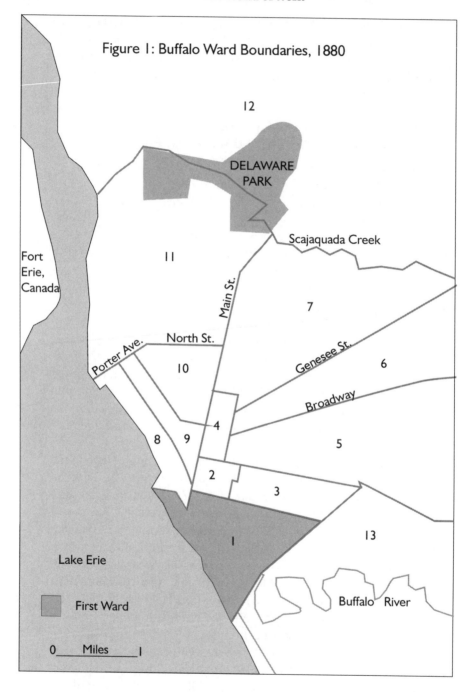

Figure 1: Buffalo Ward Boundaries, 1880

TABLE 1
ETHNIC ORIGIN OF FIRST WARD
HOUSEHOLD HEADS, 1880

Ethnic origin	N	%
Irish	202	70.4
German	30	10.5
American	13	4.5
English	18	6.3
Scottish	9	3.1
Canadian	9	3.1
Other European	6	2.1
Total	287	100.0

Source: U.S. federal census manuscripts, 10 percent household sample.

American laborers, painters, printers, and sailors regularly broke the ethnic monotony, however.

The spiritual center for the Irish Catholic inhabitants of Buffalo's First Ward was initially St. Bridget's Church. Its genesis dates from 1850 when Bishop Timon organized a Society of St. Vincent de Paul to administer relief and spread the catechism among impoverished famine immigrants. The parish dedicated a proper brick church in 1860, replacing the initial small frame structure. The parish priests, with names like McMullen, O'Connor, Gleason, Quigley, Lanigan, and O'Brien, were clearly of an Irish background.[20] In addition, the establishment of two churches marked the presence of a minority Protestant population: St. Mark's Methodist Episcopal (1856) and St. Thomas' Episcopal (1876).

Tenement life, the everyday domain of thousands of Irish families in New York City at this time, had little parallel in Buffalo. While tenement buildings housing three or more families were part of the First Ward's housing stock, they were exceptions. In a sample of 185 first- and second-generation Irish households in 1880, 94 (50.8 percent) lived in modest frame-built single-family dwellings, 53 (28.6 percent) in two-family dwellings, and the remaining 38 (20.5 per cent) in buildings housing more than two families. Inspection of the Sanborn fire insurance maps for the city in 1881 reveals that because only a few houses in the area were more than two stories high, the remainder were extended further into the lot to cope with the demand for space. Number 191 Elk Street, for example, was a two-story structure that housed ten families in 1880, seven of whom had Irish heads of household.

Despite its outward character as an Irish working-class neighbor-hood, the inhabitants of the First Ward seldom perceived the area as a homogeneously "Irish" space. Community was present on a variety of spatial scales and a process of differentiation, based primarily on occu-pation and the length and street of residence, became inscribed into the district's social geography. Many among the Irish-born in Buffalo had grown up in the Catholic parishes of western and southern Ireland, where the townland and parish defined locality. Within such divisions, place-names were bestowed informally on landmarks such as fields and crossroads, many of which escaped official cartography by the Ord-nance Survey. While the official title "First Ward" (or simply "The Ward") was adopted by its Irish-American inhabitants as the general name of their neighborhood, informal local names were created by the immi-grant generation (Figure 2).[21] "Haker Town" was apparently christened by immigrants from Cork and Kerry "where they ate much hake-fish."[22] "Uniontown" was named after the dominating Buffalo Union Furnace, and in some respects those who worked in that steel mill inhabited a world separate from the rest of the ward. To the east of the grain eleva-tor district and in a somewhat isolated location, the company built more than sixty frame houses on stilts with board sidewalks and dirt streets. To offset occasional floods, the land underneath the houses was filled in with slag, a by-product of iron. The mill had an employment capacity of five hundred men, and excess funds from dances held in local board-ing houses went to needy families whose fathers were ill or injured.[23]

The working-class Irish on "The Beach" were isolated from the rest of the city by a maze of freight yards, grain elevators, docks, slips, and rail-roads. Inhabiting city-owned land and not troubled by deeds or taxes, the Irish shared this strip, nicknamed "Wall Street," with a smaller num-ber of Portuguese families. Lake Erie fish, caught all year round, was cen-tral to the diet of these families. They were served by a Roman Catholic church between 1873 and 1915, after which the city evicted the inhabi-tants in favor of railroad development.[24]

Although a working-class community overall, the tightly knit social milieu and subtle class or lifestyle distinctions in the First Ward gener-ated a lack of privacy and a small-town snobbery similar to those found in rural Ireland. Dooley's novel, *Days Beyond Recall*, proves valuable evi-dence in this regard:

> There were few [families] whom the Shanahans did not know, at least among the families who had always lived here. Tenants might come and go, forever moving from one back yard to another or living in flats over Elk Street stores, but the families who owned their own houses, they who

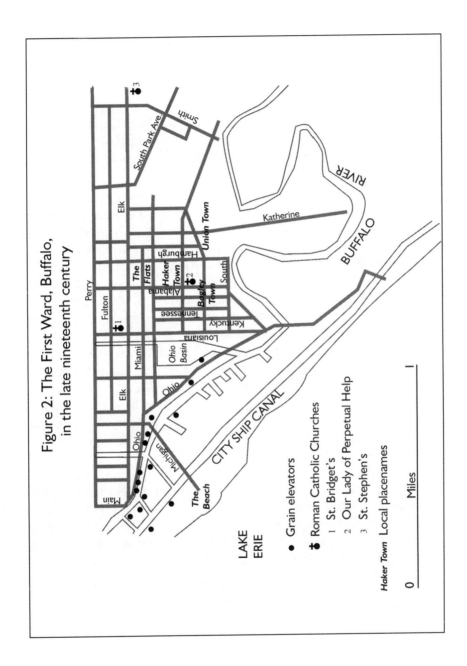

Figure 2: The First Ward, Buffalo, in the late nineteenth century

had formed St. Bridget's nearly fifty years ago . . . these were still the backbone of the parish, and the ones who rated a greeting from Mary Ellen
Shanahan.[25]

To some First Warders, not all of their fellow Catholic Irish were alike. In
the eyes of pious and respectable locals of long standing, such as Mary
Ellen, the novel reveals further that the absorption

> of the population of The Beach by a parish restructuring had consider-
> ably lowered its standing in the eyes of St. Bridget's parishioners. It might
> boast many comfortable families, but it also numbered a great many
> more like . . . former Beachers, newer from the old country or more
> menially employed on the docks and in the mills.[26]

Other institutions of the First Ward shaped its social life. As with Barrett's intimate portrayal of Chicago's Packinghouse district, the saloon,
often doubling up as a boarding house, a grocery, or both, was a common commercial establishment and key point of reference socially.[27]
Possessing a vibrant port culture, Buffalo was not noted for its lack of
saloons. In 1880, the city directory enumerated a total of 1,042 saloons,
with 6.72 saloons per 1,000 individuals.[28] In the First Ward for that year,
there were 24 boarding houses and 119 saloons listed. "No nice Irish
woman would set foot inside one," said Rose Shanahan, noting the surprise of her Uncle Otto, a German, in whose culture the saloon was a
place for the family as a whole.[29] Irish dock laborers rubbed shoulders
with the aldermen they helped elect in these dimly lit and male-domi-
nated spaces. The irregular nature of grain scooping and other dock-
based work meant that workers often utilized the saloon as a cafeteria,
a hiring location where networks were forged and news was spread, a
place to sleep, and a location for general conviviality.

A wide breadth of social classes was present within the average First
Ward kin network, due to the various settlement and economic mobility experiences of individuals and families. Each family, it seems, had its
"poor" and "well-off" cousins. The often turbulent lives of Rose Shanahan's relatives suggest that alcohol-fueled domestic violence remained
a pervasive problem in the community:

> The way Paddy [O'Farrell] beat his wife when he got a bit of drink in him
> and the way she beat the children, even without any drink in her at all,
> and the language they all used, were a disgrace to St. Bridget's parish. But
> what could she expect, and they coming from The Beach? Nothing but
> squatters down there, the lot of them.[30]

In contrast, she had cousins on Buffalo's West Side—a priest, a doctor,
and a lawyer—all of whom graduated from Georgetown and, as Shana-

TABLE 2

OCCUPATIONAL DISTRIBUTION OF HOUSEHOLD HEADS

IN BUFFALO'S FIRST WARD, 1880

	All		Irish		Non-Irish	
	N	%	N	%	N	%
Professional and managerial	8	2.8	7	3.5	1	1.2
Self-employed	33	11.5	19	9.4	14	16.5
Clerical	9	3.1	5	2.5	4	4.7
Lake-based employment	25	8.7	15	7.4	10	11.7
Building trades	25	8.7	12	5.9	13	15.3
Skilled/semi-skilled	47	16.4	25	12.4	22	25.9
Unskilled labor	96	33.5	77	38.1	19	22.3
No stated occupation	44	15.3	42	20.8	2	2.4
Total	287	100.0	202	100.0	85	100.0

Source: U.S. federal census manuscripts, 10 percent household sample.

han notes, "there was no keeping up with."[31] The West Side emerged as a secondary settlement area for the upwardly mobile Irish in the 1890s, where they partly displaced an older American population that was expanding northward.[32] Activities in the labor market of Irish males and females helped to further shape these experiences and perceptions of life and territory beyond the First Ward.

The Structure of Labor in the First Ward

Nonetheless, the First Ward remained the key reception area for Irish immigrants, and it remained solidly working-class. As Table 2 illustrates, the Irish there were likelier than the non-Irish to occupy unskilled work (38.1 percent versus 22.4 percent). Conversely, the non-Irish were more concentrated in skilled trades such as machinist, blacksmith, shoemaker, and the building trades, while both groups were represented in Great Lakes-based occupations such as ship captain, ship carpenter, caulker, and sailor. The Irish shared with the other groups what little of a middle-class of grocers and saloonkeepers remained.

The Buffalo Irish middle-class in 1880, then, had become only marginally more substantial since the 1850s, when Thomas D'Arcy McGee's wife complained during their sojourn in the city that "there were few of the type of people she hoped to befriend among her fellow Irish."[33] The milieu of the First Ward was akin to a small industrial town where, rather than the Satanic mill, the Irish lived in the shadow of the grain elevator. Many Irish immigrant livelihoods depended on the latter building, developed by Joseph Dart in 1842. In 1881, the "rambler" wrote:

The grain-shovellers, of whom there are thousands, are almost all Irish-men, the "Bosses" being of the same nationality. The "Boss" yields auto-cratic sway. To him is confided the task of hiring men; and being invari-ably the proprietor of a boarding house and lager beer saloon, he protects his interests to the extent of employing no man who will not accept his board and drink his beer. . . . [Thus the scooper] very often finds himself at the end of a season, owing to the avarice and cupidity of which he is the victim, not only out of money, but deeply sunk in debt.[34]

The market for grain scoopers was, on this evidence, biased in favor of single and intemperate Irish males. The birthplace and marital status of boarders in fourteen boarding houses and family homes on Ohio Street are shown in Table 3. Most of those providing shelter were Irish, and while they did not take in Irish-born boarders exclusively, the latter dominated the scene, representing just under half the total. The non-Irish boarding house keepers still took in a lot of Irish people. The occu-pation of one of these Irish household heads, John Hoolahan, was given simply as "laborer," but his provision of space for ten boarders highlights the degree to which an informal market for shelter existed. These board-

TABLE 3

CHARACTERISTICS OF SELECTED LODGINGS
ON OHIO STREET, BUFFALO, 1880

House No. on Ohio St.	Occupation of Proprietor	Birthplace of Proprietor	Total No. of Boarders*	No. of Irish-born Boarders*
34	Boarding. Ho./Saloon	Ireland	10 (2)	4 (2)
38	Boss shoveller	Ireland	15 (3)	12 (3)
40	Boarding. Ho./Saloon	Germany	25 (4)	8 (4)
44	Boarding House	Germany	19 (2)	4 (1)
54	Boarding. Ho./Saloon	Ireland	5 (1)	4 (1)
160	Laborer	Ireland	10	7
170	Keeping house	Scotland	17	0
172	Boss shoveller	Ireland	19 (1)	18 (1)
189	Boss shoveller	Ireland	17 (1)	8
286	Grocer	Ireland	26	16
336	Saloon keeper	New York	14 (1)	0
370	Boarding. Ho./Saloon	Baden	8 (1)	0
390	Elevator boss	Ireland	32	27
496	Laborer	Ireland	4	1

Source: U.S. federal census manuscripts.
*Number of married or widowed boarders shown in parentheses; otherwise all are single.

ers contributed much to the community, bringing news directly from the Old World and, frequently later, their friends and relations also. In addition, they provided a valuable income supplement to the family-based economies of the district's working class.

Direct links between boarding house keepers and the waterfront labor market served to keep elevator jobs in Irish hands. John Haley, for example, was an elevator boss who took in thirty-two boarders, twenty-seven of whom were single Irish-born males. His lodgings were teeming with men in their twenties and thirties with last names such as Shaughnessy, Hickey, McCarthy, Griffin, O'Day, Hennessy, Dolan, and O'Grady. "Long hours for little pay," was how Kerry-born Thomas Evans described his days as a scooper.[35] With such a plentiful labor supply, this was not surprising. As one local historian has stated: "It was quite easy for a contractor to reduce wages by hiring all Mayo men and then inviting the Galway immigrants to take the jobs at a lower wage."[36]

Ownership of a saloon was viewed as a key avenue of upward mobility within the community, and Irishmen who graduated to this status had themselves worked on the docks or in the elevators and mills. Yet what became known as the "boss-saloon" system was clearly exploitative. Despite sharing a common ethnic background with their employers, class-based loyalties developed among the Irish scoopers and other dockworkers in the 1890s, culminating in the strike of 1899. The social center of St. Bridget's parish, the hall, was also the center of scoopers' meetings during the strike. Almost ten thousand were involved and the strike was successful in achieving reform of the system.[37] Thereafter, the unionized scoopers were paid in an office rather than over a saloon counter. The saloons continued to serve their social function, however, and the intemperance problem persisted within many of the ward's families.

At an individual level, the gender-based journey to work shaped a series of perceptions and experiences of the city. As in other American cities, domestic service was the principal occupation of unmarried Irish females in Buffalo in the late-nineteenth and early-twentieth centuries. The Buffalo labor market for domestic service produced a geography of movement that connected the worlds of Irish working-class families and Yankee upper-class families. This connection brought an awareness of other parts of Buffalo and their social characteristics from which most First Ward males, with shorter journeys to work, remained remote. Work on the waterfront tied the latter's everyday lives to that particular district; few were compelled to commute outside it. In contrast, John Feather has noted that First Ward girls left home (before the age of eighteen) almost always to become live-in domestic servants in the homes of the native-born citizens. However, this was not a permanent occupation for most women; by age 21, over half were married . . . women usually spent several years learning the values and ways of life of the native-born Buffalo elite.[38]

This reality is also reflected in *Days Beyond Recall,* where Rose Shanahan's eldest aunt, Biddy, works as a cook for Judge Harrison Lovett, who lives on Delaware Avenue, portrayed as a member of one of Buffalo's oldest families with New Hampshire roots. Through her aunt, "Rose knew almost as much about Delaware Avenue as she did about the First Ward, though in quite a different way. To her, the names associated with these houses were as magically remote and fascinating as those in a fairy tale."[39] The trajectories of residential movement also connected the First Ward with the city's West Side where, not surprisingly, the attempts of the "lace-curtain" Irish to impose respectable middle-class values often made them the object of scorn back in the southern district.

The Political Scene

The Irish, forming a mass proletariat in American cities by the late 1850s and 1860s, were the key ethnic group of "ex-plebes" identified by Robert Dahl who used their sheer numbers and geographical concentration to depose the business and industry men as local political leaders.[40] Their influence in local political structures, and those of the Democratic Party, in particular, served to increase the group's presence in public employment in Buffalo by the early twentieth century.

Although the Sheehan brothers, John C. and William F., the sons of a Cork-born immigrant, were key shapers of the "fortress of working-class Democrats in Irish South Buffalo," there was some degree of political pragmatism that disrupted this familiar alignment.[41] The politics of popular First Ward Republican politician Jack White, for example, was imbued with the same machine-style pragmatism of the Democrats, whereby "it was the first ward first and the party later with both Republican and Democrat leaders."[42] Joining the Republican party out of a desire to accrue the advantages of leading the minority rather than the majority party on the local scene, White remained on Buffalo's board of aldermen for almost a quarter of a century. William "Fingy" Conners was a former stevedore who, after making a fortune as a labor contractor and saloonkeeper, became a local newspaper mogul and politician. His unpopularity during the 1899 strike exposed the tensions between the Irish workers and the middle-class "élite" in the neighborhood, many of whom had little time for trade unions. Conners's political strategy was also one of pragmatism, as he switched his loyalties to Democrat from Republican, becoming deeply involved in local and state politics in the early-twentieth century.

Leadership of the Irish working-class in the First Ward was contested not only between rival political factions but often between these and local clergymen. Serving as parish priest in St. Bridget's from 1895 to 1897, when he was appointed Bishop of Buffalo, the Ontario-born Fr. James Quigley described with disapproval how "men marched like cattle to caucuses and election booths."[43] A central figure in the 1899 strike by grain scoopers and freight handlers on the city's waterfront, Quigley defended the workers against the Irish contracting and saloon-keeping interests, exclaiming, "I intend to adopt the docks as my parish, and the dockmen as my parishioners."[44] Quigley's dislike of local political corruption and patronage practices as well as his support of organized labor make him one of the key liberal figures within the American Catholic hierarchy in the late-nineteenth and early-twentieth centuries.

The numerous social networks created by Irish ward-based politics meant that political appointments were commonplace. Mark Stern has estimated that, in Buffalo, the proportion of Irish-born in government employment rose from 2 percent in 1855 to 21 percent by 1915.[45] That the public school curriculum was taught to the children of the First Ward by teachers of Irish ancestry, if not birth, owed much to the patronage of the local political system. The Republican White apparently "managed to have more teachers on the payroll than any other individual . . . during the . . . 80's when the school department was a Democratic political preserve. . . . It was the same with the police department."[46]

Contrary to an earlier school of thought, then, the Irish in Buffalo had a significant interaction with the city's public school system, not only as pupils but as teachers.[47] Irish female teachers, mainly second generation, slotted into a system of public education in Buffalo where many pupils were of Irish background. There were four public schools in the First Ward in 1880 (Figure 2). In number 34, on Elk Street near Louisiana Street, which was described as being "overcrowded with pupils" in 1881 and where apparently "all of the teachers were of Irish descent," 349/404 (86.4 percent) of the pupils' parents were Irish-born.[48] In schools 3, 4, and 33, the figures were 246/373 (66 percent), 574/903 (63.6 percent), and 185/350 (52.9 percent), respectively. The redistribution of patronage did not trickle indiscriminately down to all members of the community electorate, however. Although becoming a schoolteacher was a key aspiration for second-generation Irish-American

females, in *Days Beyond Recall,* Rose herself "might have been one, had
the Shanahans at that time commanded enough political pull to wangle
an appointment."[49]

Patronage also ensured that the "Irish Cop" was well represented at
the upper levels of the police hierarchy in Buffalo as well as at the neighborhood scale. Five of the twelve detectives at headquarters were born
in Ireland, including the assistant superintendent, Patrick Cusack,
whose family arrived in Buffalo from County Clare in 1852 when he was
thirteen years old.[50] The annual police and fire service reports provide
listings of officers by name and precinct or station. The results indicate
that the allocation of policemen and firemen followed the general ethnic geography of the city. It seems clear that those who knew their home
turf were stationed there, since most First Ward policemen were of Irish
descent. In 1890, at precinct number 7, 455 Louisiana Street, the Lieu-
tenant was Irish-born Michael Regan; of the twenty-four patrolmen stationed there, fifteen (63 percent) had distinctively "Irish" last names.
Nineteen of twenty-four staff (83 percent) at two fire engine company
stations in the First Ward, numbers 8 and 10, were of Irish extraction in
1900.[51]

The Twentieth Century: Enduring Irishness

Compared to the period 1840–1900, by the early twentieth century
Buffalo's capacity to attract Irish immigrants was in decline. By 1910, the
number of Irish-born in the city had fallen to 9,423 from 11,664 in 1890.
The share of the Irish-born in Buffalo's population fell from 10 percent
in 1870 to just 2 percent in 1910 and, during the same time period, the
Irish proportion of the foreign-born in the city fell from 24 percent to 8
percent. By this stage, Poles and Italians had replaced the Irish and Germans as the "foreigners" in the city, as seen through the eyes of the
long-established Protestant élite. Aside from the Hungarian-born furnace workers who came to Uniontown after 1900, however, new arrivals
did little to disturb the established Irish neighborhood of the First Ward
through any process of residential succession. Neither did the African-
American migrants of the 1920s, who succeeded the German population
on the city's Near East Side, dislodge the Irish-American First Warders.

By the early twentieth century, three generations of Irish were resident in the First Ward. Only the first two generations are directly meas-
urable, however, and they constituted half of all households in the area
in 1910 (Table 4). Between these two generations of Irish, the share of
households with an Irish-born head declined from 81.7 percent in 1880
to 58.2 percent in 1910. Third-generation households are subsumed

TABLE 4

ETHNIC ORIGIN OF FIRST WARD HOUSEHOLD HEADS, 1910

Ethnic origin	N	%
Irish	134	50.0
German	21	7.8
American	44	16.4
English	9	3.4
Scottish	14	5.2
Canadian	20	7.5
Other Europe	26	9.7
Total	268	100.0

Source: U.S. federal census manuscripts, 10 percent household sample.

under the "American" ethnic origin in Tables 2 and 4, a group whose share of the community rose from 4.5 percent in 1880 to 16.4 percent in 1910. Thus, the true (i.e., three-generation) "Irish" proportion of the area's ethnicity in 1910 is probably closer to 60 percent.

The Irishness of the First Ward was maintained despite high levels of out-migration from the district since its settlement in the 1840s. Rather than being an uprooted mass of disoriented foreigners, unable to adjust quickly to life in the New World, it is now clear that the Irish and other immigrants were aware of the American capitalist economic system and did not choose their destinations randomly.[52] As Golab has written, "Once in a city, immigrants did not scatter randomly around the urban landscape. Their ultimate destination was (or became) an ethnic neighborhood."[53] New arrivals to the First Ward acted as a balance to the many who departed for other, less congested parts of Buffalo, or for other cities. Of the seventy Irish-born household heads sampled in 1910 whose year of immigration was recorded, 40 percent arrived before 1880, 52.9 percent between 1880 and 1900, and 7.1 percent since 1900. New immigrants were drawn to the area for its ethnic familiarity and labor demand, particularly in grain scooping, which remained a secure employment base for newcomers along with work in the steelworks and flour mills, and on the docks and railroads. Receipts of flour, corn, and grain by the port of Buffalo all increased during the period 1886–1901, keeping labor demand buoyant.[54]

That it remained an area of primary settlement for many Irish immigrants helps to explain the First Ward's continued status as a working-class locality in the early twentieth century (Table 5). Although the Irish had improved their representation in skilled and semi-skilled labor since 1880, almost 30 percent of their household heads were still

TABLE 5

OCCUPATIONAL DISTRIBUTION OF HOUSEHOLD HEADS
IN BUFFALO'S FIRST WARD, 1910

	All		Irish		Non-Irish	
	N	%	N	%	N	%
Professional and managerial	18	6.7	10	7.5	8	6.0
Self-employed	21	7.8	10	7.5	11	8.2
Clerical	5	1.9	3	2.2	2	1.5
Lake-based employment	15	5.6	9	6.7	6	4.5
Building trades	11	4.1	6	4.5	5	3.7
Skilled/semi-skilled	84	31.3	34	25.4	50	37.3
Unskilled labor	72	26.8	38	28.4	34	25.4
No stated occupation	42	15.7	24	17.9	18	13.4
Total	268	100.0	134	100.0	134	100.0

Source: U.S. federal census manuscripts, 10 percent household sample.

engaged in unskilled labor, mainly grain scooping.[55] Chain migration
drew new immigrants to the First Ward when others moved out. Many
"greenhorns" got their start in grain scooping upon arrival in the city,
and they used their savings to finance the passage for other kin. For
example, the savings from scooping grain acquired by Thomas Evans
from Castlemaine, Co. Kerry, who arrived in 1885, were first directed
toward securing passage for his fiancée, Nora Fitzgerald. Five brothers
followed Evans to the First Ward and to unskilled work on the waterfront, while Evans's own path out of unskilled labor was, typically,
through self-employment as a saloon owner. His brother Michael did
even better: "being the best businessman of the six . . . , [he] became the
owner of a tavern . . . at 326 Ohio Street and a number of apartment
buildings and houses."[56]

    Anthony McGowan, an immigrant from Kilmihill, Co. Clare, who
arrived in 1886, also graduated from dockworker to saloonkeeper. His
story demonstrates the saliency of transatlantic kin and friendship connections that served as a form of social capital as well as the importance
of the relatively small Irish middle-class as social agents and employment brokers. McGowan followed his brother to the First Ward and,
shortly after arrival, started work as a grain scooper. He had been active
locally in the Democratic Party, working as a committeeman in the First
Ward shortly after arrival. His talents were rewarded by John J. Kennedy,
a former scooper and city alderman, saloon owner, and freight contractor, who gave McGowan a break. McGowan became the manager of
Kennedy's Seabreeze Hotel, and opened his own tavern in 1897 at 206

Elk Street. The rise of this one-time grain scooper in local politics continued in 1908 when he was appointed to the Department of Markets and served as assistant superintendent in charge of the Elk Street market for thirty-one years.[57]

Once some families had accumulated wealth, however, they moved out of the district. Although an "Irish world" in many respects, the ward had a number of undesirable characteristics. Family dissolution, crime, alcoholism, poverty, and disease were rampant. Dock-based work was hazardous. Men would fall into the harbor and drown. Air quality was poor with "the strong malty smell . . . floating through countless kitchen windows . . . as much a part of the First Ward streets as their horse-troughs and their carbon arc lights."[58] Tuberculosis and asphyxiation were widespread among the scoopers; the grain dust would get into their lungs and cause asthma. Thomas Evans witnessed the death of his wife and two children from tuberculosis; three out of five children from his second marriage also succumbed to the disease at an early age.[59] Nonetheless, many of those who chose to remain in the area were rewarded by homeowner status. Of the one hundred thirty-four Irish household heads sampled in 1910, forty-five (33.6 percent) were homeowners whose endurance helped to cement the Irish Catholic identity of the neighborhood, which was also solidified by an apparently high rate of intra-ethnic marriage. Locals had a saying, "Never throw a stone . . . you might hit your cousin."[60]

The First Ward and South Buffalo's enduring reputation as an Irish blue-collar area was further strengthened by the opening of the Seneca Street streetcar in 1896, which was followed by the eastward extension of its housing stock south of the Buffalo River. A mostly Irish-American "wedge" in the southern part of the city was thus created, with the grain elevator district of the Old First Ward as its apex. The contractor William H. Fitzpatrick, who was responsible for much of the new construction, was also a key figure in the Erie County executive of the Democratic Party, whose close involvement with municipal issues would have benefited his speculative activities. In a recent study of the New York Irish, this process of Irish-American real estate interests advancing suburbanization has been dubbed "bricks-and-mortar Catholicism."[61] In South Buffalo, Fitzpatrick "built hundreds of houses . . . laid out streets in cow pastures . . . [and] was never known to foreclose a mortgage."[62]

The Catholic parochial infrastructure expanded to meet the needs of the increasing population of communicants. "St. Stephen's-in-the-Valley" was created for the furnace workers of Uniontown in 1875 with one hundred fifteen members and a brick church with frame-built school at rear. In 1900 Our Lady of Perpetual Help (known locally as "Pet's") was carved from St. Bridget's parish and "the first Masses said . . . in a wood-frame building on Louisiana Street" with the founding priest, Father O'Connell, initially using a local saloon as a rectory.[63] Eastward population movement from the First Ward into South Buffalo was matched by parochial expansions and restructurings, with St. Teresa's and Holy Family parishes formed in 1897 and 1902, respectively. The Sisters of Mercy, invited to Buffalo by Bishop Timon, took charge of parochial schools in the First Ward. In the early twentieth century, their schools in the four parishes of South Buffalo had about five hundred pupils on average, and for the pupils of Irish-American descent, the culture of the homeland was not neglected, since in addition to learning "American songs and [idolizing] George Washington . . . they also learned Irish songs and honored the saints and heroes of Irish history."[64]

Until the 1950s, the stability of the waterfront labor market contributed to the development of a community of blue-collar Irish Catholic homeowners and their descendants in the First Ward and South Buffalo. Prior to the completion of the St. Lawrence Seaway in 1959, grain scoopers remained in demand in the First Ward, and the occupation was maintained as a mainly Irish preserve.[65] Male and female graduates of schools in South Buffalo in the 1940s and 1950s frequently described the First Ward and South Buffalo with reference to four principal characteristics: Irish, Catholic, Democratic, and blue-collar.[66] In contrast to inner-city Protestant churches, which suburbanized along with their congregations through the twentieth century, St. Thomas' Episcopal church in the First Ward was praised for resisting the temptation to move from what was "traditionally [an] Irish Catholic sector of the city."[67]

Conclusion

The First Ward established itself as the major Irish Catholic section of Buffalo in the nineteenth century. Always overwhelmingly working-class and with mainly Democratic political loyalties, it comprised a number of discrete social areas as well as a port-based labor market conducive to unskilled and semi-skilled labor. It was an area of primary settlement for Irish immigrants to Buffalo, and the close relationship between work and home produced an occasionally tense coexistence of ethnic and class loyalties, shown most clearly in the 1899 strike. Stable labor demand fused with kin-based chain migration networks, information flows, and patronage and employment practices to maintain the district's Irish identity into the twentieth century. Throughout the last one hundred fifty years or so, the residential conservatism of successive waves of homeowners has also contributed to the neighborhood, by now a sub-area of a larger South Buffalo section, so that it has become one of the oldest and most enduring blue-collar Irish Catholic neighborhoods in the United States. This neighborhood profile confounds the impression of a spatially assimilated Irish ethnic group in twentieth-century urban America. It is hoped that additional research on Irish communities using the time span studied here will sharpen our understanding of the "place" of the Irish in nineteenth- and twentieth-century American urban space.

NOTES

1. See, for example, the essays in Timothy J. Meagher, ed., *From Paddy to Studs: Irish-American Communities in the Turn-of-the-Century Era, 1880 to 1920* (New York: Greenwood Press, 1986). See also Michael F. Funchion, "Irish Chicago: Church, Homeland, Politics, and Class—The Shaping of an Ethnic Group, 1870–1900," in Peter d'A. Jones and Melvin G. Holli, eds., *Ethnic Chicago* (Grand Rapids: William B. Eerdmans, 1985); Andrew C. Holman, "Different Feelings: Corktown and the Catholic Irish in Early Hamilton, 1832–1847," *Canadian Journal of Irish Studies* 23 (1997), 41–68; Sallie A. Marston, "Neighborhood and Politics: Irish Ethnicity in Nineteenth Century Lowell, Massachusetts," *Annals of the Association of American Geographers* 78 (1988), 414–32.

2. Kenneth A. Scherzer, *The Unbounded Community: Neighborhood Life and Social Structure in New York City, 1830–1875* (Durham, N.C.: Duke University Press, 1993); Sam Bass Warner and Colin Burke, "Cultural Change and the Ghetto," *Journal of Contemporary History* 4 (1969), 173–87.

3. See Sam Bass Warner, *Streetcar Suburbs* (Cambridge, Mass.: Harvard University Press, 1962); Olivier Zunz, *The Changing Face of Inequality: Urbanization, Industrial Development and Immigrants in Detroit* (Chicago: University of Chicago Press, 1982).

4. Paul Cressey, "Population Succession in Chicago," *American Journal of Sociology* 44 (1938–39), 66. See also David Ward, *Poverty and Ethnicity in the American City 1840–1925: Changing Conceptions of the Slum and the Ghetto* (New York: Cambridge University Press, 1989) and Ernest W. Burgess, "The Growth of the City: An Introduction to a Research Project," in Robert E. Park, Ernest W. Burgess, and Roderick D. McKenzie, *The City* (Chicago: University of Chicago Press, 1925).

5. The "Old First Ward" is the modern term given to the district under study. It now forms part of a wider area of "South Buffalo," whose identity remains primarily Irish Catholic.

6. Roger B. Dooley, *Days Beyond Recall* (Milwaukee: Bruce Publishing Co., 1949).

7. William E. Mallory and Paul Simpson-Housley, "Preface" in William E. Mallory and Paul Simpson-Housley, eds., *Geography and Literature: A Meeting of the Disciplines* (Syracuse: Syracuse University Press, 1987), xi.

8. Elwin Powell, "The Evolution of the American City and the Emergence of

Anomie: A Culture Case Study of Buffalo, New York, 1810–1910," *British Journal of Sociology* 13 (1962), 160.

9. George E. Condon, *Stars in the Water: The Story of the Erie Canal* (New York: Doubleday, 1974), 150. See also 62–68.

10. Quoted in David Gerber, *The Making of an American Pluralism: Buffalo 1820–1860* (Ithaca, N.Y.: Cornell University Press, 1988), 122.

11. The Orange Order, for example, an organization that was central to political life in nearby Toronto, was weak in Buffalo. Only four lodges were in existence by the latter decades of the nineteenth century. My thanks to Professor Cecil Houston, University of Toronto, for his assistance.

12. *Buffalo Evening News*, 13 May 1972.

13. Laurence A. Glasco, "The Life Cycles and Household Structure of American Ethnic Groups: Irish, Germans, and Native-born Whites in Buffalo, New York, 1855," *Journal of Urban History* 1 (1975), 341.

14. See William Jenkins, "Geographical and Social Mobility among the Irish in the United States and Canada: A Comparative Study of Toronto, Ontario, and Buffalo, New York, 1880–1910," Ph.D. dissertation, University of Toronto, 2001, Ch. 4; Laurence A. Glasco, "Ethnicity and Occupation in the Mid-Nineteenth Century: Irish, Germans, and Native-born Whites in Buffalo, New York," in Richard L. Ehrlich, ed., *Immigrants in Industrial America 1850–1920* (Charlottesville, Va.: University Press of Virginia, 1978), 153 n.

15. Gerber, *The Making of an American Pluralism*; Andrew P. Yox, "Bonds of Community: Buffalo's German Element, 1853–1871," *New York History* 66 (1985), 141–63.

16. A second-generation Irish household was defined in terms of the head's father only.

17. *Irish Canadian*, 14 July 1881.

18. Joan Scahill, "The Mutual Rowing Club," *Buffalo Irish Times*, June/July 1999.

19. John V. Cotter and Larry L. Patrick, "Disease and Ethnicity in an Urban Environment," *Annals of the Association of American Geographers* 71 (1981), 40–49.

20. Josephus L. Larned, *History of Buffalo* Vol. 2 (New York: The Progress of the Empire State Co., 1911), 653.

21. The placing of these names is based on information given in Mary C. Bonner, "The Way of the Ward," manuscript, n.d., Special Collections, Buffalo and Erie County Public Library. See also *Buffalo Evening News*, 13 May 1972, for a special supplement on the Buffalo Irish.

22. See "Irish Immigration to Buffalo's First Ward," manuscript, n.d., Buffalo Irish Center library (hereafter Evans family manuscript).

23. See a trilogy of articles, "Uniontown: Part of the Old First Ward," by Edward J. Patton in the *Buffalo Irish Times*, January, February/March, and April/May 1993.

24. See J. David Valaik, *Celebrating God's Life in Us: The Catholic Diocese of Buffalo 1847–1997* (Buffalo: The Heritage Press, 1997).

25. Dooley, *Days Beyond Recall*, 7.

26. Ibid., 40–41.

27. James R. Barrett, *Work and Community in the Jungle: Chicago's Packinghouse Workers* (Urbana, Ill.: University of Illinois Press, 1987), Ch 3.

28. *Buffalo City Directory*, 1880, 748–54.

29. Dooley, *Days Beyond Recall*, 20.

30. Ibid., 4.

31. Ibid., 1.

32. Jenkins, "Geographical and Social Mobility," Ch. 6.

33. Gerber, *The Making of an American Pluralism*, 142.

34. *Irish Canadian*, 14 July 1881.

35. Evans family manuscript.

36. Edward Patton, "Shanty Life Along The Sea Wall," *Buffalo Irish Times*, June/July 1995.

37. See Brenda K. Shelton, "The Buffalo Grain Shovellers' Strike of 1899," *Labor History* 9 (1968), 210–38.

38. John Feather, "The Old First Ward," in Tim Tielman, ed., *Buffalo's Waterfront: A Guidebook* (Buffalo: Preservation Coalition of Erie County, 1990), 65.

39. Dooley, *Days Beyond Recall*, 23.

40. Robert Dahl, *Who Governs? Democracy and Power in an American City* (New Haven: Yale University Press, 1961).

41. Mark Goldman, *High Hopes: The Rise and Decline of Buffalo, New York* (Albany: State University of New York Press, 1983), 167.

42. *Buffalo Times*, 27 June 1933.

43. *Buffalo Commercial Advertiser*, 18 May 1899.

44. Ibid.

45. Mark J. Stern, *Society and Family Strategy: Erie County, New York, 1850–1920* (Albany: State University of New York Press, 1987), 36.

46. *Buffalo Times*, 27 June 1933.

47. Maxine S. Seller, *Ethnic Communities and Education in Buffalo, New York: Politics, Power, and Group Identity 1838–1979* (Buffalo: State University of New York at Buffalo, Buffalo Community Studies Graduate Group, Occasional Paper No. 1, 1979), 25–30.

48. John Downey, "Some of the Neglected Areas of the First Ward," manuscript, Special Collections, Buffalo and Erie County Public Library, City of Buffalo, *Annual Report of the Superintendent of Education* (Buffalo: Young, Lockwood & Co., 1882), 162.

49. Dooley, *Days Beyond Recall*, 11.

50. Mark Hubbell, *Our Police and Our City* (Buffalo: Bensler & Wesley, 1893), 315–59.

51. See *Annual Report of the Buffalo Board of Police 1890* (Buffalo: Buffalo Board of Police, 1891) and *Annual Report of the Commissioners of the Buffalo Fire Department 1900* (Buffalo: Buffalo Fire Department, 1901). Since ethnicity is not given, it was inferred by last name. While this may underestimate the numbers of Irish present, it was felt that the resulting distortion would have little effect on the pattern found.

52. John Bodnar, *The Transplanted: A History of Immigrants in Urban America* (Bloomington: Indiana University Press, 1985).

53. Caroline Golab, *Immigrant Destinations* (Philadelphia: Temple University Press, 1977), 111.

54. Richmond C. Hill, *Twentieth Century Buffalo: An Illustrated Compendium of her Municipal, Financial, Industrial, Commercial, and General Public Interests* (Buffalo: J.N. Matthews Co., 1902), 143.

55. It can be argued that some third-generation Irish-Americans could have been involved in unskilled work, thereby increasing this percentage. Unfortunately, due to problems of identification, these are subsumed within the "non-Irish" category.

56. Evans family manuscript.

57. Stephen Powell, *Rushing the Growler: A History of Brewing in Buffalo* (Buffalo: E.S. Ferguson Library, 1996), 18–20.

58. Evans family manuscript.

59. Ibid.

60. *Buffalo Evening News*, 13 May 1972.

61. Marion R. Casey, "From the East Side to the Seaside: Irish Americans on the Move in New York City," in Ronald H. Bayor and Timothy J. Meagher, eds., *The New York Irish* (Baltimore: Johns Hopkins University Press, 1997), 399.

62. *Buffalo Times*, 7 January 1932.

63. Evans family manuscript.

64. Sarah Missik, "Education in South Buffalo," unpublished paper, State University of New York at Buffalo, quoted in Seller, *Ethnic Communities and Education*, 31.

65. See the recollections of James "Jim Boy" Smith in David Isay, *Holding On* (New York: W.W. Norton, 1996), 107–10.

66. M. Carol Herwood, *All the Old Familiar Places: Memories of South Buffalo* (Buffalo: self-published, 1997).

67. *Buffalo Courier*, 28 December 1953.

Young Irish Workers:
Class Implications of Men's and Women's Experiences in Gilded Age Chicago

PATRICIA KELLEHER

DISCUSSION OF NINETEENTH- and early twentieth-century Irish Americans' "class"—their status as well as their behaviors and attitudes concerning class mobility and working-class solidarity—has been vexed and contentious. The topic's inherent complexity, in combination with the variety of perspectives brought to its analysis, has produced a welter of claims and arguments. Some historians assume a norm of upward mobility and view the Irish as laggards. In contrast, other scholars tell a success story in which Irish immigrants, and especially their descendants, struggled and eventually achieved their goals of respectability and upward mobility. Another contingent has discerned the emergence of an Irish-American radical working-class consciousness that broadened Irish workers' perspectives and encouraged solidarity with members of other groups who challenged the inequities of industrial capitalism. Still others report that a co-opted Irish working class had fallen in line behind the dictates of a hegemonic Catholic middle class by the early twentieth century.[1]

Despite these differences, most scholars' attempts to explain the Irish encounter with class in America have focused on men's experiences and perspectives. This article contributes to the discussion by clarifying Irish Americans' class standing and by demonstrating that both an appreciation of the complexity of the Irish-American population and attention to specific historical circumstances must inform any analysis of Irish responses to America's class system. I will illustrate the importance of age, generation, and gender, as well as specific context, by focusing on the experiences of young immigrant workers in Chicago in 1880— during the pivotal period known as the Gilded Age.

Class and Occupational Status in the
Late Nineteenth and Early Twentieth Centuries

This exploration must begin by assessing the class "position" of the American Irish. That task alone is a challenge, for the Irish in America were not a monolithic group, and class-based attributes that were common during the famine era were less common by the 1910s. In an effort to provide a basis from which to proceed, I will begin with some general information about both Irish emigration to North America and quantitative measures of Irish immigrants' occupational status in American society.[2]

About one million Irish crossed the Atlantic during the prefamine era (1815–45). Protestants from Ulster dominated at first; but Catholics swelled the emigrant stream by the 1830s. While moderately "better-off" people continued to seek their fortunes in America, less prosperous Catholics eventually dominated the outflow. There was some variety in class background among the prefamine Catholic Irish who established beachheads in the US. Furthermore, even those with few resources usually came from areas of Ireland that had undergone Anglicization and commercialization. They were at least familiar with, if not reconciled to, dominant cultural norms within the US. Despite these relative advantages, turbulence among Irish laborers on public-works projects and in cities broadcast high levels of poverty and dissatisfaction among North America's Catholic Irish well before the Great Famine.[3]

Famine-era migrants flattened the existing class segmentation among the Catholic Irish in North America. Repeated failures of Ireland's potato crops set off a flood of 1.8 million people into North American ports in the decade after 1845. While the most destitute could not reach America and a fair number of "better-class" Catholics abandoned famine-ridden Ireland, the migrants who reached North America during the mid- to late 1840s and early 1850s helped to create a distinctively "Irish" American lower class. Famine immigrants were, on average, even poorer and less prepared than their predecessors in terms of language, culture, and work skills to accommodate easily to American conditions. Many of them were customary rather than devotional Catholics, and between one-fourth and one-third still spoke Irish. In addition, an unusually large proportion of famine-era immigrants arrived in families with young and elderly dependents. The adjustment process was painful. Immigrant mortality was high and, decades later, survivors still bore the trauma and bitterness of their experiences.[4]

Irish emigration continued on a massive scale after the famine, ebbing and flowing in response to socio-economic stresses in Ireland

and opportunities in the US. About 3.5 million Irish arrived in North America between 1851 and 1921. Few of the middling orders emigrated, but members of the poorer farming classes poured out. The proportions of people who traveled in family groups declined while those of working-age adolescents and adults increased. Males dominated as migrants among other nationalities, but the nineteenth- and early twentieth-century Irish emigrant stream was distinctive in that the sexes reached near parity in numbers. By the turn of the twentieth century Irish immigrants were likely to be young (age fifteen to twenty-four), unmarried, technically unskilled, Catholic, and from the poverty-mired west of Ireland.[5]

Given these migration patterns, Irish-born US residents in 1880 would have included a considerable proportion of famine survivors. Large numbers of Irish arrived in the US from the 1850s to the early 1870s, but immigration dropped off sharply in response to the severe depression of 1873–78. As a result, Irish-born fifteen- to twenty-four-year-olds would have included a portion that had immigrated years earlier as children in family groups as well as very recent arrivals. Overall, the Irish-born population of the US in 1880 constituted an established group. The massive influx of Irish people into the US had begun decades earlier. Immigrants had had time to settle in, and owing to the depression of the 1870s, the proportion of "greenhorns" in the population was unusually low.[6] Establishment, however, does not imply prosperity, and "upward mobility" is an unacceptably narrow gauge for the measurement of a people's success.

Scholarly attempts to describe Irish America's socio-economic status in the nineteenth and early twentieth centuries have provoked much controversy. Implicit, and sometimes explicit, disparagement crept into some scholars' depictions of the prevalence of social problems and low-status employment among the Irish.[7] In response, other scholars, who were often Irish-American or Irish, produced studies that forced revisions of the established interpretation but did not debunk it. For example, Lawrence McCaffrey's work demonstrates that a few case studies cannot convey the complexity of an ethnic group's roles in American history. But David N. Doyle overstates the case when he claims that "Irish America in 1900 . . . had attained relative occupational parity with native white America . . . ; the same proportion of its male workforce was engaged in middle-class, lower middle-class and unskilled laboring occupations as . . . native-born whites of native parentage."[8]

The large-scale arrival of poorer Catholics who took up hard and dangerous laboring work well before the famine is now well recognized. Similarly, it is indisputable that a massive influx of famine immigrants crowded into low-status manual work. The extent to which opportunities for the Irish varied by region and the amount of upward mobility that had occurred between the 1850s and the 1910s remain debatable. Thorny methodological issues concerning occupational-classification categories complicate the discussion. Nevertheless, it is clear that immigrant males remained very heavily concentrated in low-status work. As late as 1910, about one-fifth of employed immigrant Irishmen held positions that could be classified as "nonmanual," but nearly 60 percent clustered in "unskilled" and "semiskilled" occupations. On the other hand, the maturing second generation had established a higher occupational profile as early as 1900. By then, American-born young women avoided domestic service, and their male peers were likelier to hold lower-status white-collar or skilled positions than were immigrant men.[9] Nevertheless, even the second generation had not reached occupational parity with native-stock whites at the turn of the century.

In short, the Catholic Irish in the early twentieth century were predominantly working-class and had not gained entrée into the American élite.[10] On average, first- and second-generation Irish enjoyed a better standard of living than their famine-era predecessors—but that is a low baseline for comparison. In 1880, when the US was pulling out of a fierce depression, Irish America's class situation was closer to the characteristics of the 1850s than to those of the 1910s. When confronting America's class-based power relations during the 1870–90 era, immigrants could not have assumed that either improvement in their living conditions or increased social respect was inevitable.

Class Standing and Occupational Status in the Gilded Age

In 1880, when the U.S. conducted the tenth census, the country had already entered the "Gilded Age," an era marked by raw class struggles. A number of studies have used the census-takers' door-to-door answer sheets to create detailed descriptions of Irish immigrants' living conditions during that pivotal period. Stephan Thernstrom's work on New England localities helped to set this investigatory process in motion. Thernstrom found exceedingly modest levels of upward mobility. While New England was atypical in this respect, enthusiastic descriptions of Irish "success" in the West have been overdrawn, as a review of the evidence will indicate.[11] The following tables employ status labels adopted by Thernstrom, even though the term "low manual," which includes "unskilled" and "semiskilled" occupations, is certainly infelicitous.

New England seems to have provided a narrow occupational niche for Irishmen. Brian Mitchell found that 63.7 percent of Irish male house-

TABLE 1

OCCUPATIONAL-STATUS DISTRIBUTION OF IMMIGRANT IRISH MALES,

NEW ENGLAND, 1880

(in percentages)

	Providence	Boston	Worcester
White-collar	12.6	12	5.2
Skilled	22.6	21	18.9
Low-manual	64.7	67	75.7
N	837	417	444

Source: Joel Perlman, *Ethnic Differences: Schooling and Social Structure among the Irish, Italians, Jews, and Blacks in an American City, 1880–1935* (Cambridge: Cambridge University Press, 1988), 45, 222–23 (Providence); Thernstrom, *Other Bostonians*, 187; Meagher, "'The Lord Is Not Dead,'" 159 (Worcester).

Note: The Boston data are based on employed males of all ages, while the Worcester data reflect the experiences of men aged 18 and over. The Providence findings are based on the fathers in a sample of 13- to 16-year-old children. Heads of families were typically better off than other men. I reclassified Perlman's and Meagher's findings to fit the three-status occupational scheme and recalculated their occupational distributions to eliminate dependent, unemployed, or unknown cases.

hold heads living in Lowell's "Paddy Camps" at the height of the famine era in 1850 had been classified as "laborers" in the census.[12] Three decades later, Irishmen's options in New England were still highly constricted (Table 1). JoEllen Vinyard's 1976 study of the Irish in Detroit demonstrates that conditions in New England did not represent those of the nation. However, the argument that "move west" was the best advice for ambitious Irish immigrants is not so well supported. Table 2 presents information culled from selected studies that employ differing research designs. Detroit, a fairly small city with a small Irish population, did offer more options to Irishmen than did Boston. However, Philadelphia seems to have provided as much or more scope for Irishmen's endeavors as Chicago and San Francisco.[13]

The scholarship on Irish immigrants' class standing has focused on men. However, while women constituted only 12.9 percent of all foreign-born workers, fully 20.7 percent of the 1880 Irish labor force was female.[14] The fact that women were such an important component of the Irish labor force suggests that their efforts might have enhanced the group's overall occupational standing. Yet that was not the case at all. Few scholars offer information on the full range of occupations held by Irish women in specific locales. Table 3 displays the information that is available about women workers in three cities.

Timothy Meagher reports a dismal situation in Worcester. In 1880

The World of Work

TABLE 2
OCCUPATIONAL STATUS DISTRIBUTION OF
IMMIGRANT IRISH MALES OUTSIDE NEW ENGLAND, 1880
(in percentages)

	Philadelphia	Detroit	Chicago	San Francisco
White-collar	19.5	26	21.0	19.9
Skilled	31.8	30	20.0	18.6
Low-manual	48.7	45	59.1	61.5
N	38,035	199	850	13,830

Source: Theodore Hershberg, et al., "A Tale of Three Cities: Blacks, Immigrants, and Opportunity in Philadelphia, 1850–1880, 1930, 1970," in Theodore Hershberg, ed., *Philadelphia: Work, Space, Family, and Group Experience in the 19th Century* (Oxford: Oxford University Press, 1981), 471; JoEllen Vinyard, *The Irish on the Urban Frontier* (New York: Arno Press, 1976), 135–36, 144, 350–52; Patricia Kelleher, "Gender Shapes Ethnicity: Ireland's Gender Systems and Chicago's Irish Americans" (Ann Arbor: University Microfilms, 1995), 327; R. A. Burchell, *The San Francisco Irish, 1848–1880* (Berkeley: University of California Press, 1980), 54.

Note: The Philadelphia and San Francisco information has been reclassified by combining the two manual categories beneath artisan/skilled into a single "low-manual" category. Vinyard devised her own occupational-classification schema, and her data reflects the experiences of male heads of families rather than all men. Table 2 reports Vinyard's "laborer" as "low-manual"; clothing manufacture and skilled as "skilled"; and clerk, government, business and professional as "white-collar." I also recalculated Vinyard's results to eliminate her "don't know" category. The information in Table 2 refers to employed males (Philadelphia, aged 18 and over; Chicago, aged 15 and over; San Francisco, all ages). The Chicago information derives from a data set of 14,781 cases that I created by carrying out a stratified, disproportionate sample of the 1880 manuscript population census of Chicago. The Chicago percentages reported in this article reflect weighting schema that adjust for the disproportionate nature of the sample. The Chicago Ns in Tables 2–5 denote the unweighted number of cases. For further information, see my "Gender Shapes Ethnicity," 450–67. My data are archived (access restricted) at the University of Wisconsin's Center for Demography and Ecology.

only 1.7 percent of unmarried first-generation women workers held white-collar positions.[15] Even though domestic service was Irish women's quintessential occupation, they took other available work, especially in mills and the garment trades. Irish women's wages were a crucial component of ethnic survival strategies. While second-generation girls found a somewhat broader range of occupations as early as 1880, immigrant women made their contribution by toiling in low-status, arduous work.[16] To an even greater degree than their male peers, Irish immigrant women were locked into a cramped occupational niche.

What can be made of this barrage of details? First, variation by locale

TABLE 3

OCCUPATIONAL-STATUS DISTRIBUTION OF IRISH FEMALES, 1880

(in percentages)

	Poughkeepsie 1st and 2nd generation	Chicago 1st generation	San Francisco 1st generation
White-collar	4	14.3	8.2
Skilled	15	10.7	1.3
Low-manual	79	75.0	90.5
N	670	453	3,561

Source: Clyde Griffen and Sally Griffen, *Natives and Newcomers: The Ordering of Opportunity in Mid-Nineteenth-Century Poughkeepsie* (Cambridge: Harvard University Press, 1978), 234; Kelleher, "Gender Shapes Ethnicity," 341; Burchell, *San Francisco Irish,* 54.

Note: Table 3 describes employed women, aged 15 and over in Chicago and all employed females in Poughkeepsie and San Francisco. I combined some occupational categories of the Poughkeepsie and San Francisco data to fit the three-status schema.

was real. For example, Vinyard organized published census information on male and female immigrants' occupations and then ranked the Irish experience in eighteen cities in 1880. She categorized cities by "eastern" or "western" location and found some variation between those categories. However, the same information could be used to make arguments about the significance of a city's size, economic base, and ethnic composition. Vinyard's analysis produced very similar results for New York, Philadelphia, and Chicago. Nevertheless, the basic point that conditions did vary from place to place has now been well established by numerous studies.[17] Second, nineteenth-century Irish America did develop a degree of internal differentiation by class. If "white-collar" (nonmanual) occupations are an acceptable proxy for "middle class," then about one-fifth of Irish immigrant men in cities outside New England had achieved middle-class status by 1880. On the other hand, every community showed a vast predominance of manual workers within the combined male and female Irish immigrant labor force, with "low-manual" work inevitably swamping "skilled" occupations. While conditions did vary to a degree, there was no Irish heaven in the US. Even much-praised San Francisco gave rise to Denis Kearney's viciously anti-Chinese Workingman's Party.[18]

This overview of Irish immigrants' occupational status in 1880s America provides a context for appreciating young workers' experiences and options in Chicago and offers a vantage-point on their class standing. It is important, however, to maintain a critical perspective on occupational classifications and social-mobility analyses. Occupations are at best a mediocre proxy for "class." Furthermore, the standard categorization of occupations is derived from "mobility studies" that use a group's occupational distribution as a measure of its "success" or "failure." Such studies assume that people were motivated almost exclusively by an individualistic desire for upward mobility, and that the socio-economic system operated in a generally meritocratic manner. Neither assumption seems plausible when applied to the motives and experiences of the Irish immigrant masses in Gilded Age America.[19] Another potential limitation lies in the classification of specific occupations, and people, in the three status locations of "white-collar" (nonmanual), "skilled," and "low-manual." A saloonkeeper, categorized as a white-collar proprietor, might have been a shrewd entrepreneur or a man whose friends bought drinks from him because he was too old to work or had been blacklisted for union activism.[20] Clearly, the use of this occupational-status schema to delineate any group's class standing is problematic.

Despite these limitations, the standard occupational categories are far from being simply arbitrary or ahistorical when applied to US society during the specific era from the 1830s to the 1930s. On average, people who held white-collar positions were accorded more social respect, enjoyed better living conditions, controlled more resources, and had more life options than did people who survived by manual wage work. The distinction between skilled and other manual workers could blur in practice, but, generally, skilled workers were better off in terms of social regard, living conditions, and autonomy.[21] Thus the standard schema of status categories can be used to map the general class standing of a group without either ascribing or denying aspirations for "upward" social mobility to specific individuals, let alone making judgments of "character." While most Irish immigrants surely did want access to resources that could sustain health and material comfort, these goals could be achieved by winning better conditions within the working class. Put another way, we cannot assume that working-class Irish Americans spent their time wishing that they were middle class. They had a vibrant culture of their own.[22]

Young Irish Men in Chicago

If young Irish immigrants typically found more opportunities in the US than in Ireland, they were also subjected to more physically hazardous and exhausting work than was the norm at home. As Kerby Miller notes, immigrants' letters were replete with warnings about the toll that labor took on bodies in America. Furthermore, while wage rates were higher

TABLE 4

OCCUPATIONAL-STATUS DISTRIBUTION

OF IMMIGRANT IRISH MALES IN CHICAGO, 1880

(in percentages)

	All Men: Age 15+	Young Men: Age 15–24
White-collar	21.0	10.6
Skilled	20.0	20.7
Low-manual	59.1	68.6
N	850	107

Source: Kelleher, "Gender Shapes Ethnicity," 327; Kelleher sample.

than in Ireland, so were prices, and employment was often scarce.[23] Young men were particularly likely to relocate in search of work.[24] As a result, the June 1880 census registered a strikingly unbalanced gender ratio among Chicago's young adult (aged fifteen to twenty-four) Irish immigrants, with only sixty-eight men for every one hundred women.[25] The second generation had a more balanced gender ratio, as well as a more comfortable occupational profile; but young immigrant men scrambled for jobs. By June many would already have taken up offers such as one employment agency's promise of "free fare" and work for one thousand railroad laborers in Iowa, Wisconsin, Michigan, and Illinois for $1.35 to $1.50 a day, or another's promise of $1.75 a day for "tie choppers."[26] A glance at the occupational profile of Irish young men who were counted by census-takers in Chicago, in comparison with the group as a whole, helps to explain why so many youths were likely to be on the move (Table 4). While one-fifth of young immigrant men already held skilled positions, and some more would surely move into small proprietorships and other white-collar niches, most were concentrated in jobs that demanded hard physical labor.

What were the general life-circumstances of the young men who were at work in Chicago in June 1880, and how might they have understood themselves and their prospects? Virtually all (96 percent) were unmarried.[27] Roughly one-third lived as sons in families; the fact that another 12 percent were brothers or brothers-in-law of family heads probably reflects the process of chain migration. Altogether, 55 percent lived as relatives within families. The vast majority of the remainder were "non-kin" boarders who lived in family households or boarding houses. Nearly one-fourth of the total lived in the heavily Irish and working-class Fifth Ward (the Bridgeport area). Of those who lived in households, as family members or as boarders, 91 percent lived with a first- or second-generation Irish head of household. As wage earners, 16 percent contributed to households that were headed by nonemployed women. Among those who co-resided with an employed household head, 50 percent lived with an unskilled head of household, over two-thirds with "low-manual" heads, and 16 percent with skilled workers. In other words, the young immigrant workers who lived in households co-resided with heads whose occupational profile was somewhat lower than the norm. It is unlikely that such residential patterns generated much entrée into middle-class circles.

Some class differentiation existed, even within this group. Edward Cudahy, a member of the family that became prominent in meatpacking, was a twenty-one-year-old clerk who lived in his brother Michael's family. Michael had gained notoriety six months before the census date, when charges surfaced that he had bribed a priest, Father Joseph M. Cartan of Nativity parish, to undermine a militant butchers' strike. George Collins, a sailor, was also a twenty-one-year-old immigrant. Only three Irish served on his vessel, as did three African American men. By the nature of his work, Collins was a traveling man. The same supplementary census count of the lakefront that enumerated Collins also counted prostitutes. George Collins could not have been unfamiliar with the rougher side of life or diverse peoples. He might also have belonged to Richard Powers' seamen's union. Powers was a militant workers' advocate and an ardent Irish nationalist.[28] These two twenty-one-year-old Irish immigrant men illustrate the range of experience in their cohort, but most of the group gravitated toward Collins' pole.

Nearly one-third (31.3 percent) of the men were listed as general laborers. John Cunningham was one. He was twenty-four years old and stayed in a downtown boarding house with seventy other residents. Only twelve, including the boarding-house keeper, Thomas Kearney, were first- or second-generation Irish. Kearney hosted an eclectic mix of men who represented a wide variety of nationalities and occupations. Cunningham was not isolated in an ethnic enclave. He had situated himself in the hurly-burly of American urban life. Even laborers like John Cantlon (aged twenty-four) and William Henley (aged twenty-two), who resided in the heart of the Fifth Ward at William Pigott's boarding house at 3036 Archer Avenue, had not cut themselves off from cosmopolitan influences. Their co-residents were predominantly Irish, but native-stock whites, a second-generation Englishman, and a Swiss immigrant also lived there. If Cantlon and Henley wanted to converse with a wider range of people, they could easily drop into a saloon. At least three saloons operated on their block.[29]

The working men in another family, the O'Donnells, were not listed

TABLE 5

OCCUPATIONAL-STATUS DISTRIBUTION

OF IMMIGRANT IRISH FEMALES IN CHICAGO, 1880

(in percentages)

	All Women: Age 15+	Young Women: Age 15–24
White-collar	14.3	4.9
Skilled	10.7	12.9
Low-manual	75.0	82.1
N	453	165

Source: Kelleher, "Gender Shapes Ethnicity," 341; Kelleher sample.

as laborers, but their circumstances were clearly difficult. They lived in the Fifth Ward at 2646 Hickory Street with their sister Mary Hussey and her thirty-year-old husband Patrick. All the adults in the household were immigrants. Patrick was illiterate and worked for an ice company. At age twenty-five, Mary already had a seven-year-old daughter and a three-year-old son, both American-born. Her brother, John O'Donnell, was twenty-two and also worked for an ice company, probably alongside Patrick. Young Thomas, aged nineteen, worked in a packinghouse. Thomas may have been a "greenhorn," but he could not have worked in the meatpacking houses without learning about recent Irish-led strikes in the stockyards, and he may well have arrived in time to participate himself. Labor strife provided a quick orientation lesson for greenhorns.[30]

In summary, young immigrant men generally led hard lives and were not well positioned to move into the middle class even if that had been their aim. On the other hand, few would have been bewildered naifs. Many had traveled extensively; even those who were rooted in Chicago had broad access to a range of points of view. Some may have preferred to isolate themselves from "outside" influences, but that was a choice, not a necessity.[31]

Young Irish Women in Chicago

If young men struggled to secure a livelihood, so too did young women. It is fruitless to debate who suffered most, but the information in Table 5 might help to dispel the impression that women's occupational berth was relatively more comfortable than men's.[32] Young women were even slightly disadvantaged compared to all employed Irish immigrant women (aged fifteen and over). Over four-fifths of the young women were concentrated in "low-manual" work, compared with somewhat over two-thirds of employed young men. While youthful men found their way into more than fifty specific occupations in Chicago, employed young women were listed in only thirteen occupations.

Still, immigrant men and women had more in common (in terms of earning their own living and being relatively unencumbered with family-care responsibilities) during their youth than they would have as mature adults. Virtually identical proportions of the never-married young men and women who resided in Chicago were employed (89.8 percent and 85.5 percent, respectively). Indeed, a youthful immigrant worker in Chicago was as likely to be a woman as a man. Even though 77 percent of the overall Irish immigrant labor force in Chicago was male, slightly over half (53 percent) of Chicago's fifteen- to twenty-four-year-old Irish workers were women.[33] Two reasons explain this pattern. First, men sought employment throughout their lives, but job-holding was normative only for youthful unmarried women. Second, work opportunities for women were concentrated in cities, so that more young Irish women than men resided in Chicago in 1880. A remarkably high percentage of Irish women toiled for pay at some point in their lives, sharing with Irish men a personal knowledge of wage-workers' realities.[34]

Over 80 percent of young immigrant working women worked as "servants," as "hotel help," or in other comparable situations. Like their male counterparts, young immigrant women were not so well positioned in the labor force in the second generation. Unlike men, women could turn to marriage as an alternative to employment. While virtually all the young Irish men in Chicago had never married, almost 30 percent of twenty- to twenty-four-year-old women immigrants had already opted for marriage. The following discussion considers only those young immigrant women who held jobs in Chicago in 1880—99 percent of whom were single.[35] Young immigrant women had few prospects of commanding high wages or high status through their own employment. The circumstances of individuals' lives suggest the range of experiences that influenced their sense of themselves and their goals.

In many respects, young working women's lives differed enormously from young men's. While 55 percent of the men lived as relatives within families, only 18 percent of the women did so. Four-fifths found accommodations by filling menial-status positions at their places of work. Slightly over half lived downtown or in the South Side wards that contained fashionable neighborhoods (wards 1 through 4) compared with only 16 percent of their male counterparts. Furthermore, while nearly one-fourth of the young men lived in the Fifth Ward that encompassed

Bridgeport, only 7 percent of the young women did so. Paradoxically, young women's low-status work as servants took them out of working-class residential areas.

Nearly half (45.3 percent) of all employed young women worked as domestic servants and lived in households with their employers. Only 17.6 percent of Irish domestic servants worked in households headed by people of their own nationality. In contrast with young men's living arrangements, over two-thirds of domestic servants took shelter under the roofs provided by "American" or first- or second-generation British household heads. In addition, almost all domestics who served gainfully employed household heads worked for people who operated in the white-collar world. In fact, over two-fifths worked for employers who held prestigious ("high" white-collar) positions. In short, Irish servant girls resided within a sharply different cultural and class milieu from that experienced by young men.

If a young Irishwoman sought employment by consulting newspaper advertisements, she would soon confront anti-Irish prejudice. "No Irish" occasionally appeared in "Help Wanted" listings, but the same point was usually made with preferences such as those for a "Neat American or German Girl," or for a "Protestant," or for a "Good, Reliable Colored Girl."[36] While Hasia Diner provides a good description of Irish servants' experiences, David Katzman's *Seven Days a Week* still offers the best overview of the nature of the work itself—the long hours, the drudgery, and mistresses' penchant for petty supervision of servants' personal lives as well as tasks. Meeting high housekeeping standards during the Victorian era involved hard work. Despite the anti-Irish bigotry and condescension that permeated their outlook, the logic of supply and demand forced women of the "better" sort to bring Irish women into their homes to perform the most exhausting and unrewarding facets of housework.[37] Presumably, the position that exposed Irish women to the most demands and the most isolation was to be the sole "maid-of-all-work" in a household. About half (51.5 percent) of domestic servants filled that position. However, that means that nearly half the younger servants in Chicago's households did not work alone. Maggie Cooney lived and worked at 1239 Michigan Avenue. Her prosperous "American" employer kept four servants (of Irish, German, and native-stock white descent). If Maggie tired of her fellow workers' company, she could exchange confidences with Kate Grant and Mary Morgan who worked at 1241 Michigan Avenue, or with the three Irish servants who resided at 1245 Michigan. Bridget Donavin, aged twenty, may have been lonely and overworked as the sole servant at 3240 Indiana Avenue; but she was only a stone's throw from nineteen-year-old Maggie Dooley and twenty-three-year-old Katie Ruane, who were servants at 3239 Indiana.[38]

Certainly, many Irish women were exploited as servants and some were isolated. But only 23.4 percent of the young Irish women who worked in Chicago were employed as the sole servant in a household—and many of them could find company nearby.[39] It is hard to imagine that impressionable girls were simply overawed by the higher status of their often "American" or British Protestant employers. Surely, domestic servants learned a great deal about material and cultural possibilities by living on intimate terms with such people. On the other hand, servants commonly dealt with arrogance and unreasonable demands from their social "betters." The advertisements for non-Irish help suggest that Irish women were not considered tractable, let alone overawed. A contemporary's assertion that any lady who challenged "the convenience of Bridget" risked having "the dogs of war . . . loosed upon her" nicely illustrates both the prejudice and the trepidation that many mistresses brought to their relationships with Irish servants.[40]

This study's finding that so many Irish girls (45.3 percent) worked as domestic servants in a nineteenth-century American city is no revelation. What is striking is that an additional 35.2 percent were classified in the census with the "status" of servant or other menial employee, but were not "domestic" servants. That is, over one-third of the total served in non-household settings such as hotels and boarding houses. Indeed, one-fifth of all the young employed Irish immigrant women worked in hotels. Almost all were concentrated in downtown Chicago. Surrounded by hordes of young co-workers, hotel servants were at the center of the action in a vibrant city.[41]

The Commercial Hotel listed a large staff that was entirely white with the exception of one African American man. Twenty-two first- and second-generation Irish worked there. Most of the Irish were young and single. At least three sets of probable sisters or cousins clustered together. The Irish were in the minority on the Commercial's staff; most of the non-Irish staff members were native-stock white or of British or Canadian background. The palatial Grand Pacific employed over thirty African American men, but they were outnumbered by Irish staff members. The Irish were mostly women and many were middle-aged. The census counted one hundred fifty people at the Sherman House, all of them white. Dollie O'Brien, aged nineteen, may or may not have been related to eighteen-year-old Bridget O'Brien and nineteen-year-old Anthony O'Brien. In any case Dollie could hardly have been lonely. The Sherman House employed over sixty immigrant and second-generation Irish, and many staff members were in their teens and early twenties. Dollie would have worked long hours for low pay; but she was also well positioned to meet people, see the sights, and have fun. Unmarried and aged twenty-four, Annie Hackett worked at Alexander Loftus's Hotel at 52 Sherman Street. Only fifty-three people were enumerated at the "hotel," and its residents were predominantly working-class as well—it might better be described as a boarding house. Only six servants kept the hotel going. All the residents were white, most of them Irish, British, or Canadian. If Annie were husband-hunting, she had found quite a game preserve. Almost all the boarders were young, single men. If Annie had wanted to "step out" with a young man, the downtown's entertainments were close by.[42]

Like young men, young immigrant women generally led hard lives. In addition, they were even less likely to be cocooned within their own family than Chicago-based men. In contrast to their brothers, domestic servants were positioned to develop an intimate knowledge of middle- and upper-class mores. Generally, however, they did not learn about "genteel" living from the small Irish Catholic bourgeoisie, but rather from cultural outsiders who often disparaged them. Healthy young women might enjoy the camaraderie of other servants, take pride in making their own money, and marvel at the consumer possibilities that Chicago offered. On the other hand, Dollie O'Brien at the Sherman House could not have failed to note the situation of her co-workers who were in their forties and fifties. Long-term employment prospects for the average immigrant woman were bleak. A young working woman could try to encapsulate herself within the certainties of Irish Catholic advice manuals, but she was surrounded with object lessons about power and class in American society.

Class Options

As the nationwide data unequivocally demonstrate, the Gilded Age Irish were overwhelmingly working-class. While attitudes and aspirations are difficult to ascertain, this investigation of young workers in Chicago demonstrates that age, generation, gender, and specific historical circumstances must all be considered. To be a young, immigrant, unmarried, wage-earning woman or man of Irish background who lived and worked in Chicago meant exposure to a distinctive set of influences on perceptions of class options. While these influences were interactive, I will first address generation and age and then discuss gender and specific historical circumstances more fully.

Generation is crucial. Studies that combine the first and second generations into one category blur significant differences between the two. Immigrants had a low occupational profile, and youthful immigrants were especially disadvantaged. The Chicago investigation strongly supports two additional conclusions. First, young immigrants' experiences combined low occupational status with broad opportunities to sample diverse class and cultural perspectives. While the second generation may have been more sheltered within ethnic enclaves, young immigrants were exposed to the harshness and the lures of the wider world. The fact that young immigrants were not isolated in Chicago, and that this finding applies to both sexes, constitutes one of the most significant points made herein. Gender profoundly influenced life-courses and perspectives, but it did not obviate all commonalities. The second point is that acculturation through embourgeoisement was an important option, but only one option among several that beckoned Chicago's young immigrants. Gilded Age Chicago could produce consternation and exhilaration among young Irish workers. Most were exploited; many regularly witnessed ostentatious displays of wealth. Chicago also hosted the most radical working-class movement in the country, and its government was openly corrupt. Innocence was at a premium, but energy and possibilities abounded.

Scholarly deliberations about Irish-American class identity usually deal with women in a cursory manner, if at all. While nonemployed women played a crucial role in industrial class formation,[43] this article integrates women into the discussion by trying to elucidate the influences that their own wage-work experiences may have had on their strategies and goals. Irish women typically spent years of their lives in the labor force. The labor movement's denunciations of "wage slavery" could resonate with their personal experiences. Family duty and the sheer necessity of self-support obliged most to endure low-status drudge work. Women would have personally encountered anti-Irish prejudice while witnessing other people's comfortable life-styles. Evidence culled from information about Irish servants around the country indicates that many young women learned to stand up for themselves, adopted a calculating, wage-conscious job-search strategy, adored finery and fun, and used their money to help their families and themselves. Such experiences may have fostered aspirations for upward class mobility; but, typically, that strategy would have to be pursued by promoting husbands' and children's prospects. Immigrant women knew that their own potential for individual upward mobility was low. Furthermore, given the information already presented about the general socio-economic position of the Gilded Age Irish, family-based social climbing was a long-term strategy at best. Observers suggest that Irish women were resolutely practical.[44]

Surrounded by hard-pressed and irregularly employed Irish men and observing older women who labored for meager pay, women employed various strategies to better their lot. One possibility was to insist on the right to work and earn a self-supporting wage whenever circumstances dictated that they enter the labor market. It is no accident that so many late nineteenth- and early twentieth-century women labor organizers were ethnically Irish. In areas that attracted multiracial workforces, the concern for jobs could tempt Irish women as well as men to adopt a strategy of emphasizing whiteness as a qualification for decent treatment and opportunities.[45] The labor movement's demands for an "American standard of living" may also have appealed to Irish women and promoted their support for unionized men's struggles. Their well-known interest in consumer goods, even fine things, might be met by winning a higher standard of living for the working class. Women doubtless wanted better material conditions. Gilded Age immigrant women commonly encountered industrial America's material bounty in tandem with anti-Irish condescension, overwork, and deprivation. Many may well have developed their own version of respectability and a desire for the accoutrements of genteel living without having fully internalized the world-view of their "betters."[46] Such women might back strategies of either class solidarity or individual-family social climbing based on rational calculation of immediate prospects for success. Of course, some women did develop an ideological allegiance to one or the other strategy. If they were in the market for radical ideas, Chicago offered a smorgasbord of possibilities. Some young Irish women may have joined the crowd of 20,000 to 40,000 that attended a downtown commemoration of the Paris Commune in March 1879. A *Tribune* reporter insisted that "all the red-headed, cross-eyed and frowsy servant girls" in the city turned out for the occasion.[47]

Young women were not culturally isolated. Those who resided downtown lived in the vortex of a wide-open, corrupt, and dynamic city. Given the prevailing mores, however, women's opportunities to sample the city's diversity were more constrained than those of young men, who could roam the city, absorb ideas amid the banter in saloons and shifting work sites, and participate in public contests for power and influence.

What were young men's aspirations? Personal upward mobility was at least somewhat more feasible for them than it was for immigrant women. About 30 percent of Irish youths under age twenty-five held skilled or white-collar positions. Many of those young men may have lost ground in the unstable Gilded Age economy, but no doubt many entertained hope for individual advancement. The other 70 percent held jobs that tended to be exploitative, even dangerous—and, adding insult to injury, subject to layoffs. What was their perspective? Teen-aged Michael Kilcran emigrated to Chicago in the early 1880s. He encountered brutal treatment. Kilcran could not find secure employment and he went hungry. At one point he joined a union, participated in a strike, and disparaged both bosses and the workingmen who bent to the bosses' will. Later in life, Kilcran became a detective of police and seemed fairly satisfied. Was Kilcran a class-conscious worker or upwardly mobile?[48]

Such either/or categorizations are untenable for most Gilded Age Irish. As a boy, Michael Kilcran dreamed of grand success but did not want to become "heartless." Kilcran toughened up, but he still remembered the hurts of his early years in America. People's views do not simply mirror their material circumstances. If they did, we could fairly easily resolve the debates about Gilded Age Irish Americans' perspectives on class. Certainly, however, the masses of Irish immigrants would have been extraordinarily unperceptive if their own experiences failed to debunk the contemporary rationalizations of the class system. Michael Kilcran and his fellow immigrants, women and men, had seen too much to believe that virtue and prosperity were inseparable. Catholic Irish immigrants' cultural heritage, which stressed communal solidarity and bred suspicion of bald materialism, also undermined the legitimacy of the capitalist ethos. Most immigrants' experiences and heritage provided resources that might have supported a radical, working-class consciousness. However individuals resolved tensions between the promptings of ambition and solidarity, Irish participation in the contests for power and influence that roiled Chicago during this era demonstrates widespread discontent with the status quo.[49]

By the 1880s Irish workers had earned their reputation as a volatile and militant element within the labor force. Irish men, sometimes joined by women and children, literally fought for better conditions in Chicago's streets and work sites. They drew on both Irish secret-society traditions that justified coercion and violence in defense of the oppressed and on a shared sense of ethnic solidarity. Richard Schneirov has studied the impact of the combined influences of the Knights of Labor and the social consciousness associated with the Irish nationalist Land League on the Chicago Irish working class. His conclusion that Irish combativeness was being transformed into "cosmopolitan, class-aware unionism" may be overly optimistic, but some Irish workers were showing signs of class-consciousness. In the late 1870s and early 1880s Irish workers cooperated with other ethnic groups, especially Germans and Bohemians, to stage spectacular protests and to wring concessions from employers and the government.[50]

Chicago's Irish community was overwhelmingly working class. It was not under the tight control of the Democratic Party, the Irish Catholic middle class, or the Catholic church. While some Irish workers may have isolated themselves from outside influences, others participated in the broad sweep of the city's struggles and excitement. The Democrats did not have a secure lock on the Irish vote. About 30 percent of the 1878–79 Socialist Labor Party vote was Irish, and some Irish operated within the Republican Party. Irish Catholic bourgeois hegemony did not exist in Gilded Age Chicago. The middle class was small and populated with individuals of modest accomplishments whose careers often depended on political patronage. Furthermore, members of the middle class feuded among themselves. The middle class wielded influence, but it did not command the masses. The Catholic church was more formidable than the lay middle class, but even the church did not take working-class allegiance for granted. Irish men and women religious labored mightily to build a church infrastructure and to supply the spiritual and material sustenance that would cement loyalty to the church. The working class, especially the immigrant generation, was rough-hewn. No sensible member of the lay middle class or the religious underestimated the potential for trouble or disaffection among the masses.[51]

Scholarship on the Gilded Age Irish and class has been so contentious in part because there are no clear answers. The situation was fluid and confusing, for the actors themselves as well as for later scholars. Gilded Age Chicago hosted a working-class Irish population that included militants and supported a degree of rough-and-ready cosmopolitan class-consciousness. Who could doubt that the class system was unfair and cruel? On the other hand, the lure of a bountiful life and even working-class versions of self-respect and respectability could erode radical resistance. The working class was not monolithic. As circumstances and practical options changed, an individual's perspective could change too. To complicate matters, the lay middle class and the Catholic church in the Gilded Age were not monolithic either. Officially committed to supporting the established order, members of both groups were not immune to either alienation from the dominant American system or to deep sympathy for their own kind. A profound ambivalence about class permeated all elements of Gilded Age Irish America.

NOTES

1. Stephan Thernstrom, *The Other Bostonians: Poverty and Progress in the American Metropolis, 1880–1970* (Cambridge: Harvard University Press, 1973), illustrates the first view. Examples of the second perspective are Marjorie R. Fallows, *Irish Americans: Identity and Assimilation* (Englewood Cliffs, N.J.: Prentice-Hall, 1979); Lawrence J. McCaffrey, *The Irish Diaspora in America* (Bloomington: Indiana University Press, 1976), and its revised edition *The Irish Catholic Diaspora in America* (Washington, D.C.: Catholic University of America Press, 1997) as well as Andrew M. Greeley, *That Most Distressful Nation: The Taming of the American Irish* (Chicago: Quadrangle Books, 1972). Eric Foner, "Class, Ethnicity, and Radicalism in the Gilded Age: The Land League and Irish America," *Marxist Perspectives* 1 (1978), 6–55, and David Montgomery, "The Irish and the American Labor Movement," in David N. Doyle and Owen Dudley Edwards, eds., *America and Ireland, 1772–1976: The American Identity and the Irish Connection* (Westport, Conn.: Greenwood Press, 1980), 205–18, exemplify the argument for Irish working-class radicalism. Kerby Miller's lucid argument for Catholic middle-class hegemony is summarized in "Class, Culture, and Immigrant Group Identity in the United States: The Case of Irish-American Ethnicity," in *Immigration Reconsidered: History, Sociology, and Politics*, ed. Virginia Yans-McLaughlin (New York: Oxford University Press, 1990), 96–109. A more recent line of inquiry examines the extent to which the Irish contributed to race inequality by embracing "whiteness" in order to gain social acceptance and competitive advantages in American society. See, for example, Noel Ignatiev, *How the Irish Became White* (New York: Routledge, 1995).

2. Irish people who disembarked in Canada often settled in the US. George W. Potter, *To the Golden Door: The Story of the Irish in Ireland and America* (Boston: Little, Brown and Co., 1960), 134–38.

3. William Forbes Adams, *Ireland and Irish Emigration to the New World from 1815 to the Famine* (New Haven: Yale University Press, 1932), 193–201, 224, 268–76; Kerby A. Miller, *Emigrants and Exiles: Ireland and the Irish Exodus to North America* (New York: Oxford University Press, 1985), 193–201, 224, 268–76; David Fitzpatrick, "Emigration, 1801–70," in W. E. Vaughan, ed., *A New History of Ireland*, Vol. V: *Ireland Under the Union, I, 1801–70* (Oxford: Clarendon Press, 1989), 565–41; Peter Way, "Shovel and Shamrock: Irish Workers and Labor Violence in the Digging of the Chesapeake and Ohio Canal," *Labor History* 30 (1989), 489–517; Paul A. Gilje, "The Development of an Irish American Community in New York City before the Great Migration," in Ronald H. Bayor and Timothy J. Meagher, eds., *The New York Irish* (Baltimore: Johns Hopkins University Press, 1996), 70–83.

4. Miller, *Emigrants and Exiles*, 291–97, 331; Oliver MacDonagh, "Irish Emigration to the United States of America and the British Colonies during the Famine," in R. Dudley Edwards and T. Desmond Williams, eds., *The Great Famine: Studies in Irish History, 1845–52*, (Dublin: Browne and Nolan, 1956), 322, 328–29, 385–86; Robert James Scally, *The End of Hidden Ireland: Rebellion, Famine, and Emigration* (New York: Oxford University Press, 1995).

5. Fitzpatrick, "Emigration, 1801–70," 575–77, 617; Miller, *Emigrants and Exiles*, 346, 349–53, 407, 469–70, 581; Timothy W. Guinnane, *The Vanishing Irish: Households, Migration, and the Rural Economy in Ireland, 1850–1914* (Princeton: Princeton University Press, 1997), 101–11; David N. Doyle, "Unestablished Irishmen: New Immigrants

and Industrial America, 1870–1910," in Dirk Hoerder, ed., *American Labor and Immigration History, 1877–1920s: Recent European Research* (Urbana: University of Illinois Press, 1983), 199–201.

6. Miller, *Emigrants and Exiles*, 569–82; W.E. Vaughan and A.J. Fitzpatrick, eds., *Irish Historical Statistics: Population, 1821–1971* (Dublin: Royal Irish Academy, 1978), 259–353; Ireland (Eire), Commission on Emigration and Other Population Problems, 1948–54, *Reports* (Dublin: Stationery Office, 1954), 314–19. In this context "greenhorn" means recently arrived immigrant.

7. For examples, see Oscar Handlin, *Boston's Immigrants: A Study in Acculturation*, rev. ed. (New York: Atheneum, 1970), 72; Carl Wittke, *The Irish in America* (Baton Rouge: Louisiana State University Press, 1956), vi, 23, 27; Thernstrom, *Other Bostonians*, 140.

8. McCaffrey, *The Irish Diaspora in America*, 76–82; David N. Doyle, *Irish Americans, Native Rights, and National Empires: The Structure, Attitudes, and Division of the Catholic Minority in the Decade of Expansion, 1890–1901* (New York: Arno Press, 1976), 46. Doyle revises his position somewhat in "Unestablished Irishmen," 193–95.

9. Brinley Thomas, *Migration and Economic Growth: A Study of Great Britain and the Atlantic Economy*, 2nd ed. (Cambridge: Cambridge University Press, 1973), 142–55 (1910 data, 147). The government did not publish tabulations of occupations by country of birth for 1910. A census official supplied Thomas with previously unpublished tabulations. E. P. Hutchinson describes occupational patterns in 1900 in *Immigrants and Their Children, 1850–1950* (New York: John Wiley & Sons, 1956), 174, 184. For information on specific locales, see, for example, Martin G. Towey, "Kerry Patch Revisited: Irish Americans in St. Louis in the Turn of the Century Era," in Timothy J. Meagher, ed., *From Paddy to Studs: Irish-American Communities in the Turn of the Century Era, 1880–1920* (New York: Greenwood Press, 1986), 145–49; Timothy J. Meagher, "'The Lord Is Not Dead': Cultural and Social Change among the Irish in Worcester, Massachusetts" (Ann Arbor, Mich.: University Microfilms, 1982), 157–63.

10. Frederic Cople Jaher, *The Urban Establishment: Upper Strata in Boston, New York, Charleston, Chicago, and Los Angeles* (Urbana: University of Illinois Press, 1982).

11. See especially Thernstrom, *Other Bostonians*, 130–44. Thernstrom's other study of a locale in New England (Newburyport) is *Poverty and Progress: Social Mobility in a Nineteenth-Century City* (Cambridge: Harvard University Press, 1964). On San Francisco, see Timothy Sarbaugh, "Exiles of Confidence: The Irish-American Community of San Francisco, 1880–1920," in Meagher, ed., *From Paddy to Studs*, 161.

12. Brian C. Mitchell, *The Paddy Camps: The Irish of Lowell, 1821–61* (Urbana: University of Illinois Press, 1988), 162.

13. Dennis Clark, *The Irish in Philadelphia: Ten Generations of Urban Experience* (Philadelphia: Temple University Press, 1973), 70–87.

14. My calculation, based on Hutchinson, *Immigrants and Their Children*, 98.

15. Meagher, "'The Lord Is Not Dead',"" 225.

16. For example, in Troy, women in the collar industry worked as laundresses or sewers. A recalculation of information provided by Carole Turbin, *Working Women of Collar City: Gender, Class, and Community in Troy, New York, 1864–86* (Urbana: University of Illinois Press, 1992), 54, shows that in 1880, 57.4 percent of Irish immigrants performed the more grueling laundry work, while 65.0 percent of the second generation found positions as sewers. Nationwide, as late as 1900, 60.5 percent of first-generation Irish women workers were servants or laundresses. David M. Katzman, *Seven*

Days a Week: Women and Domestic Service in Industrializing America (Urbana: University of Illinois Press, 1976), 67.

17. JoEllen Vinyard, *The Irish on the Urban Frontier: Nineteenth-Century Detroit, 1850–1880* (New York: Arno Press, 1976), 315–16. She notes the salience of factors in addition to region on 323–24. See also Dennis Clark, *Hibernia America: The Irish and Regional Cultures* (New York: Greenwood Press, 1986).

18. Ira B. Cross, *A History of the Labor Movement in California* (Berkeley: University of California Press, 1935), 88–129; Alexander Saxton, *The Indispensable Enemy: Labor and the Anti-Chinese Movement in California* (Berkeley: University of California Press, 1971). R. A. Burchell, *The San Francisco Irish, 1848–1880* (Berkeley: University of California Press, 1980) celebrates prominent Irish individuals and argues that San Francisco provided a positive environment for the Irish. However, he does make it clear that the Irish experienced a broad range of conditions in the city; see 1–11, 64, and 155–57.

19. Stuart M. Blumin, *The Emergence of the Middle Class: Social Experience in the American City, 1760–1900* (Cambridge: Cambridge University Press, 1989), 1–16; James A. Henretta, "The Study of Social Mobility: Ideological Assumptions and Conceptual Bias," *Labor History* 18 (1977), 165–78.

20. James R. Barrett, *Work and Community in the Jungle: Chicago's Packinghouse Workers, 1894–1922* (Urbana: University of Illinois Press, 1987), 82, 85.

21. Jeanne Boydston, *Home and Work: Housework, Wages, and the Ideology of Labor in the Early Republic* (New York: Oxford University Press, 1990), 56–74, 120–41; Stephanie Coontz, *The Social Origins of Private Life: A History of American Families, 1600–1900* (London: Verso, 1988), 172–80, 187–97, 200–09, 251–329; Nell Irvin Painter, *Standing at Armageddon: The United States, 1877–1919* (New York: W.W. Norton & Co., 1987), xvi–xxvii; Blumin, *Emergence of Middle Class*, 258–75, 285–97; Thernstrom, *Other Bostonians*, 289–302.

22. While the majority of Irish Americans in this period were working class, there was a small and growing middle class as well. Few Irish were professionals; the Irish middle class was heavily concentrated in small proprietorships (e.g., saloons, groceries, ice and coal delivery) and patronage positions. Saloonkeepers, petty politicians, and priests all wielded influence, but they had to contend with the basic reality that they depended on a working-class clientele. Nor was their middle-class standing by any means secure: downward mobility was a constant threat.

23. Miller, *Emigrants and Exiles*, 316–17, 320, 357–59, 502–06; Timothy J. Hatton and Jeffrey G. Williamson, "After the Famine: Emigration from Ireland, 1850–1913," *Journal of Economic History* 53 (1993), 579–80.

24. Michael B. Katz, Michael Doucet, and Mark J. Stern, *The Social Organization of Early Industrial Capitalism* (Cambridge: Harvard University Press, 1982), 102–30; Miller, *Emigrants and Exiles*, 316–17; Thernstrom, *Other Bostonians*, 39, 221–32.

25. The youthful labor force in Chicago was not overwhelmingly female because a considerable proportion of the young women had married and were not employed. Kelleher sample.

26. Kelleher sample; *Chicago Tribune*, 1 June 1880.

27. Enumerators failed to note the marital status of a few individuals; 95 percent were explicitly recorded as single. I used contextual information to code 1.3 percent as "presumed single." Unless otherwise noted, all statistics in the text from this point forward derive from my sample.

28. U.S. Census Office, Tenth Census (1880), Manuscript Population Census, Chicago, Enumeration District 24, 48, and ED 8, 64. It is difficult to differentiate vessels in the supplementary pages of enumeration district 8. Collins' vessel apparently includes persons listed on lines 39 through 50. Louise Carroll Wade, *Chicago's Pride: The Stockyards, Packingtown, and Environs in the Nineteenth Century* (Urbana: University of Illinois Press, 1987), 125; Richard Schneirov, *Labor and Urban Politics: Class Conflict and the Origins of Modern Liberalism in Chicago, 1864–97* (Urbana: University of Illinois Press, 1998), 101, 107–08, 125.

29. Tenth Census (1880), Manuscript Population Census, Chicago, ED 10, 46, and ED 45, 6; Thomas Hutchinson, comp., *The Lakeside Annual Directory of the City of Chicago* (Chicago: Chicago Directory Company, 1880), 1266, 1461–73.

30. The last name is spelled as O'Doneil in the manuscript census. Hutchinson, *Lakeside Annual Directory* (1880), lists Patrick Hussey (576) and John O'Donnell (848) at 2646 Hickory Street. Young Thomas was not listed in the directory. Tenth Census (1880), Manuscript Population Census, Chicago, ED 48, 66; Wade, *Chicago's Pride*, 122–26; Schreirov, *Labor and Urban Politics*, 106–10; James R. Barrett, "Americanization from the Bottom Up: Immigration and the Remaking of the Working Class in the United States, 1880–1930," *Journal of American History* 79 (1992), 997–98.

31. Howard P. Chudacoff, *Mobile Americans: Residential and Social Mobility in Omaha, 1880–1920* (New York: Oxford University Press, 1972), 35, 41–42, 61–110.

32. Hasia R. Diner, *Erin's Daughters in America: Irish Immigrant Women in the Nineteenth Century* (Baltimore: Johns Hopkins University Press, 1983), 71.

33. Percentages derived from Kelleher sample. See note to Table 2.

34. Faye E. Dudden, *Serving Women: Household Service in Nineteenth-Century America* (Middletown, Conn.: Wesleyan University Press, 1983), 8, 50–51, 62.

35. Less than 1 percent were enumerated as married or widowed. Enumerators were especially lax about specifying marital status when recording information about downtown hotel workers. Overall, 86.5 percent of the employed young women were recorded as single, I used contextual information to code 12.6 percent as "presumed single." Kelleher sample.

36. See *Chicago Tribune*, 6, 13, 27 June 1880, for "no Irish" examples, and *Chicago Tribune*, 3, 6, 13 June 1880, for examples of preferences for non-Irish employees.

37. Diner, *Erin's Daughters*, 70–94; Katzman, *Seven Days a Week*, 44–183. See also Dudden, *Serving Women*, 44–183. Kevin Kenny, *The American Irish: A History* (London and New York: Longman, 2000), 149–54, also emphasizes the degree of labor exploitation involved in domestic service.

38. Tenth Census (1880), Manuscript Population Census, Chicago, ED 13, 7, and ED 26, 35, 47.

39. Dudden, *Serving Women*, 230–32, discusses camaraderie among domestic servants.

40. *Chicago Tribune*, 6 July 1878.

41. The Commercial Hotel advertised itself as "First Class" and boasted of "All Modern Improvements." The Sherman House was "Elegantly Furnished" and "Strictly Fireproof." The opulent Grand Pacific occupied an entire city block. Republican Party, *The Republican National Convention Catalogue and Visitors' Guide* (Chicago: Blakely Marsh Printing Co., 1884), 67, 84–85; A.T. Andreas, *From the Fire of 1871 until 1885*, vol. 3 of *History of Chicago* (1886; reprinted New York: Arno Press, 1975), 354.

42. Tenth Census (1880), Manuscript Population Census, Chicago, ED 1, 16–18

(Commercial); ED 4, 33–37 (Grand Pacific); ED 1, 28–30 (Sherman House); ED 6, 21–22 (Loftus Hotel).

43. Boydston, *Home and Work*, 120–41.

44. Arnold Schrier, *Ireland and the American Emigration, 1850–1900* (Minneapolis: University of Minnesota Press, 1958), 30, 104–08; Dudden, *Serving Women*, 50–59, 62, 65–66; Diner, *Erin's Daughters*, 70–105.

45. Diner, *Erin's Daughters*, 92–93, 100–05; Turbin, *Working Women of Collar City*, 38–39; Kathleen Banks Nutter, "Organizing Women during the Progressive Era: Mary Kenney O'Sullivan and the Labor Movement," *Labor's Heritage* 8 (1997), 18; Martha Mabie Gardner, "Working on White Womanhood: White Working Women in the San Francisco Anti-Chinese Movement, 1877–1890," *Journal of Social History* 33 (1999), 73–95.

46. Lawrence Glickman, "Inventing the 'American Standard of Living': Gender, Race, and Working-Class Identity, 1880–1925," *Labor History* 34 (1993), 221–35; Colleen McDannell, "Going to the Ladies' Fair: Irish Catholics in New York City 1870–1900," in Bayor and Meagher, eds., *New York Irish*, 239–41, 246–47; Kerby A. Miller, with David N. Doyle and Patricia Kelleher, "'For Love and for Liberty': Irish Women, Migration, and Domesticity in Ireland and America, 1850–1920," in Patrick O'Sullivan, ed., *The Irish Worldwide: History, Heritage, Identity*, Vol. IV: *Irish Women and Irish Migration* (Leicester: Leicester University Press, 1995), 54–61.

47. *Chicago Tribune*, 23 March 1879, quoted in Bruce C. Nelson, *Beyond the Martyrs: A Social History of Chicago's Anarchists, 1870–1900* (New Brunswick, N.J.: Rutgers University Press, 1988), 79.

48. Nelson, *Beyond the Martyrs*, 9–26; Eric L. Hirsch, *Urban Revolt: Ethnic Politics in the Nineteenth-Century Chicago Labor Movement* (Berkeley: University of California Press, 1990), 1–10; Wade, *Chicago's Pride*, 119–22; Barrett, *Work and Community in the Jungle*, 20–31; Miller, *Emigrants and Exiles*, 499, 503, 505, 509; Michael Kilcran, "Journal," Kerby A. Miller Collection, History Department, University of Missouri-Columbia. My thanks to Professor Miller for sharing the Kilcran journal with me.

49. Miller, *Emigrants and Exiles*, 3–4, 111, 325, 493; Kilcran, "Journal."

50. Barrett, *Work and Community in the Jungle*, 119–31; Schneirov, *Labor and Urban Politics*, 35–40, 48–53, 70–94, 109–38, ("cosmopolitan," 119); Hirsch, *Urban Revolt*, 21–42, 62–85, 117–43.

51. Schneirov, *Labor and Urban Politics*, 86, 99–161; Michael Funchion, *Chicago's Irish Nationalists, 1881–1890* (New York: Arno Press, 1976), 42–55; Stephen P. Erie, *Rainbow's End: Irish Americans and the Dilemmas of Urban Machine Politics, 1840–1985* (Berkeley: University of California Press, 1988), 21–22, 27–33, 40–45; Bruce C. Nelson, "Revival and Upheaval: Religion, Irreligion, and Chicago's Working Class in 1886," *Journal of Social History* 25 (1991), 233–35, 242–49; Ellen Skerrett, "The Development of Catholic Identity among Irish Americans in Chicago, 1880–1920," in Meagher, ed., *From Paddy to Studs*, 117–38.

"Come You All Courageously": Irish Women in America Write Home

RUTH-ANN M. HARRIS

WHAT WE KNOW ABOUT IMMIGRANTS has too often been seen through official lenses. Documentation beyond official sources is scarce because few immigrants conducted their lives with an eye to the biographer. If the world of immigrants is to be recovered, historians must be innovative in identifying and using nonconventional sources. Personal documents like letters are an especially appropriate source for research on immigrant and ethnic women, whose lives are so often hidden. In this essay I examine some of the themes that appear in letters written by Irish women.[1]

In Ireland two scholars based in Ulster were responsible for emigrant letters being given due place as historical documents. The late Rodney Green of Queen's University, Belfast, was the first to collect emigrant letters systematically, and it was he who first alerted many of us to their importance as documentary sources. Brian Trainor, while director of the Public Record Office of Northern Ireland, also ensured the collection and preservation of emigrant letters, encouraging researchers such as myself to work in a receptive atmosphere. Drawing attention to their documentary significance, Professor Green said that while emigrant letters are highly subjective material as historical documents, they do nevertheless allow one to make some valuable generalizations about the emigration/immigration experience.[2] Among other conclusions, he noted "the favourable reaction of the emigrants to American conditions. . . ."[3] Most emigrants would have agreed that, on balance, America offered more than had Ireland. Their letters, replete with statistical information about wages and prices, are valuable sources for economic history, demonstrating that immigrants often had a sophisticated awareness of local as well as international markets.

Emigrant letters have been extensively used by some American scholars. Arnold Schrier used letters as historical documents in his pioneering and evocative study, *Ireland and the American Emigration, 1850–1900*, published in 1958.[4] Drawing on 222 emigrant letters as documentation, he opened what has become a lively and continuing discussion about the use of letters as sources. Twenty-five years later, Patrick O'Farrell used emigrant letters to document the lives of the Irish in Australia, while Kerby Miller drew on a wide array of letters in his influential study, *Emigrants and Exiles: Ireland and the Irish Exodus to North America*, published in 1985.[5] Donald Harmon Akenson challenged the adequacy of these earlier approaches in an article drawing on a selection of letters from the Irish in Australia, New Zealand, and North America.[6] More recently, David Fitzpatrick has used detailed and informed textual analysis to elucidate Irish-Australian letters, extending the range of what historians can achieve with such sources.[7] My own method has been to use textual analysis to create a computerized database with five main categories: family name, letter author name, collection, recipient, and characteristics of each letter. The letters were analyzed in terms of subcategories such as push-and-pull conditions, mention of remittances, evidence of bad family relations, renewal of ties, choice of spouse, poetry, religion, and education. The themes were analyzed in two different ways, one using individual letters, the other using individual authors as the unit of observation.

Collections of emigrant letters are likelier to contain letters from men than from women, although some evidence suggests that women tended to write more often. Thus my research efforts located only ninety-five letters from forty-five female authors, while there were five hundred forty-four letters from one hundred seventy-six male authors on which to base an analysis.[8] The letters were collected from several sources in Ireland and America.[9] Following an examination of how the letters of women and men differed, I will explore a number of themes appearing in women's letters. With the exception of a memoir and one letter, all the women's letters in this collection were written in the nineteenth century. For reasons that are not entirely clear, letters from males generally contained a greater number of topics than did those from females. One explanation may be that men wrote fewer but longer letters than women.[10]

Differences in interpreting emigrant letters relate most frequently to what we do not know about those who made the decision to go to America. What we cannot avoid knowing, however, is that Irish families sent their children to the emigrant ship partly in order to protect those who remained at home, a strategy that necessitated the departure of those most able to remit funds home—i.e., the ablest members of the family. The information that such individuals chose to write home about may have been very selective, skewing the conclusions we can draw from their letters. As the immigrant Henry Johnson warned his wife back in Ireland, "Beware of most American letters you may hear. They either greatly overrate the matter or through ignorance put a false face upon the nature of things altogether."[11] Despite this warning, the "American letter" (as Irish families respectfully called it) has certain advantages over oral history in reconstructing what it meant to be an immigrant. While oral-history interviews are inevitably determined by retrospection, letters reflect immediate concerns and retain a proximate link with the past.

There are, however, some considerations that should be kept in mind when using letters as sources. Such documents frequently reveal the writer's inexperience in communicating the details of personal life on paper, and thus appear to have been neither a familiar nor a common form of expression for most immigrants. The tradition of emigration began earliest among Protestants from Ulster, many of whom ardently desired that family and friends would join them in America. In communicating this desire, they had the advantage of a higher degree of literacy than in other parts of the country, based largely on biblical instruction. The religious traditions of Nonconformists emphasized the value of personal experience, encouraging a distinct facility of observation and expression. Finally, most Protestant emigrants belonged to extensive social networks based on congregational, mercantile, and extended family links sustained by correspondence. Catholic emigrants, on the other hand, were far likelier to depart as individuals and were much less involved in continuous social networks.[12] Religious affiliation aside, it should also be remembered that emigrants who did produce letters were either literate or had had access to someone who was, and had family or friends in Ireland who valued their letters sufficiently to preserve them. Only those who had received some schooling and retained contact with literate family members in Ireland met these conditions; the poorest emigrants clearly did not.

Individual letters or collections of letters were preserved for a variety of reasons. Occasionally, letters appear to have had quasilegal aspects. In one case a letter and the fragment of a second from County Londonderry emigrant Catherine Ann McFarland was quite possibly preserved by her family as a kind of legal document affirming that whatever claims this daughter may have had on them had been discharged. The maintenance of counterclaims between family members was important in an age when parents could be left destitute in their old age if their emigrant children chose not to send money home. This threat is evident when Catherine states that her mother, a remarried widow, may some day need to call on her daughter. Referring to her mother's promise to send some household items, Catherine writes: "You [k]now you promised me something and perhaps i may send you as mutch yet no i mother if you can doo this for me, i now you will."[13]

Letter writers may also have been representative of the somewhat less-assimilated immigrant, their output diminishing as they became more accustomed to life in America and increasing as they became dissatisfied with life there. If this were so, it would impart a significant bias to the interpretation of letters. This is not to imply that letter writing was solely a matter of dissatisfaction and unhappiness; most migrants simply wanted to keep all options open, and writing home to family and friends was a way to maintain connections that could be drawn upon in the future, particularly if the writer sought to return to Ireland. Others have interpreted the restlessness expressed in emigrants' letters in terms of an alienation, fatalism, and passivity rooted in Irish Catholic culture. Yet this restlessness could just as well be seen as the pursuit of opportunity.[14]

Motivation, Expectation, and Realities

Concentrating on events within the family and household, women were less likely than men to discuss conditions either in America or in Ireland. And all letter writers, both male and female, were likelier to discuss the reasons that *drew* them to America than the conditions in Ireland that had *pushed* them abroad. Few single women would have been courageous enough to leave Ireland had there been attractive prospects to remain, which suggests that a primary motivation for women's emigration to America was the desire to improve their status. Until the demand for hand-spun yarns declined at mid-century, women were of considerable economic importance to the family as spinners, a contribution considered essential to the survival of many families in the west of Ireland. As the demand for hand-spun products diminished, Irish daughters lost their economic importance within the family, with the result that families wishing to preserve their status increasingly exported their surplus daughters to the emigrant ship. Thus one can conclude that the lack of the incentive or ability to remain within their families, coupled with rising levels of education and social expectation, led large numbers of Irish women to seek opportunity by emigrating.[15]

What were the emigrants' expectations, and how did they accord with the reality of life in America? According to Hasia Diner, young Irish servant girls expected great things on coming to America and enthusiastically corresponded with friends and relatives back home, endorsing their migration. Thus, for example, a seamstress in Connecticut wrote: "I am getting along splendid and likes my work. . . . I will soon have a trade and be more independent . . . ; you know it was always what I wanted so I have reached my highest ambition."[16] Widow Ellen O'Dea wrote to her "Beloved Son" that

> we was only four days landed in Washington when my two daughters was employed by two ladies living in Washington. They are employed at the rate of six dollars per month, that is £1 4s British currency. So now I expect as we are all together that coming on the following harvest we will join together and send as mutch as will bring Alisa out here as nothing would give us more pleasure than to have her with us.[17]

Another young emigrant, Margaret McCarthy from County Cork, sought to lure her family to join her in New York, telling them that "any man or woman without a family are fools that would not venture and come to this plentiful country where no man or woman every hungered or ever will and where you will not be seen naked."[18]

Other writers, however, warned of the dangers to be encountered in America. Julia Field wrote to her friend, Mrs. Corrigan, in Dublin, about her arrival in New York: ". . . it is every one for himself and who shall with each so that the desolate are sometimes at an unknown nonpluss [sic] but however as fortune ordained it I happened to be one of the favored children."[19] Alicia Shaw wrote home to her brother Richard in 1851 relating the hardships that their family was facing in antebellum Mississippi: "Our country in general has been quite sickly this last summer and fall. We had a new disease amongst us . . . which was very fatal."[20] Alicia's Aunt Sarah, who had assisted eight nieces and nephews to emigrate, when contemplating another request for assistance, wrote: "Poor girl, she little knows how hard it is for females without a father to get along in this country, close hard work and in many instances looked upon as hirelings." Margaret Gault, writing during the American Civil War, felt that the war had ruined opportunity for the immigrants: "This country is in a very bad state at present . . . ; [the Americans] have ruined the best country in the world. It was home for everybody, the distressed and down trodden of all nations. . . . I humbly pray that the Stars and Stripes will still wave over the land of the free and the home of the brave."[21]

The theme of expectation versus reality comes through strongly in the letters. Once in America, letter writers had to make the decision whether to be encouraging or realistic in relating their experience. America meant many things to incoming immigrants. It was a land of promise and opportunity, but also a land of shattered dreams and broken families. Julia Field recognized this when she informed her friend that

> this country in general is very good and markets cheap—but all persons coming here has to encounter abundance of hardships and difficulties unknown when they land on the shore unprovided—and destitute of friends or money, and no matter how clever they may be at home in abilities of earning bread they must here begin anew for they are in a new world among multitudes of strangers possessed of customs and laws entirely foreign—and it is a second apprenticeship.[22]

Mary Anne and Ann Jane Sinclair's letters to their cousin, Mary Ann Graham, diminished in number as they assimilated into American life, ceasing after about three years. In contrast, the letters written by their father John S. Sinclair continued for another ten years until he made a return visit to Ireland. While Mary Anne and Ann Jane's letters told of the newness and novelty of life in America, those of their father, with his land claims at home, dwelt on old grievances and events in Ireland.[23]

Soon after arriving in California, both Sinclair sisters found work with families in the San Francisco Bay area. Mary Anne Sinclair's first letter, undated but believed to have been written around 1879, shortly after the family's arrival, described the journey from Philadelphia across the continent by train as exciting—"I could tell you a great many things that would keep you laughing for a month"—and went on to describe her work as a servant in positive terms.[24] Ann Jane's first letter also describes how much she enjoyed her work as a maid: "I have a nice place her[e]," she wrote, prefacing the description of her tasks with the phrase "I have only" to do such and such.[25] In Mary Anne's next letter, dated 11 February 1880, her only reference to her job was that her employer had given her a silver thimble for Christmas.[26] Ann Jane's next letter, in the same month, discussed the many outings she had taken.[27] A year later, Ann Jane had changed her employer because she wanted to live in the country and was now working for an East Oakland family. She described her new employment as "a pleasant place and bigger wages" and said that she was taking three lessons a week on the family's piano.[28] By June 1882 Mary Anne also had new employers. She was working for a childless couple, and her "lady" had taught her to do all kinds of cooking and housework so that she was, as she said, much too busy to be homesick any more.[29] The absence of further letters from either of the sisters suggests that part of the motivation in writing had been to retain the contact with home, and that once they had begun to settle into their new lives in America, there were fewer incentives to write. Home had become America.

Mary Gayer Anderson, a clergyman's daughter from Rostrevor, Co. Down, brought a servant, Margaret, with her when she came to America with her husband and four children in the early 1870s. While Margaret had not worked for the Andersons in Ireland, she came well recommended. Mary Anderson would have been accustomed to obsequious behavior from servants and so was scarcely ready for the changes in Margaret after the family began to settle into life in America. At first she could not have praised Margaret more. Throughout the voyage to America, when all the family was seasick, Margaret's care of them was beyond compare: "Margaret is a great comfort, so strong and willing, very fond of the children, also very sensitive and intelligent."[30] Servants were so scarce on the frontier that Mary said that some chose to live in hotels rather than manage a household without staff. After the Andersons had been in Wichita, Kansas, for a while, there appeared the first hint that Margaret had begun to compare her life with that of other servants, chafing at the wide range of responsibilities that she was expected to undertake, including child care. Mary wrote:

> Margaret is doing very well—and since I spoke to her about keeping her Irish ways and manners, has behaved very well—but it is quite "infra dig" for a "Help" to work with children and she is not going to do it. She is, however, very friendly with and I think fond of them. She has an easy time here. I make the beds, settle the rooms and do anything I can of that sort. She goes out after 6 o'clock tea every Sunday and does not come in till 10.[31]

Later, she wrote:

> Margaret does very well in all she does for us and is always cheerful and good-tempered but each week I see less inclination to do things, trying to put more and more on me and do less and less herself. She has a fine time of it—constantly out and so little work to do, she never touches the children, nor my room, nor the drawing room nor the parlor except to lay the table. She makes the nursery bed, but does not sweep the floor unless told to do so. Would not put coal on the fire. . . . However it is a blessing to have her, so few have any help. Aunt M. says it is the way always with girls brought from home. When Henry [Mary's husband] was explaining to her how much wages she was to have, in paying us back for her expenses he said, "You agreed to come for £30 a year, I will make it $3 a

week, that is about £33 a year, the usual wages here." She said quite
coolly, "Girls here who do the washing get $4 a week." Henry said, "Well,
I will not give you $4 a week."[32] Later, "Margaret sometimes satisfactory,
sometimes careless. I am sure I shan't keep her very long—she also has
sweethearts!"[33]

Many years later, she wrote in her memoir that Margaret had left the
family's employ because she "got into trouble." Whatever may really
have finally happened to sever the relationship, there is no doubt that
after a few years in America Margaret could never again be the grateful
serving maid who had followed her mistress to America.

Work, Remittances, Family, and Marriage

Women's letters demonstrate an intense determination to save. The
incentives for saving varied, but the evidence suggests that most Irish
women saved in order to send money back to families in Ireland. In the
letters represented here, women were likelier than men to enclose remittances of either money or prepaid passage tickets for other family members. These remittances were part of a network of reciprocal relationships among family members. Margaret McCarthy's letter to her family
in Cork illustrates the reiterated understanding of mutual claims
between family members that accompanied remittances. She enclosed
a sum of money, but her letter also carried the threat that she would
send no more until she saw her family in America. Margaret emigrated
from the Kingwilliamstown crown estate in the parish of Nohavaldaly,
near Kanturk on the Cork-Kerry border, during the famine years as one
of a group of poor tenants whose passages were financed by the crown
as a way of clearing the estate of "uneconomic tenants." In her letter,
dated 22 September 1850, she sought to persuade her family to take the
next opportunity for assisted emigration:

> Have courage and prepare yourself for the next time that that worthy
> man Mr. Boyan is sending out the next lot; and come you all together
> courageously and bid adieu to that lovely place the land of our Birth. . . .
> So prepare as soon as possible for this will be my last Remittance until I
> see you all here.[34]

Hers was a typical "American letter," representing what David Fitzpatrick has called "a carefully coded political statement, rich in half-
articulated signals and warnings, and minutely studied by its audience."[35] Margaret's intention was to convince and inspire her family to
join her, although there is no evidence that she was successful in per-
suading them to do so. Her letter reiterates the theme of mutual obliga-

tion—in this case, her family must now reciprocate by joining her in America. Margaret McCarthy confidently assured her parents:

> I believe that we will all do well Together So as that I am sure it's not for slavery I want you to come here. No, it's for affording . . . an opportunity of Showing our Kindness and Gratitude and Coming on your seniour days that you, my D[ea]r Father and Mother could walk about Leisurely and independently without Requiring your Labour, an object which I am Sure will not fail even by myself if I was obliged to do it without the assistance of Brother or Sister.[36]

Desire to reunite with siblings and family members was pervasive among Irish female emigrants. Vere Foster learned that by the 1870s most women who applied for assistance to emigrate already had relatives, usually siblings, in North America. That the sibling relationship was a very strong one can be seen in the advertisements that Irish persons placed in the *Boston Pilot* in search of relatives, 65 percent of which were placed by siblings.[37] In the distinctive rural society that emerged in postfamine Ireland, sibling relations, especially between sisters, seem to have been especially strong.[38] Kathleen and Nora Corr's father discouraged his daughters from emigrating in the 1920s, for example, because he believed that moving to America would expose them to all sorts of immorality. However, the sisters were determined to have a different life. Kathleen borrowed money from a relative and emigrated to New York, where, after having established herself, she sent for her sister. Once Nora had arrived, the sisters were roommates until Nora married. In Kathleen's letter home, in which she described Nora's wedding in minute detail, she wrote:

> I needn't tell you I'm lonesome, as you can imagine how I feel after four years constantly together—I actually imagine I'm cut in two sometimes, but it won't be so bad when she comes back as Bill has such long hours she'll be able to spend almost as much time with me as heretofore.[39]

Diner suggests that sibling bonds may even have strengthened as a result of emigration because the siblings were no longer rivals for the family inheritance: "The importance of sibling relationships in adulthood also survived the transoceanic journey. . . . They succored one another and provided support in the cycle of crises of poverty and illness, desertion and widowhood."[40]

The ten children of the Shaw family, five brothers and five sisters, remained exceptionally close. Only Richard and Mary remained in Ireland, which suggests that they were the first-born children, one to inherit the land and the other the dowry. The letters to Richard were preserved, and they discuss the well-being of the sisters and brothers scattered around antebellum Mississippi and Texas. They tell of Matilda's marriage, their brother George's death, and the financial status of James, who, as he prospered in Texas politics, drew away from the rest, a cause of much grief to his Aunt Sarah, who wrote, "As for James we never hear from him. We have all written to him but it is all the Same he will not let any of us hear from him. So I suppose we must give him up."[41]

As in the case of Kathleen Corr, many young Irish women sought to finance the emigration of their siblings. In one study Maureen Murphy found that among women going to America for the first time at the turn of the twentieth century, 75 percent had their passage paid by a sister, and 100 percent were going to a sister.[42] There is no evidence in the letters that the tie with their Irish families was a burden for women, but men did not always relish the connection. Patrick Magill, who was bitter about his obligation to support his family, eventually broke off all contact with his Donegal family:

> I never for a moment thought of keeping all my wages for myself. Such a wild idea never entered my head. I was born and bred merely to support my parents, and great care had been taken to drive this fact into my mind from infancy. I was merely brought into the world to support those who were responsible for my existence. Often when my parents were speaking of such and such a young man I heard them say: "He'll never have a day's luck in all his life. He didn't give every penny he earned to his father and mother."[43]

Letters renewing ties after an absence were about evenly divided between men and women, but women were likelier to attempt to renew ties broken by emigration. One example of this appears in the letters of Rose McCormick Williams when she wrote to her aunt twenty-seven years after arriving as a famine immigrant in New Orleans. Her letter is a graphic account of the misfortunes that could separate a family as well as the kindness of strangers who ensured the survival of the remaining children. She told her aunt in 1879:

> You ask me to tell you how long my Mother and father are dead, also my brothers. It has been so long and I was so young that I have but a faint recollection of what transpired. We had been ten weeks on sea and had a very rough voyage of it. We all landed in New Orleans safe, sound, and healthy, [indecipherable] everything seemed to be prosperous for us, but unfortunately it did not remain so long, for seven days after we landed Mother and James died and were buried the same day. They all died with a sort of cholera, which was at the time raging here. We had a priest to attend to them in their last moments.

Williams then related what had happened to her remaining siblings in America:

> Being in a strange land, amongst strangers and not being able to help one another we had to separate and do the best we could. Of course being young we did not miss the loss of our parents but many and many a time since have I missed them. Patrick was taken in charge by a gentleman who took him to Cincinnati, where he remained for some years when he came back to New Orleans, and then learned the trade of ship carpenter. He remained in N[ew] O[rleans] for some time, and then went off travelling and finally settled [in] Columbus, Georgia, where he still resides. He is married, and has three children. . . . William remained in N[ew] O[rleans] for a long time. A few years previous to our late rebellion he went to Texas, and I had not seen him for some years when he was taken prisoner by the Federal forces and brought to N[ew] O[rleans]. So I went to see him nearly every day during his imprisonment here. He was kept a captive here for a long time, and when released went to a place called Lake Charles where he resides at present, and engaged in business there for himself. He also is making a good living . . . ; if possible I am going to send my son out to see him in a few weeks. tom and myself remained in N[ew] O[rleans] and therefore have always seen one another. . . .

Finally, she told her own story:

> As to myself, I was taken in charge by a lady from the County Cavan, and remained with her until I was capable of going to work. After working around for some time, I was married and lost my husband some years after. . . . I having been keeping a grocery store for the last four years, and all of my children remain at home with me. Business is very dull, therefore not making any money, just a living. My brothers and I had a rough time of it, but always managed to make an honest living.[44]

In Ireland marriage could be considered only if males and females each brought sufficient resources to establish a viable union. Males generally brought land, while females brought a dowry, used in part to capitalize the new unit and in part to enable the groom's family to provide dowries for other daughters. Sons without land and daughters without dowries either worked as unpaid labor on the family farm or sold their labor in the cash economy. The distribution of land and dowry was the prerogative of the senior males of the family, and this kept unmarried children subject to patriarchal control. Nevertheless, possession of a dowry gave women power within the household because women maintained individual claims on their dowries.[45] As the landholding system of partible inheritance began to give way to primogeniture, so was the custom of distributing dowries to all the daughters transformed. Families increasingly sought to consolidate their resources by giving a dowry to only one daughter. As early as the 1830s observers such as John Revans, secretary to the Poor Law Commission, noted how important it was for women to marry in order to secure their survival.[46] The declining wage-earning capabilities of both men and women in the postfamine era made things even worse.

That Margaret McCarthy would have known the resulting difficulties at firsthand is attested to by Michael Boyan, who attributed the great poverty of many tenants to the large numbers of married daughters forced to return to their natal families when there husbands fell into debt, thereby exhausting the family's already precarious resources.[47] The result was that young people married less frequently and at later ages, while the choice of marriage partners was determined and restricted by the dowry system. Irish families and the Catholic church together enforced this system of female dependence and sexual repression.[48]

While marriage may have been more easily attainable for Irish women in America, their letters back to Ireland demonstrate a caution bred of their experience prior to emigration. This caution is evident, for example, in the letters of Sarah Shaw and Margaret Jane Moore. In Sarah's letter to her nephew she referred to a prior letter announcing her niece's impending marriage:

> Matilda [is] to change her name to that of Bell. he is of stable . . . habits but poor which was a very great Objaction with me, if she was of a strong constitution with his Industry the[y] might do well . . . but I trusts the Lord will bless their endeavours and with that if the[y] are not rich the[y] will be happy.[49]

Her niece, Margaret Moore, looked kindly on the marriage of the Lackart family, with whom her aunt lived because the couple appeared to be prosperous:

> He is an Irish man, and a very fine little woman for his wife . . . , very attentive to her, and is very comfortably [situated]. The[y] have a son large enough to drive to Lexington [Mississippi] every two or three weeks . . . very good salary . . . gay and very fine of dress.[50]

Women's letters demonstrate that they sought to maintain their economic independence by marrying cautiously and relatively late. Their access to cash income made them more able to control their own fates and determine the course of their lives, altering gender relations between immigrant men and women. Marriage and family formation were now subject to a different set of rules. In a letter to her mother, Catherine Ann McFarland emphasized that Hugh Hutchinson, who had offered her marriage, did not expect her to bring a dowry. While pressing her mother to send her promised household items, she said that Hugh "does not want anething but my selfe but still I think its hard not to have my own bed."[51]

According to Christiane Harzig, many immigrants discovered or could enjoy romantic love for the first time in America, the concept having been either alien or impracticable in their natal countries.[52] Mary Harlon learned in America that if a suitor did not please her, she could refuse to marry him, telling Vere Foster: "The man I told you about that ast me to marie him, I did not care for him."[53] Because women could afford to be selective in choosing a husband, some men suffered because of their adherence to old ways of marrying. After losing an opportunity for marriage, William Shanks reflected: "All I can say I lost my darlin with the courtin too slow. The next one that I spark will not have that to say. I will put marriage to her at once and have done with it." His uncle did not like the American ways of marriage and planned to return to Ireland for a wife: "Uncil William is coming home this fall for a wife. He hopes you will have on[e] picked out for him."[54]

For some young Irish women, coming to America was clearly a safety valve. Margaret McCarthy considered her dismal prospects had she remained in Ireland: "Oh how happy I feel and am sure to have looke[d] as[at?] the Lord had not it destined for [me] to get married to Some *Loammun* [a man of poor prospects] that after a few months he and I may be an incumberance upon you or perhaps in the Poor House by this [time]."[55] Julia Field fled to America to escape someone who was probably her husband. Working as a domestic in the New York household of the elder brother of Robert Emmet, she wrote to her friend Mrs. Corrigan:

> [I] do require your friendship and truly rely on it to send me as you have promised a full and particular account of Christ[opher?] and his relatives conduct and opinion of me since my abrupt departure. Bye and part from him I never would, only for his Brothers for firstly they disrespected me and that unjustly—Nevertheless my feelings are not estranged from my fated partner and I hope in my God we shall yet meet and be happy and in a short time hence I have not forgot my duty to him and never will. My Brother has not at all sanctioned my separation and it is his utmost wish to see us united—My friend much depends on your answer to your far distant but faithful old friend till death.[56]

Some believed that in Ireland couples married for riches while in America they married for love and worked for riches. As the letters illustrate, the decision to marry was still a very important one. The new economic opportunities in America disturbed traditional ideas of marriage, but what was missing was the financial necessity that often forced women to marry. Nevertheless, in some regions of North America women were in high demand as marriage partners. One of Vere Foster's informants said of Irish girls:

> Many, especially at the West, report the customary position of such girls in the family as that of daughters, sitting at the same table, dressing as well or better, riding to the village church in the same vehicle, and say that they appear to marry even quicker than the ladies. The tendency throughout the West to *immediate marriage* is a subject of general *complaint.* One counts over his girls on his fingers with this curious statistical result: "In the last eight years I have had in my employ 23 girls, 19 of whom have married out of my house."[57]

Conclusion

The Margaret McCarthys and Mary Harlons of Ireland were expected to display a forelock-tugging humility in the presence of their "betters," not because they were Irish or even because they were female but simply because they were poor. Mary's letters show that she knew what was expected of her. Nevertheless, while she obeyed her brothers and her priest, she also learned in America that she did not have to remain where her efforts were not appreciated. She used the newspaper to find new employment and in a later letter told of refusing a suitor who had failed to please.

The generally positive view of domestic service in the letters is corroborated in Joy Lintelman's study of immigrant letters from Swedish domestic servants in America.[58] Lintelman found that Swedish immigrants considered their work "attractive and rewarding." Rather than feeling trapped in a job that lacked respect as well as opportunities for individual growth and personal recreation, these women capitalized on their ethnic networks to counter problems common to household workers. Most were not eager to leave domestic service and expressed greater satisfaction in domestic service than did white, native-born women.[59] For most Irish women domestic service offered advantages unavailable at home and so was a mostly positive experience.

On the other hand, domestic employment was less satisfactory for women for whom it marked a deterioration in their standard of living. And Irish women's strong commitment to education for their children would suggest a deliberate strategy to create opportunities so that their daughters would not have to become domestic workers. Even the abandonment of the name Bridget by the second generation of Irish Americans suggests a deliberate distancing of Irish immigrants from a name connoting the archetypal female domestic worker.

Research on Irish emigration increasingly suggests that emigrants were not drawn primarily from the most impoverished groups but from those who saw their opportunities declining and sought to re-create in the New World what was slipping from them in Ireland. This is certainly true of the letter writers. It would also appear to be true of many of those in the "Missing Friends" sample drawn from advertisements placed in the *Boston Pilot*, which suggests that the approximately 31,000 persons sought from 1831 through 1863 were not the most impoverished. Almost 14 percent of those sought were reported as having pre-industrial skills; the males were blacksmiths or masons or coopers.[60] John Mannion's study of males emigrating to Newfoundland from the 1760s through the 1870s concludes that the majority of those migrating from southeastern Ireland were the children of comfortable Catholic farmers whose family strategy was to encourage noninheriting sons to emigrate and thus keep the family farm intact.[61]

Emigrants' letters do, of course, have their limitations as sources. Emigrants did not always describe their true feelings and circumstances, nor were they inclined to admit failure in the new land, so that the immigrant who urged others to beware of the news carried in the "American letter" was partly correct. Yet the value of women's letters lies in how often they express common themes, thereby suggesting that there was a collective experience of what it meant to be an immigrant over time and across space. The letters of these women speak to a wide audience. They suggest that the problems of Irish women relate to the problems faced by all immigrant women. Women's voices have powerful messages for us when they are allowed to speak, and when we can find ways to give them expression.

NOTES

1. I conducted some of the research on the emigrant letters while Senior Research Fellow at the Institute of Irish Studies, Queen's University, Belfast, in 1994–95. I wish to thank my colleagues there and at the Public Record Office of Northern Ireland, Belfast (PRONI).

2. E. R. R. Green, "Ulster Emigrants' Letters," in E. R. R. Green, ed., *Essays in Scotch-Irish History* (London, 1969), 87–103.

3. Ibid., 96.

4. Arnold Schrier, *Ireland and the American Emigration, 1850–1900* (Minneapolis, 1958).

5. Patrick O'Farrell (with Brian Trainor), *Letters from Irish Australia, 1825–1929* (Sydney and Belfast, 1984); Kerby A. Miller, *Emigrants and Exiles: Ireland and the Irish Exodus to North America* (New York, 1985). See also Kerby A. Miller, with B. Boling and D. N. Doyle, "Emigrants and Exiles: Irish Culture and Irish Emigration to North America, 1790–1922," *Irish Historical Studies* 82 (September 1980): 97–125.

6. D. H. Akenson, "Reading the Texts of Rural Immigrants: Letters from the Irish in Australia, New Zealand, and North America," in *Canadian Papers in Rural History* 7 (Kingston, 1989), 387–406.

7. David Fitzpatrick, "'An Ocean of Consolation': Letters and Irish Immigration to Australia," in Eric Richards, Richard Reid, and David Fitzpatrick, eds., *Visible Immigrants: Neglected Sources for the History of Australian Immigration* (Canberra, 1989), 56–86.

8. There is a disparity between the total of all authors (227) and the total number of letters (650) because six authors and eleven letters cannot be identified by gender.

9. I have located letters in the National Library, Dublin; the Quit Rent Office (QRO) of the Public Record Office (PRO), Dublin; and PRONI, Belfast. In America the letters I have collected were donated by individuals.

10. Unlike men, women rarely made connections between their private and public lives, which may also help to account for why fewer women's letters were preserved by their families.

11. Johnson to his wife Jane McConnell Johnson, in Louise Wyatt, ed., "The Johnson Letters," *Ontario History* 11 (1948), 40. Hereafter referred to as Johnson family letters.

12. I am assuming here that a single individual striking out on his or her own had somewhat less incentive to maintain a correspondence with home than did those who saw themselves as part of a web of immigrants. David Doyle has drawn attention to the fact that the eighteenth-century emigration from the southern counties of Ireland was primarily that of single males, many of whom assimilated into mainstream America when they married non-Irish women.

13. PRONI, D1665/3/6, Catherine Ann McFarland to her mother, 5 March 1855. Hereafter referred to as McFarland letters.

14. PRONI, D1665/3/6. Cf. Miller, *Emigrants and Exiles*, with its emphasis on the "exile motif." If writing letters home to family and friends in Ireland was a way to maintain connections that could be drawn upon, and single women had fewer social as well as economic reasons for maintaining those connections, they may also have had correspondingly fewer incentives to maintain lengthy correspondences with family and friends in Ireland. This may also help to account for the lower number of extant women's letters.

15. For a discussion of this, see Joseph J. Lee, "Women and the Church since the Famine," in Margaret MacCurtain and Donncha Ó Corráin, eds., *Women in Irish Society: The Historical Dimension* (Dublin, 1978), 37–45.

16. Hasia R. Diner, *Erin's Daughters in America: Irish Immigrant Women in the Nineteenth Century* (Baltimore, 1983), 71.

17. PRONI, D3618/D25/5, Mrs. Ellen O'Dea to her unnamed son, 27 May 1858, Vere Foster papers.

18. QRO file 11821, PRO, Dublin. Margaret McCarthy to her parents, 22 September 1850. Hereafter referred to as Margaret McCarthy letter.

19. Field letter.

20. Sarah Shaw to her nephew Richard Shaw, 10 January 1852. Hereafter referred to as Shaw family letters. Private collection.

21. Margaret Gault to "Friends," 11 December 1858. Hereafter referred to as Gault letters. Private collection.

22. Field letter.

23. PRONI, D1497, Sinclair family. The sisters' letters are part of a large file of correspondence from various members of the Sinclair family who emigrated in the late 1870s from Draperstown in the parish of Ballynascreen, Co. Tyrone, to Healdsburg, California. The Sinclair family letters may have been preserved for quasilegal reasons because many of John Sinclair's letters maintained claims over Irish land that he believed still to be his. Hereafter referred to Sinclair family letters.

24. PRONI, D1497, Sinclair family letters.

25. PRONI, D1497/4/2, Sinclair family letters.

26. PRONI, D1497/4/3, Sinclair family letters.

27. PRONI, D1497/4/4, Sinclair family letters.

28. PRONI, D1497/4/7, Sinclair family letters.

29. PRONI, D1497/2/2, Sinclair family letters.

30. PRONI, T3258/4, Mary Gayer Anderson to her parents, 8 September 1884. Hereafter referred to as Anderson letters.

31. Ibid.

32. Ibid.

33. PRONI, T3258/4/7.

34. Margaret McCarthy letter. Michael Boyan was the estate agent.

35. David Fitzpatrick, "The Irish in America: Exiles or Escapers?" *Reviews in American History* (June 1987), 272–79.

36. Margaret McCarthy letter.

37. Ruth-Ann M. Harris, Donald Jacobs, B. Emer O'Keefe, eds., *The Search for Missing Friends: Irish Immigrant Advertisements Placed in the Boston* Pilot, 8 vols., 1831–1916 (Boston, 1989–2000).

38. Diner, *Erin's Daughters*, 15.

39. Kathleen Corr to her parents, 5 October 1925. Private collection.

40. Diner, *Erin's Daughters*, 45.

41. Sarah Shaw, Shaw family letters.

42. Maureen Murphy, "The Fionnuala Factor: Irish Sibling Emigration at the Turn of the Century," in Anthony Bradley and Maryann Gialanella Valiulis, eds., *Gender and Sexuality in Modern Ireland* (Amherst, Mass., 1997), 85–101.

43. Patrick Magill, *Children of the Dead End: The Autobiography of a Navvy* (London and New York, 1914), 48.

44. PRONI, T3258/28, Rose McCormick Williams to her aunt, 10 July 1879. Hereafter referred to as McCormick Williams letters.

45. For a study of the significance of the dowry in the Carrickmacross region of County Monaghan, see Ruth-Ann M. Harris, "Negotiating Patriarchy: Irish Women and the Landlord," in Marilyn Cohen and Nancy J. Curtin, eds., *Reclaiming Gender: Transgressive Identities in Modern Ireland* (New York, 1999), 215–16.

46. John Revans, *Evils of the State of Ireland: Their Cause and Their Remedy: A Poor Law* (London, 1835).

47. QRO correspondence file 11821, PRO, Dublin. Michael Boyan to Commissioner of Woods, Charles Gore.

48. For the best recent discussion, see Timothy Guinnane, *The Vanishing Irish: Households, Migration, and the Rural Economy in Ireland, 1850–1914* (Princeton, N.J., 1997).

49. Shaw family letters.

50. Margaret Jane Shaw Moore to her brother Richard, 1 August 1848. Shaw family letters.

51. McFarland letter.

52. See Christiane Harzig, "Women Move from the European Countryside to Urban America," in Christiane Harzig, ed., *Peasant Maids, City Women: From the European Countryside to Urban America* (Ithaca and London, 1997), 16–17.

53. PRONI, D3618/D/25/10, Mary Harlon to Vere Foster, 16 October 1865.

54. PRONI, D2709/1/15, Williams Shanks to his mother, 26 June 1875.

55. Margaret McCarthy letter.

56. Field letter.

57. As quoted in Vere Foster, *Work and Wages; or, The Penny Emigrant's Guide to the United States and Canada* (London, 1851), no pagination.

58. Joy K. Lintelman, "'America Is the Woman's Promised Land': Swedish Immigrant Women and American Domestic Service," in George E. Pozzetta, ed., *The Work Experience: Labor, Class, and Immigrant Enterprise* (New York and London, 1991), Vol. 6, 385–99.

59. Ibid., 395.

60. See R. A. Harris, "Introduction," in Ruth-Ann M. Harris and Donald M. Jacobs, eds., *The Search for Missing Friends: Irish Immigrant Advertisements Placed in the Boston Pilot, Volume 1, 1831–1850* (Boston, 1989), and R. A. Harris, "Introduction," in Ruth-Ann M. Harris and B. Emer O'Keefe, eds., *The Search for Missing Friends: Irish Immigrant Advertisements Placed in the Boston Pilot, Volume II, 1850–1853* (Boston, 1991).

61. See John Mannion, "The Regional and Social Origins of Irish Emigrants to Newfoundland, 1780–1830." Unpublished paper delivered to the Social Science History Association, New Orleans, Louisiana, November 1991.

Relinquishing and Reclaiming Independence: Irish Domestic Servants, American Middle-Class Mistresses, and Assimilation, 1850–1920

DIANE M. HOTTEN-SOMERS

BETWEEN THE ONSET OF THE Great Famine and the restriction of immigration in the 1920s, some five million Irish people emigrated to North America. Roughly half of these emigrants were female, and most were young and single.[1] In America's rapidly developing industrial society Irish women, even more than Irish men, were highly employable.[2] For women of the newly emerging American middle class, employing a servant became a badge of respectability and class legitimacy. No longer directly engaged in the production of wealth, these women were becoming increasingly involved in consuming it instead; and to be active as consumers and members of the public sphere they needed surrogates to run their households. The flood of Irish immigrant women readily met this demand. And because most Irish female immigrants arrived impoverished, unskilled, and single—and were apparently unaffected by the social stigma attached to domestic service—they eagerly accepted the opportunity to work in service. Thus by the turn of the century the Irish "Bridget" had become an integral part of the middle-class American home.[3]

Many historians have interpreted the Irish woman's emigration to America and her work in domestic service as a liberating experience. Both Hasia Diner and Janet Nolan, for example, emphasize the new-found autonomy of young Irish women in the US.[4] While Nolan focuses her argument on the idea that through emigrating and working within America, Irish women hoped to "regain the freedom that women had had in pre-Famine Ireland," Diner concentrates on showing that Irish women's emigration to America was an exercise in "cultural persistence," freeing young women to express themselves once they had escaped abroad.[5] Thus, while domestic service certainly carried some disadvantages, the consensus is that it was certainly an improvement over Ireland, and that, from the secure setting of the middle-class household, the young women involved could carve out for themselves and for their children a better life in America.

While this interpretation does discuss the nature of domestic work at some length, it does not adequately consider how Irish women's "working" relationships with their American middle-class mistresses shaped their immigrant experience. The Irish servant and the American mistress are treated almost as separate entities who barely interacted and almost never influenced each other's identities. This perspective, of course, serves well the argument for independent Irish womanhood. But it does not adequately address the process of assimilation, a critical aspect of the immigrants' lives. When the mistress and maid are brought together, rather than treated as separate entities, what becomes apparent is that the mistress-maid relationship not only defined the Irish woman's process of assimilation into American society, but also greatly helped American middle-class women to renegotiate their identities in the public sphere that became increasingly open to them during the second half of the nineteenth century.

This essay will consider both sides of the mistress-maid relationship as a single social process. Did the relationship between American mistresses and Irish maids force the latter to appropriate the values of their middle-class mistresses, thereby sacrificing much of the independence pointed to by previous historians? And in what ways were the experiences of both maids and mistresses shaped by the social, political, and economic changes in American culture that freed the mistresses to roam the public sphere? By considering firsthand accounts by Irish domestics, along with descriptions by contemporary observers, I will argue that the *interdependent* relationship between these two classes of women reveals, among other things, middle-class America's prejudice toward the Irish and the manner in which a significant portion of Irish immigrants were taught to replace their so-called uncivilized Irish character with a proper, "civilized" American one. Yet these same sources, firsthand accounts, and contemporary descriptions also suggest an evolution in this relationship in tandem with larger socio-economic and cultural changes in American history. As the Progressive Era (1900–17) of social and political reforms provoked a revolution in the domestic-service industry, servants increasingly became "live-out" rather than "live-in" household employees. The mistress-maid relationship changed accordingly from interdependence to one defined by much greater independence on both sides, whereby the maid, now freed from living in the confines of the American middle-class home, could reconnect with her Irish community and cultural ways; and the mistress, freed from supervising a full-time maid, turned at least part of her attention back to the household.

-1-

By the late nineteenth century millions of women had taken permanent positions as servants in American households. No longer was domestic service simply a fleeting position agreeably taken on by young women prior to setting up their own households.[6] It had become a serious business that women entered into, often permanently and always with the intention of economic gain.[7] According to the calculations of Lucy Salmon, an expert on domestic service and Professor of Home Economics at Vassar College, by 1897 the service industry had become a multimillion-dollar business, with employers paying out $160 million in wages to domestic servants around the country.[8]

Why did American middle-class households hire "live-in" servants by the hundreds of thousands? Employing servants had become an integral part of the new middle-class culture that arose in the second half of the nineteenth century. There was a theatricality to middle-class social conduct, according to cultural historian Karen Halttunen, that mandated that its actors wear specific clothing, fill their homes with appropriate material goods, and interact in a particular manner in public, all in the name of self-identifying as members of the middle class. Violating this code of conduct might entail the loss of middle-class status. One of the most important signs that identified one's family as part of middle-class culture was the employment of a servant; and the more servants one had, the higher up the social ladder one climbed.[9] Thus, as thousands of American families moved into the middle classes in nineteenth-century America, the need for able-bodied servants grew accordingly.[10]

Hand-in-hand with this growing need for servants went the renegotiation of the American middle-class woman's domestic responsibilities. As the industrial revolution moved middle-class families' means of economic gain out of the home and into workshops and factories, middle-class American women were freed of many of their former work responsibilities. Before the onset of industrial America women had been an integral part of the domestic economy. As their husbands assumed the role of primary or exclusive providers, however, middle-class women were freed from direct involvement in production. These women were increasingly free to enter the public sphere as "leisured wives," both as consumers and as activists for social and political reform.[11] Yet this freedom could be double-edged, for these women were by no means absolved of the responsibility for making their homes sites of pure and peaceful domesticity. On the contrary, they were still obligated to participate in the "cult of true womanhood," whereby women ensured that their homes were a "haven in a heartless world" for their husbands and children.[12] Thus the middle-class woman found herself in quite a predicament. On the one hand, society expected her to continue her role as arbiter of domestic moral and material well-being; on the other hand, she had a new-found opportunity—in her mind perhaps even a responsibility—to leave the household and participate in the public sphere. One of the ways that middle-class women attempted to resolve this dilemma was by hiring domestic servants. As David Katzman argues, "The greater liberty of these middle-class women was achieved at the expense of working-class women, who, forced to work, assumed the tasks beneath, distasteful to, or too demanding for the family members."[13]

Irish female immigrants provided the perfect source to fulfill the middle-class woman's need for domestic help. It is estimated that 1.2 million Irish women emigrated to America between 1851 and 1920.[14] Between 1860 and 1920 the number of female workers claiming domestic service as their occupation in the US census climbed from 559,908 to 1,012,133.[15] According to a report by the Women's Education and Industrial Union (a Boston-based organization whose work for the advancement of women made them one of the nineteenth century's most successful and influential social-reformist groups), Irish women held close to 15 percent of all domestic-servant positions nationwide. In areas densely populated by Irish immigrants, like Massachusetts, the Irish made up more than half of the domestic-service work force.[16] At the same time, looking at these figures from the Irish point of view, fully 60.5 percent of all Irish-born women in the US (i.e., the immigrant generation) worked as domestic servants in 1900.[17]

Irish women's entry into domestic service, however, was far from smooth. Though many of them had been "servants," in Ireland they were accustomed to working on farms, not in middle-class urban households. They had little prior knowledge of the modern cleaning, cooking, or laundry techniques that were the backbone to maintaining the middle-class home. Nor had they much if any grasp of the complicated code of morals and values that these American homes were meant to embody. When an Irish girl arrived in America, her skills as a servant reflected her native culture's idea of domestic work. Harriet Prescott Spofford, a prominent and prolific contemporary writer on the problems in domestic service, outlines the cultural disparity that existed between housework in Ireland and America:

> Does your maid waste the food, scattering here, giving away there, saving nowhere, spoiling everything? . . . Do mop and broom in her hands . . . [do] their task slightingly, the one sparing corners, and the other leaving windows of sweeping behind it? If you reflect that her floors at home were earthen ones, you will think it remarkable that she has learned to use such implements with half the skill she does. Does your treasured china slip through her fingers, does she nick the edges of your cut glass and break more than the values of her wages? Perhaps if you yourself had done no more dainty work all your life than the farm-work of the fields, hoeing, weeding, binding sheaves, all that is so picturesque in the fancy of Ireland and Scotland . . . , then china would slip through your fingers too.[18]

If the Irish woman's ignorance of American middle-class ways constituted one-half of what would come to be known as the "servant girl problem," the other half came from the negative sentiments that Americans held for the Irish. Of course, the two cannot always be separated in practice; but Irish women did objectively lack knowledge of American middle-class mores, while American women harbored preconceptions about Irish character and culture transcending this specific lack. Many American middle-class women, for example, expressed their revulsion at what they saw as the dirty and uncivilized nature of Irish women. At the same time they feared that the Irish women's "popery" would contaminate their highly moral Protestant homes. Thus many mistresses joined the ranks of the American nativists, stating in their advertisements for servants that "No Irish Need Apply."[19]

Mrs. Caroline Barrett White's experience with Irish servants exemplifies the frustration of many American mistresses. In her diary she records that between the months of April and June 1859 she hired and fired three Irish cooks, claiming that their uncontrollable tempers, erratic work schedules, and ignorance of proper cooking techniques and dinner menus made them worthless servants. White's irritation was mild at first. After firing her first cook, she wistfully wrote: "I do wish I might find some good Protestant girls of some other nation besides Irish." However, by the time that her third cook left, White was beyond irritation and began to express disdain for the entire Irish people: "I am heartily sick of the Irish."[20] Sentiments like these reinforced the cultural disparity between mistresses and maids, erecting obstacles to Irish women's desire to learn how to cross the great cultural divide between them and their American employers.

One way that mistresses sought to resolve the "servant girl problem" was to take the time to train their Irish maids thoroughly in the ways of properly maintaining their middle-class homes. However, this "training" clearly implied a kind of coerced assimilation into the American middle-class value system. As Katzman has argued, "The employer required conformity to the standards and overt values of the family; whether or not the servant accepted these, she would have to live by the standards and rhythms of the middle-class employers."[21] Ensuring that the Irish girl appropriated these values was of the utmost importance for the mistress, because as she spent more time outside the home attending to both her leisure activities and professional or social responsibilities, she needed to have a domestic surrogate fulfilling her obligations at home. If the servant did not learn to uphold the expected standards in the absence of her mistress, the class status of the family might be in danger. For the middle-class mistress, then, the ideal Irish servant would embody middle-class domesticity.

Many American women voiced their belief that it was the mistress' responsibility to build the moral and ethical character that Irish women needed to adopt to become their surrogates. As Harriet Prescott Spofford wrote, the mistress was in the perfect position to shape her maid into an image of herself: "Yet only a little observation of contagious example will convince you that as the mistress is, the maid is. . . . Where she is energetic and industrious the maid will be likewise; where she is slack, slack will be the maid; and where the mistress is a tidy body the maid is a tidy body too."[22] Harriet Beecher Stowe, whose writing shaped America's idea of middle-class domesticity, echoed Spofford's sentiments in her article entitled "Ireland's Daughters in Their New Home." Discussing the precarious nature of the Irish girl in America and the important role that the mistress played in her life, Stowe remarked that "thousands of young Irish girls have landed on our shores, utter strangers, far from advice and protection of fathers and mothers. . . . A kind, consistent, watchful, careful mistress will keep her servants in the way of honesty; a careless or incompetent one tempts them to fall."[23] Mistresses, according to Stowe, were in the most important position to ensure the moral development of the Irish servant girl and guarantee that their Irish domestics appropriated their middle-class values—most importantly, hard work and the development of a high moral character.

Mistresses' attempts to assimilate their Irish maids into an American middle-class Protestant "culture of character" were detailed in several nineteenth-century domestic-service instructional manuals and popular periodicals.[24] Both *Plain Talk and Friendly Advice to Domestics* (author unknown) and *Letters to Persons Who Are Engaged in Domestic Service* by Catherine Beecher, a sister of Harriet Beecher Stowe and a prolific writer on the merits of domestic morality, extol the merits of frugality, a particularly Protestant middle-class value, in order to warn servants of the evils in squandering their money on silk dresses and gaudy personal ornaments.[25] Beecher urged servants both to place the wages they saved from not buying "showy dresses" into a savings account where interest would be earned, and to spend their free time educating themselves through reading daily to their mistresses rather than going shopping. The suggestion of acceptable free-time activities was a staple of the campaign to develop these women into exemplary middle-class women. Catherine Beecher advised domestic servants that attending religious meetings in the evenings was perfectly acceptable, provided that the intention was serious worship rather than meeting members of the opposite sex.[26] Beecher's sister, Harriet Beecher Stowe, continued this line of advice by outlining some rules for domestics' leisure times:

> Rule the first is that no young servant should be out alone after dark giving reasons for this rule that are easily understood. Rule the second, that no one comes to the back door after a certain hour, because their friends are quite welcome to come to the front door; and once it is dark, bad characters are about and young girls are easily frightened.[27]

In an ultimate expression of domination over the servant's recreational hours, one master wrote in *Old and New*, a popular but short-lived literary and political magazine, that their Irish servant should participate in all of the family's leisure activities, "For I mean that Mary . . . shall go out into company with us, to evening parties when we attend them, and to tea when we go out to tea; . . . [she] reads loud to us in the evening, or sits beside you when I am reading loud."[28] Mary's actions, in other words, were to be a mirror image of those of her master and mistress. She would work and play under prescribed rules, leaving no time for individual expression. Here, at least, domestic service for Irish women was clearly a matter of servility and coerced assimilation.

-2-

Did these Irish maids heed their mistresses' advice? Was the mistress–maid relationship truly as influential as these mistresses hoped it would be? The answer to both of these questions seems to be glaringly affirmative. In several interviews, surveys, and articles written about the social activities of Irish maids, the servants appear to have appropriated all the morality lessons taught to them by their "concerned" mistresses. Mary Meehan, an Irish woman who spent all her working years as a household cook, described how she and the other maids only dressed as her mistress wanted, in the traditional black sturdy frock during working hours and in modest dresses with fashionable ribbons in their hair during hours of leisure.[29] In a survey conducted by the Women's Educational and Industrial Union, 113 Irish servants in Boston claimed to have spent their leisure time and their money just as Beecher, Stowe, and others had instructed them to do. They used their free time to read, sew, or attend church services or socials, and they diligently placed their money in secure savings accounts or sent it back to their families in Ireland.[30] An article in *Donahoe's Magazine*, one of the most widely read Irish-American monthlies, detailed the monetary support that Irish maids gave to their homeland:

> Mr. Patrick Donahoe furnishes us with a significant fact. There are numerous offices in Boston for the transmission of money order[s]. . . . During the four weeks ending on Dec. 20, 1879, drafts to the number of 2,250 and representing 5,376 pounds, passed through his hands. The senders were almost exclusively servant girls.[31]

In a letter home to Ireland household servant Mary Harlon proudly explained that after only a few short months in New York City she was "happy in her present post, she now had a bank account of eighty dollars, and was putting aside money for a new silken dress."[32] Granted, Harlon did have a desire for the "showy dresses" that Catherine Beecher advised servants to avoid purchasing, but Harlon's ability to prioritize saving over spending may also signify her partial adoption of the middle-class values of frugality or thrift. Each of the above examples suggests that through entering into a relationship with a mistress and adhering to her advice, Irish maids were successfully assimilated into the ways of America's middle-class culture.

The "Americanization" of Irish maids thus accomplished its main goal—freeing the mistress from her domestic responsibilities and providing her with a domestic surrogate. However, what these middle-class women gained, Irish domestic servants lost: personal freedom. Many historians have seen the movement from Ireland to America as one from social constraint to personal autonomy. Yet the stultifying nature of postfamine Irish society should not be overestimated, and neither, clearly, should the liberating effects of service in America. That young

Irish women were in several senses better off in America than they would have been in Ireland does not mean that they were free or independent. Irish immigrant women who chose to live as maids in middle-class households relinquished much of their personal freedom, at least for the duration of their service. Many Irish women had little choice but to enter service, of course, but that merely underscores the absence of freedom involved in the relationship.

As Irish women began to recognize the sacrifices that they had made to become servants, they simultaneously began to realize the hypocritical nature of their mistresses. Servants observed their mistresses behaving exactly as domestics were trained not to act. By the turn of the century these maids began to voice their frustrations with the paradox in which they lived. In an April 1912 edition of *Outlook* magazine, an extremely successful weekly that ran a series of articles written specifically to address the domestic-service crisis, one maid voiced her dissatisfaction with her mistress as follows: "Perhaps the lady goes downtown in the morning, has her own nice lunch at a restaurant, and tells me I can give the children a pick-up lunch, and I am lucky if I have enough in the pantry to give them fried bread."[33] In a September 1916 edition of *The Living Age*, a weekly magazine that tended to print the voice of the dominant mistress, the editors broke with tradition and portrayed the life of servants in very sympathetic terms:

> Her working day is all day in a sense in which this is not true of a shop-girl or a female clerk in the Post Office. She has, no doubt, idle hours on her hands, and may read Shakespeare if she will in the kitchen while her mistress is drinking tea. But she is bound to the house as an old serf to the land. She cannot go sailing down the road for an hour in the middle of the day. She is not free for the evening, with its excitements of the streets, the cinemas, and the soldiers in the park. She has to live other people's lives from the moment she gets up till the moment she goes back to bed. She is at best a well kept prisoner.[34]

What domestics began to realize was not only the unfairness of their position, but also that they wanted a certain amount of personal time and similar forms of freedom to those enjoyed by their mistresses. Irish domestics had worked hard for their money and were finally in a position where they could afford to spend a bit on themselves, but both their working hours and the demands of their mistresses left them with little free time to enjoy themselves. Gradually, however, the life of the servant began to change through a combination of servants' struggles for more personal freedom and, ironically, the rise of middle-class women's social-reform groups concerned with questions of child and

female labor, among other issues. Together, maids and social reformers
began to call for a restructuring of domestic service.[35]

Domestic service had traditionally demanded extremely long hours
of service from its maids. In an investigation conducted by the School
of Housekeeping, the range of working hours for maids was between
twelve and fifteen hours per day. In contrast, shop and factory workers'
hours ranged from eight to ten hours per day.[36] Aware of this, many
maids began to leave their service jobs in the early twentieth century,
claiming that they would find shorter hours, greater individual freedom, and more time for leisure in other lines of work. In an investigation of New York City women wage-workers, entitled *Prisoners of
Poverty: Women Wage-Workers, Their Trades, and Their Lives*, Helen
Campbell, a dedicated urban and social reformer, chronicled former
domestics' reasons for leaving the service industry.[37] The former maids'
complaints ranged from loneliness, to abominable living quarters, to
unruly children. And each ex-servant mentioned in her interview the
lack of freedom involved in such work. One interviewee exclaimed that
she hardly minded being called twenty times a day to serve her mistress, and she was quite satisfied with her room and board, but what
she really longed for was time for herself when she could either enjoy
the company of her friends or simply relax on her own. Another maid
captured the sense of imprisonment and lack of freedom inherent in
service: "'It's freedom that we want when the day's work is done. . . . [In
service] you're never sure that your soul's your own except when you
are out of the house.'"[38] What these maids seemed to crave most was
time for themselves, away from the ever-watchful eyes of their
mistresses.

Articles written by maids and social reformers in such popular middle-class periodicals as *Harper's Bazaar, Ladies' Home Journal, Atlantic
Monthly*, and *Outlook* called for a radical change in the domestic-service industry. In a March 1905 edition of *Ladies' Home Journal*, Annette
Jaynes Miller claimed that the reason she never had any trouble with
her servants was that she treated them as both professionals and
human beings, standardizing their work hours and duties while giving
them time off to do things such as visit the dressmaker. A thankful husband writing in *Harper's Bazaar* explained that the main reason why his
wife managed to sustain a long and continuous relationship with her
maids was simply that she gave them ample time to socialize. In a letter
in *Outlook* one servant wrote that she continued to work for her mistress
because this woman treated her very much like one of her equals, giving her a room as beautifully decorated as her own and allowing her

some time every day for recreation or study. And finally, another article in *Ladies' Home Journal* by Mrs. Christine Broderick went so far as to suggest that the remedy for the servant-girl problem was to have them "live-out." Broderick claimed that "living-out" would give them ample time to socialize with friends or spend a whole day shopping, before returning to their work at seven o'clock each morning.[39]

These articles gave evidence of the changes occurring in domestic service in the early twentieth century. Through the work of women's social-reform groups such as the Domestic Reform League of Boston, combined with the pressures that the flight of women workers from the service industry placed on middle-class women and their households, servants' hours were gradually shortened, domestic responsibilities were made more manageable, and living conditions began to be renegotiated. While no labor laws were enacted to legalize these changes, the work of domestic-service professionals, such as Lucy Salmon and Frances A. Kellor, helped to initiate changes within domestic service. These professionals suggested myriad options including the drawing up of contracts that detailed the mistresses' and maids' responsibilities, the mandating of an eight-hour workday for servants, and the creation of a "living-out" system. Another reformer, Mrs. C. H. Stone, called for the establishment of household training schools where maids and mistresses alike could receive a thorough education in how to conduct themselves in their respective roles. That some mistresses responded to these recommendations is suggested by the growing testimony of servants that they were working shorter hours, were being given verbal confirmation of their work responsibilities before they accepted positions, and were in many cases beginning to "live-out." In cities like Fall River, Massachusetts, and Providence, Rhode Island, where the Irish dominated service, the number of servants "living-out" almost doubled between 1900 and 1920.[40]

Although these changes may appear as minor adjustments, they greatly and positively affected the life of the servant. With shorter hours maids found themselves with the freedom to live their lives as they pleased. This freedom allowed them to reconnect with the Irish community from which they had been forced to separate when they entered service during the nineteenth century. Domestic service had isolated these women from their ethnic communities, which by the twentieth century had become a very large part of almost every major urban center in America. Most of these Irish neighborhoods were re-creations of Irish cultural life, as they offered pubs, dance halls, theaters, and homes with an open-door policy. Thus, many of the Irish domestic servants who emigrated in the early twentieth century discussed in their interviews how they spent their leisure time with their Irish relatives and friends in the community. Katherine Donoghue and Catherine Keohane explained how they and their sisters, all of them domestic servants in the Boston area, would spend their "days out" visiting each other and their aunts, uncles, and other relatives. Elizabeth Linehan remembered spending her leisure time taking fresh baked breads and soups over to a neighbor's house for a friendly chat.[41] And Mrs. John Wesst vividly recalled how her Sundays were spent singing folk songs from the Emerald Isle.[42] These kinds of leisure activities were certainly not the ones prescribed by their mistresses. By participating in such activities, the "new" Irish domestic servant countered the thrust of forced assimilation.

At the same time, Irish servants increasingly entered the public sphere as consumers, emulating their mistresses, though not necessarily on the same terms. Irish women were among the most avid theater fans, dance-hall attendees, and shoppers for the latest fashions.[43] Mary Meehan, a domestic servant who had once strictly followed the guidelines that her mistress set out for her, recounted that with the onset of a "living-out" service industry, she and her friend spent much of their free time dining in restaurants with the traveling salesmen who passed through their town of Brookfield.[44] Irish immigrants' entrance into consumer culture was also reflected in the rising quantity and variety of goods advertised in prominent Irish-American newspapers such as the *Irish Echo* and the *Boston Pilot*. In the nineteenth century advertising in these papers was limited to a very small space, mainly offering myriad medicines for any ailment that one might have.[45] By the early twentieth century these papers began advertising products that ranged from pianos to corsets, rosaries to prayer books, and parlor suits to furnaces. By exercising their own consumer choices, Irish domestic servants could express a distinctively Irish-American identity, thereby countering once again the drive toward coercive assimilation. Besides buying Irish bank bonds, linens, and novels, they purchased such "American" commodities as hats, chandeliers, candlesticks, and organs.

By the 1920s, the mistress–maid relationship had come full circle. Domestic servants had, for the most part, become "live-out" employees, reestablishing a sense of personal freedom and ethnic community that had been lost when the maid became a permanent part of the household as a "live-in" servant. With her own home to return to at the end of the working day, the maid finally had her own space and time, free from the demands of the American middle-class home and mistress. And, ironically, with the onset of the "live-out" maid, even middle-class women rediscovered some of the personal freedom they had once enjoyed through running their own households, if only in the negative sense of no longer having to supervise a "live-in" servant. In the words of one very insightful mistress, the household had now become a site of independence for both the maid and the mistress: "Freedom lies in that quarter, privacy and individuality for the maid; freedom, too, for the household to joke, to meddle, to be noisy, to have company; freedom to lock the house and with a clear conscience prolong the motoring trip and sup at an inn."[46] As the age of social reform began to usher the servant out of the house and the mistress back in with a redefined idea of domesticity, their comings and goings signaled that the mistress–maid relationship had evolved from one of interdependence to one in which each party was much more independent of the other. Yet even within this newly defined relationship the dialectic between maids and mistresses continued.

NOTES

1. Kerby A. Miller, *Emigrants and Exiles: Ireland and the Irish Exodus to North America* (New York and Oxford: Oxford University Press, 1985), especially Chapters 7 and 8; Kevin Kenny, *The American Irish: A History* (London and New York: Longman, 2000), especially Chapters 3, 4, and 5.

2. Hasia R. Diner, *Erin's Daughters in America: Irish Immigrant Women in the Nineteenth Century* (Baltimore: Johns Hopkins University Press, 1983), 83–85.

3. During this same time that Irish women emigrated to America, so too did German, Scandinavian, Italian, and Eastern European women. However, this article concentrates on Irish domestic servants precisely because Irish women seemed to pay no mind to the fact that becoming a servant implied being of the lower class; they simply wanted to find work that paid high wages. The other immigrant groups, especially Italian and Jewish women, refused to enter domestic service, mainly because they emigrated either as married women or as part of a strong patriarchal family, and also (perhaps) because they shared with American-born women a sense of the stigma attached to domestic service. The only other groups of women heavily concentrated in domestic service were African Americans and Swedish immigrants. For further discussion of this topic, see Diner, *Erin's Daughters,* 82–83; David M. Katzman, *Seven Days a Week: Women and Domestic Service in Industrializing America* (New York: Oxford University Press, 1978), 271–73; and the Women's Educational and Industrial Union (hereafter WEIU) investigations of the nationality of domestic servants at the Schlesinger Library at Radcliffe College, Cambridge, Mass.

4. Diner, *Erin's Daughters,* 80–94, and Janet A. Nolan, *Ourselves Alone: Women's Emigration from Ireland, 1885–1920* (Lexington: University Press of Kentucky, 1989), 73–90. Other scholars, such as Maureen Murphy and Ruth-Ann Harris, argue in the same vein as Diner and Nolan, interpreting documents either from or about Irish women as pointing to the sense of independence and power that domestic service

gave them. Kevin Kenny questions this thesis, emphasizing the social inequality inherent in the labor relationship between mistress and servant. See Ruth-Ann M. Harris and B. Emer O'Keefe, eds., Introduction to *The Search For Missing Friends: Irish Immigrant Advertisements Placed in the Boston* Pilot, *Vol. 4. 1857–1860* (Boston: New England Historic Genealogical Society, 1995) i–xxxiv; Kenny, *American Irish,* 149–54; Maureen Murphy, "Bridget and Biddy: Images of the Irish Servant Girl in *Puck* Cartoons, 1880–1890," in Charles Fanning, ed., *New Perspectives on the Irish Diaspora* (Carbondale and Edwardsville, Ill.: Southern Illinois University Press, 2000), 152–75; Íde O'Carroll, *Models for Movers: Irish: Women's Emigration to America* (Dublin: Attic Press, 1990), 17–19.

5. Diner, *Erin's Daughters,* xvi; Nolan, *Ourselves Alone,* 89–90.

6. Faye E. Dudden, *Serving Women: Household Service in Nineteenth-Century America,* (Middletown: Wesleyan University Press, 1983), 1–55.

7. While Irish women eagerly accepted positions as "live-in" servants, many of them viewed this work as a stepping-stone to a better life for either themselves or their children. Some women spent their whole lives serving in various homes (with a select few staying in one home throughout their entire working lives), but their children often went on to work in other industries or in semiprofessional positions. As for the first-generation serving women themselves, they often left service to take higher paying jobs or to marry. Thus service was often viewed as a convenient and economically advantageous but temporary first position. Diner, *Erin's Daughters,* Chapter 4; Katzman, *Seven Days a Week,* Chapters 1, 6, and 7.

8. Lucy M. Salmon, "Domestic Service from the Standpoint of the Employee," *Cosmopolitan* (July 1893), 346.

9. Karen Halttunen, *Confidence Men and Painted Women: A Study of Middle-Class Culture in America, 1830–1870* (New Haven and London: Yale University Press, 1982), 191–97.

10. Dudden, *Serving Women,* 1–11, 44–47.

11. For discussion of the kinds of work that women engaged in throughout the nineteenth-century, see Lois W. Banner, *Women in Modern America: A Brief History* (New York and Chicago: Harcourt Brace Jovanovich, 1974); Barbara J. Harris, *Beyond Her Sphere: Women and the Professions in American History* (Westport, Conn., and London: Greenwood Press, 1978); Linda K. Kerber and Jane Sherron De Hart, eds., *Women's America: Refocusing the Past,* 5th ed. (New York and Oxford: Oxford University Press, 2000); Nancy Woloch, *Women and the American Experience* (New York: Alfred A. Knopf, 1984). The "leisured wife" was a woman who had the means and time to undertake activities that were purely for enjoyment and not for economic gain. The "leisured wife" was an important aspect of the middle class because by engaging in the activities of the "leisured wife," a woman's activities validated both her husband's professional and economic success and her family's middle-class standing. For further discussion of this topic, see Elaine S. Abelson, *When Ladies Go A-Thieving: Middle-Class Shoplifters in the Victorian Department Store* (New York and Oxford: Oxford University Press, 1989), 3–41, and Cordery, "Women in Industrializing America," 111–31.

12. See Cordery, "Women in Industrializing America," 112; Nancy F. Cott, *The Bonds of Womanhood: "Woman's Sphere" in New England, 1780–1835* (New Haven and London: Yale University Press, 1977), 63–100.

13. Katzman, *Seven Days a Week,* 270.

14. W.E. Vaughan and A.J. Fitzpatrick, eds., *Irish Historical Statistics: Population,*

1821–1971 (Dublin: Royal Irish Academy, 1978), 261–66. There is no exact record of how many Irish women emigrated to America during this period. This figure is an estimate based on the total male/female emigration statistics and the total number of emigrants from the destination chart.

15. Joseph C. G. Kennedy, *Population of the United States in 1860* (Washington: Government Printing Office, 1864), 675, and William C. Hunt, *Fourteenth Census of the United States Taken in the Year 1920*, Vol. IV: *Occupations* (Washington: Government Printing Office, 1923), 358.

16. "Number and Nationality of Women in Domestic Service" in *Bulletin of the Domestic Reform League*, III (October 1908). Bulletin found in WEIU Papers, Box 1, Folder 5.

17. Diner, *Erin's Daughters*, 89.

18. Harriet Prescott Spofford, *The Servant Girl Question* (Boston: Houghton Mifflin and Co., 1881), 44–45.

19. Diner, *Erin's Daughters*, 80–94; Dudden, *Serving Women*, 55–71.

20. Caroline Barret White's story can be found in Elizabeth H. Pleck and Ellen K. Rothman, "The New American Families: The Irish, 1840–1860," in *Legacies: An Audiocourse on the History of Women and the Family in America, 1607–1870* (Washington D.C.: Annenberg/CPB Project, 1987).

21. Katzman, *Seven Days a Week*, 275.

22. Spofford, *Servant Girl Question*, 53.

23. Stowe, "Ireland's Daughters in Their New Homes," *Donahoe's Magazine* (January 1879), 53–54.

24. Warren Susman coined the phrase "culture of character" in his book *Culture as History: The Transformation of American Society in the Twentieth Century* (New York: Pantheon, 1989). Susman argues that nineteenth-century America was a culture obsessed with obtaining and developing citizens who had a high character. The "culture of character" emphasized the development of one's character through strict adherence to the Protestant work ethic and morally acceptable recreational activities.

25. Catherine E. Beecher, *Letters to Persons Who Are Engaged in Domestic Service* (New York: Leavitt & Trow, 1842); *Plain Talk and Friendly Advice to Domestics, with Counsel on Home Matters* [author unknown] (Boston: Phillips, Sampson, and Co., 1855).

26. Beecher, *Letters*, 122–25.

27. Harriet Beecher Stowe, "Mistress and Maid," *Donahoe's Magazine* (May 1885), 442.

28. Rev. Eli Hartness, "Wanted: A Domestic," *Old and New* (July 1871), 493–94.

29. Mary Meehan, "Irish Cook–Brookfield," interview by Louise Bassett, *American Life Histories: Manuscripts from the Federal Writers' Project, 1936–1940*, available from <http://www.loc.wpaintro/wpahome>.

30. *Social Conditions in Domestic Service*, prepared by the Massachusetts Bureau of Statistics of Labor in collaboration with Women's Educational and Industrial Union of Boston (Boston: Wright & Potter Printing Co., 1900), and found in WEIU Papers, Box 1, Folder 5.

31. "What Is Thought of Our Irish Girls Abroad" [author unknown], *Donahoe's Magazine* (May 1880), 437.

32. Harlon's letter as cited in Harris and O'Keefe, eds., *Search For Missing Friends*, IV, xxxii.

33. "The Experience of a 'Hired Girl'," *Outlook*, 6 April 1912, 778–79.

34. "On Being a Servant," *Living Age*, 9 September 1916, 821.

35. Ironically, the employment of servants freed middle-class women to engage in social-reform movements, and these movements eventually agitated for better wages and working conditions for children and women, including domestic servants. See Adele Heller and Lois Rudnick, eds., *1915, The Cultural Moment: The New Politics, the New Woman, the New Psychology, the New Art, and the New Theatre in America* (New Brunswick: Rutgers University Press, 1991); Lucy Maynard Salmon, *Domestic Service* (New York: Macmillan Company, 1897).

36. *Social Statistics of Working Women*, prepared by the Massachusetts Bureau of Statistics of Labor, with information collected by the School of Housekeeping (Boston, 1901). Found in WEIU Papers, Box 1, Folder 5.

37. Helen Campbell, *Prisoners of Poverty: Women Wage-Workers, Their Trades, and Their Lives* (Boston: Little, Brown and Co., 1900).

38. Ibid, 224.

39. Annette Jaynes Miller, "Why I Never Have Trouble with My Servants," *Ladies' Home Journal* (March 1905), 4, 52; "How My Wife Keeps Her Maids" [author unknown: a thankful husband], *Harper's Bazaar* (December 1909), 1231; "An Ideal Mistress" [author unknown: a servant], *Outlook*, 10 August 1912, 838–39; Mrs. Christine Broderick, "Suppose Our Servants Didn't Live with Us," *Ladies' Home Journal* (October 1914), 102.

40. Domestic Reform League Papers, in WEIU Papers, Box 1, Folder 5; Katzman, *Seven Days a Week*, Chapters 1, 6, 7 and p. 297; Salmon, *Domestic Service*, Chapters 11, 12, and 15; Mrs. C. H. Stone, *The Problem of Domestic Service* (St. Louis: Nelson Printing Co., 1892).

41. Katherine Donoghue, interview by Eugenia Kaledin on 10 December 1982, tape available at the Schlesinger Library, Radcliffe College, Cambridge, Mass.; Catherine Keohane and Elizabeth Linehan, "The Íde O'Carroll Collection," Box 1, Inventory Folder, also available at the Schlesinger Library.

42. Mrs. John Wesst, "Pioneer Life in Nebraska," interview by Frederick W. Kaul and L. A. Rollins, *American Life Histories: Manuscripts from the Federal Writers' Project, 1936–1940*, <http://www.loc/wpaintro/wpahome>.

43. *The Irish in America: The Long Journey Home,* Part II, a film made by National Public Television, 1998.

44. Mary Meehan, "Irish Cook–Brookfield," <http://www.loc/wpaintro/wpahome.>

45. For examples of advertisements, see *Irish Echo, Vol. 4, 1890–1984; Boston* Pilot, 1900–20.

46. "A Maid in the House" [author unknown], *Atlantic Monthly* (May 1920), 715.

Part 4

*Representation,
Memory, and Return*

Editor's Introduction

THE TWENTIETH CENTURY WILL BE the next growth area in the study of Irish America. The nineteenth century will always be central, for it was then that most Irish migrants came to the United States and the main patterns of Irish-American history were laid down. The post-1920 period has not been entirely neglected, but it remains largely unstudied and presents the best opportunities for new scholarship. Given that transatlantic migration during this period was relatively small, the appropriate object of inquiry is no longer the immigrant generation but the multigenerational ethnic group—its economic and social progress, cultural and political achievements, retention of an Irish sensibility, and development of an American one. Historians of the twentieth century continue to study central themes like social and geographical mobility, labor, religion, politics, nationalism, and various forms of identity, but their focus is on those who were born in America rather than Ireland.

A second central topic for twentieth-century historiography is the back-and-forth movement between Ireland and America of money, people, and ideas, in a way that had been rare before the 1920s. At the turn of the century, return migration to Ireland had been negligible (well under 10 percent of those who had left, compared to more than 50 percent for Italians and Eastern Europeans at the turn of the twentieth century). With the significant exception of nationalist movements, transatlantic cultural and political interactions across the Atlantic had been uncommon. All of this changed after the 1920s, with considerable back-and-forth migration, economic and political engagement, and cultural interpenetration between Ireland and America. One central theme in this new history is the simultaneous convergence and divergence of the two

245

interconnected but separate Irish cultures that now flourish on opposite sides of the Atlantic Ocean. The resulting tensions in how these two cultures perceive each other—politically, economically, culturally, and intellectually—are central to the essays presented in this final section.

These tensions have been conspicuously evident in the writing of history itself. In the 1970s and 1980s, a new generation of historians in Ireland, known retrospectively as "revisionists," set out to dismantle what they saw as the received orthodoxy of Irish history. The standard nationalist interpretation, these historians argued, reduced the rich complexity of the Irish past to a one-dimensional story of British oppression culminating in the heroic birth (or rebirth) of the Irish nation. And Irish America, it was alleged, represented one of the last bastions of this point of view. Of the various aspects of Irish history that came under debate, the Great Famine was predictably one of the most important. Was the Famine the great turning point in Irish history that the received wisdom suggested? Did it, as many people believed, cause the decline of the Irish language, the consolidation of large landholdings, and the onset of mass emigration? Did the British government deliberately engineer the catastrophe, or at least bear passive responsibility once the unforeseeable disaster of potato failure had begun? Merely posing these questions called into question the dominant narratives of Irish history.

While this revisionist challenge significantly improved the standard of Irish historical scholarship, some recent historians have argued that it went too far, at least in the case of the Famine. If, in the old view, the Famine had assumed an exaggerated importance, in the new version it threatened to become just one of many equally important events in nineteenth-century Ireland. And, while few, if any, historians in Ireland today would endorse the idea of British genocide (in the sense of conscious intent to slaughter), this does not mean that government policies, whether adopted or rejected, had no impact on starvation, disease, mortality, and emigration. On the contrary, a close examination of those policies reveals that the Famine, despite its overwhelming awfulness, had an internal history that can be analyzed and judged. An emphasis on this internal history is among the defining characteristics of the most recent school of Famine historiography, which (for want of a better name) is often referred to as "postrevisionism."

Viewed in retrospect, historical controversies tend to arrange themselves into the familiar dialectic of thesis, antithesis, and new synthesis, with the last of these generally retaining the best aspects of the two positions it transcends. Accordingly, in the 1990s the postrevisionists offered a compelling new interpretation of the Famine that, while it rejected the idea of genocide, insisted nonetheless that the British government bore responsibility for its decisions and further emphasized that the events of the 1840s transformed the social and economic history of Ireland. Postrevisionism, however, is scarcely a term one would use to describe how the Irish potato famine is currently taught in American schools. In the 1990s, several states passed laws mandating the inclusion of the Famine on their curricula, generally under the heading of "human rights" or "holocaust and genocide" studies. So far, only New York and New Jersey have implemented this legislation, but the curricula these states proposed ignited a political controversy.

Even as this controversy indicated the continuing divergence of Irish and Irish-American culture, Ireland and the United States were both enjoying the unprecedented economic prosperity of the 1990s. Driven by a combination of European Union funding, intelligent government planning, and recruitment of foreign business, the Irish economy expanded rapidly after 1990. In the context of this booming economy, affectionately known as the "Celtic Tiger," something remarkable happened: for only the second time since the Famine, the number of people entering Ireland exceeded the number of people leaving. While many of Ireland's new immigrants came from Europe and North Africa, substantial numbers of them were Irish people who had left the country during the economically depressed 1980s. Now they were coming home—from London, continental Europe, Australia, and the United States. Their adjustment was not always easy. Having idealized Ireland while they were away, they found that it did not always measure up. Indeed, it had changed markedly during their absence, its pace of life intensifying with the booming economy. In some ways it was more like the countries they were now departing than the Ireland they had left. Ireland, moreover, was saturated by American popular culture, and the economic boom that allowed the former emigrants to come home was based largely on American corporate capital. As the twenty-first century began, Irish and Irish-American culture were in some ways drawing further apart, but in others they were more intertwined than ever.

Culture, Commodity, and Céad Míle Fáilte: U.S. and Irish Tourist Films as a Vision of Ireland

HARVEY O'BRIEN

IN 1966, BORD FÁILTE, the Irish Tourist Board, sponsored a documentary intended to update the international profile of "The Emerald Isle." Robert Monks's 1966 *Ireland: The New Convention Country* would emphasize the modern facilities available to conference holders and delegates, especially in Dublin city. The film did indeed publicize the hotels, airports, and advanced technical equipment that would expedite such events. But at one point roughly half way through, the voice-over suggested conspiratorially: "Take a day off from your conference: you won't be missed." It then proceeded to detail the range of sporting and leisure activities within easy reach of the urban center (neglecting to mention that some of them were over a hundred miles away). It featured images of Quin Abbey, Bunratty Castle, angling on the river Shannon, and rural roads the voice-over claimed were "the most traffic free in Europe." Many of these were the standard scenes used in the promotion of tourism in Ireland since tourism began, images familiar from paintings, postcards, and photography before the inception of the cinema.[1] Modern it may have been, but this was still "friendly, leisurely Ireland" where culture, history, and geography could be reduced to a series of commodities and services malleable and marketable according to the expectations of sponsors and potentially international audiences.

The Paradoxes of Tourism

Projecting images of the country designed to achieve specific ends, tourist films give perhaps the strongest indication not necessarily of what a country thinks of itself, but of what its cultural industries believe is expected of it. It should come as little surprise then that when international cinematic representations search for cues in the native culture to guide their own promotional films, they should yield similar results to one another, albeit in films filtered through the sensibilities of their producers. Tourist films are promotional and engage a different set of expectations from those documentaries which attempt to explore the identity of a place and its people in a more introspective manner. Though they may be poetic in style and feature and document some essential characteristics of the land and its inhabitants, their concern is not with the satisfaction of the desire to mimic the forms seen in nature. Instead, as Terry Lovell has observed, they are interested in the creation of a desire to control and commodify reality. In Lovell's words, "The cultural producer is keenly interested in the proliferation of wants which will lead consumers to seek out the commodities sold to satisfy those wants."[2] He identifies here a central paradox of the tourism industry. Tourism is a definite site of cultural production, both employing and promoting aspects of "culture" to encourage visitors. As T.J.M. Sheehy observed in the Irish film journal *Vision* (1967) regarding the increase in production of tourist films at that time: "Sponsors of tourist films are not philanthropists. Their interest is tourist publicity. In the films they sponsor they want quality and artistic integrity, but in their approach art, desirable as it may be, takes second place to publicity needs."[3]

Yet tourism is not merely the result of a capitalist conspiracy. The desire to travel and visit places of which we have no direct experience has always been central to human behavior, though it was only organized within an industrial infrastructure and a capitalist mode of production in the mid-nineteenth century. Tourism capitalizes on that which already exists: on one hand the desire for new experiences, and on the other the qualities of the place in question. In promoting a particular location, it must draw on the frames of reference familiar to the intended audience. Lovell notes that consumers must seek out "the commodities sold," not the commodities created to meet the wants. Tourism is tailoring: it matches product to market in a way that engages both the qualities of the place in question and the expectations of the consumer. There may be grains of truth and elements of reality contained within tourist films, but they require closer analysis to separate form from content and understand what wants are being satisfied and how.

Derek Paget identifies another important paradox.[4] While he acknowledges that tourism is an expression of the economic supremacy of the tourist and draws attention to its colonialist origins, he is not so naïve as to suggest that countries which are popular tourist destinations are wholly victims. He asks, "Who, exactly, is exploiting whom in the Greek taverna on Rhodes or Corfu (intertextual with the film *Zorba the Greek*)? It is difficult to say but quite likely that both tourists and 'ethnic entertainment' understand each other."[5] He observes that the recourse for a nation whose economic outlook is less than salubrious is often to fall back on its past. So-called "Heritage Industries" are a significant collective contributor to the economies of most European countries in the late-twentieth century, Ireland included. Paget does not suggest an absence of exploitation in this process, but his point about the partly willing nature of this retreat into the historical twilight is well taken, especially in Ireland.

Exploitation is a common theme in writing about postcolonial societies, as is the labeling of touristic self-caricature as a symptom of colonialism. In one sense, representations that replicate the clichés of the colonizer are part of the process of regression to tribalism described by Frantz Fanon.[6] Fanon argued that though the emergent postcolonial society seeks to shed itself of its colonial baggage, its attempts to cultivate a national concept of self are frequently a retreat into tribalism and myths of racial purity. Meanwhile the economic and administrative institutions and procedures used by the educated middle-classes to sustain the emergent state tend to follow the templates established by the colonial authority. The result, he explained, is often less a break with the past than a period of mimicry and assimilation that attempts to (re)construct a primordial nationality. This period eventually segues into a "national" culture, but only after a period in which the nature of that culture is negotiated using the superstructures inherited from the colonizer. The cost of this process for an independent and indigenous identity is often most clearly seen with the onset of tourism, which can be viewed as a type of neocolonial conquest. In representing itself in a form that is pleasing to the former colonizer (because it corresponds with colonizers' preconceptions), the tourist destination commodifies itself and reduces the specifics of culture and heritage to generic objects. As Paget notes:

> The act of tourist photography converts indigenous subjects into consumed objects, objects to be possessed (at one remove, it is true, but possessed in important ways). The resultant objects are passed into a kind of currency back in the camera owners' home countries, where they have become indicators of economic power, or sophistication, or of well-traveled knowledge of foreign lands, or of all of these things in conversations and slide-viewing sessions. If the Grand Tour was an index of nineteenth-century sophistication, foreign travel is just as important now.[7]

Speaking specifically of Ireland, Declan Kiberd, whose work follows and often cites Fanon and Edward Said in this regard, takes a similar view. He discusses, for example, how Synge portrayed the Aran Islands as a living tableau of cultural stereotype, where "every man and woman becomes a sort of artist."[8] He notes of Synge's writing on the Aran Islands that "English typology has encouraged this stage Irishman to mimic a stock type—with no saving sense of irony—and to confuse this type with 'personality'."[9] The comment about irony may be unjust, or at least unduly restrictive. The Irish have long been aware of the necessity to commodify their culture. Though it may represent a colonial stain on national identity in general terms, this awareness deepened over time into a form of counter-exploitation, as evinced in Micheál Ó Siochfhradha's 1930 short story, "An Corp,"[10] in which Irish villagers stage a phony wake to defraud a visiting author eager to document Irish customs and rituals.[11]

Though it may not have been elevated to the level of an articulated concept of self, this approach is at least evident in the schism between the image of Ireland promoted by the tourist industry from the 1950s (*Bord Fáilte* was established in 1955), which actively proposed a romantic, pastoral ideal, and informational films made for distribution within Ireland, which emphasized industry and progress. In time, a clumsy hybrid of the two became common (and remains so), with many such films attempting to posit Ireland as a "land of contrasts" where the traditional and the modern peacefully co-exist in a Celtic fantasia with all the trappings of contemporary civilization. Even in the enormously high-profile television series *The Irish Empire* (1999), the documenting of the international influence and experiences of the Irish diaspora was accompanied by a soft-spoken, brogue-ish narration by Fiona Shaw and sentimental, overbearing music by Deborah Mollison.[12]

It may be argued, of course, that such developments were indicative of ongoing cultural schizophrenia of the type identified by Fanon rather than an articulate attitude toward cultural representation. There is nonetheless a consistency in the vision of Ireland proposed by both tourist and informational films right to the present day, not only visually, but in terms of argument. Like *Ireland: The New Convention Country*, they represent an Ireland struggling with its self-image. Then, as now, the country was willing to exploit its well-worn conventions while also attempting to promote a more modern, progressive image of a successful, independent nation. This is partly because it was the appeal of those conventions that attracted the interest of visitors in the first place. Yet even in the era of the so-called "Celtic Tiger," when industrial and social progress seem to take center stage, tourism continues to be a significant source of revenue, and tourist films are still produced. In 1960, IR£41 million in foreign exchange earnings came from tourism. By 1998 the figure had risen to a total of IR£2.281 billion. With this kind of money at stake, it was and is obviously vital that the image of Ireland projected in films sponsored or otherwise endorsed by the tourist industry should continue to encourage visitors, regardless of the cost in cultural terms. This is no longer motivated out of a desperate need to plunder one's own history for the sake of survival; rather, it is part of an articulated strategy for economic growth and the exploitation of expectation.

As Luke Gibbons notes of the image of Ireland proffered by *Bord Fáilte* and the Industrial Development Authority (IDA) in the 1980s, this process is indicative of a cultural industry learning how to exploit its raw materials. It is the distillation of the pro-filmic realities of Ireland as a geographical and social space and the psychic conception of the country long established by representation throughout the centuries. As Gibbons says:

> This is not a reassertion of vestigial ideology, as if 'prehistoric planning' was part of an ancient cultural legacy which survived into the contemporary world. It is instead an invented tradition, a recourse to the past which exceeds even the most imaginative flights of nationalist history in its desire to confer an aura of permanence on the new information order. The facility with which distant aeons are collapsed into the present has more in common with the ersatz history of American wax museums than with the lingering traces of rural values. Traditionalism looks to history for continuity: neo-traditionalism abolishes not only continuity but history itself.[13]

Here Gibbons identifies the dichotomy of traditionalism and neo-traditionalism, also elaborated upon by Kiberd, which is also part of the process of cultural (re)construction discussed by Fanon.

The tourist film falls on the side of what Gibbons terms "a fabricated relationship to the past"[14] resultant from the underdevelopment of smaller nations in the late-twentieth century. This ties in with Paget's assessment of the heritage industry in Britain and what Lovell refers to as "the proliferation of wants." Whether deliberate and conspiratorial or part of a process of economic evolution, it is clear that tourism endorses a representation of the country amenable to the need to generate revenue regardless of its relationship with either an invented or existing reality. The revenue generated in turn contributes to the overall economic growth of the country, in theory resulting in greater levels of modernization.

The question is, of course, what do tourists think they're paying to see and how does the tourist film cater to their needs? If, as Paget argues, the tourist and the ethnic entertainment industries understand one another, what precisely is at stake in tourist films? How do U.S. and Irish visions of Ireland as a tourist destination differ, and what can this difference tell us about how culture becomes commodified through the proliferation of wants rather than the representability of the product?

Glimpsing Erin:
The View from the United States in the 1930s

Ireland is far from being the sole producer of images of itself. Tourist films originating in other countries extend back to the origins of the medium, beginning with Lumière films shot in Ireland in 1896. British and U.S. travelogues were commonplace throughout the first decades of the twentieth century. In 1934 American producer James A. Fitzpatrick made one in his famous series of illustrated travel lectures in Ireland. Fitzpatrick's films were widely distributed as filler material for theatrical exhibition throughout the thirties and forties. All of them tended toward affectionate condescension, and each one ended with his narration, "And so we say farewell to ___," which became a recognized catchphrase among audiences of the time. Fitzpatrick's 1934 *Glimpses of Erin* represented the country as a land of thatched cottages, peasants, and donkeys—a place where people were poor but happy. A brief visit to Dublin notwithstanding, most of the images were of a quaint and picturesque agrarian society. Overall the film painted a picture of Ireland in the 1930s in which impoverished farmers struggled gamely in difficult conditions but always came up smiling. At the conclusion Fitzpatrick bade farewell to "the Emerald Isle" (despite the black & white photography) and the audience was left with the impression of a rural idyll in which simple folk with simple needs lived simple lives.

In order to understand the type of needs fulfilled by a film like *Glimpses of Erin*, it is necessary to study the context of its production and reception. As ever, there is more than one side to the story. In this case we must consider both the U.S. and Irish situations. *Glimpses of Erin* was released into American theatres in 1934, two years after the drought that marked the beginning of the spread of the Dust Bowl. Striking photographs of the destruction of the American rural landscape had already begun to circulate. The efforts of photographers such as Dorothea Lange and Walker Evans would eventually become even more organized with the establishment of the Resettlement Administration (later Farm Security Administration) in 1935, and the social, economic, and physical decimation of the plains would be dramatically documented on film by Paré Lorentz in 1936.[15] The Great Depression was also hitting hard at this time, driving the cinema-going public to ever more escapist entertainment. It is not difficult to see the appeal of Fitzpatrick's travel talks in this kind of environment, especially one in which happy Irish peasants and green fields struck such a contrast with what Americans were seeing coming out of their own rural landscape.

There is another side to the story. The Irish Free State had achieved partial independence from the British Empire in 1922 following a protracted struggle for political freedom and a bloody civil war. Irish cinema had developed haltingly throughout the first decades of the twentieth century, given no support by the indigenous government and working with very limited resources.[16] By the early 1930s the majority of cinematic representations of Ireland originated abroad, and though the government showed no interest in supporting their production, it did not object to the making of films including the British-produced *Man of Aran* (Robert Flaherty, 1934) or *Glimpses of Erin*. On the contrary, as has been argued by Kevin Rockett, the Irish government wholeheartedly endorsed the interpretation of the country espoused in Flaherty's film, the production and screening of which he describes as "an Irish national event."[17]

Man of Aran raises many questions of its own regarding the authorial content of documentary film and a long and involved production history incorporating both American and British determinants. Fuller analysis of the film and its maker can be found in a variety of books on documentary film.[18] The most important point worth raising in the context of the present discussion is, as Richard Barsam puts it, that "[a]ll of Flaherty's films are variations on one ideal: happiness exists when man is free and lives simply and harmoniously with nature."[19] As is only to be expected when the nature and character of a country are seen through the filter of an individual's psychological and emotional perspective, *Man of Aran* says more about Robert Flaherty than it does about Ireland. Yet Flaherty's romantic impression of the relationship between long-suffering fishing families and the sea that sustained (and challenged) them also corresponded with the Irish government's view of the Irish people as a self-sustaining, independent race with a tradition of determination and courage.

The same is true of *Glimpses of Erin* which, though lacking the grandeur and epic vision of Flaherty's film, presented Ireland within similar terms. Its images of an elderly woman bent double feeding chickens, or of a grotesquely overweight man cheerfully leading his donkey and cart loaded with turf, demonstrated an indefatigable "personality," which, as in the case of Synge's Aran Islanders (which partly inspired Flaherty's film), a stock type was being mistaken for an exemplar of the real people. But whereas Flaherty's film served a more personal set of motivations, Fitzpatrick's was merely the latest in a series of such views of different parts of the world that he had reduced to a few simple iconic images and happy platitudes designed to provide emotional comforts to the American cinema-goer of the 1930s dreaming of faraway places untouched by the ravages of depression and environmental disaster.

Cultural Tourism: Selling Yeats Country

During his visit to Dublin, James A. Fitzpatrick had been careful not to over-emphasize the presence of the urban in the blissful rural idyll that made up the greater part of *Glimpses of Erin.* It was, he told us, "a cosmopolitan city," and images of its main streets and both human and motorized traffic were shown. Urban imagery had been relatively sparse in travelogues produced in Ireland after the initial Lumière films (which were mostly shot in Dublin and Belfast). Fitzpatrick was among the first to devote any time at all to life in the capital, and also among the first to sidestep the problem of dealing with an urban Ireland by recourse to its past. Dublin was also, he explained, steeped in history. With reference to its great men of letters, including Swift and Yeats, the film linked the municipal edifices of Dublin city to its literary traditions. "When you pass through the gates of Trinity College, you pass into the seventeenth century," said Fitzpatrick, erasing three centuries of progress in the name of identification with cultural heritage.

This theme continued to surface even in indigenously produced documentary films such as Liam O'Leary's 1951 *A Portrait of Dublin* and remains current today. The most striking example of how it has been even more strenuously applied in the marketing of Ireland and Irish culture both at home and abroad can be seen in the many films about the poet W.B. Yeats. Arguably the two most important, *W.B. Yeats—A Tribute* (George Fleischmann, John D. Sheridan, 1950) and *Yeats Country* (Patrick Carey, 1965), were made within fifteen years of each other. They illustrate the process by which the commodification of culture for the purposes of selling an image of a country can be extended to films not nominally "touristic" in nature.

W.B. Yeats—A Tribute was the most high-profile non-fiction film of its time. It was made under the auspices of the National Film Institute, a body founded in 1943 with the support of Archbishop John Charles McQuaid.[20] It was produced in conjunction with the Cultural Relations

Committee and the Department of External Affairs, thereby also representing the endorsement and support of the Irish government. The film neatly combined the process of cultural commodification and international marketing under the banner of celebrating the life and work of the poet and statesman who had died in 1939. It was to be an exemplar not so much of Irish film making, but of Ireland itself, specifically the Ireland represented by the poetry of W.B. Yeats and the landscape of Sligo which the film argues inspired him. Paradoxically, while it therefore presents an interrelationship between man and landscape, the film demonstrates the capacity evinced by the majority of tourist films to strip the geographical space of its actual inhabitants. It envisions, as Robert Ballagh noted of such films in general, "a country nobody lives in."[21] The sole inhabitant of this landscape of mountains, waterfalls, trees, lakes, and even urban edifices is a dead man: the disembodied presence of W.B. Yeats.

The film was nonetheless (or perhaps consequently) a considerable success abroad. It was awarded a Certificate of Merit at the Venice Film Festival in 1950, and it was also shown at the Edinburgh Film Festival that year. While not significant honors in themselves, these represent an important step forward for Irish documentaries in terms of having an international profile. Prior to this commendation, few enough Irish films had had such exposure, let alone ever won any kind of award. The distribution of the film to festivals of this kind may be seen as part of the project of giving people an Irish view of Ireland.

Yet *W.B. Yeats—A Tribute* exhibits the same paradoxical fascination with Ireland's achievements in the past as a medium of promoting its future (tourism) that *Glimpses of Erin* and other films citing the literary tradition did. Though Yeats was not long dead, his status as an icon of Irish cultural heritage was already assured, central as he was to ideas both of the romantic and mythic past and the mythology of more recent history. The film was part of an attempt to present Yeats as a paragon of Irish identity, an appeal ironically undermined by the unproblematic approach it takes. It charts only his artistic career and his inspiration by the places being shown, which are photographed beautifully. These are obviously offered as sites where prospective tourists might find their own inspirations endowed with similar profundity simply by being there, as if it were characteristic of the Irish landscape to produce great poetry. The film lacked a study of Yeats's political status, not only in terms of 1916 and the search for national form, but even as a statesman in his latter years, and failed to delve even into his personal life to make him anything more than an abstract figure of admiration.

Yeats Country was virtually a remake and achieved even greater international recognition.[22] The film restated the correlation between landscape and poetry, adding only color photography to its predecessor's weaponry of nostalgic evocation. Its purpose was to locate Yeats firmly within the physical and cultural landscape of Ireland, as the first film had. Essentially it is the same in style, content, and approach, though its tone is more reflective. There are several sequences in the film that abandon voice-overs and linger on the natural beauty of the landscape. Carey's marvelous color cinematography and excellent use of natural sound are evocative and lyrical, and there are many stunning images of the eponymous locale. Yet, like its predecessor, *Yeats Country* is, on another level, a consciously promotional document of the Irish landscape. Though Yeats's poetry may have importance on a world scale in literary terms, neither film explores this in any detail. Neither film attempts to examine the political context of his work, or his changing beliefs over the course of his life (which admittedly did mirror some of the phases of the development of the state). Instead Yeats becomes a "mere" poet, a product of the inspiring landscape which he so often described in his poems, himself a commodity being utilized by the forces of cultural production to inspire admiration for and interest in the country itself. Ironically, the only film of this era to examine Yeats in political terms was George Morrison's 1959 *Mise Éire*, a historical document of the struggle for Irish independence. But this film reduced Yeats to a nationalist icon by dealing only with his influence on the 1916 Easter Rising, failing to note his latter-day rejection of many of the ideals of that generation.[23]

Come Buy with Me: *O'Hara's Holiday*

The 1950s brought a renewed interest in Irish travelogues in the U.S., primarily because of the production of John Ford's 1952 *The Quiet Man*. Winton C. Hoch's Oscar-winning color cinematography had fired the imagination of the U.S. cinema-going public, now emerging from the post-war period into an era of exuberant excess characterized by a cheerful consumer culture that is still the object of homage and parody today. James A. Fitzpatrick made a return trip to Ireland around this time to make two more of his postcard films, *Roaming Through Northern Ireland* and *Ireland— "The Emerald Isle."*[24] Distributed now by MGM and granting Fitzpatrick himself the title of "the voice of the globe," these color shorts found an Ireland that seemed to have stubbornly resisted change of any kind. "The picturesque little villages that are so characteristic of old Erin form a colorful background for a country folk who live in modest circumstances. They find in their humble thatched cottages pleasures that are unknown in the palaces of kings," Fitzpatrick claimed while viewers were treated to images of donkeys, pigs, cattle, and people that seemed identical to those pictured in 1934.

All was not as it seemed, though. As Erik Barnouw has observed, the selection and arrangement of footage in a documentary film inevitably reflects the subjective choices of the filmmaker in representing the subject.[25] Having had difficulty incorporating Dublin into his vision of Ireland in 1934, Fitzpatrick chose to exclude it on this occasion. The film features no urban imagery whatsoever and seems to have deliberately sought out the more remote parts of the country to provide it with its imagery. Evidence is found in the inordinate amount of time spent in Claddagh village in the Connemara Gaeltacht, which Fitzpatrick admits has been "forgotten by the rest of Ireland." Without explaining the linguistic and cultural specifics of this Irish-speaking area, Fitzpatrick lovingly details the simple life lived by the simple people here "untouched by modern influence," and only occasionally mentions that this community is in fact unusual and almost unique.

While Fitzpatrick's view remains a familiar one, a slightly more contemporary version of it is featured in Peter Bryan's 1959 *O'Hara's Holiday*. In the mold of many 1950s advertising films, this one used a fictional narrative and a central character to hold the audience's attention. It followed the story of a New York traffic cop with Irish roots who elects to take a trip to "the old country" to trace his long-lost relatives and "have a darn good holiday." In the course of his trip he meets up with a lovely Irish "colleen" (in reality an employee of *Bord Fáilte*) who accompanies him on parts of it. He is also later joined by two of his American friends, and all four enjoy the delights of various products and services available to the average tourist.

For the most part *O'Hara's Holiday* is concerned with the marketing of various commodities and locations, from Shannon Airport and angling in the west of Ireland to Irish coffee, Limerick ham, and hotels and restaurants in Dublin. It is filled with lush rural imagery and scenes of general tourism specifically designed to whet the appetite of prospective visitors. It also comes with moments of light comedy to sustain the tone of happy escapism that prevails throughout. Its most interesting aspect concerns the fate of the lovely colleen, called "Kitty." She is introduced wrapped in a shawl, sitting alone in an otherwise suspiciously empty green field. The image is faintly reminiscent of the introduction of Maureen O'Hara's character in *The Quiet Man*, only without the quasi-parodic observation "Is that real?"[26] In the course of the narrative,

O'Hara and Kitty enjoy much time together, until at the climax we are informed that along with his gifts bought in duty free for his friends at home, he has a gift for himself, namely Kitty. The two board the plane for the United States, confident that they will be back "with lots of little O'Haras" before long.

Though extraordinary to our eyes at the outset of the twenty-first century and in the wake of decades of feminism, this treatment of the female character is merely a logical extension of the consumerist project of this film and others like it, including those about Yeats. *O'Hara's Holiday* posits Ireland as a bucolic paradise that, as Fitzpatrick would put it, is "untouched by modern influence" at least insofar as this implies a simplicity and innocence far from the world of late-1950s America. The film is a prime example of the typical attitude to Ireland propagated by domestic and international tour operators throughout the twentieth century. It is an idealized, romantic vision of the landscape as the antidote to contemporary urban culture, which is similar to that suggested by *Glimpses of Erin* but comes from a very different contextual background. It explicitly posits Ireland as a virtually premodern, certainly old-fashioned, "old country" where the "down home," as it were, values lost to contemporary urban America were still alive and well, and which can be visited and enjoyed at one's leisure—while also availing of the "modern" facilities that are part of this "modern" culture.

Though it is often believed that Americans are solely responsible for this type of image of Ireland, it has its roots in a much earlier British colonial interpretation of both Ireland and the rural landscape in general. The tradition of the picturesque dates back to paintings and depictions from centuries earlier, which portrayed peasants and farmers as happy, apple-cheeked characters working in harmony with the land. Commenting on such depictions, Margaret McCurtain writes:

> Nineteenth-century artists saw the peasant as a subject associated with a receding but passionately remembered scene: the haywagon, the communal harvesting of the crops, the patient figures with bowed heads reciting the Angelus—all the romantic evocations of a countryside before the railways swept peasants into the noisome, crowded ghettos and factories of the Industrial Revolution.[27]

This same vision of rurality was, as noted, espoused by the Irish government *itself* in the 1930s when it suited its political purposes to lionize self-sufficiency and agricultural labor. Therefore, it was not surprising that promotional films should seize on both the specific, visual cues provided by nineteenth-century paintings and on the notion that such imagery was an antidote to modernization. For indigenous filmmakers, this was a form of self-exploitation, using the audience members' expectations to enhance their desire to visit Ireland. For international promoters, it provided a convenient set of preexisting representational conventions. These appealed both to visitors from England (the former colonial authority) and the United States (the final destination of so many of the diaspora) because they relied on established imagery and romantic myths of rurality which corresponded with their view of the country formed in the past. Yet this was also a view continually proffered by the Irish tourist authority precisely because it appealed to potential visitors, which made it, at least on some level, a form of counter-exploitation that eventually generated earnings in excess of £2 billion.

Luke Gibbons observes that such manipulation is inevitably the result of a modernized and urban sensibility rather than a primordial nationality:

> ... idealizations of rural existence, the longing for community and primitive simplicity, are the product of an *urban* sensibility, and are cultural fictions imposed on the lives of those they purport to represent. In the United States, for example, it was not cowboys who sang the praises of the Old West but rather writers and ideologues from the East, intent on establishing a mythology of the last frontier. By the same token, it was urban-based writers, intellectuals and political leaders who created romantic Ireland and perpetrated the myth that the further west you go, the more you come into contact with the real Ireland.[28]

O'Hara's Holiday is quite explicitly based on this type of ideal. It features an individual coming first of all from the United States, the economic and social hub of twentieth-century modernity, and secondly—and more specifically—from New York. This place (with its own links to the history of Irish emigration) is portrayed as a busy metropolis of taxi cabs and skyscrapers (using a combination of stock footage and cheating camera angles shot on location in Ireland). It is, as O'Hara tells us, a place of "exhaust fumes" from which he wants to be "a whole world away." His trip to Ireland is a trip to what Gibbons terms "a vanished pre-industrial era,"[29] a place where the comforts of modernization exist insofar as an airport allows travel, visitors can move around by car, the roads are empty, the land is unspoiled, and the women are virtuous, simple-minded, and beautiful. Kitty is, by extension, like Yeats in *W.B. Yeats—A Tribute* and *Yeats Country*, a symbol of the desirability and accessibility of Ireland for the international visitor. She, like the landscape itself, is a commodity for purchase and possession, one that reduces the specifics of personality and culture to an exchange of currency: tourist dollars for eternal bliss.

Conclusion

Tourism is a two-way process of exploitation. Both U.S. and Irish tourist films seek to promote the consumption of a product which has been tailored to meet the demands of the target market. Despite some surface differences, the underlying logic is the same. Though the films discussed in this paper come from a particular era, it is fair to say that the basic questions posed by contemporary promotional films are no different. Today, it is clear from the numerous in-flight magazines, informational films, and direct-to-retail videos that are so widely distributed as to defeat cataloguing that the lessons of James A. Fitzpatrick have been well learned and well used. The tourist film invites you to the land of a hundred thousand welcomes, but it is just as happy to bid you farewell when your visit is over and your money is spent. It is not unlike a dance where the partners couple for a while and then respectfully part company. In the words of Yeats himself, "How can we know the dancer from the dance?"[30]

NOTES

1. See Adele M. Dalsimer, ed., *Visualizing Ireland: National Identity and the Pictorial Tradition* (Boston and London: Faber & Faber, 1993).

2. Terry Lovell, *Pictures of Reality* (London: BFI, 1983), 58.

3. T.J.M. Sheehy, "The Tourist Film," *Vision* 3 (Summer 1967), 5.

4. Derek Paget, "Tales of Cultural Tourism," in Alan Rosenthal, ed., *Why Docudrama? Fact-Fiction on Film and TV* (Carbondale and Edwardsville, Ill.: Southern Illinois University Press, 1999), 47–63.

5. Ibid., 48.

6. Frantz Fanon, *The Wretched of the Earth* (London: MacGibbon & Kee, 1965).

7. Paget, "Tales of Cultural Tourism," 48.

8. Declan Kiberd, *Inventing Ireland: The Literature of the Modern Nation* (London: Jonathan Cape, 1995), 288.

9. Ibid.

10. Micheál Ó Siochfhradha, *Seo Mar Bhí* (*Baile Átha Cliath: Ó Fallamhain i gcomhair le hOifig an tSoláthair*, 1930).

11. Problems ensue when the "corpse" is tormented by his drunken friends, who eventually light matches and stick them between his fingers. He jumps "to life" and terrifies the author. The character of the author is most probably modeled on Seán Ó Súilleabháin, whose researches into the customs of Irish wakes from 1921 eventually resulted in *Irish Wake Amusements*, translated by the author from the Irish original, *Caitheamh Aimsire ar Thórraimh* (*Baile Átha Cliath: An Clóchomar Teoranta*, 1961).

12. A Little Bird, Café, Hilton Cordell Productions production for RTÉ, BBC Northern Ireland, and SBS Independent (Australia), co-directed by Alan Gilsenan, Dearbhla Walsh, and David Roberts.

13. Luke Gibbons, *Transformations in Irish Culture* (Cork: Cork University Press/Field Day, 1996), 89.

14. Ibid.

15. *The Plow That Broke the Plains* (Paré Lorentz, 1936). Further reading on this period and the films and photographs to emerge from it can be found in Richard M. Barsam, *Non-Fiction Film* (Bloomington: Indiana University Press, 1992), and Robert L. Snyder, *Paré Lorentz and the Documentary Film* (Reno, Las Vegas, and London: University of Nevada Press, 1994).

16. The history of Irish film has been extensively documented by Kevin Rockett, Luke Gibbons, and John Hill, *Cinema and Ireland* (London and New York: Routledge, 1988) and, more recently, Martin McLoone, *Irish Film: The Emergence of a Contemporary Cinema* (London: BFI, 2000), and Lance Pettitt, *Screening Ireland* (Manchester: Manchester University Press, 2000).

17. Rockett, Gibbons, and Hill, *Cinema and Ireland*, 71.

18. See Barsam, *Non-Fiction Film*, Erik Barnouw, *Documentary: A History of the Non-Fiction Film* (New York and Oxford: Oxford University Press, 1993) and Alan Rosenthal, ed., *New Challenges for Documentary* (Berkeley, Los Angeles, and London: California University Press, 1988).

19. Richard Barsam, *The Vision of Robert Flaherty* (Bloomington: Indiana University Press, 1988), 7.

20. For more detail on this body and on the development of Irish cinema in this era, see Rockett, Gibbons, and Hill, *Cinema and Ireland*; McLoone, *Irish Film*; and Pettitt, *Screening Ireland*.

21. Robert Ballagh, quoted in Gibbons, *Transformations in Irish Culture*, 86.

22. The film won a Golden Bear at the Berlin Film Festival, a Diploma of Merit at the Edinburgh Film Festival, First Prize at the Chicago Film Festival, and First Prize for Best Color Short at the Barcelona International Film Festival. It also was nominated for an American Academy of Motion Picture Arts and Sciences Award in 1966.

23. For a fuller discussion of *Mise Éire* and the use of Yeats's image in the film, see Harvey O'Brien, "Historical Documentary in Ireland," *Historical Journal of Film, Radio, and Television* 20 (Autumn 2000), 335–50.

24. The exact dates of production of these films is uncertain. Sources at the Irish Film Archive of the Film Institute of Ireland estimate they were made either in the late 1940s or early 1950s. The archive does not possess prints of these films (only a videotape), and thus cannot stock-date the material.

25. See Barnouw, *Documentary*, 348.

26. Recent analyses of *The Quiet Man* by McLoone, *Irish Film*; Pettitt, *Screening Ireland*; and James MacKillop, "The Quiet Man Speaks," in James MacKillop, ed., *Contemporary Irish Cinema From The Quiet Man to Dancing at Lughnasa* (New York: Syracuse University Press, 1999) have redeemed this film from its pariah status in the history of the representation of Ireland on film by emphasizing its elements of self-parody and irony, including this famous moment and the cited line, spoken by John Wayne.

27. Margaret McCurtain, "The Real Molly Macree," in Adele Dalsimer, ed., *Visualizing Ireland*, 11.

28. Gibbons, *Transformations in Irish Culture*, 85.

29. Ibid., 204.

30. W.B. Yeats, "Among Schoolchildren."

Nationalism, Sentiment, and Economics: Relations between Ireland and Irish America in the Postwar Years

MARY E. DALY

Ireland is a country whose sons and daughters hold her dearly above all, and it is evident in your great country as in others, that their love does not wither because the soil beneath their feet is foreign soil. St Patrick planted more than the shamrock when he came to Ireland—he planted in the hearts and minds of her people a spiritual fire that nothing can extinguish—a fire which still burns brightly in the hearts and minds of Irish men and women and those of Irish descent the world over.

ST. PATRICK'S DAY GREETINGS FROM THE *TAOISEACH*,

JOHN A. COSTELLO,

TO THE FRIENDLY SONS OF ST. PATRICK IN HAWAII, MARCH 1957[1]

DESPITE MANY ASSERTIONS to the contrary, Mary Robinson was not the first Irish leader to reach out to the Irish diaspora.[2] W.T. Cosgrave, President of the Executive Council of the Irish Free State from 1922 to 1932, broadcast a St. Patrick's Day message to the United States in March 1926, several years before King George V began his annual Christmas broadcasts to the British Empire.[3] Cosgrave's first live broadcast in March 1931 seems to have attracted a large audience, judging by the many letters and postcards that he received from listeners throughout the United States and Canada.[4] De Valera continued the tradition of sending St. Patrick's Day greetings to the United States until 1938, when he relinquished the honor to Ireland's first President, Douglas Hyde. This is not the only evidence that independent Ireland kept in touch with the American Irish. During the late 1930s de Valera and Eoin MacNeill explored the possibility of establishing Irish cultural centers throughout the United States, so that Irish Americans and other Americans might learn "something about our past and present," but the plan was abandoned at the outbreak of World War II.[5] In February 1946 de Valera entertained four Irish-American prelates—Spellman of New York, Mooney of Detroit, Stritch of Chicago, and Glennon of St. Louis—in Killarney, when they visited Ireland en route to Rome, where they were consecrated as cardinals. The party included James Farley, who had served as Post-Master General in Franklin Roosevelt's cabinet, and Fr. Robert Gannon, the President of Fordham University.[6]

Visits to the United States by leading Irish politicians became more common in the 1950s, with the introduction of regular trans-Atlantic flights; in 1956 John A. Costello became the first Irish head of government to spend St. Patrick's Day in the United States, inaugurating a pattern that many later *Taoisigh* have followed. In the morning he presented shamrocks to President Dwight D. Eisenhower at the White House, before flying to New York to preside at the St. Patrick's Day parade; that evening he was guest of honor at the annual dinner of the Friendly Sons of St. Patrick in Philadelphia.[7] Yet, despite evidence of regular contact between the Dublin government and Irish America, there is some validity in the belief that independent Ireland failed to keep in contact with the wider Irish community. This distancing seems to have happened during the 1950s and the 1960s because of changes in the Irish community in the United States, and in political and economic policies in Ireland. This essay concentrates on the perspective of the Irish government.[8]

-1-

Mass emigration from Ireland to the United States came to a halt in 1929, following the Wall Street crash. By the late 1930s Britain had become the dominant destination for Irish emigrants, and by 1950 there were more people of Irish birth living in Britain than in the United States. Between 1951 and 1961 more than 400,000 men and women are believed to have emigrated from Ireland, but only 62,400 went to the United States. During this period, Irish immigrants filled less than 50 percent of the annual quota of 17,853 U.S. visas earmarked for Ireland in every year except 1957 and 1958, when a recession in Britain created greater interest in other destinations and the numbers emigrating to the United States increased to 9,124 and 10,383, respectively.[9]

Because of the small number of postwar emigrants to the United States, and the physical distance between the two countries, the Irish in America were seen in a very different light from the Irish in Britain. By the 1950s all the leading Irish newspapers had appointed London correspondents, and they carried regular reports about the social problems experienced by Irish emigrants in Britain. Irish politicians and church-men relayed similar information on many occasions, in the hope that it would discourage young people from leaving Ireland.[10] Reports about the Irish in America were much more upbeat. While some local news-papers, such as the *Western People*, carried a regular column about Mayo emigrants in the greater New York area, most newspapers were more concerned with social and sporting events. The only reference to current emigration in the briefing notes prepared for visits by Irish min-isters to the United States during the 1950s concerned the non-recogni-tion of Irish medical degrees by the U.S. authorities, and the liability of Irish citizens for military service.[11] Most Irish politicians seem to have regarded emigration to the United States as a matter of history, and they tended to invoke Irish America as evidence that there were some bene-fits from emigration: it gave Ireland an influence throughout the world that was disproportionate to its size. In 1948 during the debate on the Republic of Ireland Bill, the then-*Taoiseach*, John A. Costello, noted:

> We are a small country. Our material wealth is comparatively insignifi-cant. . . . Though we are a small nation, we wield an influence in the world far in excess of what our mere physical size and the smallness of our pop-ulation might warrant. We are sometimes accused of acting as if we were a big nation. But, in fact, we are a big nation. Our exiles have gone to practically every part of the world and have created for their motherland a spiritual dominion which more than compensates for her lack of size or material wealth. The Irish at home are only one section of a great race which has spread itself throughout the world, particularly in the great countries of North America and the Pacific area.[12]

Such consolatory images were particularly important during the 1950s, when the population of the Irish Republic fell to a postfamine low. When the 1956 Irish Nationality and Citizenship Act extended citizen-ship to the descendants of Irish emigrants on very liberal terms, the Northern Ireland Minister for Home Affairs, Captain Terence O'Neill (a future prime minister), claimed that this "attempt by a small pastoral republic to create a vast empire of citizens" was designed to compensate for the falling population in the Irish Republic.[13] If so, it was not very successful; until the late 1960s fewer than one hundred people a year claimed Irish citizenship by descent.[14]

Although Irish America had provided substantial funds for nation-alist causes from the mid-nineteenth century onward, the new state made little effort to tap the economic and financial power of the Irish emigrant community until after World War II.[15] By the late 1940s, how-ever, the dollar shortage was preoccupying most governments throughout Western Europe, and Ireland was forced to consider all possible means of increasing dollar earnings. Emigrant remittances and legacies provided substantially more dollars than merchandise exports to the United States, and this remained the case until the late 1950s.[16] The 1950 Treaty of Friendship, Commerce, and Navigation relieved bequests and the U.S. estates of returning emigrants of the threat of double-taxation, but the declining number of Irish-born residents of the United States meant that this was a dwindling source, so alternatives had to be explored.[17] Efforts to increase the value of Irish exports to the United States immediately after World War II did not prove very successful. In 1952 a team of U.S. consultants who were asked to select ten Irish products that could be marketed successfully in the United States failed to identify any suitable products. They also remarked on the smugness of Irish businesses and on "the illusion of appealing to Irish sentiment in the United States."[18]

Tourism appeared to offer better opportunities. When U.S. airlines were attempting to secure landing rights in Dublin in 1948–49, they held out the prospect that thousands of Irish-Americans might visit Ireland as part of a pilgrimage to Rome during the 1950 Holy Year. Although the Irish government refused to grant U.S. airlines landing rights in Dublin, because they had invested heavily in trans-Atlantic runways at Shannon, a committee of civil servants charged with identifying possible sources of dollar earnings decided to open an Irish tourist office near the Vatican to target some of the 15 million Irish Americans who were expected to visit Rome. Their report drew a distinction between visitors who had been born in Ireland or were first-generation Irish Americans, and others, who either had no Irish connections or were "but remotely of Irish origin" and whose tie to Ireland was "one only of vague sentiment." U.S. visitors with close family connections were expected to stay with relatives and to spend less money *per diem*, though they would remain in Ireland for a longer period than other tourists. As they would not require hotel accommodation, were not reliant on publicity to persuade them to visit Ireland, and would probably travel by the cheapest means of transport, by sea rather than by air, it was decided that any promotional campaign should be directed at the wealthier second- and third-generation Irish Americans.[19] It is not clear whether this proposal was implemented; government files in this period contain many promising ideas that were not put into effect for many years, and the frequent changes of government between 1948 and 1957 meant that decisions were often amended or reversed.

In 1951 tourist marketing in the United States took an entirely new direction when Pan American Airlines submitted proposals to Seán Lemass, Minister for Industry and Commerce, who was responsible for tourism and transport, for a national festival that would serve as a device to extend the tourist season. The festival, to be known as *An Tóstal* (pageant, muster, array, display), would be marketed using the slogan "Ireland at Home" and the shamrock symbol. John Leydon, secretary of the Department of Industry and Commerce, remarked that the "English phrase 'at home' will be used in connection with the event to convey the idea that the whole country will be at home to Irish exiles and friends from abroad." He advised against using Irish terms such as *céilí* or *cuaird*; the word *craic* was not commonly used until the 1980s. Leydon added that the scheme "is based largely on the sentimental attachment to this country of Irish Americans."[20]

Pan American Airlines planned to target the 20 million Irish Americans who were believed to "have a strong sentimental tie with the 'Old Sod,' especially members of Irish fraternal organizations, church societies, and the marching groups that took part in St. Patrick's Day parades. They claimed that the "overseas Irish want and deserve recognition by the Irish Republic for their contribution to the advancement of their nation and the prestige of their people. Any recognition by the Irish Government will be returned ten-fold." The festival would serve the dual purposes of "drawing the Irish world more closely together with the mother country, and secondly, of developing visitor traffic to Ireland among these people who are most receptive to such an appeal." They recommended that the weeks immediately after St. Patrick's Day should be known as COME BACK TO ERIN MONTH, "in recognition of the exploits of Irish people overseas and as an expression of appreciation for their contribution to the creation of a free Ireland." This slogan would appeal to "an emotional desire on the part of people of Irish descent to visit Erin." The festival should offer a range of sporting and cultural events, including a world cup in hurling and Gaelic football, a special program at the Abbey Theatre featuring performances by actors and actresses of Irish descent, and an exhibition at the National Museum dedicated to the spread of the Irish people and their influence throughout the world from the earliest times. Visitors would be encouraged to travel to the county or counties of their ancestors.[21]

One of the most interesting suggestions was the compilation of a register of all the Irish overseas. Names would be inscribed on a scroll to be kept in the National Museum. Persons of Irish ancestry would be encouraged to register their children's names at birth. While the register would constitute an emotional record, it would also provide useful mailing lists for promoting tourism and exports.[22] Irish residents would be encouraged to write to relatives overseas "about the old sod," inviting them to visit Ireland. Another proposal was for a beauty contest, in Ireland and the United States, to choose "a typical Irish coleen," with Irish-born Hollywood stars Maureen O'Hara and Maureen O'Sullivan among the adjudicators. Shannon Airport would be promoted using the shamrock, "the most significant symbol of Ireland in the minds of people throughout the world." A large map at the airport should indicate where different family names originated. Pan America was also keen to construct a special national park beside the airport, called "The Valley of the Fairies or the home of the Leprachauns," complete with a slab showing the print of a tiny foot, but Seán Lemass regarded this as one marketing gimmick too far.[23]

The most remarkable feature of this proposal is the extent to which it defined the marketing strategy for Irish tourism in the United States for many years to come, with the mixture of sentiment, leprechauns, sport, references to "the old sod," and encouragement to visit the ancestral birth-place.[24] Although Lemass also vetoed the Irish-American beauty contest, the concept re-emerged some years later as the "Rose of Tralee." The origins of the Dublin Theatre Festival can also be traced to this document.

The first *An Tóstal* opened on Easter Sunday 1953 with a three-week program of events. The official brochure promised "magnificent parades, colorful displays, bright attractions, spectacular exhibitions and a gay and joyous mustering of the Irish Clans from near and far." The decision to move the opening date from St. Patrick's Day to Easter meant that the festival became associated with the commemoration of the 1916 Rising. In 1953, as part of the opening ceremonies, de Valera laid a wreath at the 1916 memorial at Arbour Hill, before attending a memorial mass for the Old IRA. Religion and nationalism featured prominently in the 1953 program, though the only reference to these in the original proposal was the suggestion that the festival should recognize the part that Irish Americans had played in "the creation of a free Ireland." The centerpiece of the 1954 *Tóstal* was a historical pageant at Tara. This was such a logistical nightmare that the 1955 pageant was held at the GAA stadium at Croke Park in Dublin. The 1953 souvenir handbook emphasized the festival's aim of "keeping 'open door' to men and women of Irish birth and origin from all parts of the world, who have come back to renew their contact with our country." And the 1954 program included a special section listing local *Tóstal* Centres, which was preceded by a note: "Visitors if you are Irish Born or if your kinsfolk were exiles you may wish to visit the places in Ireland most dear to you." But the large numbers of U.S. tourists failed to materialize, and by 1955 there was less emphasis on attractions for overseas visitors, and more on local participation.[25]

-2-

An Tóstal combined Catholicism, nationalism, nostalgia, and sporting events in a representative cocktail of Irish culture. Politics lurked in the wings in the form of the anti-partition campaign, which raised some troubling issues for the tourist drive. Should *Bord Fáilte*, the state tourist board, encourage visitors to travel to Northern Ireland? Would anti-partition campaigners be permitted to participate in *An Tóstal*? Seán Lemass was unenthusiastic on both fronts, and one official in his department urged that the anti-partition league should be kept "ten thousand miles away from all the events," though he would not object to "an authoritative lecture" on partition being included in the program. However, Minister for External Affairs Frank Aiken recommended that the anti-partition league avail itself of "the excellent opportunity" that *An Tóstal* presented to distribute its leaflets. He also believed that the festival would provide an opportunity for cross-border cooperation in promoting tourism, but he had few supporters.[26]

The Irish Anti-Partition League was founded in Dungannon, Co. Tyrone, in November 1945. By 1949 all the main Irish political parties had joined the anti-partition campaign through the all-party Mansion House Committee.[27] There was a concerted effort to persuade foreign governments and the wider public of the moral case for a united Ireland.[28] Irish exiles in Britain, Australia, and the United States were especially targeted; when de Valera lost office in 1948 he toured all three countries to drum up support for the cause. After he addressed a large crowd at New York City Hall, the *Irish Press* noted that his first reference to partition brought deafening cheers from the crowd. They claimed that "the United Irish Societies are delighted, as they have made the Partition problem Number One in the scheduled publicity program."[29] John Bowman, however, has claimed that the audiences for de Valera's anti-partition speeches "were largely composed of the converted."[30] The anti-partition campaign attracted considerable support from Irish-American organizations in its early years. In November 1947, three thousand delegates representing organizations from thirty-eight states met in New York at an Irish Race Convention to form the American League for an Undivided Ireland (ALUI) — a loose confederation that would coordinate a U.S. campaign against partition.[31] Within a short time they had collected 200,000 signatures on a petition asking President Truman to use his efforts to end partition.[32] The U.S. government took the predictable line that partition was a matter for Britain and Ireland to resolve, and Irish efforts to link the ending of partition and NATO membership—by promising to join NATO if Ireland were united—proved an utter failure.[33] However, the American League for a United Ireland had some success in raising the anti-partition cause in Congress. In 1949 four congressmen and one senator moved unsuccessful resolutions on Capitol Hill against partition and in March 1950 Congress voted to withhold ERP (Marshall Plan aid) funds from Britain as long as partition continued, though the vote was later reversed.[34] Resolutions in favor of a united Ireland were tabled in the House of Representatives, the Senate, and several state legislatures in 1951.[35] Although the international campaign against partition had waned by 1953, the ALUI was distributing literature outlining the evils of partition to Catholic schools throughout the United States.[36]

References to partition seem to have been mandatory in all speeches by visiting Irish ministers during the 1950s.[37] In October 1953 Seán Lemass, *Tánaiste* and Minister for Industry and Commerce, gave a speech to the National Press Club in Washington about the Irish economy, in which he mentioned that the U.S. consultants who had advised the Irish government on tourism, trade development, forestry, mineral exploitation, and industrial development "were often very frank and outspoken in their comments on Irish conditions . . . which is the way we wanted them." Lemass went on to argue that Ireland's progress, both in economic terms and in international relations, was "seriously impeded by the persistence of Partition. . . . Ireland's economic and social problems cannot be completely solved until the re-unification of the national territory has been brought about."[38]

In 1954, Joseph Brennan, counselor in the Irish Embassy in Washington, asked the Irish consuls in New York, Chicago, Boston, and San Francisco to report on the level of commitment to the anti-partition campaign among recent emigrants. Brennan claimed that priests and others who were in regular contact with new Irish emigrants had reported that "these native-born Irish are rather less zealous and less interested in the anti-partition movement than one might expect or even hope."[39] John Conway and Paul Keating, the Irish Consuls-General in Chicago and New York, respectively, confirmed that this was correct. Keating acknowledged that there was "a certain amount of conflict" between new emigrants and established members of the Irish and Irish-American community:

One reason for this I think is that the attitude of people who grew up in an Independent Ireland is different to that of people who knew Ireland before 1922, or perhaps only by hearsay. I think a great deal of the sentimentalism and romanticism of so many Irish-Americans grates on the younger people coming to this country. I think they are also at times irritated by the assumption which prevails in some quarters that they know nothing and I certainly know of some who resent very much being told that it was the Irish Americans who won the war for Independence in Ireland. On this account there is a clash.[40]

Conway claimed that recent emigrants had little difficulty in adjusting to life in America, because they had "come from a modernized Ireland in which even the rural areas have felt the impact of urban culture." The majority were not interested in joining Irish societies.[41]

"Operation Harvest," the IRA border campaign that began in December 1956, ended any residual support by the Irish government for the anti-partition campaign.[42] Internment was introduced in 1957. The Irish Embassy in Washington was expressing concern about the extremist tendencies of the ALUI some years before violence erupted. In 1953 the ALUI issued a press release that "congratulates the Irish patriotic men and women in the British-occupied six counties who protested by deeds and words against the official visit of the British Queen to their homeland . . . and are willing to substitute deeds for words in speeding up the day of liberation."[43] In 1958 John Conway, the Irish Consul General in New York, reported that relations between the New York county clubs and the Irish government were cool because the Irish Institute, which acted as an effective headquarters for the county clubs, disagreed with the Irish government's stance toward the IRA's border campaign, and the director of the Irish Institute—Mayo-born lawyer Paul O'Dwyer, the brother of former New York mayor William O'Dwyer—had adopted an attitude toward the Dublin government that was "unfriendly and at times even offensive." Conway claimed that most of the membership of the county clubs shared O'Dwyer's attitude.[44]

When Seán Lemass, now *Taoiseach*, accepted an invitation in 1963 to speak at a dinner organized by the Irish Fellowship Club in Chicago (the most exclusive Irish Society in that city, which was controlled by Mayor Richard Daley), the Consul-General Seán Ó hEidéain, advised that:

> Partition and the need for territorial re-unification should be mentioned, at least briefly. Such a mention is important because as Taoiseach Mr. Lemass will represent the integral Irish tradition. Moreover, any old IRA men and Old Clan na Gael men present, on reading the speech afterwards will expect it and others will be interested to hear it as the *Time*

Magazine article, which so many read was a bit out of focus on the non-economic side, and on pre-1959 history.[45] Moreover there is a numerically small so-called Clan na Gael group in Chicago who if the government policy on a peaceful solution of Partition is not publicized appropriately may fill the vacuum with violent and non-violent words with possible grave results in deeds in perhaps a year or two. The other formerly intransigent group in Chicago, the Ulster Irish Liberty Legion has this year given up any pro-violent aims and has switched its energies to cultural activities.[46]

Lemass's speech concentrated on economic matters. His government was firmly committed to developing the Irish economy, and attracting U.S. industrial investment was an essential element in the overall development plan. The *Time* magazine coverage concentrated on these matters. Lemass was also keen to promote closer cooperation between the Dublin and Belfast governments. Economic development and policy toward Northern Ireland were closely linked, because Lemass believed that economic success in the Irish Republic would be a major factor in reducing the opposition of Ulster unionists toward a united Ireland.[47]

-3-

What role did the Dublin government envisage for Irish America in this new political and economic strategy? In June 1958, some months before the publication of the decisive 1958 *Programme for Economic Expansion*, Irish Consul-General John Conway, and his third secretary, Eamonn Kennedy, compiled a report on the political and economic influence of the Irish and Irish Americans in the New York area.[48] References to a "long-range program" suggest that this report formed part of the background material drawn up by government departments for the *Programme for Economic Expansion*. Conway claimed that the Irish carried little political or economic influence in the New York area. With the number of residents of Irish birth falling rapidly, Conway concluded that "influence solely through them is a diminishing possibility. Any long range program based only, or even largely, on their goodwill would probably have poor prospects of success." Although recent emigrants from Ireland had a somewhat higher economic status than earlier generations, it was probably below the general average, "although by no means poor by Irish or, for that matter, British standards." The county clubs, the main organizations for Irish immigrants, had only "a few thousand" members, and the numbers attending their social events, such as annual dances, were falling. Membership was overwhelmingly drawn from blue-collar workers; the clubs made no real effort to attract professional and white-collar immigrants. For this reason Conway believed that the leadership and membership of the county clubs carried "little economic or social weight," and, as already noted, they disagreed with the Irish government's attitude toward the IRA border campaign.[49]

Conway lamented the absence of a non-political organization "of a middle-class social or cultural nature" that would attract professional and white-collar emigrants. Because no such organization existed, the influence of middle-class Irish immigrants was "scattered and virtually valueless." He ended this section of the report, concerning Irish-born residents of the New York area, by noting that they had "little political power, little social status, little financial or economic worth, and such cultural importance in the educational and theatrical field as individuals may exert. The leadership of the principal Irish organizations seem neither skilful enough nor dedicated enough to arrest the decline of our influence here if directed solely through our own Irish-born people."[50]

Conway was also skeptical about the possible influence that the estimated 29 million Irish Americans might exercise in favor of Ireland, because he believed that for the majority of Irish Americans Catholicism was more important than Irishness. He described the New York St. Patrick's Day parade as "a demonstration of Catholic presence with some Irish overtones." Although many Irish Americans worked in radio and television, he doubted that they exercised much influence, because radio and television were dominated by liberals, and "the 'liberal' point of view is not essentially an Irish-American characteristic." While Irish Americans prominent in New York financial circles were active in Catholic church organizations, Conway found that "with one or two exceptions . . . their interest in Ireland is limited to a sentimental regard for their ancestry, which does not involve financial expenditure."[51] As to politics, he claimed that Irish-Americans "have not quite reached the top political rung," and he predicted that John F. Kennedy was unlikely to become president of the United States. The enhanced economic and social status of Irish Americans meant that they were no longer voting en masse for the Democratic party; and their political influence was fading as a consequence. Conway summarized the position as follows:

> Our influence in the United States is a function of the amount of interest Irish-Americans have in Ireland, rather than in being *Irish*. Being "Irish" means merely having Irish ancestry, feeling a sentimental regard for it and displaying the "green" on St. Patrick's Day. It is remarkable the extent to which being *Irish* does *not* involve any particular enthusiasm for, or even interest in, *Ireland*. Ireland's problems have small place in the consciousness of Irish-Americans. 1916 is a dim memory.[52]

Intermarriage and assimilation, Conway continued, inevitably brought a lessening of interest in Ireland. Although there was "a natural race relationship" between Ireland and Irish America, he suggested that "our contact with Irish-Americans is so limited that we are in danger of losing any real connection with them." While some Congressmen and other politicians would give "us [presumably Irish diplomats] a casual hearing," he warned that "it would be a mistake to expect too much of them." Irish Americans were not interested in Irish domestic affairs, and Ireland's international position was not sufficiently important to attract their interest. The best approach would be to nurture their "friendly interest" through some type of cultural organization. Affluent Irish Americans might display a greater interest in Ireland "if social cachet were provided." As for influencing U.S. policy, Conway believed that "our one vote" at the United Nations "exercised the United States State Department considerably more than any resolution passed by an Irish-American organization."[53]

As to the economic potential of the Irish-American market, tourism was the only sector in which ethnicity seemed to be a promising selling point, although *Bord Fáilte* believed that the ethnic market was limited and declining. *Córas Tráchtála*—the state-owned Irish trade board—described the level of interest shown by Irish emigrants and Irish Americans in Irish produce as "disappointing." The Industrial Development Authority—the state organization that promoted foreign industrial investment in Ireland—reported that Irish-American industrialists were disinclined to show any particular enthusiasm for Ireland "merely because of their racial background." With the possible exception of tourism, "Irish Americans undoubtedly represent tremendous economic power but such power is neither concentrated enough nor 'Irish' enough to risk very much for Ireland's benefit."[54]

When Secretary of the Department of Finance T.K. Whitaker convened a group of senior Irish civil servants in 1960 to consider the merits of establishing an Irish Chamber of Commerce in the United States, they decided that "the Irish Chamber of Commerce in the United States should not be an Irish-American organization"; instead, "the members should be the heads of important American business, commercial and banking organizations; they need have no Irish connections, but it is desirable that some at least are well disposed towards Ireland."[55] Instrumentalism had triumphed over sentiment; Irish America was being redefined on the basis of economic interest, rather than ethnicity. When the establishment of the Irish-American Council for Industry and Commerce was announced in January 1963, it was determined that membership would be strictly limited both in terms of numbers and status.[56] While it would be too extreme to suggest that "No Irish need apply," applicants would be carefully vetted before being admitted. In 1962 the Irish Embassy in Washington reopened dusty files dating from the 1930s concerning a proposed Irish-American cultural foundation. Officials determined that the first step should be to form a fundraising committee consisting of "influential and wealthy persons" in the United States. They expressed hopes that the foundation would provide "a welcome outlet for the vague—and even at times misguided—desires of so many existing Irish bodies in the US to promote the well-being of "'the old country.'" Once again the emphasis was on wealth and status, with Irish ancestry an optional qualification.[57]

Official efforts to project an image of Ireland as a modern, economically successful nation took full advantage of the election of John F. Kennedy as President of the United States. Seán Lemass's visit to the United States in October 1963 was a deliberate attempt to capitalize on Kennedy's triumphant visit to Ireland some months earlier. The Kennedy family history and the targeting of affluent Americans, whose links with Ireland were often rather tenuous, led to an emphasis on famine-era emigrants and their descendants who had achieved fame and fortune. In May 1963, Aedán O'Beirne of the Irish Embassy in Washington reported that Cecil Woodham-Smith's best-selling book, *The Great Famine*, had a very beneficial impact on American attitudes toward Ireland, because it had succeeded "in putting into focus Irish emigration into the United States and generally of winning a sympathy and respect for the Irish emigrant who was the victim of the Famine and its consequences in the ensuing Century."[58] The Irish consulate in San Francisco began to compile profiles of successful citizens of California with Irish ancestry, in the hope of targeting them for membership of business or cultural organizations.[59]

The success achieved by the descendants of nineteenth-century emigrants, who left a poverty-stricken Ireland, was consistent with the image of a modern successful Ireland, whereas the reality of continuing emigration was not. This may explain why Irish officials adopted such a sanguine attitude toward proposals to reform U.S. immigration laws, including an end to national quotas. In 1963 an official in the Irish embassy in Washington noted the widely held belief that the existing immigration quotas were "outmoded, unjust and should be revised."[60] In 1965 Irish officials concluded that proposed legislation did not appear to be contrary to Irish interests. Although national quotas would end, they believed that Irish applicants would be in a favorable position, because of their comparatively high level of education, their fluency in English, and the large number of Irish people with relatives who were U.S. citizens.

When the new immigration law came into effect in 1968, however, the number of immigrant visas awarded to Irish immigrants fell sharply. Only two hundred twenty-seven emigrant visas were awarded to Irish citizens during the first six months. The overwhelming majority of successful applicants were close relatives of American citizens, who did not require a labor clearance; or they fell into special categories such as ministers of religion, and emigrants who had formerly resided in the United States for some years, but had not taken out U.S. citizenship. The Irish Embassy in Washington acknowledged that if the new immigration act were not in force, Irish immigration in 1969 would have been in the region of four thousand, more than twice the actual figure. Contrary to the belief expressed in 1963 that Irish emigrants had a high standard of education, most applicants were the sons and daughters of small farmers, who had few job skills and only elementary education; they ranked very low in U.S. immigrant preferences.[61]

In 1954 Paul Keating, the Irish Consul-General in New York, had noted that the Irish consulate made no effort to keep in contact with the emigrant community: "Generally speaking we are embarrassed by callers who have nothing to recommend them except their Irish citizenship." Keating added that "We cannot afford to entertain them . . . we do not have even a St. Patrick's Day reception for Irish citizens and are forced by our financial circumstances to avoid them rather than to associate with them."[62] By the 1960s Irish government finances were less straitened, but Ireland's official hospitality was increasingly directed at wealthy and influential men and women, who did not necessarily have strong ethnic connections to Ireland. Those who had "nothing to recommend them" were left to their own devices. The longer term consequences of this official indifference can be seen in the widening gulf between the Irish government and Irish-American organizations over the Northern Ireland crisis that erupted in 1969, foreshadowed by the differing views over "Operation Harvest." It would be evident also in the belated response by the Irish authorities to the problem of illegal or "undocumented" Irish immigrants in the 1980s.

NOTES

1. National Archives of Ireland (hereafter NAI), Department of the *Taoiseach* files, S5683.

2. Helen Burke and Olivia O'Leary, *Mary Robinson: The Authorised Biography* (London: Hodder & Stoughton, 1998), 189–205. On 2 February 1995, President Robinson addressed both Houses of the Oireachtas, delivering a speech entitled "Cherishing the Diaspora."

3. NAI, Department of the *Taoiseach* files, S5111/1, Broadcast Messages by President. King George V made his first broadcast at Christmas 1932. Ross McKibbin, *Classes and Cultures: England 1918–1951* (Oxford: Oxford University Press, 1997), 9.

4. NAI, S5111/7, S5111/8. This broadcast was on the CBS network. Cosgrave recorded a separate St. Patrick's Day message that was broadcast on 15 March by NBC in Chicago; the text was published in the *Chicago Tribune* (S5111/6). Earlier addresses were either pre-recorded, or read on Cosgrave's behalf by a U.S. broadcaster.

5. NAI, S9215A, Irish-American Cultural Foundation.

6. Sean Cronin, *Washington's Irish Policy 1916–1986: Independence, Partition, Neutrality* (Dublin: Anvil Press, 1987), 166.

7. NAI, Department of Foreign Affairs (hereafter DFA), Washington Files, D22-I, Visit of Taoiseach John A. Costello to the United States, 1956.

8. For Irish America see Kevin Kenny, *The American Irish: A History* (New York: Longman, 2000), ch. 6, and David M. Reimers, "Overview. An End and a Beginning," in Ronald H. Bayor and Timothy J. Meagher, eds., *The New York Irish* (Baltimore: Johns Hopkins University Press, 1996), 419–38.

9. Patrick J. Blessing, *The Irish in America: A Guide to the Literature and Manuscript Collections* (Washington: Catholic University of America Press, 1982), Table 13, 308; Thomas J. Archdeacon, *Becoming American: An Ethnic History* (London: Collier Macmillan, 1983), 175. Estimates of net emigration derived from the Census of Population suggest that emigration reached 197,000 during the period 1951–56, and 212,000 in the years 1956–61. Robert E. Kennedy, *The Irish: Emigration, Marriage, and Fertility* (Berkeley, Calif.: University of California Press, 1973), 212–13.

10. Eamon de Valera gave a speech in Galway on 29 August 1951, in which he claimed that the living conditions of many Irish emigrants to Britain were far inferior to what they would have enjoyed in Ireland. de Valera drew on reports that he had received from an English social worker. His speech was widely reported in British and Irish newspapers, provoking hostile comments from the local authorities in many English cities. See NAI, S11582B, Irish labor emigration to Britain and Northern Ireland.

11. The United States recognized medical degrees awarded by British medical schools and by Queen's University Belfast, but Irish medical graduates had to undergo an internship year and sit the examinations of state medical boards. Although the 1950 Irish-American Treaty of Friendship, Commerce, and Navigation exempted Irish nationals from military service, this exemption was not observed by local draft boards. By the 1960s, and perhaps earlier, successful applicants for immigrant visas to the United States were required to waive their right to exemption. NAI, DFA, Washington Files, D23, Visit to the USA by Seán Lemass, 1953.

12. John A. Costello, *Taoiseach*, during the second stage of the Republic of Ireland Bill, Published Debates of Dáil Éireann, 24 November 1948, cols. 392–93.

13. Northern Ireland Parliamentary Debates, 10 October 1956, col. 2.

14. Mary E. Daly, "'Cherishing all the Children': Irish Citizenship and Nationality Laws," *Irish Historical Studies* (forthcoming).

15. In 1927 $15 million of the $25 million Second Irish National Loan was raised in the United States, but the cost of interest and loan repayments rose by 20 percent following the 1931 devaluation of sterling, and this deterred the Irish government from repeating the exercise; the depressed state of the U.S. economy was a further consideration. NAI, S563, Second National Loan.

16. Statistics on dollar exports and remittances and bequests from the dollar area can be found in the various Statistical Abstracts, an official publication that has been issued annually since 1931; 1958 was the first occasion that the value of merchandise exports, £7.48 million, exceeded the value of remittances and bequests, £6.5 million.

17. *Irish Trade Journal and Statistical Bulletin*, March 1950, 8.

18. NAI, S14818 B/2.

19. NAI, S10325 C/1, Report of interdepartmental committee on dollar earnings. Report on tourism.

20. *Irish Press*, 7 April 1952. The harp was the national symbol of the Irish state, but was even more widely identified with Ireland in the United States. Leydon quotes, NAI, S15297A, *An Tóstal.*

21. NAI, S15297A, *An Tóstal.*

22. The Irish export board also attempted to promote exports of altar vestments and religious objects in the United States around this time.

23. NAI, S15297A, *An Tóstal.*

24. Ibid.

25. *An Tóstal* Program and Souvenir Handbook, 1953; *Bord Fáilte* Calendar of Events, 1954–58. Dollar revenue from tourism was £4.6 million in 1952 but fell to £1.7 million in 1953. Many Americans who traveled to Ireland for *An Tóstal* complained about the unsettled weather.

26. NAI, S15297B.

27. *An Taoiseach* John A. Costello invited the leaders of all parties in *Dáil Éireann* to a meeting at Dublin's Mansion House in January 1949 in response to the militant language of the Ulster Unionist party during an election campaign in Northern Ireland. See David McCullough, *A Makeshift Majority: The First Inter-Party Government, 1948–51* (Dublin: Institute of Public Administration, 1998), 114–16.

28. John Bowman, *De Valera and the Ulster Question, 1917–1973* (Oxford: Oxford University Press, 1982), 258–60.

29. N.a., *With de Valera in America and Australia* (Dublin: Irish Press, 1948).

30. Bowman, *De Valera and the Ulster Question*, 274.

31. NAI, DFA, D23, Washington Embassy, Official American Attitudes to Partition, briefing paper prepared for visit by Seán Lemass in 1953.

32. Cronin, *Washington's Irish Policy*, 194.

33. Ronan Fanning, "The United States and Irish Participation in NATO: The Debate of 1950," *Irish Studies in International Affairs* I (1979), 38–48.

34. Cronin, *Washington's Irish Policy*, 274–75. The resolutions were moved by Congressmen John Fogarty (Rhode Island), Thomas Lane (Massachusetts), Enda Kelly (New York), Mike Mansfield (Montana), and Senator Everett Dirksen (Illinois). Fogarty moved the successful resolution linking partition and ERP funding for Britain.

35. NAI, DFA, D23.

36. Ibid.

37. This was not necessarily the case before World War II, though in 1932, within days of taking office, de Valera broadcast a speech to mark the birthday of Abraham Lincoln, which he devoted to the theme of a united Ireland.

38. NAI, DFA, D23, Speech by Seán Lemass to National Press Club, Washington, 1 October 1953.

39. NAI, DFA, Washington Embassy, P115/1, Brennan to Pat Hughes, Consul of Ireland, San Francisco; copies to Irish Consuls General in Boston, Chicago, and New York, 15 July 1954.

40. NAI, DFA, Washington Embassy, P115/1, Keating to Brennan, 22 July 1954.

41. NAI, DFA, P115/1.

42. Thomas Hennessy, *A History of Northern Ireland 1920–1996* (Dublin: Gill & Macmillan, 1997), 105–7.

43. NAI, DFA, D23, Official American attitudes to partition, briefing paper prepared for visit by Seán Lemass in 1953.

44. NAI, DFA, P115/1.

45. The article appeared as a cover story on 12 July 1963, with a picture of Lemass on the cover. The article, which concentrated on Irish economic development, did not refer to partition, and said little about political developments after 1922, though it mentioned Irish neutrality during World War II.

46. NAI, DFA 22/I, Washington Embassy.

47. See Lemass's speech to Dublin Chamber of Commerce, May 1961.

48. The "Programme for Economic Expansion" outlined a strategy for regenerating the Irish economy that involved switching government capital spending from social investments such as housing and hospitals to programs that would generate an economic return. It also proposed to move the Irish economy from protection toward free trade, in anticipation of Ireland joining the proposed European Economic Community at some future date. A drive to encourage overseas investment, particularly investment by U.S. industrial firms, formed part of this strategy. The program, which was launched in November 1958, is generally seen as a key factor in transforming the Irish economy.

49. NAI, DFA, P115/1, 27 June 1958.

50. Ibid.

51. Ibid.

52. Ibid.

53. Ibid. It is also possible that Ireland's independent stance at the United Nations may have damaged relations with some sections of Irish America.

54. Ibid.

55. NAI, S15245A, Irish Chamber of Commerce in USA.

56. NAI, S15245/B/63.

57. NAI, S9215/B/62.

58. NAI, DFA, P115/1, 25 May 1963.

59. Ibid., June 1963.

60. NAI, DFA, C32, Campbell to Rush, 10 April 1963.

61. NAI, DFA, Washington Files, C60, Irish Immigration.

62. NAI, DFA, P115/1.

The Irish Famine in
American School Curricula

THOMAS J. ARCHDEACON

ᎶᏁ Examining how people remember the past has become for historians as important as analyzing the events on which those collective memories are based.[1] On one level, the trend extends the established method of intradisciplinary self-critique known as "historiography" to a parallel study of changing opinions over time among the consumers, rather than the producers, of historical knowledge. On another, it exemplifies the epistemological doubts of the late-twentieth century that scholars can create histories that are accurate in any positivistic sense. What lasting role the history of memory may have in the discipline of history cannot yet be discerned. It has at least underlined how important, in any given era, the popular memory of the past is to current political discourse. It has also shown that the relationship between memory and discourse is two-way rather than one-way, and that the shaping of memory is partly a political process.

Fifty-year anniversaries and their multiples tend to be important moments in the reshaping of memories, and the sesquicentennial of the Great Irish Famine of 1845–52 has generated an interesting opportunity to observe a contemporary example of the phenomenon.[2] The reshaping has reflected historians' updated judgments about the famine. In the 1980s and 1990s, a series of scholars undercut the interpretation that the famine had been a natural calamity severely aggravated by unwise social and economic practices among the Irish people.[3] With much greater nuance, they again made central to the catastrophe stories about the inadequacies and even hard-heartedness of Britain's response to the Irish crisis. Of course, the stance of the "revisionist" historians whom they criticized had been a reaction to older, nationalist arguments that had made the famine primarily the product of conscious English policy.[4]

The sesquicentennial of the Great Famine also took on special importance on account of the contemporary political contexts in which it occurred. How society observed the famine had implications for various groups involved in the Northern Ireland debate. Hard-line nationalists could use evidence of mean-spirited English behavior in the famine era as an indication of English perfidy and modern English denials of responsibility as reason for distrusting today's British government. From the English point of view, the advantages of viewing themselves as helpless bystanders inevitably blamed for misfortunes that the Irish brought on themselves were equally obvious.

In the United States, the famine commemoration occurred in an era characterized by revived expressions of ethnicity and perceptions among cultural groups that they must consciously protect the presentation of their heritages in the history of the nation. For Irish Americans from backgrounds that might be included under the umbrella terms of "Catholic" or "nationalist," it was an opportunity to present an alternative depiction to that which portrayed them as racist adjuncts to the dominant culture.[5] Although they would reject politicized charges that they were claiming "victimhood," remembering the famine allowed Irish Americans to remind the nation of their initial pariah status and prolonged period of assimilation.

Given the broader cultural context of the United States in the late-twentieth century, efforts to create a niche for the famine in the American memory not surprisingly included techniques developed in the preceding generation by African Americans eager to establish their share of the nation's history and by Jews anxious lest the lessons of World War II be forgotten. Whether or not the Irish enjoyed the irony in their use of tactics associated with their ethnic competitors is not clear. Some in those other groups, especially among the Jews, definitely did not enjoy it.

One key element of the Irish-American initiative to create a famine memory in the United States was a campaign to include instruction about it in the curricula of several school systems, especially in states with large Irish or Irish-ancestral populations. The push generated multiple kinds of friction. Persons sympathetic with the Irish causes and officials of the British government clashed over the propriety of treating the famine as an issue relevant to Americans. Experts divided over how the famine would be presented. Finally, tensions rose further when proposed interpretations included terms like "genocide," which not only infuriated interested British parties but also threatened to undermine the special connection that had been established between the curricula and the history of the Holocaust.

This essay presents an overview of the effort to incorporate the Irish Famine into the curricula of American schools. It focuses, in particular, on the struggle in New Jersey and New York. The debate was high pitched and well documented in those two states, and I became involved in the New York contest in a minor way, when I responded to a request for advice from the Office of the Governor.

-1-

According to the United States Holocaust Museum, which is located in Washington, D.C., six U.S. states—California, Florida, Illinois, Mississippi, New Jersey, and New York—"mandate" that schools teach about the Holocaust of World War II. Ten more states—Connecticut, Georgia, Indiana, North Carolina, Ohio, Pennsylvania, South Carolina, Tennessee, Virginia, and Washington—recommend teaching about the subject. Only three states specify the grade levels at which students should receive instruction: California provides for instruction in grades 7 through 9 (middle school) and 10 through 12 (high school); Mississippi includes a course in the high school curriculum; and New Jersey broadly calls for inclusion of lessons across the elementary (1 through 8) and high school years (9 through 12). Curricula and guides for teachers that ten states have developed, however, seem best suited for students of middle-school and high-school ages.[6]

Mandatory or officially recommended Holocaust courses first appeared in the 1980s. From the beginning, a few states included, under the rubric of such offerings, opportunities to examine topics besides the extermination of Europe's Jews. Mississippi called for "a course of instruction in human rights" that "must emphasize the study of slavery, genocide and the Holocaust." New York, which developed a curriculum in 1985–86, passed a law in 1994 requiring "courses of instruction in patriotism and citizenship and human rights issues, with particular attention to the study of the inhumanity of genocide, slavery, and the Holocaust."[7]

Political pressure grew to include in Holocaust courses the experiences of peoples other than Jews. As Florida moved toward the adoption of its mandatory course in 1994, the *Miami Times* agreed that the Jews "suffered terribly" at the hands of the Nazis and that the lessons of their Holocaust are "universal in their application." The paper argued, however, that "the Jews were not the only ones on whom major human rights violations have been committed in recent history." It would be "unfair," the *Times* wrote, "for, say, an African American or a Native People child to be taught merely that the Jews suffered as a people, without, at the same time, being made to learn about the suffering of his or her own people."[8]

In New Jersey, which developed its first state curriculum on the Holocaust in 1983, inclusion of other episodes of recognized or alleged genocide became part of the political compromise necessary to win approval for mandatory instruction on the experiences of the Jews during World War II. In 1993, Garabed "Chuck" Haytaian (Republican), then Speaker of the State Assembly, had sponsored a bill to mandate studies about the Nazi-era Holocaust, the slaughter of Armenians by Turks in World War I, and the massacres in Cambodia by the Pol Pot regime. The state legislature became deadlocked, however, when Senator Ronald Rice (Democrat, Essex) attempted to add to the list the famine endured by Ukrainians under Soviet rule in 1932–33.[9]

To avoid a repetition of such internecine bickering, New Jersey legislators pursued a more inclusive strategy when they next took up the issue of a mandatory Holocaust curriculum. Senators Jack Ewing (Republican, Somerset), James McGreevey (Democrat, Middlesex), and Jack Sinagra (Democrat, Middlesex) sponsored a measure that required "instruction on the Holocaust and genocides." The purpose of the instruction would be, in part, to help students "understand that genocide is a consequence of prejudice and discrimination" and to recognize "the personal responsibility that each citizen bears to fight racism and hatred whenever and wherever it happens."[10] Governor Christine Todd Whitman signed the New Jersey measure in April 1994. Whitman said the seriousness of the bias problem overcame her Republican reluctance to impose curriculum mandates on localities. "Our children and their children," she said, "need to learn the truth about intolerance—to know that racial, religious, and ethnic hatred can lead to genocide."[11]

Jewish spokespersons were divided regarding efforts in New Jersey and elsewhere to add the experiences of other groups to Holocaust courses. Writing in *The New Republic*, Deborah E. Lipstadt condemned approaches that linked teaching about the Holocaust to discussions of other injustices such as the Armenian genocide or American racism. In her opinion, such efforts undermined the unique character of the Holocaust. Lipstadt argued that the Nazi extermination marked the only time a state tried to annihilate an entire people without regard to the ages, sexes, locations, occupations, or beliefs of the persons targeted. Likewise, it was the only such event in which the aggressors carried out their violence for no ostensible material, territorial, or political gain.[12]

Many Jewish commentators, however, quickly made peace with the inclusion of other topics under the Holocaust curriculum. In Israel, Dr. Yair Oron of Tel Aviv's Hakibbutzim Teachers Seminary called for the inclusion of other genocides in courses about the Holocaust taught in his own nation's schools. "If I demand that the world know about the Holocaust," he stated, "I have to also demand that my own people address the genocide of the Armenians and Gypsies." Sounding a somewhat different note, Oron also expected that inclusion of such genocides would highlight how special the Jewish experience of World War II was. "How can we know why and how the Holocaust was unique," he asked, "if we don't know what happened to other people?"[13] Other Jewish leaders willing to make Holocaust courses more ethnically inclusive expressed similar confidence. According to Michael Berenbaum, the director of the United States Holocaust Research Institute, "to understand the uniqueness of the Holocaust, a student must also understand how it contrasts and compares to other events of genocide."[14]

New Jersey's Irish were latecomers to the debate about Holocaust education. In 1995, James Mullin saw in the *Philadelphia Inquirer* a report that the New Jersey Commission on Holocaust Education was studying genocides in connection with developing a curriculum to meet the state's new educational mandate. A librarian who had served as president of the South Jersey Irish-American Unity Conference and as a member of other Irish-American organizations, Mullin contacted Commission Executive Director Paul Winkler. According to Mullin, Winkler was initially skeptical of his suggestion that the Great Irish Famine should be included in the curriculum. So too were some other members of the commission, including Luna Kaufman, a survivor of the Cracow ghetto and a founding member of the Commission on Holocaust Education. "Face it," she remarked. "The Irish could come to America. There was an escape route. The Jews could not."[15]

Mullin set out to change minds. Jack Worrall, a professor of economics at Rutgers University–Camden and president of the Federation of Irish-American Societies, also took a leading role in the effort. Both believed that extending the curriculum to include the Great Irish Famine not only would give proper recognition to a formative era in the history of Irish America but also was necessary to the success of the overall program. They argued that, in confronting a tragedy akin to genocide in their own history, the many New Jerseyans of Irish descent would become more sympathetic to analogous experiences among other groups.[16] As chair of the Irish Famine Curriculum Committee, Mullin took steps to create a famine component for the New Jersey curriculum. Dr. Nancy Omaha Boy of Rutgers University–Camden, who had designed the curriculum for the Native American experience, supplied Mullin with lesson plans that served as a guide. An assortment of Irish-American groups, including the Irish Action Coalition, the American Irish Political Action Committee, and the Ancient Order of Hibernians also gave support.[17]

In September 1996, the New Jersey Commission on Holocaust Education accepted the document produced by the Irish Famine Curriculum Committee and arranged for its distribution to three hundred eighty-four public high schools throughout New Jersey. The curriculum will be a resource for teachers, but how exactly New Jersey schools will incorporate the famine in instruction remains unclear. State authorities do not dictate precise course content, and only one of the seven units in the recommended school curriculum deals with atrocities other than the Holocaust. In that rather small intellectual space, the Great Irish Famine will be vying for attention with slavery, the treatment of Native Americans, the fate of the Armenians, the Ukrainian Famine, the Cambodian genocide, and possibly with events in Rwanda and Bosnia.[18]

The New Jersey curriculum episode undoubtedly reveals aspects of American ethnic politics. The ability to gain recognition in school curricula is partly a function of political strength, and the Irish are strong in New Jersey. Subsequent to the inclusion of the famine, James Mullin sought nomination to the Holocaust Education Commission and, in December 1996, Jack Collins (Republican), Speaker of the New Jersey General Assembly, named Mullin to a three-year term on the twenty-one-member body.[19]

New Jersey has also been the source of an effort to propel the Great Irish Famine to attention in national politics. Members of the state's delegation to the U.S. House of Representatives have sponsored a resolution proclaiming it "the sense of the Congress that the Department of Education should develop a model curriculum designed to educate elementary and secondary school-aged children about the Irish Famine and its effects, and that this model curriculum should be readily available to educational institutions and the public." The movement has been ethnically ecumenical. Robert Menendez, a Cuban-American Democratic congressman, has been the principal spokesperson for the movement, and a number of other representatives, including Robert E. Andrews (Democrat), Rodney Freylinghausen (Republican), Bill Martini (Republican), Frank Pallone (Democrat), Donald M. Payne (Democrat), Robert G. Torricelli (Democrat), and Richard A. Zimmer (Republican) have joined him.[20]

Trivializing the famine curriculum movement because it involves ethnic politics would be wrong. Denying a group its history is a means of reducing its political and social influence. Among academics in the United States, the trend in recent years has been to demonize Irish immigrants for their role in American racism rather than to see them in a sympathetic light.[21] That the sesquicentennial of the potato famine would be the occasion for a reassertion of Irish consciousness is not surprising. Activists in states beyond New Jersey also took up the cause. Representatives Steven Tolman and Kevin Honan joined Senators Warren Tolman and Edward J. Clancy in putting forward legislation to incorporate the famine in the school curriculum of Massachusetts. Representative Michael McGeehan sponsored a similar bill in Pennsylvania, as did other lawmakers in Illinois.[22]

-2-

Developments in New York State soon overshadowed those elsewhere. There, the members of the American Irish Teachers Organization were eager to mark the sesquicentennial of the famine. The teachers argued that the famine deserved attention as the greatest social catastrophe of nineteenth-century Europe, and they called attention to its obvious impact on the history of the United States. Moreover, they believed that recalling U.S. efforts to relieve the famine victims of the 1840s carried important lessons about America's role in fighting world starvation today.[23]

The teachers thought that the most constructive option lay in an emendation of the 1994 state law mandating courses of instruction in human rights. Accordingly, Ann Garvey, the president of the organization, approached Assemblyman Joseph Crowley (Democrat, Queens). Crowley, whose mother is from Ireland, agreed to sponsor legislation that would make instruction about the Great Irish Famine a mandatory part of the curriculum in the public and private schools of the state.[24] His measure was an ingenious amendment (A.6510) that inserted ten words at two points in subdivisions of section 801 of the state's education law. The key section read:

> In order to promote a spirit of patriotic and civic service and obligation and to foster in the children of the state moral and intellectual qualities which are essential in preparing to meet the obligations of citizenship in peace or in war, the regents of The University of the State of New York shall prescribe courses of instruction in patriotism, citizenship, and human rights issues, with particular attention to the study of the inhumanity of genocide, slavery, [and] the Holocaust, *and the mass starvation*

in Ireland from 1845 to 1850, to be maintained and followed in all the schools of the state.[25]

Bipartisan support grew quickly for the amendment. In the Assembly, Richard Keane (Democrat, Buffalo), Elizabeth Connelly (Democrat, Staten Island), Donna Ferrara (Republican, Long Island), and Michael Balboni (Republican, Long Island) joined Crowley, who is the secretary of the American Irish Legislators' Society. Jewish leaders in the chamber, including Speaker Sheldon Silver (Democrat, New York) and Steven Saunders (Democrat, New York), endorsed the bill. Jeffrion Aubry (Democrat, Queens), who was the chair of the legislature's Black and Puerto Rican Caucus, likewise agreed that a clear connection existed between the famine and the human rights subjects already singled out for inclusion. "It comes from a realization of the connections that human beings have in both the enormous good and the enormous bad that they're capable of doing," Aubry stated, "and that they're not limited to any one racial group."[26]

In the State Senate, Michael Hoblock (Republican), whose wife is an Irish American, sponsored parallel legislation (S.4880). "Being from Ukrainian ancestral ties, I am keenly aware of the necessity to inform New York's children of the sacrifices and injustices suffered by many of New York's ethnic population," Hoblock said. "We must ensure that our children are educated to learn from past wrongs so that people of different ethnic origins are treated with respect and mutual understanding."[27]

Not everyone agreed with Crowley's initiative. Representative Bernard Mahoney (Republican, Syracuse) led the opposition to it in the Assembly. He saw no time for add-ons when schools lacked adequate time to teach the basics. Carl Hayden, the chancellor of the State Board of Regents, complained that the bill "sets in motion a set of ethnic rivalries that almost always is counter-productive." Mandating "every individual legislator's favorite piece of historical information," Hayden charged, would create "an unmanageable set of demands on schools."[28] The New York State School Boards Association objected, arguing that "it is the Regents' responsibility, and not the Legislature's, to decide what should be taught in the state's schools."[29] Not surprisingly, the amendment also disturbed British officials stationed in New York, and they carefully monitored its progress through the legislature.[30]

New York's Assembly passed Crowley's bill after three hours of debate. The Senate assented to the measure without prolonged discussion. The bills then proceeded to the desk of New York's governor.[31] Governor George E. Pataki (Republican) quickly signed the Crowley bill. The governor said:

By making instruction on the mass starvation in Ireland a part of New York State curriculum, it is my sincere hope that our State's pupils—a great many of whom descended from Irish immigrants—will develop a respect and universal concern for human rights, the sanctity of human life and a tolerance of other races, religions and points of view. To instill these moral and ethical values in New York State's youth, it is imperative they receive a full appreciation of the lessons of history, however troubling they may be.[32]

"The years from 1845 to 1850 were a time of great tragedy for the Irish people," the governor added. "During this period, often referred to as the Great Irish Hunger, more than one million Irish men, women and children starved to death after a blight caused the potato crop—the food upon which the poor tenant farmers and their families subsisted—to fail. Millions more were forced to flee their native land to obtain food, with many of these emigrés succumbing during the arduous, transoceanic voyage."[33]

Other remarks by Pataki contained more controversial judgments:

During this very time period, while millions of Irish were suffering and dying, large quantities of grain and livestock were being exported from Ireland to England, under the supervision of the British government. While the Great Hunger often is characterized as a famine, a severe shortage of food resulting from an act of God, the concurrent export of food from Ireland to England demonstrates that the tragedy could have been avoided if the British had allowed Ireland to retain sufficient grain and livestock to feed its own people.

A press release separate from the governor's formal statement quoted Pataki as saying, "History teaches us the Great Irish Hunger was not the result of a massive failure of the Irish potato crop but rather was the result of a deliberate campaign by the British to deny the Irish people the food they needed to survive."[34]

Pataki's fervor caught many by surprise. To them, he was mainly a moderate politician who, in the Republican landslide of 1994, had unseated Governor Mario Cuomo, the charismatically enigmatic icon of liberal Democratic politics in New York. Pataki, however, has strong—although not publicly paraded—ties to Irish America. His surname is Hungarian, and his maternal grandfather was Italian. Pataki's grandmother, however, was Agnes Lynch, a native of Blackrock, which lies south of Dundalk in County Louth. She lived with the Pataki family in New York's Hudson Valley and played a central role in caring for the future governor during his youth.[35] Nor was family Pataki's only tie to Irish-American affairs. As a member of the state legislator, he had been active in the American Irish legislators' society. He was a strong supporter of the McBride Principles. Moreover, a number of the governor's top aides, including Chief Counsel Michael C. Finnegan, are Irish Americans with similar attitudes.[36]

Pataki immediately received criticism from many fronts. Leading the charge against him was John Kerr, the ambassador of the United Kingdom to the United States. Kerr's line of attack had three elements. He alleged that the governor had equated the Great Famine with the Holocaust, and denied the comparison. He challenged Pataki for supporting an outdated nationalist line of historical argument and offered an alternative "revisionist" interpretation. Kerr chided the governor for endangering the peace process in Northern Ireland. Moreover, Kerr's letter of 17 October 1996 to Pataki began "I was surprised to see that you had signed into law an Act which, in requiring New York public schools to teach courses on the Irish Famine, appears to equate it with the Holocaust."[37] The governor had made no direct mention of the Holocaust, but a press release from the Executive Chamber had perfunctorily—and correctly—noted that "the study of the mass starvation" would be added to an existing law that required "courses of instruction in patriotism, citizenship, and human rights issues, with particular attention to be devoted to the study of genocide, slavery and the Holocaust."[38] Having set up that straw man, Kerr continued, "it seems to me rather insulting to the many millions who suffered and died in concentration camps across Europe to imply that their man-made fate was in any way analogous to the natural disaster in Ireland a century before."[39]

To support the claim that the Irish Famine was primarily a "natural disaster," Kerr called Pataki's attention to the work of "so-called 'revisionist' Irish historians, both Catholic and Protestant," who "now probably predominate" in Irish universities, "on both sides of the old divide." According to Kerr, "When it comes to the Famine, some of them tend to stress the role of well-meaning and earnest Britons in the provision of relief." The ambassador conceded that "it is easy to argue that different policy decisions in Dublin and London, by those fighting the Famine, might have been more effective in reducing its scale." But, he added, "[u]nlike the Holocaust," the Famine "was not deliberate, not premeditated, not man-made, not genocide."[40]

Kerr expressed concern that "[t]his battle over history has echoes in today's political argument over the future of an island of conflicting loyalties." "Surely what matters now," he added, "is not to re-open the wounds of the Famine, not to try to ascribe more clear-cut responsibility than the historians allow, but rather to work together for a better future in Northern Ireland, in which the 20th century tragedy of bombs and guns will also become a subject of discussion only among historians." Advising Pataki that the governments of England and Ireland were seeking reconciliation, Kerr concluded, "I hope New York schools will teach that too."[41]

Concern over Northern Ireland remains high on the British agenda regarding what Americans learn about the famine. A cordial conversation turned testy when I asked spokespersons at the British Consulate in New York if Her Majesty's government was concerned that the inclusion of the famine in school curricula could have policy implications regarding the North. Construing my comment in a way other than I intended, they sternly responded that nothing—presumably nothing emanating from the United States—would change British policy. When I clarified what I meant, they conceded that the United Kingdom was naturally concerned that "Brit bashing" by Irish Americans could create "misperceptions" in the United States.[42]

Not surprisingly, persons involved in the curriculum movement and in other initiatives to call attention to the dark side of British policy during the famine era rarely are Unionists. James Mullin describes himself as a "nationalist" but an opponent of violence. Jack Worrall believes that self-defense is sometimes a necessity and accepts the label "republican."[43] They deny, however, that their efforts regarding the curriculum in New Jersey reflect any direct agenda regarding the North. Governor Pataki would likewise make it clear in his eventual response to Ambassador Kerr that his administration viewed inclusion of the famine in the curriculum as a matter separate from Northern Ireland. New York's always lively *Daily News* moved to Pataki's defense, with the suggestion that Kerr was having a "hissy fit." England's inadequate response to the crisis was at best "monumentally stupid," and its historic mistreatment of Ireland made it "no mystery as to why the word 'genocide' creeps into discussions of the famine." The editors advised the ambassador, "With all due respect, Excellency: Put a sock in it."[44]

Other news organizations were not as supportive of Pataki. The issues raised followed lines of argument cited earlier in connection with the New Jersey initiative. The *Trenton Times* claimed that the Holocaust was "an event unique in world history" and that "arbitrarily resurrecting an ancient group grievance" such as the Irish Famine reflected a "current fascination with group grievances" that would "dilute" the New Jersey curriculum's effectiveness.[45] Rupert Murdoch's *New York Post* editorially condemned the New York legislation as an "Irish-American quest for victimhood." The *Post* urged that the Irish instead "hold themselves up as an example to others" of overcoming the obstacles faced by one's ancestors.[46] The *Times* of London lumped Pataki among those politicians "who play on people's ignorance to grub ethnic votes."[47]

Commentators did not hesitate to give Pataki history lessons. Herb London, a professor at New York University and an old rival of the governor within the Republican party, reminded readers of the *Albany Times Union* that he had "written a dissertation about Irish history in the 1840s." He dismissed Pataki as a candidate unworthy to be "dogcatcher" and a "flimflam artist when it comes to historical scholarship." Conceding that English actions in Ireland were "sometimes unfair and unreasonable," London nevertheless noted that there was "considerable evidence suggesting the Peel and Russell governments attempted to assist in alleviating the effect of famine." He recommended that Pataki read up-to-date accounts, including those by William Forbes Adams and Roy F. Foster.[48]

Active historians tended to be more circumspect in their criticism. "As an historian and a teacher, I believe that people ought to know about the Irish famine," said Eric Foner of Columbia University. "But I'm not thrilled about the state legislature deciding what should be considered historically important."[49] Robert Scally, the historian and director of Ireland House at New York University, agreed that the famine had important implications for American history and should be in curricula. He remarked, however, that legislating history by popular demand made it difficult "to draw the line between history and propaganda." Scally disagreed with Governor Pataki's allusion to a "deliberate campaign" against the Irish, and demanded a "full and open forum" on the famine before the final curriculum was written.[50]

Despite the pieties of historians regarding the importance of the famine for American as well as Irish history, their voluntary curricula have paid little heed to it. An examination of standard textbooks on my bookshelf shows that, even at the university level, the famine gets short shrift—with England's role minimized. The best coverage, by far, appears in the text by Bernard Bailyn and his associates. *In toto*, it states:

> In 1845 the Irish potato crop—which provided most ordinary Irish with their basic food supply—failed disastrously. Five years of famine followed. Many Irish thus had little choice but to emigrate or starve. . . . And the British landlords who controlled Ireland helped to subsidize emigration in the hope of reducing taxes that were being levied for the support of workhouses, which were spilling over with starving laborers who had been evicted from the land.[51]

Irwin Unger's account is sympathetic but even briefer. *In toto*, it states: "Denied economic and political rights, [Catholic Irish peasants] lived as impoverished tenants on lands owned by rich Protestant landlords. . . . When the potato crop failed during the mid-1840s, hundreds of thousands of Irish fled to escape starvation."[52]

Other scholars are less judgmental. Paul Boyer and his co-authors state that

> between 1845 and the early 1850s, a blight destroyed every harvest of Ireland's potatoes, virtually the only food of the peasantry, and spawned one of the most gruesome famines in history. The Great Famine inflicted indescribable suffering on the Irish peasantry and killed perhaps a million people. . . . To escape the ravages of famine, 1.8 million Irish migrated to the United States in the decade after 1845.[53]

They do, in another context, refer to the eviction of "superfluous" Catholic tenants by Protestant landlords. Winthrop Jordan and Leon Litwack devote two sentences to the famine. "In 1845," they note, "Catholic Irish peasants were devastated by a blight that struck the potato crops, the mainstay of their miserable diets. The blight brought famine that was only partly relieved by massive emigration to America."[54] George B. Tindall keeps himself under one sentence with the remark that "after an epidemic of potato rot in 1845 brought famine, the flow of Irish immigrants rose to a flood."[55] Alan Brinkley, in his own textbook and in his revision of Current, Williams, and Friedel, does not mention the famine.[56]

Among historians working in the field of famine history, statements at least indirectly supportive of the thrust of Pataki's argument emerged. Speaking at an Irish-government sponsored Famine Commemoration at NYU's Ireland House, Luke Gibbons of Dublin City University dismissed the claim that the Famine was primarily a natural calamity. He stated, "Mass starvation would have been unthinkable in the imperial heartland, not just for humanitarian reasons, but for reasons of national pride." Its outbreak in Ireland confirmed English suspicions of Irish inferiority, and many hoped the outcome of the event would serve as a "desperate remedy" for the island's economy:

> . . . the fact that a benign outcome was anticipated, however perversely, and that, accordingly, there need be no imputation of direct genocidal intent towards the Irish, has misled some commentators into seeking to absolve officials at the Treasury, and the British administration, of any responsibility for the catastrophe in Ireland.[57]

Angered by what they saw as Ambassador Kerr's distortion of the New York legislation, and stung by critiques from other quarters, the

Pataki administration refrained from an immediate response. In the months that followed the October blow-up, officials consulted with academics and others in an attempt to present in the most effective manner the state's rationale for the curricular legislation. Although I was not living in New York and had had no previous contact with Governor Pataki, his staff requested and received my cooperation in their effort.[58]

From my point of view, the first step was to eschew oversimplified and exaggerated charges of British responsibility for the famine. Direct accusations of "genocide"—a word that the governor had not used—did not seem sustainable, at least as the term is understood by most people. The English may have taken advantage of the famine to foster what they considered desirable changes in the society and economy of Ireland. They may have been callously willing to accept very high levels of collateral damage among the Irish population in order to prosecute their war on the island's poverty. The high level of vacillation in English policy during the famine years, however, and the existence of even niggardly efforts at relief, are inconsistent with a prior intent to exterminate and a systematic pursuit of that goal.

The second step was to jettison arguments that rested on shaky evidence. Governor Pataki's presentation seemed most vulnerable at the point where the allegation of a "deliberate campaign by the British to deny the Irish people the food they needed to survive" relied on claims about the exportation of large amounts of grain and livestock. Christine Kinealy is apparently re-examining the question of exports, and the pendulum may soon swing toward a less "revisionist" interpretation. Scholars, however, will not likely return to a full embrace of John Mitchel's point of view: "The almighty indeed sent the potato blight, but the English created the Famine."[59]

-3-

Governor Pataki's eventual response to Ambassador Kerr focused on disarming the British emissary's most misleading charges and on re-expressing why the Great Irish Famine was suitable material for a course on human rights. Pataki described as "indefensible" Kerr's assertion that the New York legislation equated the famine with the Holocaust. "Nothing in the bill purports to make such an equation," the governor wrote. Rather, the bill simply requires that the famine "be included (with genocide, slavery and the Holocaust) in the human rights issues to be taught in New York's schools."[60]

Pataki also distinguished the famine from slavery and from genocide, but he nevertheless called it "a worthy subject of instruction." He defined the famine as "a subject of vital importance because of its profound human rights implications." The governor condemned, as an insult to the dead, Kerr's description of the famine as a "natural disaster" and the implication that "the British government was blameless." "Assuming that the famine was but a 'natural disaster,'" the governor commented, "ignores at least two important issues: how the Irish became so utterly dependent on the potato, and the adequacy of British relief efforts." Elaborating on the latter point, Pataki called attention to "underlying racism" that colored attitudes toward the Irish, and he effectively marshaled familiar quotes from Charles Trevelyan, Edward Twistleton, and Lord Clarendon.[61]

At the end of his letter, Pataki denied that his actions endangered the situation in Northern Ireland. "I, too, eschew bitterness and violence," he advised the ambassador, and "am strongly committed to the Peace Process, reject terrorism, want reconciliation and share your hope that New York schools will teach these things." But Pataki's message to Kerr ended on a combative note: "While I, too, want no more 'battles over history,' I want the truth above all to be taught. If it is, the children of New York will learn that the Great Irish Hunger was no mere 'natural disaster.'"[62]

Ambassador Kerr opted to declare victory and retire from the field. "I am delighted that you do not equate the Irish Famine with the Holocaust, or with slavery, or with genocide," he wrote to Pataki.[63] In other correspondence, the ambassador continued to claim that the governor had made the allegation and had "withdrawn" it.[64] Kerr reminded Pataki of the governor's most problematic statement, advising him that his references to a "deliberate campaign" constituted "a grossly misleading over-simplification, amounting to an accusation of genocide." "It was because your office's press release attributed these words to you," Kerr remarked, "that I felt obliged to write. Your disavowal of the accusation is doubly reassuring."[65] Regarding his own "natural disaster" interpretation, Kerr made a modest concession. "I certainly would not wish to minimise the scale of the disaster in mid-19th century Ireland," Kerr wrote, "or to maintain that the relief effort, intended to counter its effects, was adequate." The ambassador accepted "that we can all learn from history," but chose not to continue to "trade texts" with the governor.[66] The concluding paragraph of Kerr's letter referred to reconciliation and the Peace Process, ending with a gratuitous insinuation that Pataki had been encouraging the IRA. "The IRA's apparent preference for murder rather than negotiation," Kerr commented, "means that Sinn Fein, alone of all the parties successful in last year's election, are absent [from the resumed multi-party talks]. I hope that you will add your voice to those of the great majority of the Irish people, and their many American friends, who—with the Administration and the two Governments—call on the IRA too to pursue the path of peace."[67]

The *New York Times* chose to ignore the exchange of letters between Pataki and Kerr, but the city's Irish-American press followed the story. A bold, red headline on the front page of the *Irish Voice* announced that "Pataki Backtracks on Famine." The spin was unwelcome, but not completely unexpected in the Pataki camp, inasmuch as Niall O'Dowd's paper is seen as closely tied to New York's Democratic Party. Emer Mullins's article on the inside was a factual summary of the governor's letter.[68] Coverage in the *Irish Echo* was more favorable to Pataki. Ray O'Hanlon's column went under the headline "British 'delighted' with Pataki reply," but its contents accurately summarized the latest Pataki–Kerr exchange. The *Echo's* editorial page accepted the governor's interpretation of the whole affair and endorsed his letter. "No, Pataki may be ducking and weaving a bit as he deals with a skillful adversary," the *Echo* stated, "but he has yet to give ground on the significant British responsibility, if not for the potato blight, but most certainly for the unacceptable level, by any era's standard, of mass death that followed in its wake."[69]

Despite his disavowal of the word "genocide," Pataki received support from the Irish Famine/Genocide Committee. Led by Owen Rodgers, an immigrant from County Tyrone, the committee has embarked on a campaign to have a tribunal established to adjudicate England's responsibility for the outcome of the famine. The committee's efforts have received support from O'Dwyer and Bernstein, a New York City law firm with a tradition of engagement in civil rights, Irish, labor, and radical causes.[70] In a letter to the *Irish Echo*, Rodgers and Eamon Dornan, an attorney associated with the committee, accepted Pataki's rejection of the word "genocide, as it is employed in everyday language." They noted, however, that the word has a broader definition in International Human Rights Law.

Their arguments ran parallel to those associated with Charles Rice of the Notre Dame University Law School.[71] Rice has argued that, although the Geneva Convention of 1948 cannot be applied to events occurring a century earlier, British policies during the famine may fit its definition of genocide. The convention outlaws "acts committed with the intent to destroy, in whole or part, a national, ethical, racial, or religious group." Proscribed acts include "causing serious bodily or mental harm to members of the group," and "deliberately inflicting on the group conditions of life calculated to bring about its physical destruction in whole or in part." According to Rice, "wanton indifference" can supply the intent required by the convention.[72]

The pro-curriculum side has also taken satisfaction from the remarks delivered, on behalf of Prime Minister Tony Blair, by Veronica Sutherland, the British Ambassador to the Republic of Ireland, and read by the actor Gabriel Byrne at the Great Irish Famine Event in Millstreet, County Cork. The Prime Minister's remarks captured the essence of their position:

> That one million people should have died in what was then part of the richest and most powerful nation in the world is something that still causes pain as we reflect on it today. Those who governed in London at the time failed their people through standing by while a crop failure turned into a massive human tragedy. We must not forget such a dreadful event.[73]

The *Albany Times Union* applauded Blair's statement about the famine. "In the absence of nourishment then, there is vindication now," the editors opined. "Vindication, most recently and most prominently, of Governor Pataki, who was criticized by the Brits, unfairly and inaccurately, last year upon the passage of a state law directing that the Great Famine be made part of New York's public school curriculum."[74] Assemblyman John J. McEneny (Democrat, Albany) called the message "a good step toward the reconciliation of the two nations," and noted "I think it has to be very well received by Governor Pataki in light of the abuse he took."[75]

Implementation of the famine curriculum remains a matter of serious contention. Supporters of the curriculum have desired the publication of a fourth volume, to join the three put out in 1985 and 1986 by the Bureau of Curriculum Development of the New York State Education Department for its "Human Rights Series." Volume I contained chapters on "The Roots of Intolerance and Persecution" and "Precursors of the Holocaust."[76] Volume II had chapters on "The Nazi Holocaust" and "Implications for the Future," as well as a bibliography.[77] Volume III had six chapters, including a bibliography, on "forced famine in Ukraine" and the "killing of Cambodia."[78] Those three, and another Education Department volume entitled *United States History: The Black Perspective. A Guide for Eighth Grade Social Studies*, were available when the 1994 act was passed.[79]

Assemblyman Crowley had hoped that the New York State budget for the 1998 fiscal year would include an allocation of approximately $150,000 to support the creation of the curriculum. That did not happen.

To date the Education Department has committed itself only to sending a "field memorandum" to inform teachers that instruction on the famine is mandatory for grades 7–8, 9–10, and 11, and to providing a bibliography. Such limited action probably does not meet the law's mandate that the Board of Regents "prescribe a course of instruction." Assemblyman Crowley and others are currently seeking a more satisfactory response.[80]

What would constitute an appropriate curriculum for the targeted grade levels is debatable. The New Jersey curriculum focuses on the history of England's colonial subjugation of Ireland and on the failures of the English government to provide adequate relief to famine victims. It contains six chapters, which have the following titles: "Laws That Isolated and Impoverished the Irish," "Racism," "Mass Eviction during Famine," "Mortality Rates and 'The Horror'," "Emigration: Departure, Crossing, and Arrival," and "Genocide." The accompanying description states that the last chapter "gathers together several definitions of genocide, as well as statements by historical figures and historians, and asks the students to relate facts, opinions, and definitions."[81]

The New Jersey curriculum includes much pertinent material and draws on the writings of major students of the famine. The authors featured in the "Genocide" chapter, for example, are Dennis Clark, James S. Donnelly, Jr., Edward Twistleton, Lord Clarendon, Nassau Senior, Lady Jane Wilde, R. Dudley Edwards and T. Desmond Williams, and John Mitchel. The excerpts taken from their works are strongly condemnatory of England, but some, including those from Clark, Donnelly, and Edwards and Williams argue that British actions did not fully meet the criteria of genocide.[82]

British spokespersons are strongly displeased with the New Jersey curriculum, which they see as one-sided. They informally suggest that works like the collection of essays recently published by Cathal Poirtéir would offer a more satisfactory balance of materials.[83] At the same time, however, they explicitly disavow any desire to re-open the debate over the legislation or to interfere in the shaping of curricula for American schools.[84]

Students in junior high and secondary schools have neither the knowledge nor the maturity to deal with historiographical issues of the kind discussed in volumes like that edited by Poirtéir. Moreover, the curricula, under the laws, purposefully emphasize the human rights dimensions of the famine, particularly insofar as they reveal problems that frequently arise when the interests of the powerful and the weak— be they people or nations—clash. Nevertheless, most historians would see in New York's curriculum a more nuanced presentation than that currently encountered in the New Jersey materials.

Historians will want closer attention to some technical issues. For example, whether or not they believe any food should have left Ireland, specialists on the Great Famine will want the New York volume to address better how much livestock and grain was exported and how much of a difference retention of foodstuffs would have made. Perhaps most important, they will want to provide at least the teachers with some insight into what the most recent generation of "postrevisionist" historians have learned about social and economic changes that were occurring within Ireland on the eve of the famine and that took place there consequent to it.[85]

NOTES

1. Kerwin Lee Klein, "On the Emergence of Memory in Historical Discourse," *Representations* 69 (2000), 127–50.

2. See, for example, *Éire-Ireland* 32:1 (1997).

3. Joel Mokyr, *Why Ireland Starved: A Quantitative and Analytical History of the Irish Economy, 1800–1850* (London and Boston: Allen & Unwin, 1983); Cormac Ó Gráda, *The Great Irish Famine* (Cambridge, U.K.: Cambridge University Press, 1997); Margaret Kelleher, *The Feminization of Famine: Expressions of the Inexpressible?* (Durham, N.C.: Duke University Press, 1997); Christine Kinealy, *This Great Calamity: The Irish Famine, 1845–1852* (Dublin: Gill and Macmillan, 1994); James S. Donnelly, Jr., *The Great Irish Potato Famine* (Stroud, Gloucestershire, and New York: Sutton Publishing, 2001).

4. James S. Donnelly, Jr., "The Construction of the Memory of the Famine in Ireland and the Irish Diaspora, 1850–1900," *Éire-Ireland* 31:1–2 (1996), 26–61.

5. See, for example, Noel Ignatiev, *How the Irish Became White* (New York: Routledge, 1995).

6. United States Holocaust Memorial Council, "States with Holocaust Education Legislation" (typescript document updated in June 1996; received from Council in June 1997); Edna Greene Brabham, "Holocaust Education: Legislation, Practices, and Literature for Middle-School Students," *The Social Studies* 88 (May/June 1997), 139–42.

7. United States Holocaust Memorial Council, "States with Holocaust Education Legislation."

8. "Teach about All Holocausts," *Miami Times*, 31 March 1994, 4A.

9. Walter Bodnar, "Jersey's Genocide Curriculum is an Opportunity to be Used," *The Ukrainian Weekly*, 8 May 1994, 7.

10. *New Jersey Statutes*, Title 18A, ch. 35.

11. Bodnar, "Jersey's Genocide Curriculum is an Opportunity to be Used."

12. Deborah E. Lipstadt, "Not Facing History: How Not to Teach the Holocaust," *The New Republic*, 6 March 1995, 26–27.

13. Larry Derfner, "Not Only Jews: Will the Holocaust Be Diminished if Israeli Schools Include Lessons on Other Genocides?" *Baltimore Jewish Times*, 8 April 1994, 48.

14. Ellen Friedland, "Jews Split on Additions to Holocaust Ed Curriculum," *Metrowest Jewish News*, 11 April 1996, 8.

15. "Interview with James Mullin and Jack Worrall," New Brunswick, N.J., 30 July 1997; Ellen Friedland, "Jews Split on Additions to Holocaust Ed Curriculum."

16. "Interview with James Mullin and Jack Worrall," New Brunswick, N.J., 30 July 1997.

17. Ibid.; "Great Irish Famine Taught alongside Jewish Holocaust: New Jersey Law Used as Model for Nation," *An Scathán* 1 (30 September 1995), 6.

18. "Hibernia: Bits & Pieces; Irish Famine for New Jersey Schools' Curricula," *Irish America* 12 (30 April 1996), 20; Ellen Friedland, "HS Curriculum Includes Seven Units," *Metrowest Jewish News*, 20 April 1995, 22.

19. "Interview with James Mullin and Jack Worrall," New Brunswick, N.J., 30 July 1997; News release, Irish Famine Curriculum Committee and Education Fund, 30 December 1996.

20. U.S. House of Representatives, "House Congressional Resolution 226," 105th Congress, 1st Session.

21. See, for example, Ignatiev, *How the Irish Became White.*

22. "AOH-Ancient Order of Hibernians Massachusetts Hibernian News," *Boston Irish Reporter*, 1 January 1997, 12; "Hibernia: Bits & Pieces; Irish Famine for New Jersey Schools' Curricula."

23. Telephone interview with Ann Garvey, 4 September 1997.

24. Telephone interview with Assemblyman Joseph Crowley, 29 July 1997.

25. A.6510, "An Act to amend the education law, in relation to instruction on the subjects of human rights violations, genocide, slavery, the Holocaust, and the mass starvation in Ireland from 1845 to 1850" (28 March 1995). Material in brackets is to be deleted from, and underlined material to be added to, existing law.

26. Telephone interview with Assemblyman Joseph Crowley, 29 July 1997; Joel Stashenko, "Teach Irish Famine History, Pol Urges," *New York Daily News*, 24 April 1996.

27. Telephone interview with Assemblyman Joseph Crowley, 29 July 1997; State of New York Executive Chamber, press release, 9 October 1996.

28. Stashenko, "Teach Irish Famine History, Pol Urges."

29. Louis Grumet (Executive Director of School Boards Association) to Michael C. Finnegan (Counsel to the Governor), 5 August 1996 (letter in bill jacket for A.6510/S.4880).

30. Interview with Peter Reid and Dr. Ray Raymond, British Consulate, New York City, 14 August 1997.

31. Telephone interview with Assemblyman Joseph Crowley, 29 July 1997.

32. State of New York, Executive Chamber, "Memorandum of Approval for Assembly Bill Number 6510," press release, 9 October 1996.

33. Ibid.

34. Ibid.; State of New York, Executive Chamber, press release, 9 October 1996.

35. Interview with Jack Irwin (Assistant to Governor Pataki for Irish Affairs), 13 August 1997.

36. Ibid.

37. John Kerr to George Pataki, 17 October 1996.

38. State of New York, Executive Chamber, press release, 9 October 1996.

39. Kerr to Pataki, 17 October 1996.

40. Ibid.

41. Ibid.

42. Interview with Peter Reid and Dr. Ray Raymond, British Consulate, New York City, 14 August 1997.

43. Interview with James Mullin and Jack Worrall, New Brunswick, N.J., 30 July 1997.

44. Editorial: "Irish Still Hunger for An Apology," *New York Daily News*, 26 October 1996, 18.

45. "Elastic Curriculum," *Trenton Times*, 28 February 1996.

46. "An Irish-American Quest for Victimhood," *New York Post*, 12 March 1997.

47. The *Times* (London), 11 October 1996.

48. Herb London, "Pataki Should Take Time to Check Facts," *Albany Times Union*, 26 November 1996.

49. Helen O'Neill, "Legislating History," Associated Press Report, 17 October 1996.

50. Emer Mullins, "Born Astride of a Grave," *Irish Voice*, 17 December 1996, 10.

51. Bernard Bailyn, et al., *The Great Republic: A History of the American People*, 4th ed. (Lexington, Mass.: D.C. Heath and Company, 1991), I, 380.

52. Irwin Unger, *These United States: The Questions of Our Past*, 5th ed. (Englewood Cliffs, N.J.: Prentice-Hall, 1992), 318–19.

53. Paul S. Boyer, et al., *The Enduring Vision: A History of the American People*, 2nd ed. (Lexington, Mass.: D.C. Heath and Company), I, 417.

54. Winthrop D. Jordan and Leon F. Litwack, *The United States*, 6th ed. (Englewood Cliffs, N.J.: Prentice-Hall, 1987), 263–64.

55. George Brown Tindall, *America: A Narrative History*, 2nd ed. (New York: W.W. Norton & Company, 1988), I, 473.

56. Alan Brinkley, *The Unfinished Nation: A Concise History of the American People* (New York: McGraw-Hill, Inc., 1993); Alan Brinkley, Richard N. Current, Frank Friedel, and T. Harry Williams, *American History: A Survey*, 8th ed. (New York: McGraw–Hill, Inc., 1991), I.

57. Luke Gibbons, "Doing Justice to the Past: The Great Famine and Cultural Memory," in Tom Hayden, ed., *The Irish Hunger: Personal Reflections on the Legacy of the Famine* (Boulder, Colo.: Roberts Rinehart Publishers, 1997), 258–59.

58. My colleague and longtime friend James S. Donnelly, Jr., also provided advice, sometimes directly and more often indirectly, through me.

59. Quoted in Kerby Miller, *Emigrants and Exiles: Ireland and the Irish Exodus to North America* (New York: Oxford University Press), 306.

60. George E. Pataki to John Kerr, 24 January 1997.

61. Ibid.

62. Ibid.

63. John Kerr to George E. Pataki, 29 January 1997.

64. John Kerr to James Mullin, 30 January 1997.

65. Ibid.

66. Ibid.

67. Ibid.

68. *Irish Voice*, 29 January–4 February 1997, 1; Emer Mullins, "Pataki: Famine not Genocide, After All," *Irish Voice*, 29 January–4 February 1997, 3.

69. Ray O'Hanlon, "British 'delighted' with Pataki reply," *Irish Echo*, 5–11 February 1997, 5; "George and genocide" (editorial), *Irish Echo*, 5–11 February 1997, 8.

70. Interview with Owen Rodgers, Dorothy Bukantz, and Sean Grealy, 25 July 1997.

71. Owen Rodgers and Eamon Dornan, letter to the editor, *Irish Echo*, 19–25 February 1997, 9.

72. Charles E. Rice, letter to the editor, *Irish Echo*, 12–18 February 1997, 18; Charles E. Rice, "A Proposal for a Tribunal of Inquiry into the Irish Famine," unpublished paper of 20 August 1996, sent to the author by Professor Rice.

73. Tony Blair, "The Irish Famine," press release, British Information Services (New York), 2 June 1997.

74. Editorial, *Albany Times Union*, 6 June 1997, A12.

75. Shawn Pogatchnik, "Britain Admits Role in Irish Potato Famine," *Albany Times Union*, 3 June 1997, A1.

76. Clayton Adams, et al., *Teaching about the Holocaust and Genocide: Introduction*, The Human Rights Series, Volume I (Albany: New York State Education Department, Bureau of Curriculum Development, 1985).

77. Adams, et al., *Teaching about the Holocaust and Genocide*.

78. Walter Litynsky, et al., *Case Studies: Persecution/Genocide*, The Human Rights Series, Volume III (Albany: New York State Education Department, Bureau of Curriculum Development, 1986).

79. New York State Education Department, Bureau of Secondary Curriculum Development, *United States History: The Black Perspective. A Guide for Eighth Grade Social Studies* (Albany: New York State Education Department, 1970).

80. Telephone interviews with Assemblyman Joseph Crowley, 29 July and 3 September 1997; James Mullin, "Update of New York's Law Mandating Education on Irish Mass Starvation" (unpublished memo sent to Jack Irwin).

81. Irish Famine Curriculum Committee (James Mullin, Chair), *The Great Irish Famine* (photo reproduction in binder, 1996).

82. Irish Famine Curriculum Committee (James Mullin, Chair), *The Great Irish Famine*.

83. Interview with Peter Reid and Dr. Ray Raymond, British Consulate, New York City, 14 August 1997; Cathal Poirtéir, ed., *The Great Irish Famine* (Cork: Mercier Press in association with Radio Telefís Éireann, 1995).

84. Interview with Peter Reid and Dr. Ray Raymond, British Consulate, New York City, 14 August 1997. Despite the protests of British spokespersons, rumors were rife this summer of English efforts to reach out to education officials in New Jersey and New York. The Irish Famine/Genocide Committee and the Irish Famine Curriculum Committee jointly responded by seeking copies of all correspondence between the British government and the State Department of Education. (Owen Rodgers, Eamon Dornan, Sean Grealy, and James Mullin to Chancellor Carl T. Hayden and George M. Gregory, 24 June 1997.)

85. See, for example, Donnelly, *The Great Irish Potato Famine*; Peter Gray, *The Irish Famine* (New York: Henry N. Abrams, Inc., 1995) and *Famine, Land and Politics: British Government and Irish Society, 1843–1850* (Dublin and Portland, Oreg.: Irish Academic Press, 1999); Cormac Ó Gráda, *The Great Irish Famine* and *Black '47 and Beyond: The Great Irish Famine in History, Economy, and Memory* (Princeton, N.J.: Princeton University Press, 1999).

The Process of Migration
and the Reinvention of Self:
The Experiences of Returning Irish Emigrants

MARY P. CORCORAN

IRISH MIGRATION AT THE END of the twentieth century encompasses complex and multidimensional processes. Whereas Irish emigrants were once drawn almost exclusively from the agricultural and laborer classes, in the closing decades of the twentieth century emigration came to permeate the entire social system. Thus, Irish migrants are to be found not just among the ranks of skilled and semi-skilled labor, but also among the transnational professional élite that crisscrosses the globe. Current migration trends suggest a radical departure from the pattern that has characterized Irish demography for more than two centuries. Nowadays, more people are entering Ireland than leaving, bringing the country's migratory profile more into line with its European partners. Indeed, Irish government agencies are currently engaged in campaigns to recruit non-national immigrants in key labor market niches *and* to attract Irish emigrants home. Furthermore, there has been a significant increase in the numbers of non-nationals seeking asylum in Ireland over the last ten years. The study of migration and its meaning in the context of the unprecedented buoyancy of the Irish economy directs us to new concerns about multiculturalism, immigration policy and practices, Ireland's position in the global economy, and the relationship between the Irish diaspora and the homeland.

This article is based on a set of qualitative interviews involving a cross-section of emigrants who left Ireland in the 1980s and returned in the 1990s. Particular attention is paid to their motivations for leaving and their experiences abroad in terms of professional and personal development. Analysis of the data reveals that these returners have been able to exercise considerable autonomy in terms of making decisions about their careers, and that in many instances they have used their time abroad to reinvent themselves in terms of their professional career trajectory. Yet, they are drawn back to Ireland in a quest for "community" and better "quality of life," both of which have become more elusive in the fragmented and deeply individualized society that underpins the "Celtic Tiger."

Emigration Trends and Return Migration

In the sixty years after the foundation of the Irish State, Ireland on average lost 0.5 percent of its population annually through net emigration. In the 1950s, the emigration rate rose to 1.5 percent of the population, a rate of outflow that was previously surpassed only in the 1840s and 1880s.[1] The post-1958 opening up of the Irish economy to foreign investment brought a significant increase in the growth rate and a rise in living standards. Average annual net emigration fell from 43,000 per annum between 1956 and 1961 to 16,000 between 1961 and 1966, and to 11,000 between 1966 and 1971. This corresponds to a drop from an annual gross emigration rate of 14.8 percent to 3.7 percent of the population.[2]

Between 1971 and 1979, Ireland for the first time experienced net *immigration*, reversing a two-centuries old trend. Arrivals exceeded departures by about 109,000 people, mainly due to Irish emigrants returning from Britain to take advantage of opportunities in the resurgent economy. But, significantly, net emigration from Ireland persisted even in this period in the 15 to 24 age group and among men in the 25 to 34 age group.[3] That suggests that many newly created jobs went to returned emigrants who brought with them skills and experience, while Ireland's youth continued to seek work abroad. The relative prosperity that marked the 1960s and 1970s in Ireland was short-lived and, by the mid-1980s, unemployment and emigration were both increasing. The annual average migratory outflow rose to nearly 34,000 between 1986 and 1990.[4] As emigration began to rise inexorably in the 1980s, the focus of attention shifted away from returners and toward the burgeoning diasporic communities in the United States and elsewhere. Overall, then, Ireland's migratory profile up until the last decade of the twentieth century can be characterized as one of emigration rather than immigration, with the exception of the 1970s, when a pattern of return emigration was identified.

In the 1990s, however, more people entered Ireland than left it, bringing the national migratory profile more into line with that of the European Union. Between 1991 and 1998 Ireland experienced an average inflow of some 37,000 immigrants each year. In 1998 arrivals exceeded departures by 22,800, a historical high point. The combined effect of this flow and the excess of births over deaths in the same period resulted in a population figure of 3.7 million in April 1998, up 1.2 percent on the previous April. More than half (53 percent) of all immigrants to Ireland in 1998 were Irish nationals, most of whom (43 percent) were concentrated in the 25 to 44 age category.[5]

TABLE 1

ESTIMATED NET MIGRATION, 1995–2002

1995	− 1,900
1996	+ 8,000
1997	+ 15,000
1998	+ 22,800
1999	+ 18,500
2000	+ 20,000
2001	+ 26,300
2002	+ 28,800

Source: Central Statistics Office

There is a dearth of literature on return migration to Ireland. Fiona McGrath suggests two reasons that this is the case: the fact that much of the nineteenth-century movement involved little return, and the statistical elusiveness of the return flow.[6] Hence, our knowledge about returners remains extremely limited. Matthew O'Brien, using census data and labor force surveys among other sources, has identified a circulating migratory pattern between Great Britain and Ireland during the 1950s.[7] Highly qualified emigrants, whose movement abroad was prompted primarily by career considerations, returned to Ireland in significant numbers in the 1950s. O'Brien suggests that this decade marked an important (and thus far overlooked) quantitative and qualitative transition between earlier types of outflows and contemporary migratory trends.

A second study is that of Gmelch, who examined the experiences of return migrants in the 1970s, focusing on return migration to eight western counties—Cork, Kerry, Clare, Galway, Mayo, Sligo, Leitrim, and Donegal—all located on the predominantly rural and relatively impoverished western seaboard.[8] Gmelch questioned his sample of over six hundred returned emigrants on a range of issues, including their circumstances before emigration, the emigration experience, their reasons for return, and post-return adjustment. He found that the majority experienced problems with readjusting to Ireland, although only 20 percent still regretted their decision to return at the end of the second year. The problems of readjustment especially in the first year home were attributed to the false or unrealistic expectations returners had about life in Ireland. Respondents cited the slow pace of life and widespread inefficiency as their biggest problems on return. The perceived backwardness of the local population and the difficulty in establishing relationships also impeded successful readjustment. An overwhelming majority (85 percent) felt that they had been changed by the experience of emigration. More than two-thirds felt that they had a broader outlook than those who had never left Ireland.

A study conducted by McGrath some ten years later echoed these findings.[9] McGrath conducted one hundred forty-two interviews with returned emigrants on Achill Island, off County Mayo, in 1988. Among the primary readjustment problems for this cohort were the poor economic situation, the attitudes and gossip of locals, inefficiency, and the slow pace of life. McGrath also found corroborating evidence to support O'Malley's claim that returned emigrants tended to find fault with everything in Ireland, thereby creating an unnecessary mental barrier between themselves and the home setting.[10]

According to Barrett and Trace, the current cohort of returning emigrants have higher levels of educational attainment than the resident population.[11] Furthermore, there appears to be a selection process whereby the returners are those with the higher levels of education among the group who left. The current population of returners, therefore, can be broadly described as a highly educated group that has amassed considerable cultural capital and career experience during their sojourns abroad. Statistics alone, however, cannot provide insight into the motivations, decision-making, and experiences of those who left Ireland and have now returned. Rather than viewing migrants' experiences purely "in behavioural terms as manifest responses to particular configurations of opportunity and constraint," I am interested in the deeper question of how emigrants make sense of their lives.[12] For that kind of information we need more qualitative techniques for data collection and analysis.

The Methodology

My aim at the outset of the current study was simply to illuminate the experiences of returned emigrants who feature in statistical calculations but not elsewhere. Yet the statistical elusiveness of this group demands more informal techniques. My training as a sociologist has been very much in the tradition of qualitative research methodology, in which the research participant is enabled "to define the situation." During the second half of the 1980s I researched the Irish immigrant community in New York City, making and sustaining relationships with a wide cross-section of Irish emigrants.[13] Drawing on these social networks, along with familial and work networks in Dublin, I have generated a population frame of returners. In addition, I was able to contact returning emigrants through an advertisement placed in the newsletter of the High Skills Pool distributed to prospective and recently returned emigrants.[14] To broaden the population I have asked each returned emigrant interviewed to refer me to another who is unknown to me. This is a form of "snowball sampling" often used when particular populations are difficult to access in a random way.

Between July 1997 and March 1998 I conducted twenty-three in-depth interviews with returners. My stipulation was that the emigrant must have left Ireland in the 1980s and returned in the 1990s. The majority of those interviewed either had advanced educational qualifications before leaving Ireland or had completed advanced—mainly postgraduate—qualifications on their return. So, strictly speaking, my population falls into the relatively privileged category of "credentialized" emigrants. However, a study of the educational level in 1992 of a sample of young people who left school in 1986, carried out by the Dublin-based Economic and Social Research Institute, suggests that my sample is not unrepresentative. This study showed that only 5 to 6 percent of those young people who left school without a qualification were abroad, 15 percent of those with a Junior or Leaving Certificate were outside the country, while about 25 percent of those with a higher education qualification had emigrated.[15] Furthermore, Barrett and Trace's analysis confirms that returners have a relatively high level of educational attainment compared to that of the general population.[16]

Interviews with respondents lasted approximately ninety minutes and covered a range of issues including motivation for leaving, decision-making processes, goal attainment, self-identification and ethnic identification, perceptions about Ireland, adjustment problems, and so on. Interviews were conducted in the interviewee's home, my home, or a neutral public venue such as a café or bar. All of the interviews were tape-recorded and transcribed. In this paper, I focus on a number of themes that emerged from analyzing the data. These themes suggest that a key aspect of the migratory experience for returners was the opportunity afforded them to reflexively "reinvent the self." This opportunity, of course, is predicated on the confluence of a number of different factors, including high levels of cultural capital on the part of the emigrant, the presence of a risk-taking/entrepreneurial culture, and more flexible labor markets. The ability to make meaningful choices in relation to one's life-plan is characteristic of a particular type of Irish emigrant at a particular historical point in time.

The process of reinvention tended to occur in three stages: a growing sense of self-awareness and the need for self-actualization; a review of existing goals, the setting of new goals, and goal attainment; and the reconfiguration of the self, based on newly acquired skills and experiences.[17] The following section details the experience of returning emigrants in terms of these three themes.

Self-awareness and Self-actualization at the Professional and Personal Levels

All of the returners interviewed were highly self-aware. Prior to the interview, most had reflected at length on the kinds of issues I wanted to raise. Indeed, all of the respondents had engaged in self-conscious monitoring of the self on an ongoing basis, a trait identified by Beck and Giddens as being quintessentially part of the modern individualization process.[18] This meant developing a perspective or explanation as to why they had left Ireland, reflecting on what the experience of emigration had actually meant to them, and rationalizing the decision to return home. In choosing to go abroad, most of the interviewees were responding to a need to self-actualize, that is, to fulfill their potential in ways not possible at home, because of a variety of structural and social constraints. For example, Kieran earned a degree in electrical engineering and moved to London in 1988.[19] There he worked for a London financial institution in banking software, before moving to a British university to complete a Ph.D. He returned to Ireland in 1997 and took up a position as a lecturer at an Institute of Technology:

> At first I was going to work for a couple of years in banking and then go travelling, but then I decided to start saving so that I could do a postgraduate degree. I guess what triggered that was that I was getting a bit cheesed off with work. Work was good in that conditions of service were good, good pay, foreign travel, and good benefits. But on the downside the work was very boring. Well, writing banking software wouldn't be the most productive job in terms of doing anything useful apart from making fat-cat bankers fatter, do you know what I mean? It was like, do I really want to do this? I could see the future, and the future was backache, ulcer and 90K a year if you wanted. I could see people at that stage — doing well financially but quite bored. I thought in academia there would

be more opportunities. The financial rewards wouldn't be as good but it is a bit more satisfying.[20]

Similarly, Peter, a science graduate, spent almost a decade in London doing a variety of short-term contractual work related to the arts-based courses he took while living there. He eventually returned to Dublin and opened his own art gallery:

> The context of my initial decision to go away was that I had finished a degree in Science which I realized I wasn't going to use. I wasn't going to seek employment related to my degree. I was twenty-two years and heading off casually rather than to take up a post university post. It was easier to go to London . . . it had the bright lights, big city attraction. By the end of my second year there I was living on the dole and taking all sorts of courses in areas that had been denied to me educationally in Dublin. Typically, like a lot of Irish people I was told by the Christian Brothers at the age of thirteen, that sorry, you are too intelligent not to do Latin, Science, whatever. So in London I actually did classes on anything from tailoring and pattern cutting to jewelry making to set and costume design and explored that whole area that I hadn't explored before. It opened up a whole other part of myself.[21]

Maeve graduated with a degree in economics at the end of the 1980s and immediately went to the United States. During her five-year sojourn, she spent several years working as a waitress before going to work for a law firm. On her return to Ireland she went back to do a postgraduate degree in community work and now works in that field. She, too, was philosophical about her time spent abroad and what she hoped to gain from the experience:

> My quality of life was good in terms of the freedom, in the explorative sense, and the broadening of the mind. Being in college was like being in the Bastille really, it was narrow, limited, and you didn't meet a very wide variety of people. I felt I had to get to know other sides, other people, other ways of looking at things and I achieved that.[22]

This sense of going abroad to work as primarily a "broadening experience" was reiterated by Patrick, another engineering student, who completed his program in 1987 and subsequently worked in London in the financial services sector: "I suppose the good thing about London is that it is a real melting pot so that you get to see a bit of everything. If you want it to be, it will be a mind-broadening experience."[23] Both in professional and personal terms, then, respondents saw the experience of migration as an opportunity for self-actualization. Although leaving home and family for the unknown involved some element of risk-taking, this was more than compensated for by the chance to grasp new opportunities, make lateral rather than linear career moves, and explore hitherto unexplored parts of the self.

Goal-setting and Goal Attainment

Most of the returners did develop goals over the period spent abroad but, crucially, these goals were formed in the context of a perception of multiple choices, and the availability of alternative opportunity structures. This capacity to generate a personal biographical narrative free of constraints was perceived as a form of empowerment.

Patrick, who trained as an engineer, became increasingly disillusioned with the lifestyle that went with his job in the financial services sector in London. Although he was earning a relatively high salary, he found the job extremely stressful. After reviewing his position he opted to move into the wine trade. On his return to Ireland in 1997 he took a position as a wine store manager, the equivalent of an entry-level position in his chosen trade:

> At some point along the way I asked myself what do I want to do with my life . . . I had to set myself some goals. I had been drifting through jobs in banking services. It was very tedious. I ended up working in a big American bank as a foreign exchange dealer for four years. It was an interesting time, and an exciting trade, fast, furious and dramatic. It was very well paid so my standard of living dramatically increased. But also there was a horrible side to it . . . you worked with a lot of obnoxious, greedy people who held extremely right wing views. I decided, let's knock this on the head and try to get into something different. So I went into the wine trade starting at the bottom. I became more focused, I decided where I wanted to go, and I made some tough decisions.[24]

Rebecca's goals also evolved while she was abroad, although in her case there was a stronger focus on personal rather than strictly professional development (even if the two are often closely related). Rebecca trained as a social worker and spent several years working in that profession in a remote part of Canada. She later took time out from her profession to work as a cook on a boat. Since returning to Ireland in 1995, she has been working as a social worker and pursuing postgraduate studies:

> When I say that I didn't have goals, I mean that I didn't have professional goals when I went out [to Canada] but I had more personal goals which were to travel, to be able to experience Canada and the Canadian way of life. I didn't want to earn a lot of money and I didn't see it as a career move . . . My goal was to do something different than what I had qualified in [social work] and when I went on to do that, I did it in a way that

was enviable to others. I ended up taking something that was a hobby and skill and being able to use that as a goal, to expand that and become really good at that so that I would have another career option open to me.[25]

Similarly, Rita, who had also trained as a social worker, recognized the developmental potential of working in another country. In particular, she commented on the positive perspective she developed about her work because of the affirmative work culture she experienced. Since returning to Ireland, she continues to practice as a social worker although she feels somewhat disillusioned about the nature of social work practice in Ireland as compared to Canada:

> Work was a very different experience in Canada than it had been in Ireland. I think there was a more professional attitude toward social work. People that I mixed with professionally were very goal-oriented. It's prompted by things like going for an interview and being asked what are your goals for the next five years . . . and you have never thought of them before in your life. . . . What do you say, my career goal is to get out of bed in the morning! I had never thought in that way before, but I did develop that mentality. Within a year of being there I decided that I wanted to get more training. . . . I started on a sort of "training train." And I never got off it in a way. I did start to see myself as a professional and view myself as someone who had a career in a way that I hadn't done previously in Ireland.[26]

Self-monitoring involves a constant evaluation of the individual's life plan and goals. In the case of these returners, goal-setting and goal attainment became important benchmarks in their career trajectory, whether those goals were set personally or professionally. Furthermore, over a period of years a career path crystalized, with many graduates ending up in jobs unrelated to the discipline in which they trained. Nevertheless, there was considerable agreement among the interviewees that their general education had been a useful indirect, if not direct, resource in developing a career path.

The Reinvention of Self

All of the interviewees agreed that their lives had been enriched by the experience of emigration. They felt that they had added to their cultural capital particularly in terms of their abilities to take risks and to make choices, and in terms of the development of self-confidence and self-assurance. These qualities, they felt, made them different in a positive way from their peers who had stayed at home.

For example, Jean left school after her Intermediate Certificate and moved to London. There she worked her way up to become a senior sales executive in a British company. In 1996, after her first child was born, she and her husband returned to Ireland for quality-of-life reasons. Jean moved back to her home place where most of her family still live, and she perceives a qualitative difference between herself and her siblings who never left home:

> I am much more broad-minded [than my sisters who stayed here]. They would still have the old Irish way . . . they feel they are not good enough, and they'll never get that job, blah blah. And they are really negative about everything. Whereas I am really positive about everything, and if I applied for a job and I didn't get it, yes I would be disappointed but I would ring the person up and ask why I didn't get the job. Not because I was having a go at them but so I could find out where I went down at the interview so it won't happen again. I wouldn't have had the courage to do that when I was living in Ireland; I mean I just believe in myself now. What London has done for me is to make me realize that as a person I am valuable to somebody else in every sense of the word, relationships, work, friends, everything. It has made me a positive person. . . .[27]

Rita, the social worker, also commented on how living abroad strengthened her self-esteem:

> I have developed a more "can-do" attitude, and I am much more goal-oriented. I have a greater degree of self-assurance about myself. That is to do with the fact that I am older, but also because of my Canadian experience of self-assurance . . . being with people who were goal-directed, who were more self-assured, like being in a society where you ask people what are they good at, and they give you a list of things. Whereas in Ireland you would say not very *much*, really. That has to have an impact on you.[28]

These returners embody many of the characteristics ascribed to the individual by recent theorists. The current social formation is characterized by a collapsing of the constraints of time and space, and a concomitant interpenetration of the global and local. There is increased concentration and centralization, particularly at the institutional level, and increased fragmentation and de-traditionalization at the individual level. Individuals are increasingly being forced to negotiate lifestyle choices, or ways of living, among a diversity of options.[29] The history of Ireland in the modern era has been one of the incorporation of its workers into an international division of labor, such that Irish emigrants have contributed to the secondary labor market and the informal economies of a number of host countries. A more recent trend is the incorporation of a new type of Irish emigrant—the transnationally mobile educated élite—into primary sector positions in "global" cities.[30]

Lash and Urry, among others, argue that in the context of the new transnational economy there is greater potential for individuals to act as *reflexive agents*, to take control, in a sense, of the shaping of their own lives. "The modernisation and postmodernisation of contemporary political economies," they argue, "produce, *not just a flattening, but a deepening of the self*."[31] Mass education, the growth of information technology, the rapid expansion of the specialist service sectors, and more flexible labor markets generate new opportunities for the individual, offering greater opportunity "to reflect critically on those changes, and on their social conditions of existence, and potentially to change them."[32] Giddens' conceptualization of the "reflexive individual" is also infused with a sense of agency; we are not simply what we are, but what we make of ourselves.[33]

This concept of the "reflexive self" goes some way toward helping us to make sense of those individuals who, having emigrated from Ireland in the 1980s, chose to return in the 1990s. In their emphasis on self-awareness and self-actualization, their explicit reworking of their goals, and their desire to gain more control over their biographical narratives, they demonstrate the triumph of agency over structural constraint. The decision to emigrate and then to return seems to presage a period of "reflexive individualization" in which individuals have been empowered to invent and reinvent their personal biographical narratives. They have forged "flexible subjectivities" in the context of a transnational field of action, developing, in the words of Roger Rouse, "the capacity for rapid and dramatic processes of self-transformation, for synthesizing and recombining disparate elements and forms of personhood, and above all, for moving fluidly back and forth between markedly different modes of experience and arenas of activity."[34]

However, the interplay between culture, class, and power is critically important in understanding the panoply of Irish emigrant experiences in the transnational economy. As Rouse points out, "people destined for professional managerial activities have been equipped with attitudes to time and space, persona and sociality significantly different from people directed toward wage work."[35] Hence, any model of migration must account for class differences and concomitant differentials in cultural capital between different categories of emigrants.

The model in Table 2 is an attempt to encapsulate the impact of these differences. The élite are well positioned to make reflexive decisions about their careers, driven by the desire to self-actualize. They tend to be highly individualistic and enjoy a considerable degree of personal agency in terms of their life plans and career choices. In contrast, the more traditional Irish emigrants, whose role was to fill the gaps in the secondary labor market of global cities, are much more constrained. Their decision-making is frequently contingent and inadequately thought-through. They gravitate very much toward their ethnic group, where informal networks facilitate their entry into the labor market.[36] They may be subject to a variety of constraints ranging from prejudice and discrimination to the vagaries of the host country system of immigrant regulation.

TABLE 2

Process of migration	"Reserve army emigrants"	Professional élite
Decision-making	Contingent	Reflexive
Migratory context	Ethnicization	Self-actualization
Migrant persona	Situational ethnicity	Flexible subjectivity
Migratory experience	Structural constraint	Personal agency

What I am suggesting here is a clear demarcation between two types of emigrants who left Ireland in the 1980s: on the one hand, the "reserve army emigrants," who represent a surplus in the context of the Irish labor market and who consequently sought work elsewhere, and, on the other hand, a professional élite who are empowered to choose whether or not to stay in Ireland and whether or not to follow a linear career path. The former group make decisions that are primarily determined by the prevailing economic conditions. Furthermore, they are likely to be constrained in terms of opportunity structures because of low or non-transferable skills. The latter group makes decisions that tend to be reflexive, that is, based on an ongoing and self-conscious evaluation of personal and professional goals. The context of reception in the host country is different for each group. The "reserve army emigrants" tend to be absorbed quickly into the Irish ethnic niches in the labor market. Furthermore, they tend to live in the same neighborhoods and congregate in the same bars and cafés. In contrast, the professional élite tend to reject both symbolic and substantive ethnicity, preferring to make their way as individuals without unduly advertising their Irishness, particularly in the workplace. While the "reserve army emigrants" find that to survive in the host country they must often develop an ethnic persona in a variety of strategic situations, the professional élite are busy deploying their flexible subjectivities across a range of work and leisure arenas. Finally, it seems clear that the experiences of "reserve army emigrants" most closely mirror those of previous generations of Irish emigrants, bounded as they are by structural constraint in the form of economic and social conditions as well as legal barriers. Members of the Irish professional élite, in contrast, embody many of the attributes associated with modern individualization. Rich in cultural capital and attuned to information and communication structures, they apply themselves assiduously to the task of self-fulfillment. For many, this results in a reflexive reinvention of the self.

The Constraints on Reflexivity

For returners, a key choice that has been made is to return home. Why are these emigrants coming home? The answer lies at least in part in a quest for anchorage, for attachment to others and a sense of continuity. Often these corrections can be found in the ethnic communities that flourish in global cities. But for those among the professional élite of Irish emigrants who neither seek nor engage with the ethnic community, the quest for anchorage remains unfulfilled. The process of individualization at the heart of modern capitalist development confers on them a sense of agency. This is apparent particularly in relation to their work lives. All of the interviewees felt that the training and experience obtained abroad had contributed to their cultural capital. Most had reached points in their careers where they were in a good position to make informed choices about their next move. At the same time, the cult of individualism, whose logical extension is the application of market values across non-economic spheres of life, creates a kind of "existential isolation"—what Giddens defines as "not so much a separation of individuals from others as a separation from the moral resources necessary to live a full and satisfactory existence."[37] Put another way, "there is an increasingly felt need for some *expressive relationship to the past* and for *attachment to particular territorial locations* as nodes of association and continuity, bounding cultures and communities."[38] For the returners, this need is expressed in the desire to return home:

> It sounds corny but I just decided, this is where I belong, this is where I fit in. It just became very obvious to me, this is where I feel relaxed, this is where I feel at home. This is the social place where I seem to be myself.[39]

Or:

> There was always something that I felt was missing. I suppose you call it homesickness, but maybe it was more about me and where I was at. . . . I don't think its something that can be easily articulated.[40]

Not surprisingly, the central considerations in the decision to return to Ireland include the provision of a better quality of life for children, having more time, the ease of Irish sociability, the quality of friendship, and the slower pace of life. Paradoxically, the very pace of life that had caused the most serious adjustment problems for the returned emigrants interviewed by Gmelch and McGrath in the 1970s and 1980s is eulogized by those who returned in the 1990s. Today's returners want to feel part of something that one might describe as an organic, as opposed to a synthetic, community. There is a sense in which they want to commune with their own, with friends and family to whom they have longstanding feelings of attachment. This contrasts with their existence in global cities, which—while free of much constraint and highly flexible—was characterized by a compartmentalized lifestyle whereby the individual remained detached from groups and institutions.

Ironically, the rise of the "Celtic Tiger" economy has facilitated the return of emigrants in significant numbers but is also inextricably bound up with growing individualism. Ireland itself has been incorporated into the globalizing project of multinational capital. The private sector, in particular, now demands the same level of commitment from Irish-based employees as the parent company and its international counterparts. This puts at risk the kind of lifestyle that the returning emigrants covet. They have difficulty in acquiring reasonably priced housing, commuting times are considerably longer and more frustrating than they had anticipated, and there is less time than they had hoped for to enjoy a social life:

> Whether you are working in NY, Paris, London, or Dublin—whether it is for Rank Xerox, Jackson Stopps, or my company—people are expected to have the same work rate. A friend of mine worked for an accountancy firm taken over by a Big Six company, he worked in the UK for a while, then in Belgium and now in France, and really he is mobile within a firm rather than mobile across countries. He is just an autonomous economic unit that can be slotted in anywhere, and they expect his work rate to be the same, to hell with the social externalities. You are a little unit for us go produce the standard amount of output a day. That's very unhealthy. Because it homogenizes. We are homogenizing culturally, but we are also homogenizing economically. . . . I thought it would be different when I returned. I thought for me personally and psychologically I would get up and approach work differently, that my attitude would change. That I wouldn't be a harassed urban dweller anymore. That I would be relaxed, a less stressed individual. But because of the nature of the job, the company I am working for, and the fact that Dublin has changed that's not happening.[41]

The concept of a "positional economy" is relevant here. Fred Hirsch defines the positional sector of the economy as all aspects of goods, services, work positions, and other social relationships that are scarce in some absolute or socially imposed sense, and subject to congestion or crowding through more extensive use. The choices facing the individual in a market-type transaction in an expanding positional sector, for Hirsch, always appear more attractive than they turn out to be after others have exercised their choice.[42] In other words, the satisfaction that returning Irish emigrants may derive from goods and services depends increasingly not only on their own consumption but on others' consumption as well. In a booming economy characterized by net immigration rather than net emigration, where the demands of an expanding middle class are outstripping supply, the acquisition of positional goods becomes ever more difficult. The returning emigrants find themselves caught in a bind. Ireland's exemplary economic performance makes the dream of return possible, but that economic performance is based on the very values and practices from which these returning emigrants are attempting to escape.

NOTES

1. Brendan Walsh, "Emigration: An Economist's Perspective," Policy Paper PP88/3 (Dublin: University College Dublin Centre for Economic Research, 1988), 2.

2. J.J. Lee, *Ireland 1912–1985: Politics and Society* (Cambridge, U.K.: Cambridge University Press, 1989), 359–60. Gross emigration is the total number or rate of departures; net emigration is gross emigration minus arrivals.

3. Paul Tansey, "Figures Hid Facts of Irish Exodus," *Sunday Tribune*, 19 November 1989, B8.

4. *Central Statistics Office Annual Population and Migration Estimates, 1981–1990* (Dublin: Central Statistics Office, 1991).

5. *Central Statistics Office Annual Population and Migration Estimates, 1991–1998* (Dublin: Central Statistics Office, 1999).

6. Fiona McGrath, "The Economic, Social and Cultural Impact of Return Migration to Achill Island," in R. King, ed., *Contemporary Irish Migration* (Dublin: Geographical Society of Ireland Special Publication no. 6, 1991), 55–69.

7. Matthew O'Brien, "Migratory Patterns of the 1950s Generation." Paper presented at the international conference on "The Scattering," University College, Cork, September 1997.

8. G. Gmelch, "The Readjustment of Returned Migrants in the West of Ireland," in R. King, ed., *Return Migration and Regional Economic Problems* (London: Croom Helm, 1986), 152–70.

9. McGrath, "The Economic, Social and Cultural Impact of Return Migration to Achill Island."

10. E. O'Malley, *Memories of a Mayoman* (Dublin: Foilseachán Naisiúnta Teoranta, 1981).

11. Alan Barrett and Fergal Trace, "Who is Coming Back? The Educational Profile of Returning Migrants in the 1990s." Paper presented to the Irish Economic Association, University College, Dublin, 23 June 1998.

12. Roger Rouse, "Making Sense of Settlement: Class Transformation, Cultural Struggle and Transnationalism among Mexican Migrants in the United States," *Annals of the New York Academy of Science* 645 (1992), 26. I am indebted to Professor Eithne Luibheid for introducing me to the work of Roger Rouse.

13. Mary P. Corcoran, *Irish Illegals: Transients Between Two Societies* (Westport, Conn.: Greenwood Press, 1993).

14. The High Skills Pool is an agency funded by FAS (the State Training Agency). The agency maintains a database and channels information on industry and business opportunities in Ireland to graduates overseas. It publishes a quarterly magazine, *Inform*, which is sent to more than 5,500 graduates abroad.

15. Garret Fitzgerald, "Population Implications in our Balanced Migration," *Irish Times*, 1 February 1997.

16. Barrett and Trace, "Who is Coming Back?"

17. Once embarked on the emigration trail these emigrants attempted to sustain "coherent, yet continuously revised biographical narratives . . . in the context of multiple choice as filtered through abstract systems," to quote Anthony Giddens, *Modernity and Self Identity* (Cambridge: Polity Press, 1991), 6. The absence of structural constraint (in the form of low educational attainment, familial expectation and obligation, peer pressure, labor market inflexibility) freed them from the tyranny of a linear career path.

18. See, for example, Ulrich Beck, *Risk Society: Toward a New Modernity* (London: Sage, 1992) and Giddens, *Modernity and Self Identity.*

19. All names of interviewees have been changed to ensure anonymity.

20. Interview with returner, Dublin, 15 January 1998.

21. Interview with returner, Dublin, 17 July 1997.

22. Interview with returner, Maynooth, 17 September 1997.

23. Interview with returner, Dublin, 27 August 1997.

24. Interview with returner, Dublin, 27 August 1997.

25. Interview with returner, Wexford, 15 July 1997.

26. Interview with returner, Wexford, 17 October 1997.

27. Interview with returner, Dublin, 27 August 1997.

28. Interview with returner, Wexford, 17 October 1997.

29. Giddens, *Modernity and Self Identity*, 9.

30. See Gerard Hanlon, *The Commercialisation of Accountancy* (London: St. Martin's Press, 1994).

31. Scott Lash and John Urry, *Economies of Signs and Space* (London: Sage, 1994), 31. My emphasis.

32. Ibid., 37.

33. Giddens, *Modernity and Self Identity*, 196.

34. Roger Rouse, "Thinking about Transnationalism: Notes on the Cultural Politics of Class Relations in the Contemporary United States," *Public Culture* 7 (1995), 391.

35. Rouse, "Making Sense of Settlement," 26.

36. See Corcoran, *Irish Illegals.*

37. Anthony Giddens, *Modernity and Self Identity*, 9.

38. M. Rustin, "Place and Time in Socialist Theory," *Radical Philosophy* 47 (Autumn 1987), 33–34, qtd. in David Morley and Kevin Robins, "No Place Like Heimat: Images of Home(land) in European Culture," in E. Carter, et al., eds., *Space and Place* (London: Lawrence and Wishart, 1993), 3–31. My emphasis.

39. Interview with returner, Dublin, 27 August 1997.

40. Interview with returner, Maynooth, 18 September 1997.

41. Interview with returner, Dublin, 11 October 1997.

42. Fred Hirsch, *Social Limits to Growth: New York: Twentieth Century Foundation* (Cambridge, Mass.: Harvard University Press, 1976).

Contributors

Tyler Anbinder is Professor of History at George Washington University in Washington, D.C., where he specializes in nineteenth-century American politics and immigration. His first book, *Nativism and Slavery* (1992), a history of the Know Nothing party, won the Avery Craven Prize of the Organization of American Historians. His second book, *Five Points* (2001), tells the story of one of New York City's most colorful and heavily Irish neighborhoods in the nineteenth century.

Thomas J. Archdeacon is Professor of History of the University of Wisconsin–Madison, where he teaches the history of U.S. immigration, immigration policy, and ethnicity. He also has a strong interest in quantitative analysis as applied to historical research. His publications include *New York City, 1664–1710: Conquest and Change* (1976), *Becoming American: An Ethnic History* (1983), and *Correlation and Regression Analysis: A Historian's Guide* (1994).

Bruce D. Boling has been a professional librarian at the Library of Congress, the University of Wyoming, and Brown University and is currently Associate Professor and Principal Cataloguer in the Zimmerman Library of the University of New Mexico.

Maurice J. Bric is Senior Lecturer in History and Director of American Studies at University College, Dublin. He has written a number of works on eighteenth-century Ireland and America, and his *Economy of Irish Emigration to America, 1760–1800* is forthcoming. He is also Academic Secretary of the Irish Research Council for the Humanities and Social Sciences.

Mary P. Corcoran is Senior Lecturer in Sociology at the National University of Ireland, Maynooth. She has also held positions at New York University, John Jay College, CUNY, Trinity College, Dublin, and University College, Dublin. Corcoran's research interests are in the fields of ethnicity and migration, identity construction, and urban transformation and change. She is the author of *Irish Illegals: Transients between Two Societies* (1993) and has contributed to such volumes as *The New York Irish* (1996), *Location and Dislocation in Irish Society* (1997), *Irish Sociological Chronicles* (1998 and 2000), and *The Encyclopedia of the Irish in America* (1999). She is currently working on a book about the professional culture of Irish journalists and collaborating on a number of international projects on the dynamics of social and cultural change in European and North American cities.

Mary E. Daly is Professor of Irish History at University College, Dublin, and is the author of numerous books and articles on Irish history in the nineteenth and twentieth centuries, including *Dublin: The Deposed Capital, 1860–1914* (1984), *The Buffer State: The Historical Roots of the Department of the Environment* (1997), *Women and Work in Ireland* (1997), and *The First Department: The Department of Agriculture 1900–2000* (2001). Her essay here draws on ongoing research on the response of the Irish government to demographic issues between 1920 and 1966. In March 2000 she was elected to the office of Secretary of the Royal Irish Academy.

Catherine M. Eagan received her Ph.D. in English from Boston College. Her dissertation, "'I Did Imagine . . . We Had Ceased to Be Whitewashed Negroes': The Racial Formation of Irish Identity in Nineteenth-Century Ireland and America," was supervised by faculty in both American Studies and Irish Studies. Drawing on postcolonial theory and theories of race and ethnicity, her research examines transnational encounters between Irish and Africans, primarily in nineteenth- and twentieth-century America. Her publications include reviews in *The Irish Literary Supplement* and *American Quarterly* and an essay in the series *Working Papers in Irish Studies.*

Ruth-Ann M. Harris is Adjunct Professor of History in the Irish Studies Program at Boston College, where she teaches Irish emigration. She has also taught at Wesleyan University and Northeastern University. In 1994–95 she was Senior Research Scholar at the Institute of Irish Studies of Queen's University, Belfast. She is the author of *The Nearest Place That*

Wasn't Ireland: Early Nineteenth-Century Irish Labor Migration, a study of pre-Famine Irish migrants in England, and chief editor of the first four volumes of *The Search for Missing Friends: Irish Immigrant Advertisements Placed in the Boston Pilot, 1831–1860.* She is currently working on a study of Irish women as immigrants.

Diane M. Hotten-Somers is a doctoral candidate in American Studies at Boston University and Lecturer in the English Department at Boston College. Her research concentrates on Irish diasporic literature and history, specifically how American nationalism has shaped the Irish immigrant. She has published articles on America's response to the Famine, Irish women's immigration to America, and the future of Irish Studies.

William Jenkins received his Ph.D. in Geography from the University of Toronto. His dissertation was entitled "Geographical and Social Mobility among the Irish in the United States and Canada: A Comparative Study of Toronto, Ontario, and Buffalo, New York, 1880–1910." He has published articles in *Irish Geography, The Tipperary Historical Journal, Social and Cultural Geography,* and *The Journal of Historical Geography* and is the author of *Tipp Co-op: Origin and Development* (1999). He currently holds a postdoctoral fellowship at the Department of Geography, University of British Columbia, Vancouver, where he is revising his dissertation for publication and continuing his research on the Irish in North America.

Patricia Kelleher is Assistant Professor of History at Kutztown University of Pennsylvania. Her research focuses on the interplay of gender, class, and ethnicity. With David N. Doyle, she served as coauthor for Kerby A. Miller's article, "For Love and For Liberty: Irish Women, Emigration and Domesticity in Ireland in America, 1815–1920," in Patrick O'Sullivan, ed., *The Irish Worldwide,* volume 4, *Irish Women and Irish Migration* (1995). Her article, "Maternal Strategies: Irish Women's Headship of Families in Gilded Age Chicago," appeared in *The Journal of Women's History* 13 (summer 2001).

Líam Kennedy is Professor of Economic and Social History at Queen's University, Belfast. He is the author of *Colonialism, Religion, and Nationalism in Ireland* (1996).

Kevin Kenny is Associate Professor of History at Boston College, where he teaches U.S. immigration and labor history, with a focus on Irish transatlantic migration. His publications include *Making Sense of the Molly Maguires* (1998) and *The American Irish: A History* (2000). He is currently researching the history of popular protest movements in eighteenth-century Ireland and America and editing a collection of historical essays, *Ireland and the British Empire*, for Oxford University Press.

Kerby A. Miller is Middlebush Professor of History at the University of Missouri–Columbia and a former Senior Fellow of the Institute of Irish Studies at Queen's University, Belfast. His published works include the prize-winning *Emigrants and Exiles: Ireland and the Irish Exodus to North America* (1985) and *Irish Popular Culture, 1650–1850* (1998), coedited with James S. Donnelly, Jr. His study of early Irish immigration and identity, *Irish Immigrants in the Land of Canaan: Letters and Memoirs from Colonial and Revolutionary America, 1675–1815* (with Arnold Schrier, Bruce D. Boling, and David N. Doyle) is forthcoming with Oxford University Press.

Harvey O'Brien received his Ph.D. in Film Studies from University College, Dublin. He is currently a Government of Ireland Council for the Humanities and Social Sciences Post-Doctoral Research Fellow, researching Irish and international representations of Ireland in documentary film. Recent publications include "Historical Documentary in Ireland," in *Historical Journal of Film, Radio, and Television* (autumn 2000) and "Somewhere to Come Back To: The Filmic Journeys of John T. Davis," in *Irish Studies Review* (spring 2001). He has also contributed to *Film Ireland, Cineaste*, and Stephanie McBride and Roddy Flynn, eds., *Here's Looking at You, Kid* (1996).

Matthew O'Brien received his Ph.D. in History from the University of Wisconsin–Madison in 2001. His dissertation compares networks of Irish migration to Great Britain and the United States since 1920. He has also written on the transition from "immigrants" to "ethnics" by Polish and Irish Americans after World War I. His future research plans include work on Irish migration and national identity during the late twentieth century, as well as further study of transatlantic networks and American ethnicity.

Timothy M. O'Neil teaches twentieth-century European, British, and labor history at Central Michigan University. His dissertation, which he is currently converting into a book, is titled, "'To Undo the Conquest': Nationalism, Socialism and the Irish Revolution, 1913–1936."

Fionnghuala Sweeney is currently Lecturer in Comparative American Studies at the Institute of Latin American Studies, University of Liverpool. Her interests include nineteenth- and twentieth-century Irish, Caribbean, and Latin American literature. She wrote her doctoral thesis at University College, Cork, on Frederick Douglass's relationship with Ireland. She spent the academic year 1999–2000 in the United States as a Fulbright scholar.

Index